CALIFORNIA
COASTAL ACCESS
GUIDE

CALIFORNIA
COASTAL ACCESS
·GUIDE·

STATE OF CALIFORNIA
George Deukmejian, *Governor*

CALIFORNIA COASTAL COMMISSION
Michael L. Fischer, *Executive Director*   Melvin Nutter, *Chairman*   William Travis, *Deputy Director*

Donald B. Neuwirth, *Coastal Access Program Manager*

Editors

Madge M. Caughman
design, cartography

Joanne S. Ginsberg
research writing

Staff

Cartography
John Lentz
Mindy S. Richter
Richard L. Snyder

Research Writing
Stephen J. Furney-Howe
Sabrina S. Simpson
Jeffrey D. Zimmerman

Jane Heaphy
illustrator

UNIVERSITY OF CALIFORNIA PRESS
Berkeley   Los Angeles   London

Third Edition.

Printed in the United States of America.

Library of Congress Cataloging in Publication Data
Main entry under title:
California coastal access guide.
Bibliography: p. 232
Includes index.
1. Coasts—California—Guide-books.   2. Recreation areas—California—Guide-books.   3. Parks—California—Guide-books.   4. California—Description and travel—1951-   —Guide-books.   I. California Coastal Commission.
D859.3.C26   917.94′0453   81-14667
ISBN 0-520-04576-9   AACR2
                        2   3   4   5   6   7   8   9

Contents

Foreword

Introduction

ac·cess *n.,* liberty to approach

Foreword

The 1,100-mile California coast, from the majestic redwoods and rocky shores in the north to the palm trees and wide, sandy beaches in the south, is an area of unsurpassed beauty and diversity. A decade ago, the voters of California approved Proposition 20, the Coastal Initiative, which led to the creation of the California Coastal Commission. As a result of Proposition 20, the Coastal Commission, citizens, industrial and commercial interests, the Legislature, and many governmental agencies have worked together to conserve and manage the natural resources of the coastal zone, and to increase public access to the coast.

In 1979, legislation introduced by State Senator Barry Keene directed the Coastal Commission to prepare an access guide identifying areas on the coast that are open to the public, and explaining the public's rights and responsibilities regarding the use of coastal resources. In 1981, the Coastal Commission unveiled its authoritative guide, which was critically acclaimed and quickly became a best seller.

In 1982, the Commission revised this guide to make public access to the coast even easier and more enjoyable, and published a special hardbound edition of the guide to commemorate the tenth anniversary of California's coastal management efforts. Now the Commission presents a new revised paperback edition, which includes additional features, maps, and photographs to familiarize the public with more of the magnificent resources the coast has to offer.

Providing this comprehensive guide to an area as complex as the California coast has been a challenging and worthwhile task for the Coastal Commission. The Coastal Commission would like to express its appreciation to the University of California Press and the state, federal, and local agencies who assisted in preparing this valuable coastal access guide.

"No individual, partnership or corporation, claiming or possessing the frontage or tidal lands of a harbor, bay, inlet, estuary, or other navigable water in this State, shall be permitted to exclude the right of way to such water whenever it is required for any public purpose, nor to destroy or obstruct the free navigation of such water; and the Legislature shall enact such laws as will give the most liberal construction to this provision so that access to the navigable waters of this State shall always be attainable for the people thereof."

—Art X, Sec. 4
Constitution of the State of California

Introduction

Coastal access means getting to the coast; this Guide tells you where to go on the coast, how to get there, and what facilities and type of environment you will find at each location. It is meant for all beachgoers — hikers, campers, swimmers, surfers, divers, joggers, boaters, fishermen — and is intended to introduce the richness and diversity of the California coast.

The Guide is a thorough and easy-to-use handbook that lists and describes all open public accessways, beaches, parks, and recreational areas along the coast; it provides addresses, phone numbers, transit information, hours of use, and descriptions of facilities and type of environment for each site. The Guide is divided into sections for each county and local area, with accompanying maps that clearly locate each accessway and major streets. Photos and illustrated feature articles on history, coastal resources, and recreational activities are found throughout the book.

Natural conditions along the California coast are always changing. The width of sandy beaches fluctuates with the seasons, and the topography of coastal bluffs is altered by erosion. The heavy rain and high winds and waves that often accompany ocean storms can change the physical features of the coastline drastically in a matter of days, or even hours.

Coastal access and recreation facilities are inevitably subjected to the same physical forces as the shoreline itself. Unfortunately, these facilities often are not as resilient as the shoreline, and consequently can suffer debilitating damage. From time to time, some of the facilities described in this book, including piers, trails, stairways, parking areas, campgrounds, and restrooms, may be temporarily closed while undergoing repairs. In some cases where storm damage has been particularly severe, an entire park may be closed.

When planning any trip to the coast, but especially right after a storm, it is advisable to check ahead whenever possible to make sure that the coastal area you choose to visit is currently accessible and useable.

The Commission intends to periodically update the Coastal Access Guide to keep it current. The information in this Guide is accurate as of Spring 1983.

Coastal Access Program

Proposition 20 of 1972, and the California Coastal Act and State Coastal Conservancy Act, both enacted in 1976, contain strong access policies and programs. The Commission implements these policies through its requirement of providing access as a condition of receiving a coastal development permit, and through local coastal programs (LCPs), the coastal area plans prepared by local governments, which contain provisions for acquiring, improving, and managing access areas. The Conservancy provides grants and technical assistance to local governments and citizens' groups to acquire, develop, operate and manage new accessways.

In 1979, legislation was enacted directing the California Coastal Commission and State Coastal Conservancy to establish a comprehensive program to maximize coastal access. These two agencies are responsible for coordinating all local, state, and federal efforts to implement the access program. For example, in cooperation with the California Department of Transportation and the Conservation Corps, coastal access signs are being installed along the coast, indicating where accessways are located. Legislation also mandated that the Commission prepare this guide to all coastal accessways.

This logo has been adopted by the Coastal Commission and State Coastal Conservancy as the official symbol to appear on coastal access signs.

Public and Private Rights

The California Constitution guarantees the public's right to access to the State's navigable waters; each year, over 50 million people visit the California coast. Approximately 42% of this shoreline is publicly owned and accessible, while the remaining 58% is owned privately or is held by federal, state, or local government and is not open to the public.

The State of California owns the tide and submerged lands seaward of what is called the "mean high tide line." The precise boundary between these public tidelands and private lands is determined by using the mean, or average, of normal tides over approximately 19 years, and an analysis of the causes of shoreline changes over time. This determination is made by the State Lands Commission, which has administered these tidelands since 1938. Although it is difficult to ascertain the boundary between public and private lands, a general rule to follow is that visitors have the right to walk on the wet sand.

The public's right of access to or along the State's tidelands can be obtained by three methods. The simplest way is through the purchase of shoreline lands for public use by federal, state, and local governments, or private organizations.

Public access to the tidelands can also be obtained through deed restrictions or dedications by the landowner, which grant the public the right to cross private property. "Dedicated" lands, however, become open to the public only after an agency or private party has accepted responsibility for their management. The Coastal Commission and many local governments require access as a condition of approving development permits to assure public access to the shoreline. Access along the ocean, parallel to the shore, is called "lateral" access, and is usually provided through deed restrictions or dedications of a 25-foot wide easement landward of the mean high tide line. Access from the nearest public road or area to the shoreline is called "vertical" access, and such access through private property is usually a ten-foot wide path to the water. In almost every case, a buffer area of approximately five to ten feet exists between private structures and public areas.

Most of these "dedicated" strips of land remain undeveloped and unmanaged by government agencies and do not yet form a continuous system of access to and along the shore. Visitors are asked not to trespass onto private property adjoining public accessways and to respect the rights of property owners. If any controversy results from the use of shoreline land, please obey the requests of the property owner. You can determine the extent of public rights in the area by obtaining the street address of the parcel in question and consulting the Coastal Commission.

The public can also acquire the right to gain access to and use shoreline property through the legal doctrines of "implied dedication" and "prescriptive rights." The existence of these rights was confirmed by the California Supreme Court in 1970 (Gion v. City of Santa Cruz, 2Cal3d129). Because these rights are acquired through the use of property without the owner's permission, and because of problems associated with proving historic use, the determination of their existence is difficult and controversial.

According to court decisions, in order for the public to obtain an easement by way of implied dedication, the essential elements that must be established are that the public has used the land:

- for a *continuous* period of five years as if it were public land,

- without asking or receiving permission from the owner,

- with the actual or presumed knowledge of the owner, and

- without significant objection or significant attempts by the owner to prevent or halt such use.

The ultimate determination of prescriptive rights, if they are challenged, is in a court. The responsible public agencies, including affected local governments, the Coastal Commission, the California Department of Parks and Recreation, the Wildlife Conservation Board, the State Lands Commission, and the Attorney General, are attempting to protect these public rights. There are many areas along the California coast which may be subject to prescriptive rights. However, only those which are managed for public use have been included in the Coastal Access Guide.

Hazards, Safety, and Liability

Fritz Eichenberg, from *The Long Loneliness*, by Dorothy Day, © 1952, Harper & Row Publishers, Inc. Reprinted by permission of the publisher.

Many portions of the California coast are hazardous; steep bluffs and cliffs, agricultural and port activities, and treacherous coastal waters can all be dangerous. California's ocean waters, particularly in the north, are extremely cold, and many beaches have rip currents. A numher of beaches do not have lifeguards, and numerous drownings occur annually. Even on the calmest days, huge waves can unexpectedly crash ashore; therefore, never leave children alone on beaches or bluffs. For your own safety, consult tide tables before exploring rocky beaches and tidepools, check marine weather forecasts, and stay on trails and paths.

Formerly, public agencies responsible for improved and unimproved property open to the public were liable for injuries resulting from dangerous conditions not visible on the land. However, amendments to the law in the 1960's and early 70's granted the responsible agency immunity in the case of such injuries when the unimproved trails and accessways were being used by the public for recreational purposes.

The distinction between paved and unimproved accessways was eliminated by the legislature in 1979. The new law creates absolute immunity from liability for injuries occurring on paved as well as unimproved accessways as long as the responsible agency makes reasonable attempts, such as posting signs, to provide adequate warning of existing health or safety hazards.

Other recent legislation has created immunities under most circumstances for coastal public land trusts which maintain coastal accessways and have entered into a specified agreement with the State Coastal Conservancy. This legislation also extended the immunity which protects against liability for non-paid users of land so that it applies to owners of accessways. The trend in accessway legislation clearly indicates that the favored public policy is to increase coastal access even if that requires changes to traditional rules of tort liability.

Children and the Coast

The coast is perhaps enjoyed most by young children. The natural wonders of tidepools and marine life, and the pleasures of swimming and playing in the surf and building sand castles are our children's birthright to enjoy. This heritage, however, poses special hazards for youngsters. In addition to those safety pointers mentioned throughout this guide, parents and guardians should keep in mind the following considerations:

• Always accompany children into the water, even if it is shallow. Swim only near lifeguards.

• Do not depend on flotation devices.

• Watch out for rip currents, which are strong but narrow seaward flows. If you get caught in one, don't panic; swim parallel to shore until you get out of the current, then return to shore. If you can't escape the current, call or wave for help.

• Don't let children dive unless you know how deep the water is and whether there are any underwater hazards.

• Eating sand is not harmful unless it is contaminated by animal waste. If there is any question, see a doctor.

• Milk products and other foods spoil quickly in the sun and summer heat. Keep perishable foods in a cooler.

• When exploring tidepools, be careful on slippery rocks, avoid stepping on sea urchins, and watch for the incoming tide.

• Watch for broken glass on the beach. Please pick up and safely dispose of any sharp fragments.

• Children are especially sensitive to sunburn. Sunscreens and protective creams and oils are now rated by degree of protection. Apply higher numbered products frequently during exposure. Hats also help prevent burns and sunstroke or heat exhaustion.

• To remove tar and oil, use mineral or food oil rather than harsh turpentine or other spirits.

• Playing in firepits is dangerous. Coals can remain hot overnight when fires have been extinguished only with sand. Douse all fires with water.

• Stay away from jellyfish on land as well as in water. They can still sting after several hours on a dry beach. Children's feet are best protected from jellyfish and other debris by rubber thongs or sneakers.

• Stingrays often bury themselves in shallow water. Usually splashing feet will scare them away. However, if a stingray's tail stinger strikes, get emergency medical help as soon as possible.

• Keep children away from surf-casting fishermen. Do not attempt to pull out fishhooks from the skin, but seek medical help immediately.

• Keep small children in sight at all times. Dress your children in bright clothes and remember what they are wearing. Identify landmarks to help children remember where their group is located.

• Sea cliffs and caves are dangerous for unsupervised children. Keep young children in hand on steep trails and away from the base of cliffs where rocks may fall.

• Logs and other debris in the surf zone should be avoided because the waves can hurl them with great force.

• Children playing in deep holes in the sand can be suffocated by a cave-in. Refill all deep pits.

• Keep children away from storm water and sewage outfalls. Unsanitary and toxic wastes are health hazards.

Many educational institutions and scientific organizations provide opportunities to enrich children's visits to the coast. Several guidebooks specifically describe trips which are especially enjoyable for children, and more detailed county and regional guides are available at most bookshops. These books list local museums, historical exhibits, natural resource displays, and commercial endeavors which children will enjoy and find beneficial. For example, a visit to the artificial tidepool at Steinhart Aquarium in San Francisco's Golden Gate Park, to Pacific Grove's or Santa Barbara's Museum of Natural History, or to the Cabrillo Marine Museum in San Pedro can make a later visit to the coast more rewarding.

State Historic Parks, such as the ones at Fort Humboldt, at Fort Ross, and in Monterey, attractively present the cultural history of the coast. Several forest product companies have demonstration forests and logging museums, and offer tours of their plants. These displays show the current and historical commercial development of an important coastal industry. Marinas, ports, and commercial fishing harbors are exciting places where children can learn the importance of the coast to the economy of the state. Historical museums and displays are often provided at coastal military facilities and lighthouses.

Although San Francisco's Playland-at-the-Beach, Los Angeles' Pacific Ocean Park, and the Pike at Long Beach are gone, Santa Cruz Beach and Boardwalk, Santa Monica Pier, Marineland in Los Angeles County, and San Diego's Sea World remain popular coastal amusements for children of all ages.

Boating and Boating Safety

California's 1,100 miles of shoreline provide numerous opportunities for recreational boating, including pleasure motorboating and waterskiing. Extended fair weather periods and a number of sheltered coastal areas contribute to favorable sailing conditions, and at various times of the year fishing boats can be seen on coastal rivers and ocean waters.

Today there are more than fifty locations along the coast with berthing and launching facilities for recreational boating. However, over the years California's boating community has continued to grow, both in number and areas of boating interest; for example, canoeing and kayaking have increased in popularity in recent years. In some locations, the demand for boating facilities far exceeds the supply; waiting lists for berthing or mooring space in some marinas are years long.

With the continuing increase of newcomers enjoying various boating activities, the importance of practicing boating safety cannot be over-emphasized. Before departing on a trip, boaters should familiarize themselves with existing and predicted weather conditions and the tide stages. When leaving a slip, boaters should notify nearby craft by sounding one long blast of a horn or whistle.

In foggy weather there are standard signals that should be used to indicate a boat's location in the water: while moving in the water, motorized craft should sound a prolonged blast once a minute; sailboats should sound one blast when on starboard (right) tack, two blasts when on port (left) tack, and three blasts when the wind is from the back of the boat's beam (widest point); and all boats at anchor should sound a bell for five seconds every minute.

The International and Inland Rules are the nautical "rules of the road" applicable to all navigable waterways in California. These rules consist of standard operating procedures designed to prevent collisions, signal danger, or indicate a vessel in distress.

Generally, motorless craft have the right-of-way over motorboats. Any vessel being overtaken has the right-of-way over the passing boat. When two boats are traveling on a head-on course, each vessel should turn to the right, with the oncoming vessel passing to the left. When boats approach each other at right or oblique angles, the boat on the right has the right-of-way and should hold its course and speed. Whenever a boater does not understand the intentions or signal of another boat, or wants to indicate a dangerous condition, four or more short blasts of a horn should be sounded.

Distress signals should be used in emergency situations and when outside assistance is needed. During daylight hours, repeatedly wave an orange flag or raise and lower outstretched arms; at night ignite a red flare or rocket, or blink a flashlight or other white light. Flames on the boat (e.g., a burning tar barrel), the continuous sounding of a fog horn, and the firing of a gun are also recognized as distress signals.

It is recommended that people interested in boating enroll in one of the boating safety courses offered annually by several organizations and government agencies. Boating safety literature is available from the California Department of Boating and Waterways. For a list of available boating safety classes or copies of safety publications, send a request to:

California Department of Boating and Waterways
1629 S Street
Sacramento, CA 95814   (916) 445-2615

Access For Persons With Disabilities

The California State Department of Rehabilitation estimates that the total number of disabled persons in California exceeds four and a half million; since 80% of California's population lives within 30 miles of the coast, disabled-accessible coastal facilities should be an important part of accessway development.

Disabilities, as defined by the Department of Rehabilitation, range from visual and hearing impairments, to ambulatory and other orthopedic disabilities which limit a person's mobility, to certain mental and developmental disabilities. In addition to the four and a half million officially "disabled," countless others among the very young, elderly, and temporarily injured may require special improvements to facilities in order to be afforded access to coastal resources.

Federal, state, and local agencies and organizations throughout California are increasing their efforts to meet the needs of all of these people. For example, the State Department of Parks and Recreation is retrofitting facilities in 16 parks a year for the next four years to insure accessibility to disabled persons. Numerous piers, overlooks, and highway pull-offs allow people with all ranges of disabilities to enjoy the sight, smell, and sounds of the ocean. Wheelchair ramps and modified restrooms for the disabled are provided at many coastal accessways; these facilities are noted in the descriptive grid for each area under "Facilities for the Disabled."

Prairie Creek Redwoods State Park in Humboldt County has a nature walk for the blind, Revelation Trail, with guidebooks available in braille. At Año Nuevo State Reserve in San Mateo County, a portable trail of rubber belting can be set up across the sand to provide access to a platform from which the elephant seals can be seen in season at their rookery. The public beach in Marina del Rey is equipped with a ramp for access to the water, and wheelchairs are provided free of charge.

Tomales Bay State Park, Alan Sieroty Beach

Wheelchair accessible campsites exist at MacKerricher State Park, Pfeiffer Big Sur State Park, Morro Bay State Park, Carpinteria State Beach, and South Carlsbad State Beach. Reservations may be made in person at Ticketron outlets or by mail. For reservation request forms, contact:

California Department of Parks and Recreation
P.O. Box 2390
Sacramento, CA 95811   (916) 445-8513

Many organizations offer trips and transportation programs specifically for disabled people and are aware of facility improvements. Information about these programs and facilities can be obtained from:

The State Department of Rehabilitation
Mobility Barriers
830 K Street Mall
Sacramento, CA 95814   (916) 322-7581

The Center for Independent Living
2539 Telegraph Avenue
Berkeley, CA 94704   (415) 841-4776

National Parks and Recreation Areas

There are five national parks or recreation areas along the California coast: Redwood National Park in Del Norte and Humboldt Counties, Point Reyes National Seashore in Marin County, Golden Gate National Recreation Area (GGNRA) in Marin and San Francisco Counties, Channel Islands National Park in Santa Barbara and Ventura Counties, and Santa Monica Mountains National Recreation Area in Ventura and Los Angeles Counties.

Since each area has a variety of features, such as forests, mountains, headlands, lakes, rivers, cliffs, beaches, and tidepools, it is difficult to apply general rules to all of the parks. Normally those rules which apply to state parks apply to national parks as well. For example, animal and plant protection rules apply to all parks, while rules regarding pets are specific to each park, and often to particular areas within a park. In the Golden Gate National Recreation Area, pets are allowed to run without a leash on certain trails at Lands End; at other locations within GGNRA, they must be on a leash or are not allowed at all. Always check at park offices or information centers to be sure of rules for that park.

National Park Headquarters:

Redwood National Park
1111 2nd Street
Crescent City, CA 95531   (707) 464-6101

Point Reyes National Seashore
(Bear Valley Road)
Point Reyes, CA 94956   (415) 663-1092

Golden Gate National Recreation Area
Fort Mason
San Francisco, CA 94123   (415) 556-0560

Channel Islands National Park
1901 Spinnaker Drive
Ventura, CA 93001   (805) 644-8157

Santa Monica Mountains National Recreation Area
22900 Ventura Boulevard, Suite 140
Woodland Hills, CA 91364   (213) 888-3770

There are two other federal land areas along the coast which are open for public use. The Bureau of Land Management (BLM) operates the King Range National Conservation Area in Humboldt and Mendocino Counties; for information, write or call:

District Manager of BLM
1585 J Street
Arcata, CA 95521   (707) 822-7648

Los Padres National Forest, operated by the U.S. Forest Service, is located along the coast only in Monterey County, although it extends into five other southern California counties. For information, write or call:

Monterey Ranger District Office
406 South Mildred
King City, CA 93930   (408) 385-5434

Wood block print by Mallette Dean, *Monterey Peninsula*. Federal Writers' Project © 1941.

State Parks and Beaches

There are many beautiful state parks and beaches near or along the California coast. In order to keep them beautiful and safe for visitors, please observe the following rules and regulations:

1. Dogs with proof of rabies inoculation are permitted in state park campgrounds and day use areas, but are not allowed on most state beaches; check with the ranger. Pets must be leashed unless otherwise indicated.

2. Open fires are not allowed. Most state park camping and picnic areas have stoves or barbecues, and many beaches have fire rings.

3. Dune buggies, motorcycles, and other vehicles may be driven on the beach at Pismo State Beach/Vehicular Recreation Area. In other state park units all vehicles must stay on designated roads.

4. Many state beaches do not have lifeguards; where provided, lifeguards are usually on duty only during the summer.

5. Surfing is allowed only in designated areas at most state beaches.

6. Plants and animals in state park units are protected. Researchers may apply for collecting permits at the Department of Parks and Recreation headquarters in Sacramento at 1416 Ninth Street, 14th Floor.

7. A valid California fishing license is required in order to fish in state park units; consult the California Sport Fishing Regulations for season, size, and bag limits.

8. Individuals may collect driftwood from state beaches; commercial collection is not allowed.

9. Please stay on designated trails to prevent erosion and for your own safety.

10. Camping is allowed only in designated campsites.

11. Please don't litter — if you bring it in, take it back out.

A *Guide to the California State Park System* is available from the Department of Parks and Recreation; this guide includes a map, information on facilities at each park unit, and general park information, rules, and regulations.

To obtain a copy send $2 to:

California Department of Parks and Recreation
P.O. Box 2390
Sacramento, CA 95811   (916) 445-6477

Most campsites at state park campgrounds can be reserved in advance for a service fee at Ticketron outlets throughout the state. Reservations are recommended for popular areas. For reservation information, call toll free (in California only): (800) 952-5580.

In 1983, the Department of Parks and Recreation designated portions of existing day use parking areas in a number of coastal park units as "en route" campsites for overnight camping in self-contained recreational vehicles. En route sites are available for one-night-only stays, and cost $6.

En route sites currently exist at the following coastal parks: Westport-Union Landing State Beach and Van Damme State Park in Mendocino County; Mount Tamalpais State Park in Marin County; Half Moon Bay State Beach in San Mateo County; New Brighton State Beach, Sunset State Beach, and Seacliff State Beach in Santa Cruz County; Morro Bay State Park in San Luis Obispo County; Refugio State Beach and El Capitan State Beach in Santa Barbara County; Emma Wood State Beach in Ventura County; Bolsa Chica State Beach and Huntington State Beach in Orange County; and San Onofre State Beach and Silver Strand State Beach in San Diego County.

State park day use and camping facilities and fees listed in the Guide are current as of Spring 1983, and are subject to change.

Andrew Molera State Park

Pescadero State Beach

State Reserves, Preserves, and Refuges

Historically, the California coast has been an area of diverse landforms, vegetation, animal life, and cultural resources. Today, many coastal ecosystems and resources have been altered or destroyed by human activity. In an effort to protect and preserve remaining undisturbed areas of significant natural or cultural value, various public agencies have established a number of reserves, preserves, and refuges along the California coast. These protected areas provide excellent education and research opportunities and allow the general public to observe and develop an understanding of the state's natural environment and cultural background.

The University of California operates ten natural land and water reserves within the coastal zone ranging from the Pygmy Forest Reserve along the Mendocino County coast to Scripps Shoreline-Underwater Reserve in San Diego County; the purpose of these reserves is to protect for teaching and research purposes a series of undisturbed natural areas representing California's ecological diversity. Primary users of these reserves are public and private institutions of higher learning; other interested groups may use the reserves only if written permission has been obtained from the reserve manager, if there is no conflict with primary users, and if adequate supervision is provided.

To obtain more specific information on the U.C. Reserves System, write:

University of California
Natural Land and Water Reserves System
2120 University Avenue
Berkeley, CA 94720   (415) 644-4211

The California Department of Fish and Game is responsible for the protection and management of California's terrestrial and aquatic wildlife and their habitats. Fish and Game operates more than 40 marine life refuges and reserves within the California coastal zone, some of which are located in or adjacent to publicly accessible areas such as state parks, while others are restricted to access for education or scientific research.

The reserves and refuges have been established to protect and preserve endangered, threatened, or ecologically significant species of marine life or their habitats. As a general rule, marine reserves restrict the taking of most marine invertebrates (e.g., clams, abalone, lobster) and marine plant life. With respect to marine life refuges, it is generally unlawful to take or possess the marine life for which the refuge is named or to have in one's possession an implement designed to catch such animals.

For example, in the Pacific Grove Marine Gardens Fish Refuge, it is unlawful to catch fish or to possess any fish or fishing gear. Specific rules and regulations may vary from one reserve or refuge to another; for more specific information concerning marine life reserves and refuges, consult the Department of Fish and Game bulletins on marine resources or call or write the marine resources branch of the Department of Fish and Game office nearest you.

Entire state park units or distinct areas within them may be classified by the California Department of Parks and Recreation as reserves or preserves. The purpose of a state reserve is to provide day use areas for public enjoyment and education while preserving the reserve's unique natural features. It is illegal to disturb or take any living or non-living resource within a state park reserve except by authorized personnel for scientific or management purposes. Año Nuevo State Reserve in San Mateo County, which protects elephant seals, is an example of a natural reserve within the State Park System.

Preserves, which are distinct portions within a state park unit, are established for the purpose of maintaining an outstanding natural, scenic, scientific, or cultural feature in its natural condition. For example, a 19th and early 20th century dairy farm within Wilder Ranch State Park has been classified as a cultural preserve; the farm will be restored and operated as a museum displaying early California dairying methods.

In addition to the reserves, preserves, and refuges discussed above, other protected areas have been established by public agencies ranging from the federal government to local park districts. Visitors to any reserve, preserve, or refuge are asked to observe all rules and regulations; look for signs containing information on the proper use of the facility. Any questions concerning the use of a reserve, preserve, or refuge should be addressed to the local manager or the agency responsible for the operation of the area.

Environmental Camping

In June, 1981 the California Department of Parks and Recreation implemented its Environmental Camping Program. The purpose of the program is to provide small groups of campers with the opportunity to enjoy the scenic and natural features of California's state parks without the distractions often associated with conventional camping, such as automobiles and noise from nearby camps.

An environmental campsite consists of a tent space, table, and an enclosed pit toilet. Some campsites also include stoves or fire rings and a water source. Stoves are not provided in areas of high fire danger, but campers are allowed to use their portable camp stoves. The campsites are separated from each other and the regular campgrounds by natural features such as vegetation and landforms. Campers are required to carry in supplies from a designated parking area; automobiles are not permitted at the campsite.

Each environmental campsite has been located in an area containing significant scenic and natural qualities. Along the coast, environmental campsites currently exist at Lake Earl in Del Norte County; Prairie Creek Redwoods State Park and Dry Lagoon State Park in Humboldt County; Sinkyone Wilderness State Park and Manchester State Beach in Mendocino County; Salt Point State Park in Sonoma County; Mount Tamalpais State Park (at Steep Ravine Beach) in Marin County; Julia Pfeiffer Burns State Park in Monterey County; Montana de Oro State Park in San Luis Obispo County; Gaviota State Park in Santa Barbara County; and Point Mugu State Park in Ventura County. During the next year the Department of Parks and Recreation plans to install additional environmental campsites in other coastal park units.

Environmental camps are available to the public on a reservation basis; campsites can be reserved up to eight weeks in advance. The maximum stay at any one campsite is seven days and occupancy is limited to one family or eight people. The current user fee, as of Spring 1983, is $6 per night.

Montana de Oro State Park

Part of the environmental camping experience includes assuming responsibility for the maintenance of your campsite. Campers are expected to keep and leave the campsite and facilities clean; cleaning materials are located in the toilet structure. Garbage should be placed in trash receptacles (where provided) or carried out to the nearest trash container; do not dump garbage in the toilets. Unless otherwise posted, wood gathering in state parks is prohibited; therefore, campers should bring their own fuel. Pets are not allowed in environmental campsites in order to prevent the indigenous wildlife from being disturbed.

Conditions at the environmental camps may vary with the season and from site to site. For reservations and other information on the Environmental Camping Program, write:

California Department of Parks and Recreation
Reservation Office
P.O. Box 2390
Sacramento, CA 95811   (916) 323-2988

Coastal Hostels

Golden Gate Hostel

Coastal hostels offer travelers a distinctive type of low-cost ($4-$8) overnight lodging. Hostels vary in type and size; however, all are based on the international principle of community accommodations and on the premise that a person should leave a place in better condition than he or she finds it, whether in the natural or human-made environment.

Features generally found in hostels include a community living room; bathing, washing and laundry facilities; a fully-equipped kitchen and dining room where guests can cook and eat their own meals; dormitory rooms with bedding; and a tradition of participation in the work required to maintain the facility. Unlike their European counterparts, hostels in the United States are open to people of all ages, not specifically to "youth." In fact, many U.S. hostels now include family sleeping quarters which may be reserved in advance.

Hostels encourage non-motorized forms of tourism such as hiking, bicycling, skiing, and canoeing; however, most hostels are also accessible by public transportation or private automobile, and have limited parking available.

Since the first American hostel opened in Massachusetts in December of 1934, over 225 additional facilities have been established nationwide. The planned **California Coastal Chain of Hostels** represents one of the most innovative and comprehensive hostel programs in the United States. This unique hostel chain development serves as a model for cooperation between local, state, and federal government and hostel organizations in providing a low-cost lodging alternative.

Fourteen hostels are now open along or near the California coast. These form the backbone of the planned chain of 38 hostels located 20-30 miles apart from the Oregon border to Mexico. This chain will eventually provide non-motorized travelers with the ability to "hostel-hop" the entire length of the 1,100-mile California coastline.

The Bay Area Hostel System is currently the most well-developed link in the planned coastal chain. This network of six hostels covers over 120 miles of magnificent shoreline from the remote beaches of Point Reyes National Seashore to the urban waterfront in San Francisco and includes hostel facilities at two working lighthouse stations. Each Bay Area hostel offers distinctive accommodations in converted or renovated structures. The Golden Gate Hostel in the Marin Headlands, for example, now accommodates 60 overnight guests in a former 1902 officer's quarters building. This hostel sits amid eucalyptus trees, rolling hills, and meadows, only a short walk from Rodeo Beach and Lagoon and only four miles from the north end of the Golden Gate Bridge.

For further information on the California Coastal Chain of Hostels, on specific hostel rules and customs, or to make overnight reservations, contact the American Youth Hostels, Inc. Council in the coastal area where you will be traveling:

Golden Gate Council
Building 240, Fort Mason
San Francisco, CA 94123   (415) 771-4646

Central California Council
P.O. Box 28148
San Jose, CA 95159   (408) 298-0670

Los Angeles Council
1502 Palos Verdes Dr., N.
Harbor City, CA 90710   (213) 831-8109

San Diego Council
1031 India Street
San Diego, CA 92101   (619) 239-2644

Humboldt County

Arcata Hostel
1390 "I" Street
Arcata, CA 95521   (707) 822-9995

Marin County

Point Reyes Hostel
P.O. Box 247
Point Reyes Station, CA 94956   (415) 669-7414

Muir Woods Hostel
Muir Woods Road
Mill Valley, CA 94941   (415) 771-4646

Golden Gate Hostel
Building 941
Fort Barry
Sausalito, CA 94965   (415) 331-2777

San Francisco County

San Francisco International Hostel
Building 240
Fort Mason
San Francisco, CA 94123   (415) 771-7277

San Mateo County

Montara Lighthouse Hostel
P.O. Box 737
16th Street at Cabrillo Highway (Hwy. 1)
Montara, CA 94037   (415) 728-7177

Pigeon Point Lighthouse Hostel
Pigeon Point Road
Pescadero, CA 94060   (415) 879-0633

Santa Cruz County

Santa Cruz Hostel
P.O. Box 1241
Santa Cruz, CA 95060   (408) 423-8304
or 298-0670

Point Reyes Hostel

Montara Lighthouse Hostel

Monterey County

Monterey Peninsula Hostel
No permanent facility   (408) 373-4166

Los Angeles County

Westchester YMCA
8015 S. Sepulveda Boulevard
Los Angeles, CA 90045   (213) 776-0922

Los Angeles International Hostel
1502 Palos Verdes Drive North
Harbor City, CA 90710   (213) 831-8109

Orange County

Colonial Inn Hostel
421 8th Street
Huntington Beach, CA 92648   (714) 536-9184

San Diego County

Point Loma Hostel
3790 Udall Street
San Diego, CA 92109   (619) 223-4778

Armed Services YMCA Hostel
500 W. Broadway
San Diego, CA 92101   (619) 232-1133

Imperial Beach Hostel
170 Palm Avenue
Imperial Beach, CA 92032   (619) 423-8039

Geology of the Coast

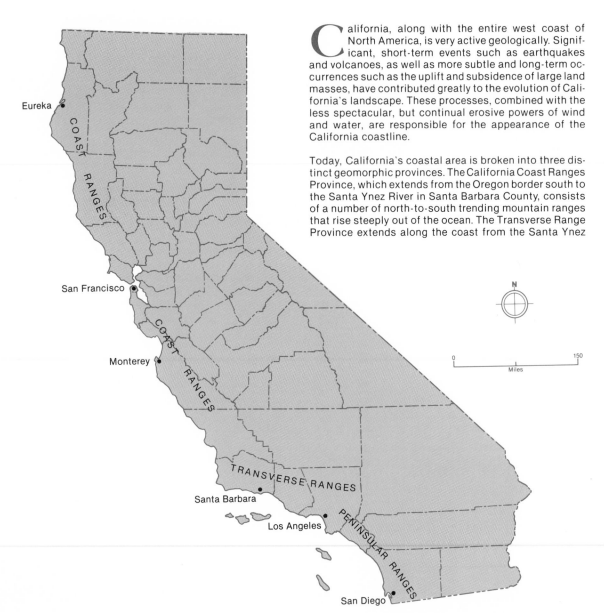

Eureka

San Francisco

Monterey

Santa Barbara

Los Angeles

San Diego

COAST RANGES

COAST RANGES

TRANSVERSE RANGES

PENINSULAR RANGES

N

0   150
Miles

California, along with the entire west coast of North America, is very active geologically. Significant, short-term events such as earthquakes and volcanoes, as well as more subtle and long-term occurrences such as the uplift and subsidence of large land masses, have contributed greatly to the evolution of California's landscape. These processes, combined with the less spectacular, but continual erosive powers of wind and water, are responsible for the appearance of the California coastline.

Today, California's coastal area is broken into three distinct geomorphic provinces. The California Coast Ranges Province, which extends from the Oregon border south to the Santa Ynez River in Santa Barbara County, consists of a number of north-to-south trending mountain ranges that rise steeply out of the ocean. The Transverse Range Province extends along the coast from the Santa Ynez Mountains in Santa Barbara County south to the Los Angeles Basin. Unlike the general north-to-south alignment of all the other mountain ranges in California, the mountains in the Transverse Range Province extend from east to west. Some of the oldest rocks in North America are found in the Transverse Range Province.

The third geomorphic province along the coast, the Peninsular Ranges Province, is one of the largest geomorphic areas in western North America. This province extends from the Los Angeles Basin south into Mexico to the tip of Baja California. Like the Coast Ranges, the Peninsular Ranges are aligned generally in a north-to-south direction.

The development of these geomorphic provinces is explained by the theory of plate tectonics. According to this theory, the earth's outermost layer, or crust, is made up of a number of rigid segments or plates that are able to move over the layer beneath it, called the mantle. Each plate may consist of a continent, an adjacent sea floor, or both, and is driven by internal earth forces.

Geologists believe that about 200 million years ago, the world's seven continents existed as one land mass. The continents have since pulled apart and slowly moved to their present locations. About 150 million years ago, the California coast was located in the area now occupied by the Sierra Nevada. As the North American plate moved westward, it overrode the Pacific Plate. Subsequently, the California coast was extended west more than 100 miles and the Coast Ranges were built from sedimentary material scraped from the Pacific Plate as it moved beneath the western edge of the North American continent.

The San Andreas fault zone, one of the most widely known earthquake-producing regions in the world, marks the current boundary in California where the North American Plate meets the Pacific Plate. Earthquakes along the San Andreas fault, such as the devastating 1906 earthquake centered near San Francisco, are caused by the friction and stress created as the two plates grind past one another. The fault runs through the interior of California from the Gulf of California until it meets the coast at Mussel Rock near Daly City. Continuing north, the fault passes through Stinson Beach, Tomales Bay, Bodega Bay, and Point Arena before leaving the coast at Shelter Cove, near Point Delgada in Humboldt County.

About 25 million years ago, the Pacific Plate began to move northward along the San Andreas fault. The central California coast was formed from a part of Baja California that attached to the Pacific Plate and moved north along the fault. Continued northward movement compressed the earth's crust and created the Transverse Range Province about five million years ago.

The two plates continue to move past each other today, as evidenced by the thousands of earth tremors that occur every year along the San Andreas and other fault systems in California. The city of Los Angeles is located on the Pacific Plate, west of the San Andreas fault, while San Francisco is on the North American Plate, east of the San Andreas fault. If the two plates continue to move in the same direction and at the same rate as they have in the geologic past, in about 10 milllion years Los Angeles will be due west of San Francisco.

The geologic units created by plate tectonics are gradually but continually being altered by other physical processes such as changes in sea level and erosion. The formation of the many lagoons in San Diego County, for example, illustrates how these processes affect the coastal landscape.

Tectonic activity resulted in the development of the Peninsular Ranges. Subsequently, ocean waves eroded the seaward edge of the ranges, resulting in the development of marine terraces. During the past ice age, sea level was lowered, thereby exposing the marine terraces. Terrestrial water runoff then cut deep channels in the newly exposed terraces. As the glaciers melted, sea level rose, and the seaward ends of the channels were flooded, creating estuaries. While streams carried water and sediment to the estuaries, the ocean currents distributed the sediments across the estuary mouths and created the bay mouth bars and lagoon systems visible today along the San Diego coast.

Marin County

San Andreas Fault, view northwest from Bolinas Lagoon to Tomales Bay.

29

Erosion

Waves, nearshore currents, and coastal sand supply affect beaches in three basic ways: first, if the amount of sand supplied to a beach is greater than the amount removed by waves and currents, the beach accretes, or extends seaward; second, if sediment supply is generally equivalent to the amount removed by the ocean, the beach is considered to be in equilibrium, although the beach's width may fluctuate in response to storm and calm periods; finally, if more sand is removed from a beach than is supplied, the beach erodes, or retreats landward.

The reduction in the amount of sand supplied to a beach may be caused by the damming of streams or the installation of structures that interrupt or inhibit the flow of sediment along the coast, such as breakwaters or jetties; the resultant erosion can have significant adverse impacts on the affected beach area. As the beach narrows from erosion, attacking waves threaten shoreline structures such as roads, houses, and other buildings. It then becomes necessary to protect these structures by installing shoreline protection devices such as seawalls, or structures designed to trap sand such as groins, or by widening the beach with sand from other sources. These protective measures are not only costly, but often increase erosion at adjacent beaches.

Coastal bluffs, which form the inland extent of many California beaches, are also subject to erosion. Advancing waves undercut the base of the bluffs, resulting in the collapse of bluff material and the subsequent landward retreat of the bluff itself. Bluff erosion is also caused by water runoff flowing over and through the bluffs; the water removes bluff material and increases the potential for landslides, slumping, or other forms of terrestrial erosion. As coastal bluffs erode and retreat landward, bluff stability, and the stability of structures located on the bluffs, becomes threatened. Subsequently, expensive stabilization, protection, and repair efforts are often required to slow or stop bluff retreat.

Many coastal access facilities include blufftop areas and trails down the bluffs to the beach. Although beachgoers can do little to stop the erosive power of waves, they can assist in reducing terrestrial erosion. Visitors should not park or walk near bluff edges except in designated locations and should use only formal trails and stairs. In addition to being unsafe, activity near bluff edges and the creation of informal trails removes vegetation and loosens bluff material, which increases erosion. Visitors who follow these simple rules will aid in reducing facility repair and maintenance costs and will prolong the availability of safe, operable access facilities.

Thornton State Beach

Pacific Palisades

Climate

California's coastal climate generally can be classified as Mediterranean — that is, characterized by temperate wet winters and warm dry summers. Only one percent of the world has this climate, and it is found nowhere else in the United States. The two chief influences on the coastal climate are the persistent high-pressure system located west of California over the Pacific Ocean, called the Pacific High, and the effect of the ocean itself.

The Pacific High is stronger and in a more northerly position in the summer. It prevents storms from approaching the West Coast and is responsible for the dry weather along the shore from May through September. In the winter this high-pressure system moves south and occasionally weakens, allowing storms to reach the state.

As storms most frequently approach from the north, that area receives more rainfall than the south, which remains partially shielded by the high, even in the winter. As a result, Crescent City receives an average of 70 inches of rain annually, while San Francisco receives an average of 20 inches, and San Diego averages only 12 inches. There are also more days with rain in the north than in the south, with San Francisco having an average of 63 days of rain per year while Los Angeles has 34. As the high migrates south, Northern California receives precipitation which is entirely blocked from the south; thus, its rainy season is longer.

As might be expected, the temperatures at the beach also vary from north to south. In Eureka in Humboldt County the average temperature in January is 47 degrees and in August 57 degrees, while in San Diego the average is 55 degrees for January and 70 degrees for August. The temperatures along the coast are limited to a relatively narrow seasonal and daily range by the moderating influence of the ocean; thus temperatures of below freezing or above 100 degrees are unusual. Long Beach, because of its south-facing shore alignment, has an average of 15 days a year of daily high temperatures above 90 degrees; however, the rest of the Southern California coast gets that warm less than five times a year.

The marine air also keeps the humidity high year-round, with 65% relative humidity being about normal. Contributing to this is the frequent occurrence of fog or low cloudiness, which is common in the spring and summer months; however, the fog and low clouds usually "burn off" by noon.

The Pacific High results in an overall wind pattern from the northwest. In most areas, onshore sea breezes increase in the afternoon. Before and during most storms, the wind shifts so that it is blowing from the south.

While the summer climate in California is fairly stable, wind, temperature, and rainfall averages can be deceptive when compared to what one actually encounters on a yearly or daily basis. In particular, rainfall usually varies greatly from year to year. Local topography has a pronounced effect on the climate as well. For example, where the shoreline is backed by mountains, precipitation is usually heavier. Another example is that south-facing shores such as those at Santa Cruz, Santa Barbara, Malibu, and Long Beach usually have warmer temperatures than the rest of the coast.

There are occasional weather patterns which, while not common, are distinctive enough that the visitor to the coast should be aware of them. When a high-pressure system builds up inland, a reversal of the usual winds can occur, the direction then being from the interior. These winds, called Santa Anas or foehns, are hot, dry, and sometimes quite strong. During the summer they can contribute to the destructive spread of brush fires. In the winter they are even stronger, sometimes of hurricane strength, but are not as warm. Santa Anas are markedly affected by local topography; for example, the winds are frequently stronger in canyons.

In the summer, tropical air may intrude even to Northern California, bringing the possibility of thunderstorms, which are usually rare along the coast. Even more uncommon are full-fledged tropical storms, which may bring heavy rains or showers to Southern California in the summer.

With moderate temperatures and dry summers, California has ideal weather for visiting the coast. Because of seasonal and geographical differences in the state, visitors should check local conditions before departing on a trip to the coast.

Russian River Estuary

History of the Coast

In 1510, the Spanish author Garcí Rodríquez Ordóñez de Montalvo wrote of a mythical island, named California, that he described as being rich in gold, located "on the right hand of the Indies...very near the Terrestrial Paradise," and inhabited only by women and man-eating "griffins." Montalvo's fictitious island, and other rumors of lands of great wealth, are thought to have led many early Spanish explorers to believe that such a land might actually exist along the uncharted areas of the west coast of the New World. One of the earliest Spanish explorers, Hernando Cortés, is thought to have been the first to apply the name California (probably taken from Montalvo's writings) to the area now called Baja California, which he explored from 1535 to 1537.

At the times of Cortés' expeditions, California was inhabited by as many as 200 to 300 thousand Native Americans; California was then one of the most densely populated Native American areas in North America, north of the present boundary of Mexico. Scattered tribes, many of which were settled along the coast, were usually peaceful and isolated from one another. More than 100 dialects of 21 distinct languages were spoken. Shell mounds indicate the presence of California Native Americans at least three to four thousand years ago; their relatively simple nomadic culture is believed to have remained unchanged until their encounters with the Spanish.

During their early explorations, the Spanish referred to all of the Spanish-claimed land from what is now Baja California in Mexico to Alaska as "California." The first European to explore the coast of California north of the state's present boundary with Mexico was Juan Rodríquez Cabrillo, a Portuguese navigator hired by the Spanish. Cabrillo sailed up the coast in 1542, charting the landmarks now known as San Diego Bay, Santa Catalina Island, the Channel Islands, Point Conception, Point Pinos, Monterey Bay, Point Año Nuevo, and Point Reyes. Because of bad weather, Cabrillo turned back near Point Reyes and returned to the Channel Islands, where he died in 1543. Cabrillo's pilot, Bartolomé Ferrelo, eventually continued the voyage north and passed Cape Mendocino, the westernmost point on the California coast; it is believed he named the cape after the Viceroy of New Spain, Don Antonio de Mendoza.

Although Cabrillo found no evidence of the riches and wealthy cities rumored to exist in California, Spain nonetheless laid claim to the entire coast. The English,

Wood block prints by Mallette Dean, *Monterey Peninsula,* Federal Writers' Project © 1941.

however, were bitter rivals of the Spanish and refused to recognize Spanish-claimed lands and rights of navigation. The English government, therefore, tacitly encouraged private adventurers to attack Spanish ships and settlements. The most famous of these adventurers was Francis Drake, who sailed up the coast of South and Central America in 1579, attacking and plundering numerous Spanish ships along the way. Drake continued northward along the California coast in a futile search for the northern passage that was thought to exist between the Pacific and Atlantic Oceans. Drake stopped along the coast to refit his vessel at an area he named Nova Albion; although the actual landing site is unknown, he may have landed at what is now called Drakes Bay off Point Reyes.

Spanish trading galleons traveling from Manila to Acapulco along the northern trade routes visited the coast in the late 1500's, in search of protective harbors where their crews could rest and gather supplies. Pedro de Unamuno anchored a galleon at Morro Bay in 1587, and Sebastián Rodríquez Cermeño landed at Drakes Bay in 1595, where his galleon was destroyed by storms. Remarkably, Cermeño and his crew traveled the remaining distance to Acapulco in a small launch, completing one of the first detailed surveys of the coast.

The Spanish again tried to find a harbor for their trading galleons in 1602, when the Spanish king directed Sebastián Vizcaíno to explore the California coast and to confirm whether there actually existed a North American passage to the Atlantic. Vizcaíno found no such passage, but he did chart a major portion of the coast and discovered what he described to be a suitably protective harbor at Monterey Bay. Many of the place names Vizcaíno gave to California coastal landmarks still exist today.

Between 1697 and 1767, the Spanish established a number of Jesuit missions in Baja California (now part of Mexico) for the purpose of converting the Native Americans to Catholicism and to strengthen the Spanish claim to the coast. In 1767, Juan Gaspar de Portolá carried out a royal Spanish decree banishing the Jesuits; the missions were then turned over to the Franciscans, led by Padre Junípero Serra.

Portolá and Serra were directed to expand the mission and presidio system northward, and in 1769 they traveled to San Diego Bay, where they established the first Alta (or upper) California mission. Portolá then continued northward on a land expedition in search of the Monterey Bay which Vizcaíno had so favorably described over a century earlier. Portolá actually camped at Monterey Bay on his first expedition, but failing to recognize it as the bay which Vizcaíno had charted, he contined north and eventually sighted San Francisco Bay. Portolá returned to San Diego and organized a second expedition which returned to Monterey Bay in 1770. Portolá was joined by Padre Serra, and they proceeded to establish the Monterey Mission and Presidio; this settlement became the first official capital of Alta California in 1775.

Between 1769 and 1823, Padre Serra, followed by Padre Fermín Francisco de Lasuén, settled a total of 21 missions on or near the California coast. The missions were usually located in the areas of the greatest Native American populations, since the missionaries' goal was to convert the resident inhabitants to the Catholic faith. However, contact with the Spanish missionaries was devastating to the Native Americans, who suffered horribly from diseases inadvertently introduced by the Europeans. The Native Americans were also forced to work on the missions' agricultural and ranch lands. Many of the Native Americans rebelled, and hostile outbreaks periodically occurred at the missions. A visiting Frenchman at Monterey in 1786, Jean Francois Galaup de la Pérouse, described the missionaries' treatment of the Native Americans as being worse than American plantation slavery in the southeast.

Mexico won independence from Spain in 1821, and California was formally declared a territory of the Republic of Mexico in 1825. In 1833, the Mexican Governor of California, José Figueroa, ordered the secularization of the missions, requiring that their lands be distributed among the mission Native Americans and the resident "Californios," most of whom were of Hispanic heritage.

However, Figueroa died in 1835, and a majority of the Native American-held land was subsequently taken by the Californios, who managed these huge land grants as livestock "ranchos."

After secularization many of the Native Americans attempted to return to their tribes and former lifestyles; those that did not were put to work as unpaid ranch hands on the ranchos. The ranchos produced hides and tallow, much of which were sold to American traders from Boston who arrived by ship. San Diego was once a principal area for collecting and curing hides obtained from the ranchos.

San Francisco Bay, before and during the gold rush.
San Francisco Archives, San Francisco Public Library

Americans began arriving on the coast in the late 1700's in search of animal furs and whales. The abundance of sea otters and fur seals created a profitable coastal fur trade, which also attracted the Russians, who built a north coast settlement at Fort Ross in 1812. New England whalers took large numbers of migrating California gray whales, which were cut and processed at land based whaling stations. Whaling stations were established on the coast at Ballast Point in San Diego Bay, Portuguese Bend near Palos Verdes, San Simeon, Moss Landing, Monterey Bay, and at Bolinas near Point Reyes. So many whales were taken (in the 1840's the patios and side-walks at the Monterey station were paved with whale vertebrae) that conservation measures were necessary in the early 1900's to preserve the remaining whale herds.

The United States did not want to be limited to land east of the Rocky Mountains, and therefore viewed California, with its desirable coastal ports, as important territory. Increasing numbers of American settlers in California, and fear that Mexico might cede its California territory to England for payment of debts, prompted the United States government to begin attempts to purchase the land from Mexico. When negotiations broke down, partly due to the war between the United States and Mexico, the U.S. helped to initiate a revolution within California.

In 1846, a small band of American settlers (who were later joined by a small army detachment led by Captain John C. Frémont) easily forced a ranking Mexican general, Mariano G. Vallejo, to surrender at Sonoma, where the Americans first raised the California Republic "Bear Flag." Commander John Sloat shortly thereafter raised the American flag at Monterey, the ex-capital of Mexican California. Skirmishes between the Californios and the Americans ended in 1847 with the surrender of the Californios. In 1848, California became a United States territory. The state's constitution was drafted at Monterey in 1849, and in 1850 California was admitted as the thirty-first state of the Union.

A discovery of gold in 1848 triggered the California gold rush, when thousands of Americans, Europeans, and Chinese flocked to the gold fields of the Sierra Nevada Mountains and the state's northern ranges. Most of the immigrants entered the state by sea, through the Golden Gate and the port of San Francisco. San Francisco grew rapidly during the 1850's, serving as an important marketplace and hub of the gold rush period.

The gold rush also initiated the development of the state's north coast, which was rich in the timber necessary to the gold mines and the state's rapidly growing towns and cities. In the 1850's, shipping timber by sea was easier than shipping it overland, and hundreds of mills and small settlements were established in the north adjacent to nearly every bay and cove that could serve as a port. The timber was mostly brought to San Francisco, Los Angeles, and through the Sacramento River Delta to the Central Valley. Major north coast timber mills are now located at Eureka and Fort Bragg.

The City of Los Angeles was incorporated in 1850, and many of the neighboring ranchos were gradually subdivided into small home and farm sites. In 1876, the Southern Pacific Railroad completed a new line, which ran between San Francisco and Los Angeles, providing a link with the transcontinental railroad system which had previously ended in the San Francisco Bay Area. In 1885, the Santa Fe railway to Los Angeles was completed, creating intense competition between the two railroads which quickly dropped fares from the midwest to Los Angeles to as low as $1 per person. Thousands of people began arriving in Los Angeles and land speculation rapidly reached a frenzied state, initiating the first of several Southern California population booms.

As Southern California developed, many areas along the coast became popular vacation spots. Beach resort communities were established at Santa Monica in 1872 (where a small hotel advertised that "a week spent at the beach will add 10 years to your life") and at Venice in 1904. Huge luxury hotels were also constructed along the coast, including the Hotel Del Coronado near San Diego, the Redondo Beach Hotel near Los Angeles, the Potter Hotel in Santa Barbara, and the Hotel Del Monte in Monterey.

Between 1860 and 1880, the Chinese formed the first marine fishing industry in California when they established a number of fishing villages on the coast from which they exported millions of dollars worth of fish (mostly abalone and shrimp) to China. Prior to 1860 the only fishermen on the coast were the Native Americans, who took fish primarily for their own consumption. After 1890 the Chinese were gradually driven from the lucrative industry by resident Italians, Japanese, Portuguese, and Yugoslavs.

In the late 1800's, Southern California experienced an oil boom, considered to be as economically important as the earlier Northern California gold rush. Exploration for oil began in the 1860's, but it was not until the 1890's (following improvements in refining, storage, and drilling) that the industry greatly expanded. In succeeding years, Southern California established itself as a producer of approximately a quarter of the world's oil and gas supply. The San Pedro Bay and Long Beach area in Los Angeles soon became, and still is, a major distribution point for the oil industry. Oil development expanded to offshore leases of the Outer Continental Shelf in the 1950's.

During the 1900's, especially during and immediately following World War II, the military built a number of coastal defense bases, including those at San Diego, Camp Pendleton, Point Mugu, Port Hueneme, Vandenberg, Fort Ord, and along the Marin County coastline. Residential and industrial development also continued along the coast; today, approximately eighty percent of the state's population lives within thirty miles of the ocean. This development created a demand for preservation of coastal public lands; the first coastal park, Big Basin Redwoods in Santa Cruz County, was purchased in 1902, and the State Park System was formed in 1927. There are currently approximately one hundred state beaches, parks, reserves, preserves, and monuments on or near the coast.

Santa Monica c. 1870's.   California State Library

Long Beach c. 1890.   California State Library

Historic Landmarks

There are virtually thousands of historic monuments, landmarks, and points of interest along the California coast; included here are descriptions of a few of the more famous and interesting historic spots.

Carson Mansion, Humboldt County: The Carson Mansion in Eureka is a famous example of Victorian Gothic architecture, built by lumber magnate William Carson in the 1880's. Having made his fortune from logging the redwood trees around Humboldt Bay, he built his mansion from choice, clear grain redwood. Carved panels, onyx fireplaces, and stained glass windows decorate the interior, while cupolas, porches, and "gingerbread" detail are part of the Queen Anne style exterior. The 18-room, three story, ornamented mansion was built for Carson by dozens of carpenters and artists, and is now a private men's club. Although the interior is not open to the public, the mansion can be viewed from Second Street in Eureka.

Fort Humboldt State Historic Park, Humboldt County: Fort Humboldt was built on a hilltop overlooking Eureka to protect the settlers from the Native Americans. The fort was occupied from 1853 to 1870; only minor battles with the Native Americans occurred during that time. There were over 14 buildings on the site, including officers quarters, a hospital, a powder magazine, a black-smith shop, a stable, and a bakehouse. The fort's most noted officer was Ulysses S. Grant, who spent six unhappy months stationed there in 1854. The commissary building still stands, and contains a small museum; there is also an exhibit of early logging tools and machinery on the fort grounds, located off Highland Avenue in Eureka.

Mendocino, Mendocino County: The town of Mendocino was first called Meiggsville after Harry Meiggs, who bought the land and opened a timber mill at the mouth of the Big River in the 1850's. Although Meiggs (and probably the name Meiggsville) departed in 1854, the timber mill operated until 1937. Around the turn of the century, Mendocino was a bustling port, boasting at least 21 saloons and 8 hotels. Because most of the residents were transplanted New Englanders, the buildings reflected the New England salt box style and early Victorian Gothic with steep roofs and clapboard walls.

After the closing of the mill, Mendocino's population declined until the 1950's, when numerous artists were lured to the town by its remoteness and inexpensive homes. The influx of artists and other people who value the charm and beauty of Mendocino continues today. Some of the notable buildings in Mendocino include the MacCallum House (1882), the Presbyterian Church (1868), the Mendocino Hotel (1878), the Joss House (1855), and the Masonic Hall (1872).

Carson Mansion, Eureka

Mendocino Hotel

Fort Ross, Sonoma County: In 1812 Captain Kuskov established a permanent Russian settlement at Fort Ross, 12 miles north of the Russian River. The settlement, one of several along the Sonoma coast, was the center of Russian activities in California. Fur harvesting and agricultural cultivation were quite successful; the surplus products were either traded to the Spanish in California, shipped up to Alaska to support Russian settlements there, or sent to Russia. The Fort Ross settlers, probably the first to commercially harvest redwood timber in California, began shipping the lumber to the Hawaiian Islands in the 1820's.

The fort's population, which never exceeded 400, was comprised of both Russians and Aleuts (natives of the Aleutian Islands). The fort included two blockades along the palisades, a chapel, and the commander's headquarters. Outside the fort were approximately 50 buildings, including the blacksmith, carpenter, and cooper shops, and a stable for cows. Because of depleted resources, the Russians gave up their colony at Fort Ross in 1841. The fort is now owned by the State Department of Parks and Recreation, and is partially restored and open to the public.

Drakes Beach, Marin County: One of the first Europeans to explore the coast was the English sailor Francis Drake, who anchored and repaired his vessel, the *Golden Hinde,* in a Northern California harbor in 1579. Drake's journal of his voyage leaves the exact location of his landing unclear; however, historians believe it was most likely either Drakes Bay at Point Reyes, nearby Bodega Bay, or along the Marin County shores of San Francisco Bay. Monuments commemorating Drake are located at Drakes Beach near the ranger's office on Drakes Beach Road, and at Drakes Estero.

Drake stayed at his landing site for 36 days, and named the land Nova Albion (New England), partly because the eroded white cliffs (such as those at Drakes Beach) reminded him of the white banks of Dover in England. Drake's crew built a stone fort at the landing site, and found the Native Americans to be extremely friendly; so friendly, in fact, that Drake reported that the Native Americans crowned him as their king and regarded the English as gods. Drake eventually returned to England, becoming the first ship's captain to circumnavigate the globe.

Golden Gate Bridge, San Francisco and Marin Counties: The entrance to San Francisco Bay was named *chrysopylae* (golden gate) by John C. Frémont in 1846. He chose this name because he expected the riches of the Orient to be shipped through the Golden Gate. Several years later, the gold riches from the Sierra foothills gave the Golden Gate a new meaning. Although the idea for a bridge spanning the bay entrance was first publicly mentioned in 1869, it was not seriously considered until 1916. Numerous problems delayed the building of the bridge, the most significant of which were design and engineering problems encountered because of severe currents caused by the tides through the gate.

In May 1937 the twin tower, single suspension bridge built by Joseph Strauss was opened. The bridge took four years to build, and although the construction claimed several lives, it was a major engineering success. The 8,981-foot bridge is red-orange, a rust-preventive shade called international orange; it is painted every year, and it takes a full year to paint. The Golden Gate Bridge is one of the few bridges which pedestrians can walk across. On May 27, 1937, when the bridge was first opened to pedestrians, 202,000 people walked across it. Two observation areas at each end of the bridge provide panoramic views of the bridge, the bay, and San Francisco.

Cliff House, San Francisco County: The Cliff House, which has a restaurant and bar and is perched on the cliffs overlooking the Pacific Ocean, Seal Rocks, and the long strand of Ocean Beach, is the third building on the site to be called the "Cliff House." The first Cliff House was built in 1863 and was a popular destination for San Franciscans. Adolf Sutro bought the building in 1883 and dispatched the rough clientele which habitually gathered there. Unfortunately, the Cliff House burned down on Christmas Day in 1894. Two years later, Sutro rebuilt the Cliff House, seven stories high, complete with spires and towers, only to have it burn down again in 1907. The present building, made of stucco, was built following the second fire and is still a popular destination point for both resident San Franciscans and visitors.

Golden Gate Bridge

San Francisco Archives,
San Francisco Public Library

City of Monterey, Monterey County: Numerous adobe buildings in downtown Monterey, dating from the 1800's, recall the town's historical importance in the development of the state. Many of these buildings are part of Monterey State Historic Park. The oldest government building on the Pacific Coast, the Custom House, was built intermittently from about 1827 to 1846. It was here that American and British traders paid duty to the Mexicans, and it is also here that the United States flag was first officially raised, on July 7, 1846. Colton Hall was the first American public building in California, and was the site of the state constitutional convention in 1849. Walter Colton, for whom the building is named, and Robert Semple started the first newspaper in California.

There are several adobe houses which typify styles popular at the time. The Larkin House, built in the 1830's, shows the typical Monterey style architecture with two stories, balconies, and verandas. This was the home of Thomas Oliver Larkin, who was the first and only U.S. Consul to Mexican California; he held this position from 1843 to 1846, and was also a key figure in initiating the American revolution in California. The Casa Gutierrez, built in the 1840's, is a home typical of average citizens during the Mexican period. Other historic buildings in the area include private houses, California's first theatre, public buildings, and a whaling station.

Hearst Castle, San Luis Obispo County: La Casa Grande in San Simeon was designed by William Randolph Hearst and his architect, Julia Morgan; construction began in 1922 and ended in 1951 when Hearst died. The house by that time had 100 rooms; 38 bedrooms, 31 bathrooms, 14 sitting rooms, a kitchen, a movie theater, 2 libraries, a billiard room and a dining room were included in this Hispano-Moresque mansion. Guests who stayed with Hearst were bound by four rules: they were required to come to the Great Hall in La Casa Grande every evening; they had to attend the nightly movie in his private theater; no liquor was permitted in the guests' suites; and no one was to mention the word death in Hearst's presence.

The grounds around La Casa Grande include 123 acres of gardens, terraces, pools, guesthouses, a small air strip, and tennis courts. The three guesthouses are Mediterranean-Renaissance style mansions; the gardens contain exotic plants from all over the world. The Roman Pool is thought to have been inspired by a first century Roman mausoleum. Hearst also had a collection of wild animals, including zebras, tahr goats, aoudad (Barbary sheep), monkeys, cheetahs, lions, leopards, panthers, and polar bears; the descendents of these animals still graze on the grounds. The State Department of Parks and Recreation now owns the property, and visits are by guided tour only.

Hearst Castle

Santa Barbara Mission, Santa Barbara County: Mission Santa Barbara was originally founded in 1786; the present structure on Los Olivos Street in the City of Santa Barbara was dedicated in 1820. The mission's well maintained features, early Spanish Renaissance architecture, massive six-foot thick walls, and the fact that it has been in continuous use for religious services since its dedication make this one of the most distinctive and attractive

California missions. The graves of approximately 4,000 Native Americans are contained within the mission's scenic old cemetery, attesting to the success of the Santa Barbara padres in recruiting the native population into the mission system.

Santa Catalina Island, Los Angeles County: Juan Rodríquez Cabrillo originally named the island San Salvador, after his ship, when he landed here in 1542. This was the first recorded landing by a European on the island. In 1602, Sebastián Vizcaíno landed on the island and renamed it Santa Caterina after a Christian martyr, the patron saint of spinsterhood. After the missions were established on the mainland, the island's Native Americans were exposed to European diseases as a result of trading with the mainland villages, and many died; measles alone killed 200 Native Americans in the early 1800's.

Until Mexico gained its independence from Spain, Catalina was a base for unlawful trade with the mainland. The numerous coves hid ships which were avoiding duty payments on trade goods. During the next few decades, Catalina had various residents; in 1887, Avalon was named by Mrs. E. J. Whitney after a Celtic paradise. In the early 1900's, Judge Joseph B. Banning, one of the island's owners, built a wharf and house on the Isthmus. This became a popular spot for filming movies; *Mutiny on the Bounty, Treasure Island,* and *The Ten Commandments* were all filmed here. William Wrigley, Jr. bought the island in 1919 and converted it into the resort it is today. He planted palm trees, cleaned the beaches, and built the famous Casino on a rocky promontory in Avalon Bay.

Dana Point, Orange County: Dana Point was named after author Richard Henry Dana, who described this point in his book, *Two Years Before the Mast,* after he had anchored his ship here in 1835. At that time, the harbor was a major port for square-rigged ships and a loading area for cattle hides brought in from the Californios' ranchos. The cliffs were steep and hard to climb, so the hides were thrown down to the harbor from the cliff tops, then carried by the sailors on their heads out to the ships. As Dana described, "It was really a picturesque sight: the great height, the scaling of the hides, and the continual walking to and fro of the men, who looked like mites, on the beach. This was the romance of hide droghing!" A new harbor with artificial breakwaters and room for 2,500 boats was completed in 1970.

Cabrillo National Monument, San Diego County: Located near the tip of Point Loma, overlooking San Diego Bay, this monument commemorates Juan Rodríquez Cabrillo, the first Europen to land in Alta California. Cabrillo sailed into San Diego Bay (which he named San Miguel) in 1542, and probably landed at what is now known as Ballast Point, originally called La Punta de Guijarros ("The Point of Cobblestones") by Sebastían Vizcaíno in 1602; the point is so named because the rocks there were used as ballast for Boston trading ships in the 1800's. Ballast Point was also the location of a Spanish fort from 1797 to 1838 (the fort was involved in the "Battle of San Diego" in 1803, a dispute between American fur traders and the Spanish), and two New England based whaling stations were established there in the mid 1800's. The old Point Loma Lighthouse, located on the hill above the Cabrillo statue and the museum, was built in 1854 but abandoned in 1891 because its elevation obscured it during periods of fog. The old lighthouse building is now open to visitors.

Hotel Del Coronado, San Diego County: This Coronado hotel, built during the 1880's, was designed by Stanford White, and is the largest wooden structure west of the Mississippi. All building materials had to be ferried to the peninsula from San Diego, then carried three miles by train to the building site. The 399-room beach resort hotel, located on 33 acres on Orange Avenue in Coronado, includes a two-acre interior courtyard, and a museum in the basement, which contains, among other things, old photographs of the hotel and famous signatures from the guest register.

Cabrillo National Monument

Hotel Del Coronado

39

How to Use the Guide

The Guide is divided into fifteen sections by county, from north to south, and into subsections by local area. Each subsection includes a map, descriptions of the accessways, and a grid which contains fifteen categories for facilities and seven for environment. The categories are defined as follows:

FACILITIES

ENTRANCE/PARKING FEE: Indicates that there is an entrance or parking fee for the area. These fees frequently apply only to summer use, and in some cases, apply only for overnight stays and not for day use.

PARKING: Indicates that there is adjacent on-street parking or a parking lot.

RESTROOMS: Noted where either flush or chemical toilets are provided.

LIFEGUARD: Lifeguards, where present, are usually on duty only in the summer.

CAMPGROUND: Indicates either a private campground or one which is part of a local, state, or federal park unit.

SHOWERS: Only noted where there are hot showers. Many beaches have outdoor cold showers.

FIREPITS: Indicates any designated cooking area, including barbeques, grills, and fire rings.

STAIRS TO BEACH: Used to indicate a stairway which leads to the beach; in certain cases, there may also be an alternate way to get to the beach.

PATH TO BEACH: Indicates that it is necessary to take a path or trail to get to the beach, as opposed to an area where access to the beach is directly from the parking area.

BIKE PATH: Indicates a paved bikeway separate from the road. Bike lanes or recommended routes are not included.

HIKING TRAILS: Indicates designated hiking trails, not simply areas where hiking is possible.

FACILITIES FOR THE DISABLED: Includes wheelchair ramps, modified restrooms, or other specific modifications which enable persons with disabilities to use the facility.

BOATING FACILITIES: Includes boat launch ramps, hoists, slips, docks, moorings, etc.

FISHING: Noted where a fishing pier or fish cleaning facility exists; also noted for any area commonly used for fishing.

EQUESTRIAN TRAIL: Noted for any area which has a designated equestrian trail.

ENVIRONMENT

SANDY BEACH/DUNES/ROCKY SHORE: Noted where the environment of the accessway includes a sandy beach, dunes, or a rocky shore; these categories are not mutually exclusive and may refer to only a portion of the area.

UPLAND FROM BEACH: Used when all or part of an accessway is upland from the shoreline. Some coastal accessways have both nearshore and upland portions.

STREAM CORRIDOR: Indicates a stream in the vicinity; sometimes the accessway is actually along the stream.

BLUFF: Used when the environment includes a bluff, although the accessway itself may not be directly on the bluff, but below or nearby.

WETLAND: Indicates a wetland in the vicinity; sometimes the accessway is actually located alongside the wetland.

CALIFORNIA
COASTAL ACCESS
· GUIDE ·

Del Norte Coast Redwoods State Park

Del Norte County

Del Norte County's two principal industries reflect its predominant natural features; the timber industry utilizes its extensive redwood forests, and commercial fishing depends on the anadromous fish rivers. Both rivers and forests provide recreational opportunities as well. The fertile Smith River plain supports dairy and Easter lily farming, in addition to providing a home to two-thirds of the county's population.

Until 1850, the Del Norte coast was home only to the Yurok and Talawa Indians. The Yurok, who lived along the banks of the Klamath River, are recognized today as having been the most advanced Indian civilization in California. In 1828, members of Jedediah Smith's expedition came overland to the coast, but permanent settlers did not arrive until 1850; in that year the Klamath area was flooded with white men seeking gold. By 1855 an Indian reservation was formed along the Klamath to contain the Yurok. Today the Hoopa (originally Hupa) Reservation on the Trinity River is the home for both Yurok and Hupa, as well as several other tribes.

Klamath recalls its Indian past each summer during the salmon festival, when ceremonial dances are performed by local Indians, in addition to logging contests and general community fair festivities. The Klamath River is famous for salmon and steelhead trout fishing; summer and fall bring hundreds of anglers to its shores.

Crescent City was also settled in the 1850's, and became an important port for the transfer of gold from the strikes in southern Oregon, and later, from those in the nearby Smith River watershed. At one point, all of Crescent Beach was staked for gold claims. By the 1870's, gold fever had subsided and the timber industry became the dominant use of the port. The timber industry in Del Norte had its most recent peak in the 1950's; now, with only a few stands of old-growth redwood remaining, cutting is slowing down to reach the rate at which new trees reach maturity.

The average temperature difference during the year along the Del Norte coast is only 13 degrees; however, coastal fog is prevalent in summer, and heavy rains in winter. In the past, huge storms have capsized many boats offshore, at times leaving no survivors. In 1964, as a result of an earthquake off Alaska, a tsunami hit Crescent City, and destroyed the business district. That same year, a storm flooded the Klamath River, washing away the town of Klamath.

The towns of Smith River, Crescent City, and Klamath are now popular tourist areas, as is Redwood National Park, which draws visitors to see the world's tallest trees and large old-growth redwood groves. Within its boundaries are two state parks: Del Norte Coast Redwoods, and Jedediah Smith.

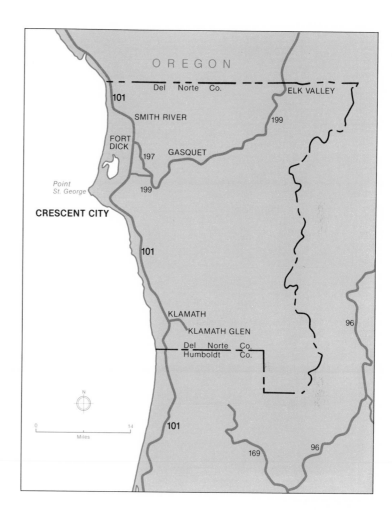

Headquarters for Redwood National Park are in Crescent City, 1111 2nd Street 95531; call: (707) 464-6101. For more information on Del Norte County, write: Del Norte Chamber of Commerce, Front and K Streets, P.O. Box 246, Crescent City 95531, or call (707) 464-3174. For information about the Del Norte County Bus, write: Del Norte Senior Center, 810 H Street, Crescent City 95331, or call (707) 464-3069.

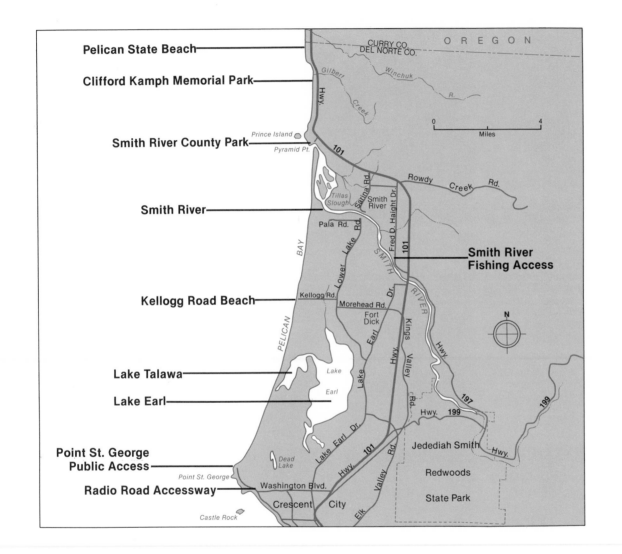

Pelican State Beach

Clifford Kamph Memorial Park

Smith River County Park

Smith River

Smith River Fishing Access

Kellogg Road Beach

Lake Talawa

Lake Earl

Point St. George Public Access

Radio Road Accessway

CURRY CO.
DEL NORTE CO.

OREGON

Gilbert Creek

Winchuk R.

0   4
Miles

Prince Island

Pyramid Pt.

101

Rowdy Creek Rd.

Tillas Slough

Sarina Rd.

Smith River

Fred D. Haight Dr.

101

Pala Rd.

Lower Lake Rd.

SMITH RIVER

Kellogg Rd.

Morehead Rd.

Fort Dick

Earl Dr.

Kings Valley Hwy.

N

BAY

PELICAN

Lake

Earl

Lake

Rd.

197

199

Lake Earl Dr.

Hwy. 199

Dead Lake

101

Jedediah Smith

Hwy.

Point St. George

Washington Blvd.

Crescent City

Elk Valley Rd.

Redwoods

State Park

Castle Rock

Smith River

Smith River County Park

Del Norte County
OREGON BORDER TO CRESCENT CITY

NAME	LOCATION	Entrance/Parking Fee	Parking	Restrooms	Lifeguard	Campground	Showers	Firepits	Stairs to Beach	Path to Beach	Bike Path	Hiking Trail	Facilities for Disabled	Boating Facilities	Fishing	Equestrian Trail	Sandy Beach	Dunes	Rocky Shore	Upland from Beach	Stream Corridor	Bluff	Wetland
Pelican State Beach	W. of Hwy. 101, 1/2 mi. S. of the Oregon border		•						•						•		•	•					
Clifford Kamph Memorial Park	W. of Hwy. 101, 2 mi. S. of the Oregon Border		•	•			•	•		•	•		•		•		•			•	•		
Smith River County Park	End of Smith River Rd., Smith River		•						•						•				•	•			
Smith River Fishing Access	2 mi. W. of Hwy. 101 on Fred Haight Dr., Smith River	•	•	•								•	•							•			
Smith River	W. of Hwy. 101, 3.5 mi. S. of the town of Smith River		•			•							•	•						•			
Kellogg Road Beach	W. end of Kellogg Rd., 5-1/2 mi. S. of the Smith River mouth		•												•		•	•	•				
Lakes Earl and Talawa	W. of Lower Lake Rd. and Lake Earl Dr., Crescent City		•	•		•	•		•					•			•						•
Point St. George Public Access	End of Radio Rd., Crescent City		•							•					•		•	•		•			
Radio Road Accessway	Off Radio Rd., 1 mi. S. of Point St. George, Crescent City		•						•	•					•		•	•					

FACILITIES — ENVIRONMENT

Pelican State Beach

PELICAN STATE BEACH: A road near the Nautical Inn leads to the beach; five acres of undeveloped shoreline, grassy dunes, and abundant driftwood.

CLIFFORD KAMPH MEMORIAL PARK: Blufftop picnic tables and benches. Paths lead to the beach; several small bridges cross a creek which empties into the ocean. The restrooms have been modified for the disabled; however, there is no paved path to the restrooms.

SMITH RIVER COUNTY PARK: Pebble beach at the mouth of the Smith River; fishing and bird-watching from Pyramid Point.

SMITH RIVER FISHING ACCESS: Picnic table; concrete one-lane boat ramp. Groceries, fishing supplies, raft rentals, bait and tackle available. (707) 464-4133.

SMITH RIVER: Part of California's Wild and Scenic River System, and one of seven stabilized river deltas in California. The year-round fishing river includes king salmon and silver salmon runs, steelhead trout and cutthroat trout, smelt, perch, and flounder. Upstream areas are safe for swimming.

Accommodations, camping, guided boat trips, water-skiing equipment, and fishing and boating supplies are available off Highway 101 mainly around the town of Smith River. Trailer campgrounds include Ship Ashore Resort, Salmon Harbor Resort, and Valley View Camper-Trailer Park. Easter in July Festival celebrates Smith River as the "Easter Lily Capital of the World."

KELLOGG ROAD BEACH: Wide, sandy beach backed by extensive dune fields and marshes. Environmental campsites are planned; for information, call: (707) 443-4588.

LAKES EARL AND TALAWA: Two freshwater lagoons of over 2,000 acres contain salmon and trout during periods of high water and rain. Duck hunting in season. Public boat ramps are located at the ends of Buzzini Rd. and Lakeview Dr., both of which are off Lake Earl Drive. Adjacent private property; do not trespass.

North of the lakes, west of Yontocket Slough off Pala Rd., a parking area with restrooms, picnic tables, and barbecues is planned for summer of 1983. Trails will lead to the beach and to several environmental campsites. Another trail to the beach is planned at Crooked Creek, west of Lake Earl, about two miles north of Crescent City. For more information, call: (707) 443-4588.

POINT ST. GEORGE PUBLIC ACCESS: A long trail leads to the beach from the bluffs. Beds of littleneck, razor, and Washington clams; rock fishing and smelt netting. The St. George light can be seen at the end of St. George reef, seven miles offshore.

RADIO ROAD ACCESSWAY: An elevated wooden walkway leads to stairs which lead to the beach. Adjacent private property; do not trespass.

Tsunami

The Japanese word *tsunami* is the word assigned to a series of waves caused by a sudden movement along a large portion of the ocean floor. Tsunamis are typically caused by underwater earthquakes, large landslides, or volcanic eruptions.

The wavelength of a tsunami may be several hundred miles, with periods ranging from 15 minutes to an hour or more. In the open ocean a tsunami is hardly noticeable. However, as the waves approach a shoreline, their height increases significantly; tsunami waves 75 feet high and greater have been observed.

Throughout history, coastal villages and towns located in the direct line of a tsunami have been completely destroyed. In California, the likelihood of a devastating tsunami with 75-foot waves is remote, largely because the waves generated in the Pacific Ocean must cross extensive stretches of shallow ocean waters as they move across the continental shelf. The result is a great loss in destructive wave energy before the waves actually reach the shoreline.

However, lesser tsunami waves are capable of causing considerable damage to developed portions of the California coastline. For example, tsunami waves generated by the 1964 Anchorage, Alaska earthquake were responsible for $27 million in damage at Crescent City in northern California. A series of waves about 12 feet high washed inland as far as 1600 feet and virtually destroyed the city's central business district, which has since been rebuilt.

Del Norte County
CRESCENT CITY

NAME	LOCATION	Entrance/Parking Fee	Parking	Restrooms	Lifeguard	Campground	Showers	Firepits	Stairs to Beach	Path to Beach	Bike Path	Hiking Trail	Facilities for Disabled	Boating Facilities	Fishing	Equestrian Trail	Sandy Beach	Dunes	Rocky Shore	Upland from Beach	Stream Corridor	Bluff	Wetland
Pebble Beach Park	W. of Pebble Beach Dr., Crescent City	•	•						•	•					•		•		•			•	
Preston Island	Condor St. and Pebble Beach Dr., Crescent City	•						•							•		•						
Brother Jonathon Park /Vista Point	W. end of 9th St., Crescent City	•	•										•						•			•	
Street Ends Leading to the Beach	W. ends of 3rd, 5th, and 6th Streets, Crescent City	•						•	•						•		•					•	
Battery Point Lighthouse	S. end of "A" St., Crescent City	•	•												•				•			•	
Beach Front Park	W. of Howe Dr., Crescent City	•	•	•						•					•		•					•	
Shoreline Campground Accessway	W. of Sunset Circle Way, Crescent City	•	•	•		•	•			•					•		•				•		•
Bike Path	W. of Hwy. 101, between Sunset Circle Dr. and Small Boat Basin, Crescent City										•								•				
Crescent City Harbor	W. of Hwy. 101 and Citizens Dock Rd., Crescent City	•	•		•						•			•	•								

PEBBLE BEACH PARK: Pebble Beach Dr. parallels the shore on a bluff overlooking the beach. There are several pull-outs for parking and viewing, with stairs or paths to the beach. A picnic table and historical marker of a Talawa Indian settlement are at the southern end.

PRESTON ISLAND: Rocky spit at the north end of Crescent City. A paved road leads down to the beach; picnic tables.

BROTHER JONATHON PARK/VISTA POINT: Grassy blufftop park and cemetery memorializes the 1865 shipwreck of the steamer Brother Jonathon. Across the street is a vista point with a picnic table and bench.

STREET ENDS LEADING TO THE BEACH: A 3/4-mile rocky beach can be reached by paths or stairways from the west ends of Third, Fifth, and Sixth Streets. All are signed, and there is parking at Third and Fifth Streets.

BATTERY POINT LIGHTHOUSE: The museum in this offshore 1856 lighthouse is accessible and open at low tides only; call for the hours. It contains a historical maritime collection and Talawa Indian artifacts. Museum: (707) 464-3089. There are picnic tables on the bluff and a view of Crescent Bay Harbor.

BEACH FRONT PARK: Howe Dr. runs the length of the park along the harbor. A bike path runs adjacent to Howe Dr. on the bay side, where there are benches; paths lead to the water. Picnic tables, both covered and open, are located on a grassy area east of Howe Drive. Adjacent Fred Endert park has a public indoor swimming pool, playground, picnic tables, shuffleboard courts, and a putting green. Del Norte County Visitors Center and Redwood National Park Information Center and Headquarters are just east of the park. Visitors Center: (707) 464-3174. Redwood National Park: (707) 464-6101.
Mass Transit: Del Norte Public Bus runs twice daily.

SHORELINE CAMPGROUND ACCESSWAY: A public path runs along the levee at Elk Creek, through Shoreline Campgrounds from Sunset Circle Dr. to the beach. There are 192 trailer campsites; all hookups. Picnic tables and campsites available. (707) 464-2473.
Mass Transit: Del Norte Public Bus.

BIKE PATH: Off-road bike path runs from the entrance of Shoreline Campgrounds to the Crescent City Small Boat Basin.

CRESCENT CITY HARBOR: Now one of the safest harbors on the north coast, protected by large rock jetties reinforced with concrete. The harbor includes lumber docks for freighters, the Small Boat Basin with boat ramps, docks and guest slips, and the Citizens Dock. This dock is a public wharf built in 1950 with private donations of materials and funds. The commercial fishing fleet, two fish processing plants, and a Coast Guard Station are based here; other facilities include a seafood restaurant, diving and marine supplies, groceries, engine and hull maintenance areas, ramp, hoist, and fuel dock.

The southern part of Crescent Bay Harbor, Bayshore Marina, has a public two-lane concrete boat ramp, sportsboat marina, two trailer parks, a sewage pump-out station, commercial aquarium, snack bar, and picnic tables. There is access to the southern jetty via Whaler Island, where there is a view area.

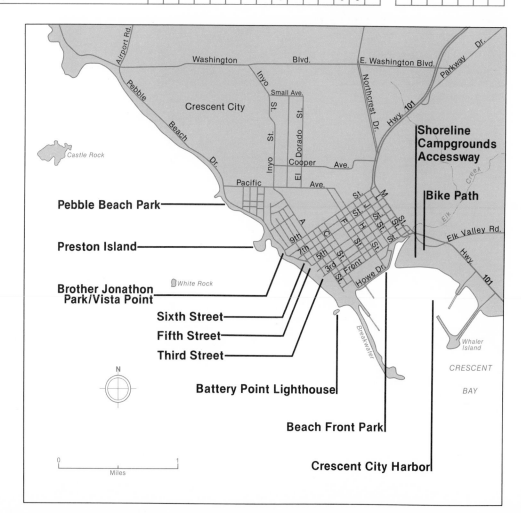

Wilson Creek Beach

Mill Creek Campgrounds

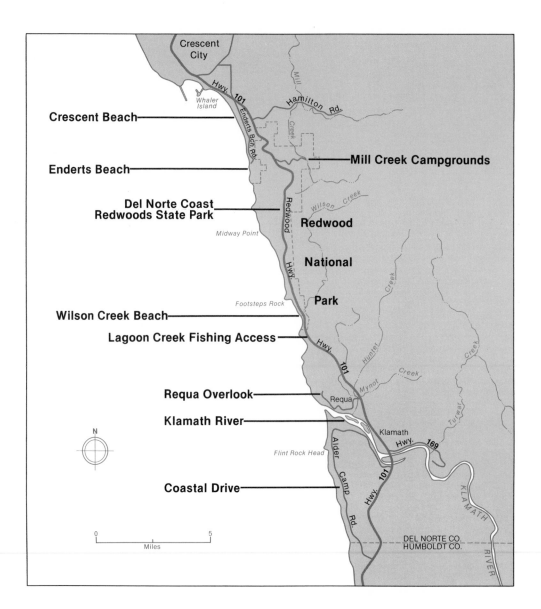

Crescent City

Whaler Island

Hwy. 101

Hamilton Rd.

Enders Bch Rd.

Crescent Beach

Enderts Beach

Mill Creek Campgrounds

Del Norte Coast
Redwoods State Park

Redwood

Midway Point

Wilson Creek

National

Redwood Hwy.

Footsteps Rock

Park

Wilson Creek Beach

Lagoon Creek Fishing Access

Hunter Creek

Requa Overlook

Mynot Creek

Requa

Klamath River

Klamath

Hwy. 169

Flint Rock Head

Turwer Creek

Alder Camp Rd.

Coastal Drive

Hwy. 101

KLAMATH RIVER

N

0   5
Miles

DEL NORTE CO.
HUMBOLDT CO.

Del Norte County
REDWOOD NATIONAL PARK/KLAMATH RIVER

NAME	LOCATION	Entrance/Parking Fee	Parking	Restrooms	Lifeguard	Campground	Showers	Firepits	Stairs to Beach	Path to Beach	Bike Path	Hiking Trail	Facilities for Disabled	Boating Facilities	Fishing	Equestrian Trail	Sandy Beach	Dunes	Rocky Shore	Upland from Beach	Stream Corridor	Bluff	Wetland
Redwood National Park	Coastal and inland areas between Crescent City and Orick		•	•		•		•		•		•	•		•	•	•		•	•	•	•	
Crescent Beach	Off Enderts Beach Rd., 2 mi. S. of Crescent City		•	•			•					•			•		•						
Enderts Beach	End of Enderts Beach Rd., S. of Crescent City		•	•		•		•		•									•	•			
Del Norte Coast Redwoods State Park	4 mi. S. of Crescent City		•	•		•	•	•		•		•	•		•		•		•	•	•		
Mill Creek Campgrounds	E. of Hwy. 101, 5 mi. S. of Crescent City	•	•	•		•		•		•		•	•		•				•	•	•		
Wilson Creek Beach	W. of Hwy. 101, 5.5 mi. N. of Klamath		•				•						•				•		•	•			
Lagoon Creek Fishing Access	W. of Hwy. 101, 5 mi. N. of Klamath		•	•			•					•	•		•				•	•		•	
Requa Overlook	Off Patrick Murphy Memorial Dr., 1.5 mi. from Requa Rd.		•	•						•		•	•								•		
Klamath River	W. of Hwy. 101 between Requa and Klamath Townsite		•		•								•	•						•			
Coastal Drive	Alder Camp Rd., S. of the Klamath River		•																	•			

REDWOOD NATIONAL PARK: Established in 1968 and expanded in 1978, the park preserves coastal redwoods, including the world's tallest trees, in virgin stands as well as new growth forests. Within its boundaries are three state parks: Del Norte Coast Redwoods; Jedediah Smith, which is inland from Crescent City; and Prairie Creek Redwoods in Humboldt County. The diverse habitats of the coastal area — redwood forests, riparian woodlands, and grassy prairie — support a comparable diversity of wildlife.

The fifty-mile long park extends through both Humboldt and Del Norte Counties. An extensive trail system throughout the park provides access to the park's natural features and recreational facilities. Headquarters for the park are in Crescent City, at Second and K Streets: (707) 464-6101. Check here for information on the two new equestrian trails, and for specific trail conditions, which may change due to heavy rains.

Redwood National Park in Del Norte County includes Crescent Beach, Crescent Beach Overlook, Enderts Beach, Lagoon Creek Fishing Access, Coastal Trail, Requa Overlook, and Coastal Drive. Del Norte Coast Redwoods State Park also lies within Redwood National Park's boundaries.

CRESCENT BEACH: Picnic tables, some modified for wheelchair use, are in a grassy area between the parking lot and the beach. There are also restroom facilities for the disabled. Crescent Beach Overlook, on a bluff off the west side of Highway 101, has parking and a picnic area.

ENDERTS BEACH: A one-half mile walk to primitive campsites and the beach; there are picnic tables and grills at the campsites. Daily tidepool walks are offered during the summer at low tide.

DEL NORTE COAST REDWOODS STATE PARK: Contains over 6,000 acres of redwoods, beaches, and rain forests. There is camping at Mill Creek east of Highway 101, and a trail system leading both inland and to the coast. Wilson Creek Beach is a day use area at the southern end of the park.

MILL CREEK CAMPGROUNDS: 145 campsites in a valley are sheltered from ocean winds and fog. Some sites can accommodate trailers although there are no hookups; there are also hike-in/bicycle sites. A sanitation station and a campfire center are provided as well as fire rings, picnic tables, and cupboards at each site. There are hiking and nature trails, and fishing in Mill Creek. For information, call: (707) 464-9533.

WILSON CREEK BEACH: Sandy beach with abundant driftwood and tidepools; picnic tables. There is fishing in Wilson Creek.

Klamath River Mouth

LAGOON CREEK FISHING ACCESS: A freshwater lagoon with picnic areas and a self-guided Yurok Loop nature trail. The lagoon is stocked with trout and is also popular for canoeing. This is the northern trailhead for the Coastal Trail, a four-mile trail which follows the bluffs south to Requa Overlook. Interpretive walks are conducted in the summer.

REQUA OVERLOOK: Views of the Klamath River valley and coastline; picnic tables and information displays. There is a trailhead to the Coastal Trail which runs north along the cliffs to Lagoon Creek.

KLAMATH RIVER: California's second largest river is one of the most well-known fishing areas in northern California. Although commercial fishing was outlawed in 1934, Klamath Indians and scores of individuals find king salmon, steelhead trout, perch, sturgeon, and flounder. From Klamath Townsite to the mouth of the river, motels and trailer parks, restaurants, fishing supplies, and boat rentals are available on both sides of the river. Requa, a small town on the north side of the river, offers a jet-boat trip 32 miles upriver into the Hoopa Indian Reservation. For information, call: (707) 482-4422.

Trailer camping near the mouth of the river, most with boat launching facilities, can be found at Kamp Klamath, King Salmon Resort, Panther Creek Resort, Riverside Trailer Park, Klamath Camper Corral, Klamath Beach Camp, Chinook Trailer Resort, Camp Marigold, High Prairie Trailer Park, Dad's Camp, Sportsman R.V. Park and Campground, Requa Resort, and Golden Bear Trailer Park. **Mass Transit:** Del Norte County Bus.

COASTAL DRIVE: An eight-mile drive which winds along the bluffs between the Klamath River and Prairie Creek Redwoods State Park in Humboldt County. Not recommended for trailers.

Patrick's Point State Park

Humboldt County

Humboldt County in northern California can claim many superlatives: The world's tallest tree, a redwood *(Sequoia sempervirens)* found near Orick; the westernmost point in the continental U.S., Cape Mendocino in southern Humboldt; the second largest enclosed bay in California, Humboldt Bay; and perhaps one of the wettest places in California, Honeydew, near Humboldt Redwoods State Park. The annual Cross-Country Kinetic Sculpture Race, from Arcata to Ferndale, is also unique to Humboldt County. All of these can be found on or near the coast.

The coastal area of Humboldt can be divided generally into three areas. In the north, steep cliffs and bluffs, and the forests of Redwood National Park and commercial timberland dominate the landscape. From south of Trinidad to the Eel River, the coastal area consists mainly of low-lying fertile river deltas and bays; the more populated areas around the Mad River, Humboldt Bay, and the Eel River are centers of dairying, fishing, and timber processing. The southern portion of the county is characterized by steep ridges rising several thousand feet from the ocean, especially in the King Range National Conservation Area, where grass, brush, and Douglas fir are the predominant vegetation.

As in much of California, Humboldt County was not settled until 1850, as a result of gold strikes on the Trinity River. Since it was easier to sail up the coast from San Francisco than to travel overland, port towns on the Humboldt coast vied for dominance. Trinidad, Arcata, and Eureka have each been the main port at different times.

Timber soon became another important industry; five months after the first settlers arrived in Humboldt Bay, a sawmill was operating in Eureka. By 1870, most of the trees around Humboldt Bay were cut. Eventually, timber and fishing industries superseded mining, and Eureka ultimately became the main port.

Today timber and fishing, in addition to tourism, remain the most important industries. Eureka's fishing industry provides about half the state's seafood; these include chinook and silver salmon, crab, sea and surf perch, several kinds of clams, oysters, rock and ling cod, cabezone, and rockfish. For the amateur angler, the numerous bays and rivers provide a fine opportunity to catch one's own.

The weather along the Humboldt coast, as in Del Norte County, is foggy in the summer and rainy in the winter; the temperature, however, rarely drops below freezing. Spring and Fall have clearer skies and warmer temperatures.

For more visitor information, write the Eureka/Humboldt County Convention and Visitors Bureau at 123 F Street, Eureka 95501, or call (707) 443-5097. The headquarters for Redwood National Park in Humboldt County is in Orick, P.O. Box 6, 95555; call: (707) 488-3461. For Humboldt Transit Authority bus schedules, write: Humboldt Transit Authority, 6700 A Highway 101 North, Eureka 95501, or call: (707) 443-0826.

Redwoods

The magnificent coast redwoods *(Sequoia sempervirens)* grow in forests along the northern and central California coast, ranging from the Oregon border to the Santa Lucia Mountains south of Monterey. These trees are the tallest on earth, with many individuals achieving heights exceeding 300 feet, and trunks measuring up to 20 feet in diameter at their base. The coast redwood is named after its dark, red-colored wood, which is highly desirable for use as lumber. The trees can be identified by their great size, stranded cinnamon-brown bark, and flat, half-inch long sharply pointed needles.

Coast redwoods only grow along the narrow strip of Pacific northwest coastline, which is frequently covered by fog. The fog, by condensing and dripping off the redwoods' leaves, may supply up to ten inches of precipitation annually; this added moisture allows the redwoods to survive in an often arid environment. Within its range, the redwood is extremely successful and nearly always dominates other trees with which it grows, such as Douglas fir, sitka spruce, tan oak, and madrone. The reasons for the coast redwood's dominance are its prolific regeneration through seed and trunk sprouting, and the fact that it is highly resistant to insects and disease and well adapted to deal with fires and periodic flooding.

Although coast redwoods produce large amounts of seed, most regeneration in redwood forests is attributed to the trees' ability to sprout from the trunk or root system. Sprouting, a redwood reproductive method which is unique among cone-bearing trees, allows coast redwoods to dominate areas where seed regeneration would not normally occur, such as forests with leaf litter thick enough to prevent seeds from reaching mineral soil. These root and trunk sprouts are also unusually hardy and fast growing because they draw water and nutrients from the already well-developed root system of the parent tree.

Another unique survival mechanism of the coast redwoods is the ability to send out new vertical roots following silt deposition from periodic flooding. Since other trees with which the redwoods compete cannot tolerate the flooding of silts on their root systems, forests of pure redwood tend to dominate along stream floodplain areas.

Low intensity ground fires, which were once common in undisturbed natural forests, also favor coast redwoods. Redwoods have an unusually thick and non-resinous bark which is more resistant to fires than competing hardwoods and Douglas fir. When periodic small fires occur, the effect is to eliminate trees other than redwoods; fire scars at the base of redwoods are evidence of previous fires which left these trees still standing.

The first commercial logging of redwoods occurred in the Oakland hills during the 1820's and in Monterey County in the 1830's. In 1848, the California gold rush began, resulting in an incredible demand for redwood lumber, and providing the first impetus for settlement of the timber-rich north coast. The first lumber mill began operating in Eureka in 1850, and within ten years approximately 300 mills had been built along the coast, the majority being in Mendocino and Humboldt Counties.

Excessive and often poorly managed logging prompted the establishment of park lands to preserve some of the most scenic redwood forests. Big Basin Redwoods State Park was purchased in 1902 to save one of the last remaining forests of old-growth redwood in the Santa Cruz Mountains. In 1906, President Theodore Roosevelt established the Monterey Forest Reserve, and designated Muir Woods in Marin County as a National Monument.

The largest park acquisition occurred in 1968 when Congress established the Redwood National Park in Humboldt and Del Norte Counties. This 58,000-acre park near the coast encompassed the Mill Creek drainage area, and the Jedediah Smith, Del Norte Coast, and Prairie Creek Redwoods State Parks. In 1978, the Redwood Creek drainage area near Orick was added to the Redwood National Park, creating a total of 106,000 acres.

Humboldt County

NORTHERN HUMBOLDT COAST

NAME	LOCATION	Entrance/Parking Fee	Parking	Restrooms	Lifeguard	Campground	Showers	Firepits	Stairs to Beach	Path to Beach	Bike Path	Hiking Trail	Facilities for Disabled	Boating Facilities	Fishing	Equestrian Trail	Sandy Beach	Dunes	Rocky Shore	Upland from Beach	Stream Corridor	Bluff	Wetland
Redwood National Park	Off Hwy. 101, N. of Orick	●	●	●		●		●		●	●		●		●		●	●	●	●	●	●	
Coastal Drive	Off Alder Camp Rd., 10 mi. N. of Orick		●							●		●							●			●	
Prairie Creek Redwoods State Park	W. of Hwy. 101, 6.5 mi. N. of Orick	●	●	●		●		●		●	●		●		●					●	●		
Butler Creek Backpack Camp	Off West Ridge Rd., 9 mi. N. of Orick			●		●		●				●								●	●		
Fern Canyon (Prairie Creek Redwoods State Park)	End of Davidson Rd.		●	●		●		●				●								●	●		
Gold Bluffs Campground	Off Davidson Rd., 5 mi. W. of Hwy. 101	●	●	●		●		●		●					●		●	●				●	
Elk Prairie Campground	W. of Hwy. 101, 6.5 mi. N. of Orick	●	●	●		●	●	●				●	●							●	●		

REDWOOD NATIONAL PARK: Over 100,000 acres of redwood forests near the coast in Humboldt and Del Norte Counties. Hiking trails and scenic drives provide access to beaches, streamside redwood groves, and overnight campsites. The world's tallest tree, a redwood towering 367.8 feet above Redwood Creek, is located near Orick. The information center at the southern end of the park is in Orick: (707) 488-3461. For more information on Redwood National Park, see Del Norte County.

Redwood National Park in Humboldt County includes Coastal Drive, Carruthers Cove, Prairie Creek Redwoods State Park, and Gold Bluffs Beach.

COASTAL DRIVE: An eight-mile drive along coastal bluffs from the Klamath River in Del Norte County to the northern end of Prairie Creek Redwoods State Park; trailers not recommended. A guide to the Drive is available at park information offices. The Carruthers Cove Trail leads from the south end of Coastal Drive to Carruthers Cove Beach on the Humboldt/Del Norte border.

PRAIRIE CREEK REDWOODS STATE PARK: A 12,384-acre park with three campgrounds: Elk Prairie along Highway 101, Gold Bluffs Beach, and Butler Creek Backpack Camp; environmental campsites are available. Ossagon Trail, just north of West Ridge Rd., leads to the north end of Gold Bluffs Beach. There are numerous hiking and nature trails, including a guided nature trail for the blind, picnic areas, fishing streams, a herd of Roosevelt elk, and interpretive talks weekends May 1–Oct. 30, daily June through Labor Day. Call: (707) 488-2171.

BUTLER CREEK BACKPACK CAMP: Located on the Butler Creek Trail, which connects to West Ridge Road. The camp is 7.5 miles from Park Headquarters, 2.6 miles from Fern Canyon, and is located in an old-growth spruce forest near Butler Creek. There are eight campsites with fire rings, one of which is large enough for small groups; stay in designated camping areas. Garbage must be packed out. All backpackers must park their vehicles and register at Park Headquarters. Call: (707) 488-2171.

FERN CANYON: Part of Prairie Creek Redwoods State Park. A short trail leads through the narrow canyon whose steep walls are covered with many species of ferns, including five-finger ferns, lady ferns, deer ferns, and chain ferns. Footbridges are installed after the heavy rains have passed each year, and are removed in the fall. The trail connects with the James Irvine Trail, which continues for four miles to the Park Headquarters. For information, call: (707) 488-2171.

GOLD BLUFFS CAMPGROUND: 25 campsites, each with a picnic table and cupboard; water nearby. 25 walk-in/bicycle sites are at the north end of the campground. Tables and fire rings are provided; restrooms and cold showers are in the adjacent campground. Campsites have direct access to the beach. Interpretive programs in the summer months.

The sand below the high cliffs of Gold Bluffs Beach was mined for gold in the 1850's; now the area is a refuge for the Roosevelt Elk.

ELK PRAIRIE CAMPGROUND: 75 campsites, each with a picnic table and cupboard; walk-in/bicycle campsites available. Campfire programs in the summer. For information, call: (707) 488-2171.

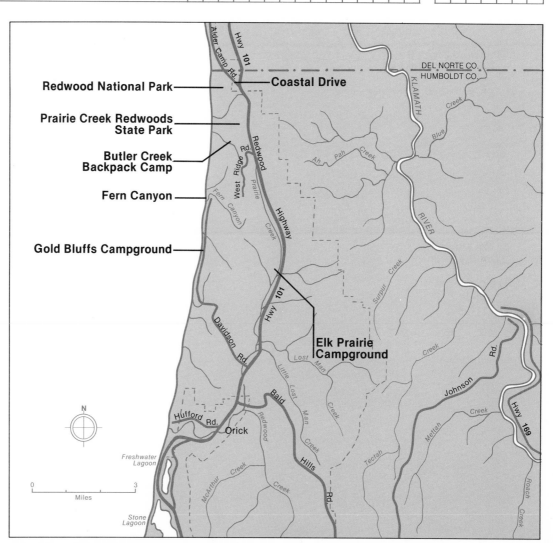

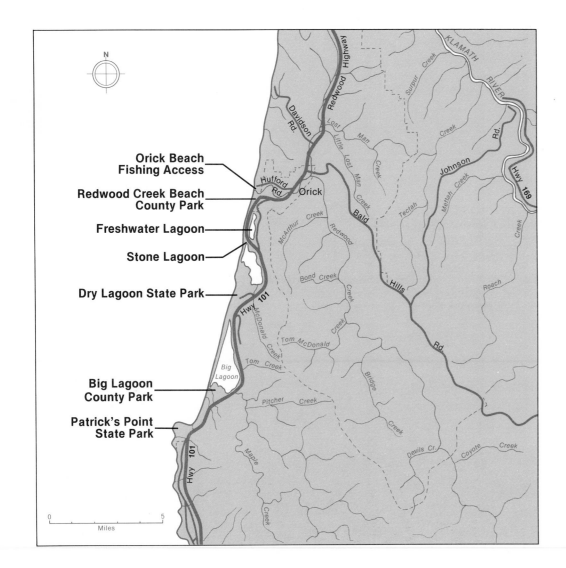

**Orick Beach
Fishing Access**

**Redwood Creek Beach
County Park**

Freshwater Lagoon

Stone Lagoon

Dry Lagoon State Park

**Big Lagoon
County Park**

**Patrick's Point
State Park**

Dry Lagoon State Park

Patrick's Point State Park

Humboldt County
ORICK TO PATRICK'S POINT

NAME	LOCATION	Entrance/Parking Fee	Parking	Restrooms	Lifeguard	Campground	Showers	Firepits	Stairs to Beach	Path to Beach	Bike Path	Hiking Trail	Facilities for Disabled	Boating Facilities	Fishing	Equestrian Trail	Sandy Beach	Dunes	Rocky Shore	Upland from Beach	Stream Corridor	Bluff	Wetland
Orick Beach Fishing Access	End of Hufford Rd., 1 mi. W. of Orick		•												•		•				•		
Redwood Creek Beach County Park	W. of Hwy. 101, 2 mi. S. of Orick		•	•													•				•		
Freshwater Lagoon	E. of Hwy. 101, 3 mi. S. of Orick		•	•										•	•		•						•
Stone Lagoon	Off Hwy. 101, 4-1/2 mi. S. of Orick	•	•	•		•								•	•		•	•					•
Dry Lagoon State Park	Off Hwy. 101, 6 mi. S. of Orick		•	•		•									•		•	•	•	•			
Big Lagoon County Park	Off Hwy. 101, 12 mi. S. of Orick		•	•				•				•		•	•		•	•		•			
Patrick's Point State Park	W. of Hwy. 101, 5 mi. N. of Trinidad	•	•	•			•	•	•	•		•			•		•		•	•	•	•	

ORICK BEACH FISHING ACCESS: At the mouth of Redwood Creek on the north side; take the left fork when Hufford Rd. splits. The road ends on a dike at the mouth of the river. The road is rough and narrow, and not recommended for campers or trailers. Fishing for salmon and steelhead trout.

REDWOOD CREEK BEACH COUNTY PARK: A day use only park with picnic tables, south of Redwood Creek, between Highway 101 and the ocean.

FRESHWATER LAGOON: Boat ramp at the north end; a small road off the east side of Highway 101 leads to the ramp and beach. The lagoon is stocked with trout. West of Highway 101, parking in the CalTrans right-of-way allows access to a sandy beach with driftwood. Popular for surf fishing.

STONE LAGOON: Camping area of Dry Lagoon State Park. A short road at the north end of Stone Lagoon leads over a ridge to a spit separating the lagoon from the ocean; small boats may be launched at the end of this road. There are 30 primitive campsites on the spit; trailers and campers are allowed. There is no water available. Environmental campsites are accessible by boat from the east shore of Stone Lagoon. Camping fee. For more information, call: (707) 488-2171.

DRY LAGOON STATE PARK: This park includes the spit between Stone Lagoon and the ocean, the marshy Dry Lagoon, and the spit between Big Lagoon and the ocean. A day use area just south of the Dry Lagoon has four picnic sites. On the east shore of Stone Lagoon there is a boat ramp and parking area at the old Little Red Hen building. Rental boats available. Migratory waterfowl and shorebirds feed at the lagoons, and anadromous fish enter the lagoons when the spits are breached during heavy rains.

BIG LAGOON COUNTY PARK: Located on a marsh which is adjacent to the ocean. Two-lane concrete boat ramp, with a 40-foot ten-ton limit. Picnic tables and an adjacent primitive camping area. Steelhead fishing; swimming.

PATRICK'S POINT STATE PARK: A 462-acre park of forests and meadows located on bluffs which are rimmed by rocky headlands and a sandy beach. There are 123 campsites including group and hike-in/bicycle sites, 43 picnic sites, and a campfire center. Nature and hiking trails include the two-mile Rim Trail, which follows an old Indian trail along the bluffs, and a self-guided nature trail through the octopus tree grove. A small museum features natural and Indian history. Shorebirds and songbirds are abundant, and migrating gray whales can be observed from the bluffs. The three-mile coastline includes Agate Beach where small pieces of agate and jade can be found, and rocky areas with tidepools. Sea lions can be seen offshore. For information, call: (707) 677-3570.

Stone Lagoon, Dry Lagoon State Park

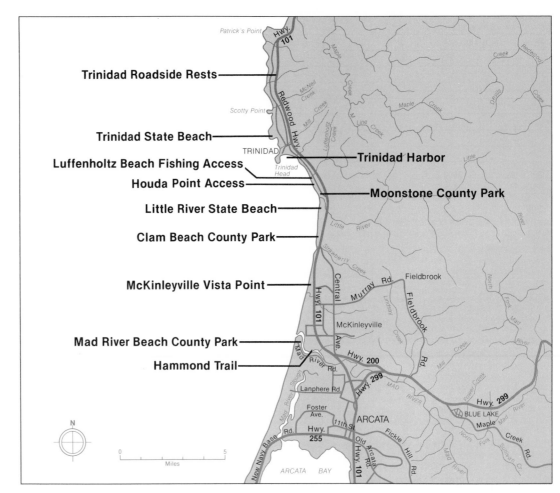

Trinidad Roadside Rests

Trinidad State Beach

Luffenholtz Beach Fishing Access

Houda Point Access

Little River State Beach

Clam Beach County Park

McKinleyville Vista Point

Mad River Beach County Park

Hammond Trail

Trinidad Harbor

Moonstone County Park

Mad River Beach County Park

Humboldt County
TRINIDAD TO THE MAD RIVER

NAME	LOCATION	Entrance/Parking Fee	Parking	Restrooms	Lifeguard	Campground	Showers	Firepits	Stairs to Beach	Path to Beach	Bike Path	Hiking Trail	Facilities for Disabled	Boating Facilities	Fishing	Equestrian Trail	Sandy Beach	Dunes	Rocky Shore	Upland from Beach	Stream Corridor	Bluff	Wetland
Trinidad Roadside Rests	Hwy. 101, 2 and 4 mi. N. of Trinidad	•	•									•	•						•				
Trinidad State Beach	Off Trinity St., N. of Main St., Trinidad	•	•					•		•			•				•		•		•		
Trinidad Harbor	W. end of Edwards St., E. of Trinidad Head	•	•							•				•	•		•		•				
Luffenholtz Beach County Fishing Access	W. of Scenic Dr., 2 mi. S. of Trinidad	•	•					•	•	•			•				•		•			•	
Houda Point Access	W. of Scenic Dr., 2.5 mi. S. of Trinidad	•								•							•		•			•	
Moonstone County Park	W. of Scenic Dr., 3 mi. S. of Trinidad	•															•						
Little River State Beach	W. of Hwy. 101, 4 mi. S. of Trinidad	•								•					•		•	•			•		
Clam Beach County Park	W. of Hwy. 101, 3.5 mi. N. of McKinleyville	•	•							•					•	•	•	•					
McKinleyville Vista Point	Hwy. 101, 2 mi. N. of McKinleyville	•																		•		•	
Mad River Beach County Park	End of Mad River Rd., W. of Hwy. 101	•	•			•		•						•	•	•	•	•			•		
Hammond Trail	W. of Hwy. 101, from Clam Beach S. to the Mad River								•	•					•		•			•	•		

TRINIDAD ROADSIDE RESTS: Northbound and southbound areas. Dog runs, nature exhibits, paths, picnic tables, and benches; trailer sanitation station.

TRINIDAD STATE BEACH: A day use park on the north side of Trinidad Point, adjacent to the town of Trinidad. The northern unpaved parking lot off Stagecoach Rd. provides trail access to the headlands and to College Cove, a sandy, clothing optional beach. There is a paved parking area, restrooms, picnic tables, and grills at the southern end of the park, adjacent to Mill Creek; trails lead to the creek, and down the bluff to the beach. Trails from the southern beach lead to the harbor area and along Trinidad Bay. There is also access to the beach from the Humboldt State University Marine Laboratory, which has a visitors area with marine exhibits and an aquarium, and is accessible to disabled persons. Marine Laboratory: (707) 677-3671.

The Humboldt North Coast Land Trust, a nonprofit land trust based in the Trinidad area, owns and operates a number of coastal trails and access points in the Trinidad area and other parts of Humboldt County. For a brochure on accessways managed by the Trust, send a self-addressed, stamped envelope to: Executive Secretary, Humboldt North Coast Land Trust, P.O. Box 457, Trinidad 95570.
Mass Transit: Humboldt Transit Authority.

TRINIDAD HARBOR: Restaurant, moorings, charter boats, and fuel dock at Bob's Boat Basin. The marine railway, used for launching small boats, is open May–October. Call: (707) 677-3625. Trails lead from Edwards St., Wagner St., and the end of Parker Creek Rd. to the harbor and bay.
Mass Transit: Humboldt Transit Authority.

LUFFENHOLTZ BEACH COUNTY FISHING ACCESS: Turn south off Main St. onto Trinidad Scenic Dr., just west of Highway 101 in Trinidad. Scenic overlook with picnic tables. Access to the beach is along steep, rocky cliffs.

HOUDA POINT ACCESS: Roadside parking area with beaches; trails lead to two pocket beaches south of Luffenholtz Beach. Owned and operated by Humboldt North Coast Land Trust.

MOONSTONE COUNTY PARK: Broad, sandy beach near Luffenholtz Beach County Fishing Access; good clamming.
Mass Transit: Humboldt Transit Authority, weekdays only.

LITTLE RIVER STATE BEACH: North end of Clam Beach County Park. Broad sandy beach, with access to the Little River delta at the north end.

CLAM BEACH COUNTY PARK: Overnight roadside stops are permitted. Facilities include restrooms and picnic tables. Good clamming area; ponds east of Highway 101 on the frontage road are stocked with trout.

McKINLEYVILLE VISTA POINT: Picnic table; panoramic view north to Trinidad.

MAD RIVER BEACH COUNTY PARK: Take the Janes Rd. exit off Highway 101, turn right on Heindon Rd., left on Iverson Rd., and right on Mad River Road. Do not trespass or allow dogs onto the adjacent private farm lands. There are two parking areas; one leads to the river and boat ramp, the other is near the ocean beach. Picnic table and restrooms are near the boat ramp.

HAMMOND TRAIL: Multi-use recreational trail that will run near the coast between Clam Beach and the Mad River, and will include an equestrian/hiking loop trail from Clam Beach to McKinleyville. Currently completed is a bridge across the Mad River, 1/2 mile east of Mad River Beach County Park, which connects bicycle lanes between Clam Beach and McKinleyville and McKinleyville and Arcata. (707) 445-7650.

Trinidad State Beach

Arcata Marsh

North Spit, Samoa Public Access

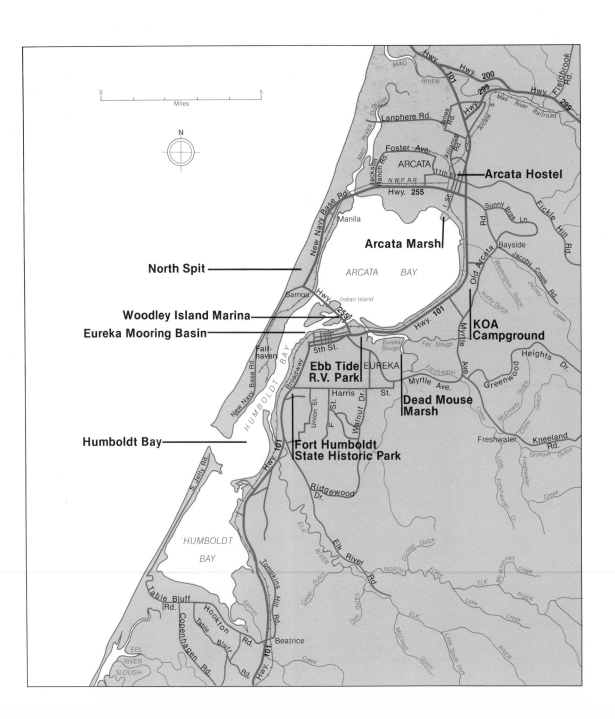

Arcata Hostel

Arcata Marsh

North Spit

Woodley Island Marina

Eureka Mooring Basin

KOA Campground

Ebb Tide R.V. Park

Dead Mouse Marsh

Humboldt Bay

Fort Humboldt State Historic Park

Humboldt County

HUMBOLDT BAY

NAME	LOCATION	Entrance/Parking Fee	Parking	Restrooms	Lifeguard	Campground	Showers	Firepits	Stairs to Beach	Path to Beach	Bike Path	Hiking Trail	Facilities for Disabled	Boating Facilities	Fishing	Equestrian Trail	Sandy Beach	Dunes	Rocky Shore	Upland from Beach	Stream Corridor	Bluff	Wetland
North Spit	Off Hwy. 255, S.W. of Arcata		•	•		•		•		•		•	•	•	•		•	•					
Arcata Hostel	1390 "I" St., Arcata	•	•	•			•													•			
Arcata Marsh	S. end of "I" St., Arcata		•									•		•									•
Humboldt Bay	S. of Arcata, S. and W. of Eureka		•			•				•				•	•								
KOA Campground	4050 N. Hwy. 101, Eureka	•	•	•		•	•						•							•			
Dead Mouse Marsh	E. end of Park St., Eureka		•																				•
Ebb Tide R.V. Park	2600 6th St., Eureka	•	•	•		•	•							•						•			•
Woodley Island Marina	Off Hwy. 255, Eureka		•	•									•	•	•								
Eureka Mooring Basin	Commercial St. and 1st St., Eureka		•	•										•									
Fort Humboldt State Historic Park	Off Highland Ave., E. of Hwy. 101, Eureka		•	•																•			

NORTH SPIT: A long spit separates Arcata Bay from the ocean. On the ocean side, there is a sandy beach which can be reached from several parking areas off Highway 255 and New Navy Base Road. There are dunes between the road and the beach. The Samoa Public Access on the bay has a ten-ton 40-foot capacity concrete boat ramp, and camping is allowed.

Manila Community Park, at Peninsula Dr. and Victor Blvd. in Manila, has a playground, baseball diamond and playing fields, picnic tables and benches, and access to the bay and marshes. Horses are allowed on trails near the bay. The Coast Guard Station at the south end of New Navy Base Rd. provides access to the jetty at the end of the spit (May–Sept. only), to the southern dune area, and to small coves along the bay. The jetty is a popular fishing area; waves can be hazardous.

An off-road vehicle recreation area, located adjacent to the Coast Guard Station and immediately north of the mouth of Humboldt Bay, is scheduled to open in fall 1983. Facilities will include trails for off-road vehicles and motorcycles, two campgrounds, picnic tables, fire rings, and a parking area; the facilities will be managed by the Bureau of Land Management.
Mass Transit: Humboldt Transit Authority.

ARCATA HOSTEL: Open mid-June to mid-September. Facilities include 20 beds, showers, kitchen, and bike storage and rentals; reservations suggested. $4.25 for members, $6.25 for non-members. Write or call: 1390 "I" Street, Arcata 95521; (707) 822-9995.
Mass Transit: Humboldt Transit Authority.

ARCATA MARSH: Recently restored freshwater marsh and wildlife sanctuary. Trails through the area are used for walking, jogging, and bird watching. Bird blinds have been constructed, and Audubon members lead Saturday morning bird-watching tours. The Arcata boat ramp, a two-lane concrete ramp, is adjacent to the marsh area and has a picnic table.

Another trail leads through the marsh along the dikes, just west of the oxidation pond; the parking lot is on South G Street. This area is adjacent to the Jacoby Creek Unit of the Humboldt Bay National Wildlife Refuge.

HUMBOLDT BAY: California's second largest enclosed bay had its first recorded discovery in 1805, although settlement by Americans did not occur until 1850. The fishing and timber mill industries now dominate the bay. The Humboldt Bay National Wildlife Refuge includes most of the south bay and some mudflats, marshes, and islands in the north bay; the snowy egret and the great blue heron are commonly sighted birds. For more information about the refuge, write or call: U.S. Fish and Wildlife Service, P.O. Box 524, Newark 94560; (415) 792-0222.

A number of access points exist around Humboldt Bay. The City of Eureka is making improvements to Waterfront Drive to provide vehicular and pedestrian access between Koster St. and Front St. at S Street. A floating dock for fishing and viewing is located at the end of F Street; other bayfront access points include the end of Commercial St. and the end of C Street. Camping is available at the nearby Redwood Acres Fairground, 3750 Harris Street; for information call: (707) 445-3037. Coast Oyster Company, at the foot of "A" Street, has a self guided tour through their processing plant; it is advisable to call before visiting: (707) 442-2947.

KOA CAMPGROUND: 165 sites; 29 sites are specifically for tent campers. $11.50/night for all hookups; $10/night for water and electricity; $8.50 for tent sites or no hookups. Other facilities include picnic tables, laundry, store, snack bar, and recreation hall. For more information, call: (707) 822-4243.

DEAD MOUSE MARSH: Trails along the dikes lead into the marsh area; good bird watching.

EBB TIDE R.V. PARK: 81 trailer sites. $9.50/night for full hookups; $9/night for electricity and water. Weekly and monthly rates are available. Laundry facilities; paths to nearby fishing areas. For more information, call: (707) 445-2273.

WOODLEY ISLAND MARINA: 237-slip marina. Two-ton hoist, work area, and sidewalk area with benches; no boat ramp. Hot pay showers and laundry facilities for tenants only; coffee shop. The rest of the island is a wildlife reserve; no public access. For more information, call: (707) 443-0801.

EUREKA MOORING BASIN: A small boat harbor with a one-lane concrete boat ramp, fuel docks, pumpout station, and berths. Picnic tables and the Humboldt Yacht Club are located in the harbor area. Adjacent 1st and 2nd Streets are part of the ongoing restoration of the Victorian buildings and businesses on the waterfront, including mini-parks and walkways; several cross-streets end at the bay. The Humboldt Bay Harbor Cruise leaves from the foot of C Street, Memorial Day through the middle of September. Information: (707) 445-1910.

FORT HUMBOLDT STATE HISTORIC PARK: Logging exhibit and museum with picnic areas and views of Humboldt Bay. Call: (707) 443-7952.
Mass Transit: Humboldt Transit Authority.

Humboldt Bay

Salmon and Steelhead Trout

Steelhead trout, king salmon, and silver salmon are three of the most important northern California fish species; all three are anadromous, meaning that they migrate from the ocean into rivers to spawn.

King (chinook) salmon are found in the ocean from Monterey northward, and run upstream from mid-July through October. Average weight at spawning is 20 lbs. To spawn, females dig nests in the gravel bottoms of cool streams and lay their eggs which are immediately fertilized by males. All Pacific salmon die shortly after spawning.

King salmon eggs hatch in 50-60 days, and several months later the young migrate to the ocean; when mature, usually at age three or four, they return to the same stream to spawn. Most king salmon migrate into fresh water in the fall and spawn from October-January. There are, however, some spring-run king salmon in certain rivers, and even some winter-run fish in the Sacramento River.

Silver salmon are mostly found north of Monterey and migrate to fresh water in fall and early winter, just before they spawn. Their habits are similar to those of the king salmon except that silver salmon usually weigh 7-12 lbs. at spawning, prefer smaller streams than king salmon, and their young remain in fresh water a year (occasionally two years) before migrating to sea in spring. Most silvers mature at age three.

King and silver salmon are caught by anglers in the ocean from Avila Beach (in San Luis Obispo County) north to Oregon, and also in the mouths and tidewater areas of northern rivers such as the Klamath, Smith, and Eel. They are best caught by trolling but may also be caught by shore casting.

Steelhead trout are found from San Luis Obispo County north to Alaska and are rarely caught at sea; they are found in smaller streams than those that salmon enter as well as in the larger rivers. Steelhead enter streams from June-November to spawn and, unlike salmon, do not necessarily die after spawning; steelhead may live up to eight years and spawn as many as five times.

After hatching, steelhead young stay in fresh water for one or two seasons and then migrate to the sea. Steelhead usually weigh 2-10 lbs. at maturity, and resemble rainbow trout when in fresh water, but change coloration, as do salmon, when entering salt water.

According to the California Department of Fish and Game, the habitats of these anadromous fish have been seriously degraded and hundreds of thousands of fish have died in recent years due to such things as the loss of stream beds to gravel and gold dredging operations; the building of dams and unscreened irrigation diversions; improper logging and road building operations; untreated industrial and domestic wastes; increased amounts of fertilizers from return irrigation waters; and higher water temperatures.

In an effort to mitigate the effects of these human activities, the Department of Fish and Game has built fish ladders to enable migrating fish to reach spawning areas upstream from dams, has aided federal agencies in constructing and operating fish hatcheries, and is currently working with the logging and lumber industry to remove barriers and pollutants from spawning streams.

Anglers should consult the current *California Sport Fishing Regulations* published by Fish and Game regarding salmon and steelhead fishing laws and regulations. Copies of the regulations, as well as *Salmon and Steelhead Fishing Maps,* are available from:

Publications Section
Office of Procurement
General Services
P.O. Box 1015
North Highlands, CA 95660   (916) 924-4800

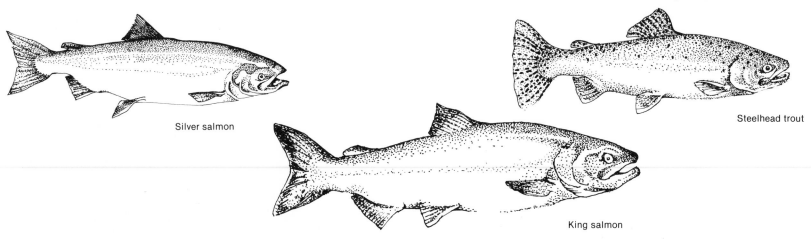

Silver salmon

Steelhead trout

King salmon

Humboldt County
HUMBOLDT BAY/EEL RIVER

NAME	LOCATION	Entrance/Parking Fee	Parking	Restrooms	Lifeguard	Campground	Showers	Firepits	Stairs to Beach	Path to Beach	Bike Path	Hiking Trail	Facilities for Disabled	Boating Facilities	Fishing	Equestrian Trail	Sandy Beach	Dunes	Rocky Shore	Upland from Beach	Stream Corridor	Bluff	Wetland
King Salmon Resort	Off Buhne Dr., W. of Hwy. 101, 1 mi. N. of Fields Landing	●	●	●		●								●	●		●						
Fields Landing County Boat Launch	Foot of Railroad Ave., Fields Landing		●	●										●	●								
South Spit and Jetty	S. Jetty Rd., N. of Table Bluff Rd.		●												●		●	●	●				●
Table Bluff County Park	Table Bluff Rd. off Hookton Rd., W. of Hwy. 101 at Beatrice		●																			●	
Crab County Park	W. end of Cannibal Rd., W. of Hwy. 101, Loleta		●						●						●					●		●	
Eel River	W. of Hwy. 101 at Fernbridge		●												●						●	●	
Humboldt County Fairgrounds Campground	W. of Main St., Ferndale		●	●		●	●														●		
Centerville Beach County Park	W. end of Centerville Rd., 5 mi. W. of Ferndale		●	●										●	●		●	●					

KING SALMON RESORT: Take the King Salmon Dr. exit off Highway 101. Sport fishing charter boats, trailer camping, fuel dock and hoists, and fishing and boating equipment are available at Johnny's Landing and R.V. Park, (707) 442-2284, and E-Z Boat Launch and Trailer Park, (707) 442-1118. A picnic area with restrooms is adjacent to the PG&E nuclear power plant on King Salmon Dr.
Mass Transit: Humboldt Transit Authority.

FIELDS LANDING COUNTY BOAT LAUNCH: Public two-lane concrete boat ramp on Humboldt Bay. The annual Cross-Country Kinetic Sculpture Race begins the bay crossing portion here.
Mass Transit: Humboldt Transit Authority.

SOUTH SPIT AND JETTY: Public fishing access open all year. Dangerously large waves; exercise caution when walking on the jetty.

TABLE BLUFF COUNTY PARK: Views of southern Humboldt Bay, including the south spit and jetty, and the Humboldt Bay National Wildlife Refuge.

CRAB COUNTY PARK: Take Loleta Dr. to Cannibal Rd. to get to the park; fishing area with access to the ocean, dunes, and river delta.

EEL RIVER: Within the Eel River delta, there are many roads which end at gravel beds along the river. Adjacent land is private property; do not trespass. Starting from the mouth of the river and moving east, the following streets end at the river: Camp Weott Rd., Dillon Rd., Tappendorf Lane, Sage Rd. and Singley Rd. near Fernbridge, and Sandy Prairie Rd. near Fortuna. One must cross through a farm gate on Sage Rd. to get to the river. Pedrazinni County Park is off Cannibal Rd. on Seven-Mile Rd., just northwest of the bridge.

HUMBOLDT COUNTY FAIRGROUNDS CAMPGROUND: Camping all year except during the fair in August. Fee $4/night; hookups and dump station are available. For more information, call: (707) 786-9511. The campground is in Ferndale, the westernmost city in the lower 48 states, noted for its many ornate Victorian buildings, which were constructed during the late 1800's. Ferndale also hosts two kinetic sculpture races in the spring.

CENTERVILLE BEACH COUNTY PARK: Four acres of park with access to the beach, reaching from the mouth of the Eel River to False Cape in the south. Private farmlands to the east; do not trespass. Four-wheel drive vehicles allowed on the beach; dangerous rip currents.

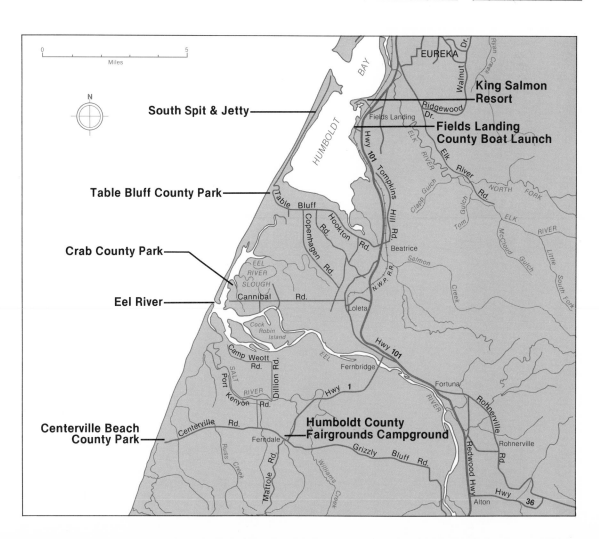

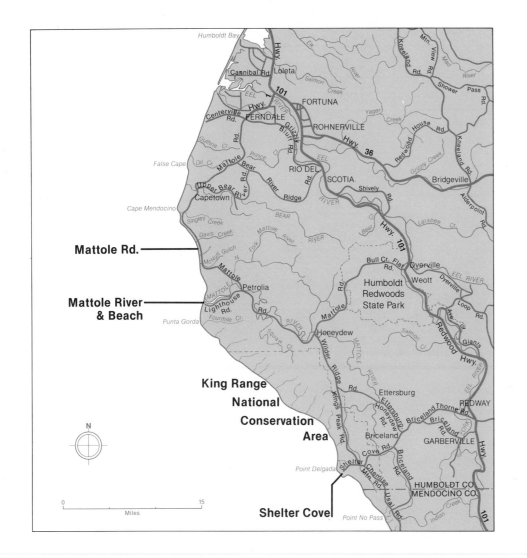

Mattole Rd.

Mattole River
& Beach

King Range
National
Conservation
Area

Shelter Cove

Humboldt Bay

Cannibal Rd. Loleta

101 FORTUNA

Centerville Rd. FERNDALE
ROHNERVILLE

Hwy. 36

False Cape
RIO DEL SCOTIA
Bridgeville

Cape Mendocino
Capetown

Bear River Ridge

Punta Gorda

Petrolia

Honeydew

Humboldt
Redwoods
State Park

Ettersburg

REDWAY

GARBERVILLE

Point Delgada

HUMBOLDT CO.
MENDOCINO CO.

Point No Pass

N

0   15
        Miles

Falls below Kings Peak, King Range National Conservation Area

Humboldt County

SOUTHERN HUMBOLDT COAST

NAME	LOCATION	Entrance/Parking Fee	Parking	Restrooms	Lifeguard	Campground	Showers	Firepits	Stairs to Beach	Path to Beach	Bike Path	Hiking Trail	Facilities for Disabled	Boating Facilities	Fishing	Equestrian Trail	Sandy Beach	Dunes	Rocky Shore	Upland from Beach	Stream Corridor	Bluff	Wetland
Mattole Road	Between Singley Creek and McNutt Gulch									●							●		●				
Mattole River and Beach	W. end of Lighthouse Rd., 5 mi. W. of Petrolia	●								●					●		●	●			●		●
King Range National Conservation Area	Honeydew to Point No Pass in Mendocino County	●	●	●		●				●					●		●	●	●	●		●	
Shelter Cove	W. end of Shelter Cove Rd.	●	●		●				●	●				●	●		●		●	●		●	

MATTOLE ROAD: The stretch of the Mattole Rd. between Cape Town and Petrolia runs along the coast at ocean level. The beach is accessible at Devils Gate and at McNutt Gulch. There are three pull-offs two miles south of Cape Mendocino at Devils Gate, a rocky point where the bluffs are close to the water. Paths to the beach cross the seawall. At McNutt Gulch, just before the road turns inland, there is a path to the beach through a gap in the fence. Each of these paths is marked by a 3/4" pipe which has *Calif. DWR* marked on it; these pipes are located where the path leaves the road. The northern paths are 50 feet wide, 25 feet on each side of the pipe; the path at McNutt Gulch is 20 feet wide, 10 feet on each side. Private property is adjacent to these paths; do not trespass.

MATTOLE RIVER AND BEACH: Lighthouse Rd. from Petrolia follows the Mattole River down to the beach. A trail leads south from the beach into the King Range, past an abandoned Coast Guard Lighthouse at Punta Gorda. It is possible to hike along the beach south to Shelter Cove; the distance is about 24 miles. Watch for rattlesnakes in driftwood and rocky areas. For more information, see the description for the King Range National Conservation Area, or contact the Bureau of Land Management Office, 1585 "J" Street, Arcata 95521, (707) 822-7648.

KING RANGE NATIONAL CONSERVATION AREA: 54,000 acres of steep coastal mountains and shoreline administered by the Bureau of Land Management (BLM). This primitive area, which constitutes part of the "Lost Coast," has very few roads; one third of the land is still privately held. BLM operates four camping areas during the summer. Facilities include picnic tables, food cupboards, grills, restrooms, and water. Numerous hiking trails cross the range, and it is possible to hike the entire coastline from the Mattole River to Shelter Cove. Permits are not required; however, backpackers are encouraged to sign trail registers near trailheads. Off-road vehicles are allowed on three miles of beach near the southern end of the park; check with the BLM for boundaries.

There are three beaches within the King Range, in addition to Shelter Cove: Mattole River Beach; Black Sand Beach off Beach Dr. north of Shelter Cove; and Chamise Cove, which can be reached by a trail from Nadelos Camp off Chamise Mountain Rd., south of Shelter Cove. Since road conditions vary during the year, check with BLM for the best routes into the King Range. Write: Eureka Resource Area, U.S. Bureau of Land Management, 1585 "J" Street, Arcata 95521; or call (707) 822-7648.

SHELTER COVE: Take Briceland-Thorne Rd. from Redway to Shelter Cove Rd.; Shelter Cove is a privately owned portion of the King Range National Conservation Area. Three areas provide access to the ocean: the main cove at the end of Machi Rd., where there is a public boat launch on the sandy beach, and parking and restrooms on the bluff; Point Delgada, where there are stairs to a rocky intertidal zone; and Little Black Sand Beach off Dolphin Drive. There are no facilities at Point Delgada or Little Black Sand Beach.

A motel, trailer park, and campsites provide accommodations. There is also a golf course and a small air strip. From May 1 to October 1, a restaurant, bar, and stores are open, with marine supplies, fishing licenses, bait and tackle. Rental boats and motors, fuel and dry storage, and a 1-1/2 ton capacity lift are also available at the cove during the summer season. For more information: Mario's Marina, Shelter Cove, Star Route, Whitehorn 95489.

Vista, North of Shelter Cove, King Range National Conservation Area

Mattole River Mouth

Near Point Arena

Mendocino County

Over 130 miles long, Mendocino County's coast is noted for its dramatically eroded sea cliffs and numerous small pocket beaches. Undeveloped terraces typically extend for miles along the coast between Highway 1 and the Pacific Ocean, interrupted only occasionally by small towns and villages, and the deep ravines of creek, stream, and river inlets.

The county's shoreline is extremely rugged, characterized by offshore sea stacks and abundant tidepool areas. Sandy beaches are usually found at the mouths of freshwater stream channels; access is often steep and difficult, but the beaches are generally secluded and protected from winds by the surrounding sea cliffs.

The rocky shores and clear waters of the coast are popular for diving. Although many people dive simply for the enjoyment of exploring undersea features such as the kelp forest off the bay at Van Damme State Park, a majority of divers are attracted by the abalone and rockfish which are prevalent here. During abalone season, which is from April to November in northern California, beaches and coastal campgrounds are often crowded with divers.

Unique to California's coastline is the north Mendocino County area known as the "Lost Coast." At Rockport, Highway 1 heads eastward, leaving the coast north of here accessible only by Usal Road, a narrow, dirt logging road with steep grades and numerous hairpin turns, which extends for 30 miles to the Humboldt County line. Although the southern half of the Lost Coast is mostly private, Sinkyone Wilderness State Park and the King Range National Conservation Area in the north provide some of the last remaining true wilderness areas in California which are adjacent to the coast.

Within the Lost Coast area the abandoned port towns of Rockport, Usal, and Bear Harbor serve as reminders of Mendocino's more populated era during the 19th century. Between 1850 and 1900, nearly every bay or anchorage large enough to harbor a ship was used along the coast as a shipping point for the valuable redwood and Douglas fir timber of the north coast, which were in high demand during and after the California Gold Rush period.

The demand for timberland resulted in the government's consolidation of the Pomo, Yuki, and Sinkyone Indian tribes, the original settlers of the coast, into the Mendocino Indian Reservation in 1856, located between the Noyo and Ten Mile Rivers. The military established Fort Bragg in 1857 to oversee the reservation. The government relocated the Indians inland to the Round Valley around 1864 due to the timber industry's interests in the reservation's forest lands. Fort Bragg was abandoned and the community subsequently became a lumber and port town. Easily harvestable timber along the coast became scarce after 1900 and many of the small towns of the north county were abandoned; remaining lumber production was eventually consolidated at Fort Bragg.

Mendocino, a former mill site established in 1852, is now an artists' community; the central town section has been designated as an historical preservation district, ensuring that its 19th century New England style architecture will be maintained.

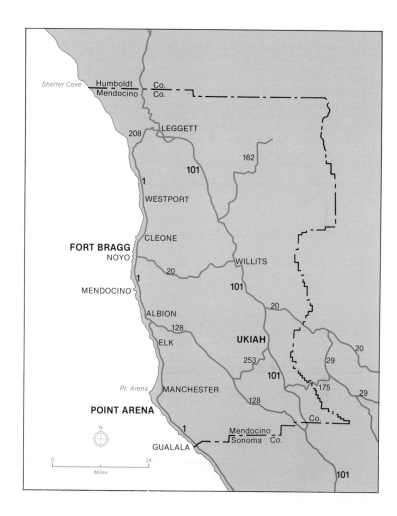

For additional information on Mendocino County's coast, contact the Mendocino Coast Chamber of Commerce, 332 N. Main Street (P.O. Box 1141), Fort Bragg 95437, (707) 964-3153. For transit information on service south of the Navarro River, contact the Mendocino Transit Authority (MTA), P.O. Box 556, Gualala 95445, (707) 884-3723. For service north of the Navarro River, contact the Mendocino Stage, Box 1177, Mendocino 95460, (707) 964-0167. Both the MTA and the Mendocino Stage buses may be boarded at regular stops or flagged at any safe location.

Coastal Landforms

Waves, wind, subsidence, and uplift are the major physical forces that act on the shoreline and which produce, over a long period of time, a variety of coastal landforms.

Perhaps the most obvious coastal landform is the beach, an area adjacent to the surf zone consisting of a veneer of sand and gravel over a bedrock base. In California, most beach sediments are carried to coastal areas by rivers and are distributed and deposited along the shoreline by waves and currents. The width and shape of a beach depend on the prevailing wave conditions and the type of sediment present at a particular location; for example, beaches made of large sand grains usually are steeper than beaches made of fine sand.

Sand spits and sand bars are formed when waves and currents deposit sand, gravel, or other sediments on the sea floor. Spits are narrow ridges or points of sand that project into the water from a point on the shore. Bars are submerged mounds or embankments of sediments that build up on the sea floor, often at the mouths of bays and estuaries. The San Francisco Bar, located offshore from the Golden Gate, is one example of a large sand bar system; this bar is formed by sediments carried from the Sacramento and San Joaquin Rivers, and if not dredged periodically, it would prevent ship movement to and from San Francisco Bay.

The erosive power of waves also contributes significantly to the creation of various coastal landforms. Breaking waves cut into the shoreline and form the bluffs and cliffs so common to the California coast. Sea caves are created when waves first remove the least resistant material, or attack the weakest areas, in a cliff face. As waves continue to advance landward, they plane, or level, the shoreline area, forming a wave cut bench, or platform, just below the water surface. Before the wave cut bench is completed, the more resistant portions of sea cliffs may project above sea level; these projections, which appear as offshore rocks or tiny islands, are called sea stacks.

The evolution of coastal landforms is demonstrated dramatically along the Mendocino County coast. Today, the shoreline is characterized by countless sea stacks located offshore adjacent to a series of promontories, or headlands, that project into the ocean. This rugged shoreline actually is the beginning of the youngest in a series of wave cut terraces, also called marine terraces, that extend inland more than two miles.

Over the last half-million years, the Mendocino coastal area has risen in response to the forces that have been building the coast mountain ranges. Thus, a terrace that was cut by the ocean more than 500,000 years ago is now elevated about 650 feet above sea level. From this oldest terrace, four more terraces step down in elevation and age as they near the present shoreline; each terrace is approximately 100 feet lower and 100,000 years younger than the preceding one.

Sea Stacks, Mendocino Coast

South Kibesillah Gulch Fishing Access

Mendocino County

NORTHERN MENDOCINO COAST

NAME	LOCATION	Entrance/Parking Fee	Parking	Restrooms	Lifeguard	Campground	Showers	Firepits	Stairs to Beach	Path to Beach	Bike Path	Hiking Trail	Facilities for Disabled	Boating Facilities	Fishing	Equestrian Trail	Sandy Beach	Dunes	Rocky Shore	Upland from Beach	Stream Corridor	Bluff	Wetland
King Range National Conservation Area	Between Honeydew in Humboldt County and Four Corners in Mendocino County	•	•		•		•			•				•	•	•	•		•	•	•		
Sinkyone Wilderness State Park	Between Four Corners and Bear Harbor			•		•				•		•			•		•		•	•	•	•	•
Overlooks	W. side of Hwy. 1, S. banks of Hardy and Juan Creeks	•																	•	•	•		
Westport-Union Landing State Beach	Frontage Rd. W. of Hwy. 1, between Howard and Dehaven Creeks, Abalone Pt.	•	•	•		•		•	•			•	•		•		•		•	•	•		
Wages Creek Beach	N.W. of Hwy. 1 at Wages Creek Beach Campground, 1/2 mile N. of Westport	•	•	•		•			•			•			•		•		•	•	•		
Chadbourne Gulch	2 mi. S. of Westport		•	•						•					•		•		•				
Bruhel Point Bluff	W. of Hwy. 1, .6 mi. S. of Bruhel Pt. Private Rd.		•	•								•							•	•	•		
South Kibesillah Gulch Fishing Access	W. of Hwy. 1, 1/2 mi. N. of Abalobadiah Creek		•	•					•	•					•		•		•			•	
Seaside Creek Beach	W. of Hwy. 1, 3/4 mi. N. of Ten Mile River	•															•			•			

KING RANGE NATIONAL CONSERVATION AREA: 54,000 total acres; 1,620 are in Mendocino County. Access is from Shelter Cove and Kings Peak Roads in Humboldt County. For additional information, see Humboldt County.

SINKYONE WILDERNESS STATE PARK: 3,600 acres of undeveloped beaches, bluffs, and coastal mountains extending from the King Range National Conservation Area to Bear Harbor; contains dense redwood forests and spectacular coastal views. Briceland Rd. (Route 435) from Shelter Cove in Humboldt County provides the best access to the park; Usal Rd. (Route 431) from Rockport in Mendocino County is narrow, winding, and often impassable. Trails at Whale Gulch and Bear Harbor lead from Briceland Rd. to narrow, black sandy beaches. Environmental campsites are located at Jones Beach, Needle Rock, and Orchard Creek. For trail maps and information, contact: Department of Parks and Recreation, Piercy Area, 1600 Hwy. 101, Garberville 95440, (707) 247-3318.

WESTPORT-UNION LANDING STATE BEACH: Blufftop day use areas are located along the two miles of frontage road just west of Highway 1 at Abalone Point. Improvements scheduled to be completed by summer 1983 include day use parking for 50 cars and camping areas for 130 vehicles; park only in designated areas. Beach access trails and stairs will lead from parking and camping areas to the beach. Wheelchair access is located at the mouths of Dehaven and Howard Creeks. Call: (707) 937-5804.

WAGES CREEK BEACH: Sandy, ocean beach at the mouth of Wages Creek is accessible from the privately run campground south of the creek, just off Highway 1; campsites are adjacent to the beach. Laundry basins, surf net rentals, and monthly trailer storage available. Camping fee is $9/vehicle; day use $4. Open all year; December–February camping requires reservations. 37700 N. Highway 1, Westport 95488, (707) 964-2964.

CHADBOURNE GULCH: Rocky cobble beach which extends 1/2 mile north and south of Chadbourne Gulch. The dirt road off Highway 1 on the north side of the gulch leads to a small parking area adjacent to the beach. Popular for surf fishing and surfing. Harbor seals are often sighted offshore.

BRUHEL POINT BLUFF: Several paths along the grassy blufftops west of Highway 1 and south of Chadbourne Gulch provide scenic views of the undeveloped headlands and rocky shore below. Access is from the small, unmarked parking area west of Highway 1, near a large grove of Monterey pine trees.

SOUTH KIBESILLAH GULCH FISHING ACCESS: Short, steep path and stairway lead from the blufftop overlook and parking area down to a sandy beach and tidepools. Popular for rock fishing and abalone diving. Bluffs are highly eroded. Due to 1983 storm damage, there is temporarily no beach access. (707) 468-4267.
Mass Transit: Mendocino Stage.

SEASIDE CREEK BEACH: Small, undeveloped ocean beach directly off Highway 1 adjoins the mouth of Seaside Creek; limited parking is at the small roadside turnout adjacent to the beach.
Mass Transit: Mendocino Stage.

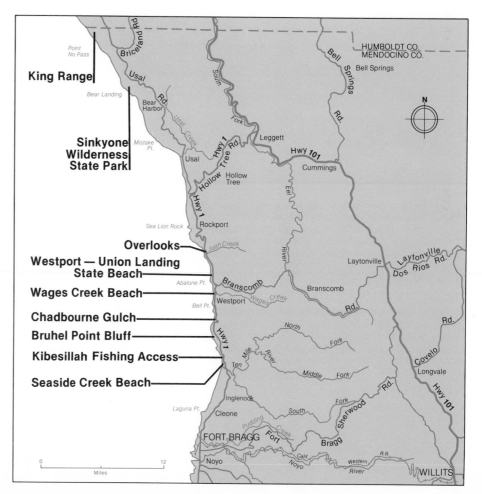

Mendocino Pygmy Forests

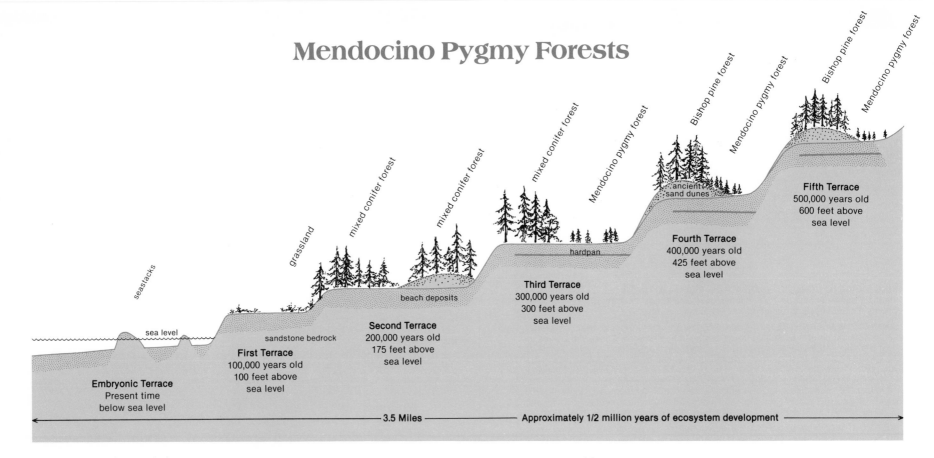

Several small forested areas known as pygmy forests are located along the Mendocino County coast between Fort Bragg and the Navarro River. These forests contain unusually dwarfed trees and shrubs which grow very slowly, typically reaching heights of only a few feet, although they may live to be over 100 years old.

The pygmy forests of Mendocino grow on landforms known as marine terraces. These terraces were created in the Pleistocene era by the periodic uplifting of the wave-eroded Mendocino coastline, resulting in a stair-case-type landform with five distinct terraces. The pygmy forests are found along the upper three older terraces where a soil condition, called podzol, has formed.

Podzol soils generally only evolve where the terraces are flat and rainwater collects and eventually drains through the sandy soils. This water is very acidic, primarily due to the decomposition of certain leaves and pine needles; as the water drains through the soil, it carries with it important plant nutrients and minerals, leaving the upper soil layers impoverished. Some of these minerals combine with the soil a few feet below the surface to form a concrete-like hardpan layer.

The iron-rich hardpan layer prevents plant roots from penetrating to the more fertile soils below. It also raises near-surface ground water levels, causing water to flood often and persist on the surface for long periods of time during the winter. In the spring and summer, however, water slowly drains past the hardpan, leaving the soils above it, where most plant roots are located, devoid of moisture. These extreme conditions of flooding in the winter, drought during the summer, lack of important nutrients; and high soil acid levels all combine to severely limit plant growth. All the plants within the pygmy forests are capable of growing to more normal heights in fertile soils.

The extremely slender and sometimes twisted and gnarled trees of the pygmy forest are a remarkable contrast to the surrounding tall forests of redwood, pine, and fir. Common pygmy forest species include the pygmy cypress *(Cupressus pygmaea),* Bishop pine *(Pinus muricata),* Bolander pine *(P. contorta* spp. *bolanderi),* and the dwarf (Fort Bragg) manzanita *(Arctostaphylos mummularia).* Except for the Bishop pine, all of these species are endemic to the Mendocino pygmy forest area.

Portions of the Mendocino pygmy forest have been formally preserved within the Jug Handle State Reserve (which contains the former Pygmy Forest Reserve), in Van Damme State Park, and in a small parcel owned by the University of California. The pygmy forests in Jug Handle State Reserve and Van Damme State Park are accessible by self-guided nature trails.

To purchase maps or literature on Jug Handle State Reserve pygmy forests, write:

Jug Handle Creek Farm
P.O. Box 17
Caspar, CA 95420.

(707) 964-4630

NAME	LOCATION	Entrance/Parking Fee	Parking	Restrooms	Lifeguard	Campground	Showers	Firepits	Stairs to Beach	Path to Beach	Bike Path	Hiking Trail	Facilities for Disabled	Boating Facilities	Fishing	Equestrian Trail	Sandy Beach	Dunes	Rocky Shore	Upland from Beach	Stream Corridor	Bluff	Wetland
MacKerricher State Park	Runs from Ten Mile River S. to Pudding Creek, Cleone	●	●	●		●	●	●	●			●	●	●	●	●	●	●	●	●		●	●
Noyo Harbor	End of Noyo Harbor Dr. at the Noyo River		●											●	●		●		●				
Mendocino Coast Botanical Gardens	18220 N. Hwy. 1, 2 mi. S. of Fort Bragg	●	●	●					●			●	●				●		●	●		●	
Path to Beach	Ocean Dr. near Hwy. 1, N. of Caspar								●						●		●		●	●		●	
Jug Handle State Reserve	E. and W. of Hwy. 1, 1-1/2 mi. N. of Caspar		●	●					●			●					●		●	●	●	●	

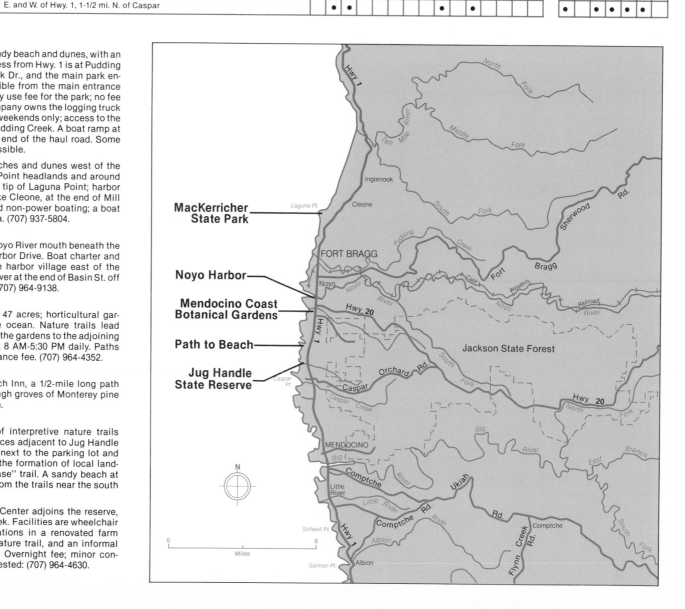

MACKERRICHER STATE PARK: Six miles of sandy beach and dunes, with an offshore underwater park for divers. Beach access from Hwy. 1 is at Pudding Creek, and at the ends of Ward Ave., Mill Creek Dr., and the main park entrance road. A 143-site campground is accessible from the main entrance road or Mill Creek Road. $6 overnight fee, $2 day use fee for the park; no fee for beach day use. Georgia-Pacific Lumber Company owns the logging truck haul road which runs along the shoreline, open weekends only; access to the haul road is west of Hwy. 1, 1/2 mile north of Pudding Creek. A boat ramp at the mouth of Ten Mile River is at the northern end of the haul road. Some campsites and restrooms are wheelchair accessible.

A six-mile equestrian trail runs along the beaches and dunes west of the haul road. Hiking trails are along the Laguna Point headlands and around Lake Cleone. A seal watching station is at the tip of Laguna Point; harbor seals are frequently seen offshore. 15-acre Lake Cleone, at the end of Mill Creek Rd., is popular for freshwater fishing and non-power boating; a boat ramp is adjacent to the parking and picnic area. (707) 937-5804.
Mass Transit: Mendocino Stage.

NOYO HARBOR: A sandy ocean beach at the Noyo River mouth beneath the Highway 1 bridge is accessible from North Harbor Drive. Boat charter and fishing equipment rentals are available at the harbor village east of the bridge; a boat ramp is on the south bank of the river at the end of Basin St. off South Harbor Drive. Boat charter information: (707) 964-9138.
Mass Transit: Mendocino Stage.

MENDOCINO COAST BOTANICAL GARDENS: 47 acres; horticultural gardens located on a coastal terrace above the ocean. Nature trails lead through the lush native and exotic vegetation of the gardens to the adjoining headlands and sandy beach. Open year-round, 8 AM-5:30 PM daily. Paths and restrooms are wheelchair accessible. Entrance fee. (707) 964-4352.
Mass Transit: Mendocino Stage.

PATH TO BEACH: Just south of the Pine Beach Inn, a 1/2-mile long path across undeveloped state park land leads through groves of Monterey pine to shoreline sea cliffs and a small sandy beach.
Mass Transit: Mendocino Stage.

JUG HANDLE STATE RESERVE: Five miles of interpretive nature trails traverse the headlands and inland coastal terraces adjacent to Jug Handle Creek. Brochures, available at the picnic area next to the parking lot and rangers headquarters off Highway 1, describe the formation of local landforms along the self-guided "ecological staircase" trail. A sandy beach at the mouth of Jug Handle Creek is accessible from the trails near the south side of the Highway 1 overpass.

Privately owned Jug Handle Farm and Nature Center adjoins the reserve, east of Highway 1 and south of Jug Handle Creek. Facilities are wheelchair accessible and include overnight accommodations in a renovated farm house and small campground, a self-guided nature trail, and an informal library. Group educational programs available. Overnight fee; minor contribution of work requested. Reservations suggested: (707) 964-4630.
Mass Transit: Mendocino Stage.

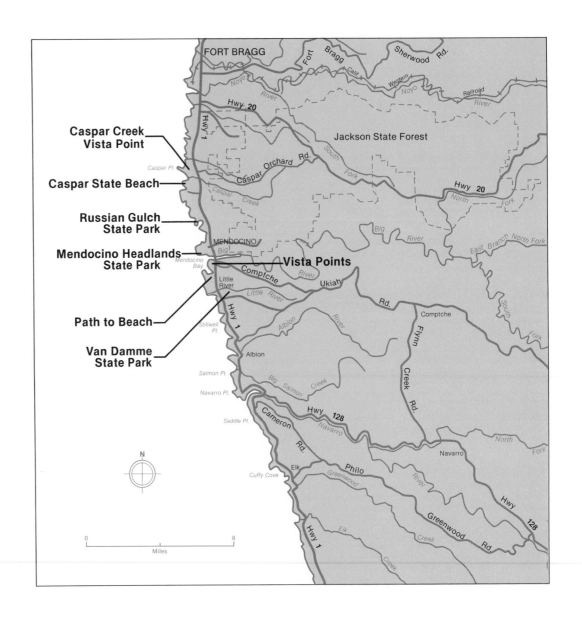

Caspar Creek Vista Point

Caspar State Beach

Russian Gulch State Park

Mendocino Headlands State Park

Vista Points

Path to Beach

Van Damme State Park

FORT BRAGG

Jackson State Forest

Hwy 20

Hwy 20

MENDOCINO

Comptche

Ukiah

Little River

Albion

Philo

Navarro

Greenwood Rd.

Hwy 128

Elk

Cuffy Cove

Saddle Pt.

Navarro Pt.

Salmon Pt.

Stillwell Pt.

Mendocino Bay

Big River

Caspar Pt.

Caspar Creek

Comptche

Flynn Creek Rd.

Sherwood Rd.

Fort Bragg

Noyo River

Western

Railroad

Big River

East Branch North Fork

South Fork

North Fork

North Fork

Little River

Cameron Rd.

Navarro River

Big Salmon Creek

Greenwood Creek

Elk Creek

Hwy 1

Caspar Orchard Rd.

N

0   8
Miles

Mendocino Headlands State Park

Mendocino County
CASPAR/MENDOCINO

NAME	LOCATION	Entrance/Parking Fee	Parking	Restrooms	Lifeguard	Campground	Showers	Firepits	Stairs to Beach	Path to Beach	Bike Path	Hiking Trail	Facilities for Disabled	Boating Facilities	Fishing	Equestrian Trail	Sandy Beach	Dunes	Rocky Shore	Upland from Beach	Stream Corridor	Bluff	Wetland
Caspar Creek Vista Point	W. side of Hwy. 1 at Caspar Creek, Caspar		•																•	•			
Caspar State Beach	At Doyle Creek, off Pt. Cabrillo Rd. (Old Hwy. 1), Caspar		•														•		•				
Russian Gulch State Park	W. of Hwy. 1 at Russian Gulch	•	•	•		•	•	•			•	•			•		•		•	•	•	•	
Mendocino Headlands State Park	Seaward of Mendocino, from Lansing and Heeser Drives to Big River		•	•						•		•	•		•		•		•			•	
Vista Points	W. of Hwy. 1, just S. of Mendocino		•																	•		•	
Path to Beach	Hwy. 1 at Gordon Lane, 1-1/2 mi. S. of Mendocino									•					•		•		•			•	
Van Damme State Park	E. and W. of Hwy. 1 at Little River, 3 mi. S. of Mendocino	•	•	•		•	•	•				•	•		•		•		•	•	•	•	•

CASPAR CREEK VISTA POINT: Overlooks the Pacific Ocean and heavily wooded Caspar Creek.
Mass Transit: Mendocino Stage.

CASPAR STATE BEACH: Small, sandy beach, located at the mouth of Doyle Creek where Point Cabrillo Rd. (Old Highway 1) runs adjacent to the ocean.
Mass Transit: Mendocino Stage.

RUSSIAN GULCH STATE PARK: 30 campsites are situated in the redwood-forested valley of Russian Gulch, below Highway 1. A sandy beach beneath the arched Highway 1 bridge is accessible from the road leading past the park's recreation hall and 40-person capacity group campsite. Horse camping is also available. There are outdoor showers near the beach. Twelve miles of hiking trails include paths along the headlands which pass a 200-foot diameter ocean blowhole, and vista points of Mendocino to the south. Inland trails lead to the 53,000-acre Jackson State Forest east of the park. $6 camping fee, $2 day use fee. Summertime reservations recommended. The offshore area is an underwater park for divers; fresh water and restrooms are available on the ocean side of Highway 1. For information: (707) 937-5804.
Mass Transit: Mendocino Stage.

MENDOCINO HEADLANDS STATE PARK: Two miles of spectacular sea cliffs, dotted with numerous wave tunnels, rim the promontory of the Mendocino headlands adjacent to the town of Mendocino and the Big River. The headlands are accessible by blufftop trails along the southern terraces or from the parking lots off Heeser Dr. to the north and west. There is a path to the beach near the Ford House, which is the ranger's residence. A sandy beach at the mouth of the Big River is adjacent to the southern headlands and is accessible from North Big River Rd.

Privately run Mendocino Campground is located just south of the Big River at Comptche-Ukiah Rd. and Highway 1. 60 sites; $6/night. Information: (707) 937-4016. Canoes can be rented hourly and daily at Catch-A-Canoe, 44900 Comptche-Ukiah Rd., just off Highway 1, on the south bank of the Big River. Call: (707) 937-0273.
Mass Transit: Mendocino Stage.

VISTA POINTS: Both of these vista points overlook the town of Mendocino, the headlands, and the Big River. One is located adjacent to North Big River Rd. at Mendocino, and the other is above Brewery Gulch Rd., 3/4 mile south of Mendocino.
Mass Transit: Mendocino Stage.

PATH TO BEACH: Located south of Mendocino Bay, a 1/2-mile long path on undeveloped state park land leads to bluffs and a small rocky beach; steep and hazardous shoreline access down the bluffs.
Mass Transit: Mendocino Stage.

VAN DAMME STATE PARK: A small sandy beach and paved parking lot is west of Highway 1, adjacent to the Little River mouth and the campground entrance; 24 en route campsites are available in this lot if the regular campground is full. Restrooms are on the beach and across the highway in the campground area. The campground contains 74 sites; reservations recommended during summer. $6 camping fee, $2 park day use fee. No fee for beach day use.

Park features include the forested valley of the Little River, and the Pygmy Forest self-guided nature trail, accessible from the 4-1/2 miles of hiking trails at the eastern end of the park, or from the parking lot at the intersection of Little River and Little River Albion Roads, 2.8 miles east of Highway 1. The Pygmy Forest is so named because of the unusually stunted mature, cone-bearing trees which grow on the hardpan soil in this area. The offshore area is an underwater park for divers. For information: (707) 937-5804.
Mass Transit: Mendocino Stage.

Van Damme State Park

Russian Gulch State Park

Albion Flat

Albion River, Albion

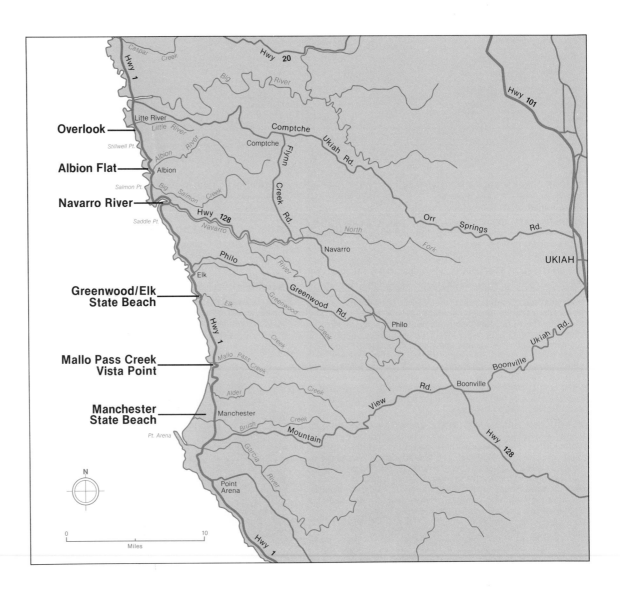

Overlook

Albion Flat

Navarro River

Greenwood/Elk
State Beach

Mallo Pass Creek
Vista Point

Manchester
State Beach

NAME	LOCATION	Entrance/Parking Fee	Parking	Restrooms	Lifeguard	Campground	Showers	Firepits	Stairs to Beach	Path to Beach	Bike Path	Hiking Trail	Facilities for Disabled	Boating Facilities	Fishing	Equestrian Trail	Sandy Beach	Dunes	Rocky Shore	Upland from Beach	Stream Corridor	Bluff	Wetland
Overlook	Bluff S. of Dark Gulch														•				•	•		•	
Albion Flat	N. bank of the Albion River, Albion	•	•	•		•	•	•		•				•	•			•					•	
Navarro River	W. end of Navarro Bluff Rd.		•	•											•			•				•		
Greenwood/Elk State Beach	W. of Hwy. 1, N. of Greenwood Creek, Elk		•	•						•					•			•		•	•		•	
Mallo Pass Creek Vista Point	W. of Hwy. 1, S. of Mallo Pass Creek, 4-1/4 mi. N. of Manchester		•																	•	•	•	•	
Manchester State Beach	Runs 3-1/2 mi. S. from Alder Creek to just N. of Pt. Arena, Manchester	•	•	•		•				•					•			•	•				•	

OVERLOOK: A dirt road, for pedestrians only, just south of Dark Gulch off Highway 1 leads to a blufftop overlook. Private property; stay on the main road. Permission to pass is by the owner and is revocable at any time.
Mass Transit: Mendocino Stage.

ALBION FLAT: Private campground and boat harbor at the end of Albion River Rd. provides access to a sandy ocean beach at the mouth of the Albion River. A boat launch to the river is east of the campground. Canoe rentals available. Overnight fee: $12 for camping and hookups; $2.50 day use fee. No fee required for pedestrian access to the beach. For reservations and information, write or call: Schooner's Landing, P.O. Box 218, Albion 95410; (707) 937-5707.
Mass Transit: Mendocino Stage.

NAVARRO RIVER: A sandy ocean beach is at the end of Navarro Bluff Rd., which runs along the south bank of the Navarro River. Navarro Bluff Rd. is unpaved and very rough; no parking permitted along the roadside. Park at the beach.
Mass Transit: Mendocino Transit Authority (MTA) Coast Van.

GREENWOOD/ELK STATE BEACH: A small, dirt parking lot is located in the town of Elk, on the west side of Highway 1. A pedestrian path to a sandy beach leads south down the bluffs from the parking lot. The path crosses leased property; vehicles are prohibited seaward of the parking lot. Private property is above this path; do not trespass. The parking lot is privately owned; permission to use the parking lot and the path is by the owner and lessee respectively, and is revocable at any time.

Scenic sea stacks are directly offshore. No camping is allowed on the beach or in the parking lot. Proposed improvements for this beach include portable toilets and picnic tables on the blufftop and at the beach. When completed, parking will be along Highway 1 only. Construction scheduled to be completed summer 1983; for information, call: (707) 937-5804.
Mass Transit: MTA Coast Van.

MALLO PASS CREEK VISTA POINT: A large paved parking lot is located on the high bluff above the south bank of Mallo Pass Creek, overlooking the rocky ocean shore to the west and the lush, riparian forests of Mallo Pass Creek canyon to the north and east.
Mass Transit: MTA Coast Van.

MANCHESTER STATE BEACH: 972 acres of beach and dunes west of Manchester. Alder Creek, Kinney, and Stoneboro Roads provide access from Highway 1 to small parking areas at the edge of the dunes; trails lead from the road ends to a long sandy beach scattered with driftwood. A 48-site campground is off Kinney Rd., 1/4 mile from the beach; $3 overnight fee. Environmental campsites are available; $6 fee. No fee for beach day use. The offshore area is an underwater park for divers' use. For information, call: (707) 937-5804.

East of Manchester State Beach is a privately run KOA campground off Kinney Road. Facilities include a store, laundry, game room, swimming pool, hot tub, and showers. Overnight fee: $10.50/two people; additional fee for hookups. Summer reservations recommended: Manchester Beach KOA, P.O. Box 266, Manchester 95459; (707) 882-2375.
Mass Transit: MTA Coast Van.

Manchester State Beach

Pier, Point Arena Cove

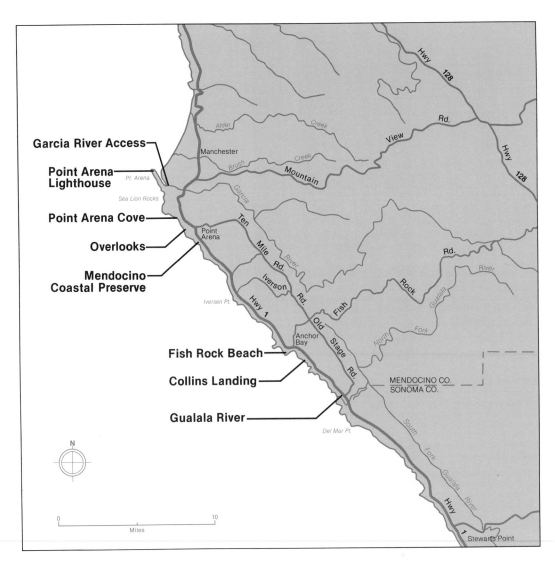

Garcia River Access

Point Arena
Lighthouse

Point Arena Cove

Overlooks

Mendocino
Coastal Preserve

Fish Rock Beach

Collins Landing

Gualala River

NAME	LOCATION	Entrance/Parking Fee	Parking	Restrooms	Lifeguard	Campground	Showers	Firepits	Stairs to Beach	Path to Beach	Bike Path	Hiking Trail	Facilities for Disabled	Boating Facilities	Fishing	Equestrian Trail	Sandy Beach	Dunes	Rocky Shore	Upland from Beach	Stream Corridor	Bluff	Wetland
Garcia River Access	End of Miner Hole Rd., 2 mi. N. of town of Pt. Arena		•							•					•				•	•			•
Point Arena Lighthouse	End of Lighthouse Rd., 1-1/4 mi. S. of town of Pt. Arena		•															•	•		•		
Point Arena Cove	W. end of Port Rd., Pt. Arena	•	•										•	•						•	•		
Overlooks	Along W. side of Hwy. 1, from Schooner Gulch to 3/4 mi. S.		•																•	•		•	
Mendocino Coastal Preserve	W. of Hwy. 1, 1 mi. S. of town of Pt. Arena		•																•	•		•	
Fish Rock Beach	At Anchor Bay Campground, .2 mi. N. of town of Anchor Bay	•	•	•		•	•	•						•		•				•			
Collins Landing	At Serenisea Lodge, 1-3/4 mi. S. of town of Anchor Bay								•	•					•				•			•	
Gualala River	W. of Hwy. 1 at Gualala		•							•	•				•						•	•	

GARCIA RIVER ACCESS: A gravel road off Highway 1 leads to the south bank of the Garcia River. Popular fishing access. The area is noted as a wintering habitat for whistling swans. No dogs, camping, or hunting permitted.
Mass Transit: Mendocino Transit Authority (MTA) Coast Van.

POINT ARENA LIGHTHOUSE: The 115-foot tall lighthouse, built in 1870, has one of the most powerful lights on the coast. Group tours, by appointment only, are given on most major holidays and occasionally Monday-Saturday. For information: (707) 882-2292.
Mass Transit: MTA Coast Van.

POINT ARENA COVE: A small rocky beach is at the end of Port Rd. within the Point Arena Cove; privately run facilities include a parking area, old fishing pier, concessions, and boat and fishing equipment rentals. Day use and boat launching fees. Open April 15–September 30.
Mass Transit: MTA Coast Van.

MENDOCINO COASTAL PRESERVE: Access to this 80-acre blufftop preserve, managed by the California Institute of Environmental Studies (formerly the Bodega Bay Institute), is restricted to educational groups and for scientific purposes by appointment only. Noted as a natural coastal grassland habitat. Group accommodations, by reservation only, available at the Pelican House at Iverson Landing. For information, contact Eric Beihl, Star Route South #20, Point Arena 95468, (707) 884-3244.
Mass Transit: MTA Coast Van.

FISH ROCK BEACH: Privately run Anchor Bay Campground, directly off Highway 1 and adjacent to the ocean, provides access to a 3/4-mile long sandy beach and tidepools; picnic tables on the beach, and boat launching and fish cleaning facilities available. Popular fishing and diving access. 76-site campground with trailer hookups is open all year. Overnight fee: $9/two people, $1 for hookups. Day use fee: 50¢/vehicle and 50¢/person. For information and reservations, contact: Anchor Bay Campground, Gualala 95445, (707) 884-9923.
Mass Transit: MTA Coast Van.

COLLINS LANDING: Rocky cove and tidepools accessible by a steep trail and stairs beginning at the north end of the Serenisea Lodge facilities; the trailhead and stairway overlook Fish Rock to the north, which is used as a haul-out by harbor seals. Use of the accessway requires the permission of the Serenisea Lodge management; the lodge office is adjacent to the accessway.
Mass Transit: MTA Coast Van.

GUALALA RIVER: West of Hwy. 1, the Gualala River runs parallel to the Pacific shoreline for two miles. Sandy beaches along the river provide freshwater swimming and views of the coastal sandspit of Gualala Point Regional Park. River access is from the dirt roads just north of the Hwy. 1 Gualala River bridge, and via the steep stairway located directly west of the Surf Motel in Gualala. The Surf Motel is west of Hwy. 1, north of Center St.; a public easement through the motel parking lot leads to the stairway. Motel facilities other than the accessway are private; do not trespass.
Mass Transit: MTA Coast Van.

Point Arena Light Station

Sonoma Coast State Beaches

Sonoma County

The Sonoma County coast, with its steep cliffs, wave-cut marine terraces, and occasional small towns, is one of the few remaining undeveloped coastal areas in California. The northern third of the coast is mostly private land with limited public access, including the ten-mile long Sea Ranch development; certain other private lands in the north county are accessible for a fee. 400-acre Salt Point State Park, 20 miles north of Jenner, is a popular area for camping, hiking, and whale watching.

Historic Fort Ross, located on a coastal bluff eight miles north of the Russian River, was occupied from 1812 to 1841 by the Russian American Fur Company, who used the fort as a base for seal and sea otter hunting, and for farming. At one time there were as many as 300 people occupying the fort. After decimating the seal and sea otter populations, however, and having little success at farming, the Russians left in 1841. Today the site is a state park with a museum, and is under reconstruction to restore the fort to its original condition.

The Russian River, which flows into the Pacific Ocean at Jenner, is noted for its spring and summer canoeing and swimming, and its winter steelhead fishing. It's a popular summer resort area, without the persistent fog found near the ocean, and there are many campgrounds and recreational facilities with river access along Highway 116, which leads inland from the coast.

The southern third of the coast is almost exclusively State Beach; the Sonoma Coast State Beaches comprise over a dozen sandy coves between Goat Rock and Bodega Bay, with headquarters at Salmon Creek Beach. These coves lead to pocket beaches which are excellent for beachcombing. This part of the coast is also popular for fishing; however, the ocean is too rough for swimming, and strong rip currents and cold water temperatures make even walking in shallow water dangerous. Lifeguards are not provided, and visitors should be very careful when walking on the beaches.

Along Highway 1 just south of these beaches is Bodega Bay, Sonoma's southernmost coastal town. The Bodega Harbor, in the north part of the bay, is a center for commercial fishing, recreation, and sportfishing, and is particularly crowded during salmon season. Bodega Bay also has piers, berths, and boat tours, and holds a Fishermen's Festival in April.

For information on the Bodega Bay Fishermen's Festival, contact the Bodega Bay Chamber of Commerce at Highway 1, P.O. Box 146, Bodega Bay 94923; (707) 875-3422. For information on Sonoma Coast State Beaches, call (707) 875-3483. For transit information, contact the Mendocino Transit Authority (MTA), 2098 Millcreek Road, Ukiah 95482, (707) 884-3723.

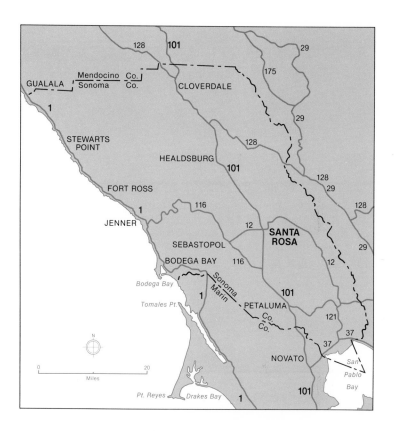

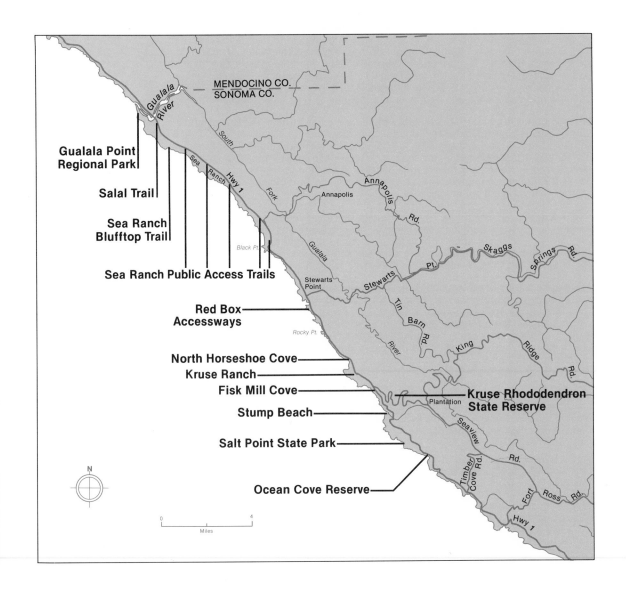

MENDOCINO CO.
SONOMA CO.

Gualala Point Regional Park

Salal Trail

Sea Ranch Blufftop Trail

Sea Ranch Public Access Trails

Red Box Accessways

North Horseshoe Cove

Kruse Ranch

Fisk Mill Cove

Stump Beach

Salt Point State Park

Ocean Cove Reserve

Kruse Rhododendron State Reserve

Annapolis

Annapolis Rd.

Skaggs Springs Rd.

Stewarts Point

Gualala

Tin Barn Rd.

King Ridge Rd.

River

Seaview Rd.

Plantation

Timber Cove Rd.

Fort Ross Rd.

Hwy 1

Black Pt.

Rocky Pt.

South Fork

Hwy 1

Gualala River

Sea Ranch

N

0   4
Miles

Stump Beach, Salt Point State Park

Sonoma County

NORTHERN SONOMA COAST

NAME	LOCATION	FACILITIES															ENVIRONMENT						
		Entrance/Parking Fee	Parking	Restrooms	Lifeguard	Campground	Showers	Firepits	Stairs to Beach	Path to Beach	Bike Path	Hiking Trail	Facilities for Disabled	Boating Facilities	Fishing	Equestrian Trail	Sandy Beach	Dunes	Rocky Shore	Upland from Beach	Stream Corridor	Bluff	Wetland
Gualala Point Regional Park	Hwy. 1, 1 mi. S. of Gualala	•	•	•		•		•		•	•	•		•	•		•		•	•	•		
Sea Ranch Blufftop Trail	Between Gualala Point Regional Park and Walk-On Beach		•							•		•					•		•	•	•	•	
Salal Trail	1/4 mi. S. of Gualala Point Regional Park		•	•						•							•		•		•		
Sea Ranch Public Access Trails	Hwy. 1 at Walk-On Beach, Shell Beach, Unit 24, Pebble and Black Point Beaches		•	•					•	•							•		•		•		
Red Box Accessways	Hwy. 1, 1/2 mi. to 2 mi. S. of Stewarts Point	•															•		•		•		
North Horseshoe Cove	Hwy. 1, 1-1/2 mi. S. of Rocky Point	•	•							•		•					•		•		•		
Kruse Ranch	Hwy. 1, 2 mi. S. of Rocky Point		•							•							•		•				
Kruse Rhododendron State Reserve	E. of Hwy. 1, off Kruse Ranch Rd.		•	•						•										•	•		
Fisk Mill Cove (Unit of Salt Point State Park)	Hwy. 1, just S. of Kruse Ranch Rd.		•	•			•	•		•		•		•			•		•		•		
Stump Beach (Unit of Salt Point State Park)	1 mi. N. of main entrance to Salt Point State Park		•				•	•	•								•		•		•		
Salt Point State Park	Hwy. 1, 20 mi. N. of Jenner	•	•	•		•		•		•		•	•		•	•		•		•		•	•	
Ocean Cove Reserve	12 mi. S. of Stewarts Point	•	•	•		•			•				•				•		•		•		

Visitors' Center, Gualala Point Regional Park

In 1980, legislation was passed to provide coastal access at six new locations within the Sea Ranch subdivision. To implement that law, the Sea Ranch Blufftop Trail and the Sea Ranch Public Access Trails are scheduled for completion by early 1984.

SEA RANCH BLUFFTOP TRAIL: A blufftop trail leads from Gualala Point Regional Park south for three miles where it connects with a trail from Highway 1 and leads to Walk-On Beach. The northernmost segment of the blufftop trail, which connects Gualala Point Regional Park to Salal Trail, is scheduled to be completed by summer 1983. Private property is adjacent; do not trespass.

SALAL TRAIL: Currently open. Parking at the trailhead and at Gualala Point Regional Park; the trail follows a creek through the Sea Ranch to a small cove. Respect adjacent private property.
Mass Transit: MTA Coast Van.

SEA RANCH PUBLIC ACCESS TRAILS: There are five public parking areas west of Highway 1 with trails that lead to the beach: Walk-On Beach can be reached by the Blufftop Trail or from a trailhead just north of Leeward Rd. Spur near Highway 1 milepost 56.75; Shell Beach is accessible by a trail that starts just south of Whalebone Reach; the pocket beach between Units 21 and 36 is accessible by a trail that begins near the Highway 1 milepost 53.96, just north of the stables; Pebble Beach is accessible by a trail south of Navigator's Reach, near the Highway 1 milepost 52.21; and Black Point Beach can be reached by a trail that starts near the Highway 1 milepost marker 50.85, just north of the Sea Ranch Lodge. Restrooms have been proposed for all trailheads. Public access rights extend to the base of the bluff or the first line of vegetation as well as the trail and parking easements. Private property is adjacent; do not trespass. Observe signs or call the Sonoma County Regional Parks Department for current status of the project: (707) 527-2041.

RED BOX ACCESSWAYS: Privately owned accessways to bluffs and coves. Red signs along the fence indicate trails; pay $2 fee in red boxes. Visitors must climb over the fence to use accessways.
Mass Transit: MTA Coast Van.

NORTH HORSESHOE COVE: The trail to the cove is partially on private land. Pay fee at the ranch house, one mile north on the east side of Highway 1.
Mass Transit: MTA Coast Van.

KRUSE RANCH: Undeveloped state park land; trails lead to the beach.
Mass Transit: MTA Coast Van.

KRUSE RHODODENDRON STATE RESERVE: 300-acre rhododendron reserve with five miles of hiking trails. Plants bloom April to June; no picnic facilities. Information: (707) 865-2391.
Mass Transit: MTA Coast Van.

FISK MILL COVE: Unit of Salt Point State Park. Scheduled to open in summer 1983; facilities include a parking lot, wheelchair-accessible restrooms, and trails along the bluff and to the beach.
Mass Transit: MTA Coast Van.

STUMP BEACH: Unit of Salt Point State Park. Picnic tables.
Mass Transit: MTA Coast Van.

SALT POINT STATE PARK: 400-acre park which includes both upland and coastal land. Camping $3-6/night; 31 sites, six environmental campsites. Day use fee $2. Marked hiking and riding trails; picnic areas, small beaches, and tidepools. Gerstle Cove is an offshore underwater preserve within the park with a boat launch.

Planned improvements for summer 1983 include 78 new, improved campsites, two group camps, one primitive camping area, extended hiking trails, and wheelchair-accessible restrooms and trails. Whale watch talks are given on weekends in January. For information, call: (707) 847-3221.
Mass Transit: MTA Coast Van.

OCEAN COVE RESERVE: Privately owned bluff and beach. Pay fee at the grocery store. Overnight camping for fee; $4 minimum. Fishing and diving area.
Mass Transit: MTA Coast Van.

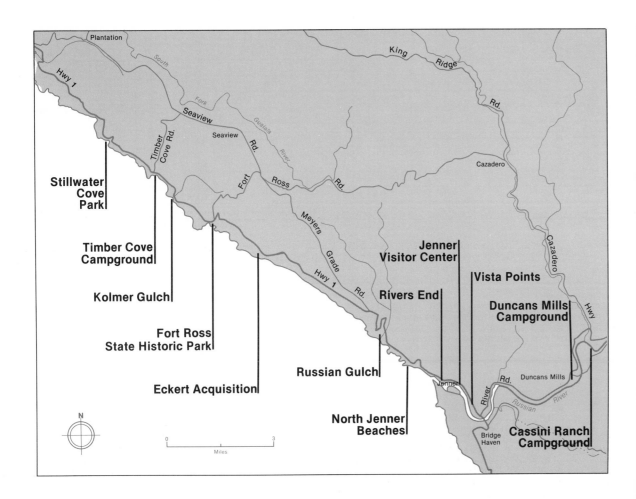

Stillwater
Cove
Park

Timber Cove
Campground

Kolmer Gulch

Fort Ross
State Historic Park

Eckert Acquisition

Russian Gulch

North Jenner
Beaches

Jenner
Visitor Center

Vista Points

Rivers End

Duncans Mills
Campground

Cassini Ranch
Campground

Plantation

Hwy 1

South Fork

Gualala River

Seaview

Seaview Rd.

Timber Cove Rd.

Fort Ross Rd.

Meyers Grade Rd.

Hwy 1

King Ridge Rd.

Cazadero

Cazadero Hwy

Jenner

Duncans Mills

Bridge Haven

River Rd.

Russian River

N

0   3
Miles

Fort Ross State Historic Park

Fort Ross State Historic Park

Sonoma County
STILLWATER COVE TO RUSSIAN RIVER

NAME	LOCATION	Entrance/Parking Fee	Parking	Restrooms	Lifeguard	Campground	Showers	Firepits	Stairs to Beach	Path to Beach	Bike Path	Hiking Trail	Facilities for Disabled	Boating Facilities	Fishing	Equestrian Trail	Sandy Beach	Dunes	Rocky Shore	Upland from Beach	Stream Corridor	Bluff	Wetland
Stillwater Cove Park	Hwy. 1, 3 mi. N. of Fort Ross	•	•	•		•	•	•	•	•		•	•				•		•	•	•		
Timber Cove Campground	Hwy. 1, 12 mi. N. of Jenner	•	•	•		•	•		•				•	•			•		•		•		
Kolmer Gulch	Hwy. 1, 1-1/2 mi. N. of Fort Ross	•								•													
Fort Ross State Historic Park	Hwy. 1, 11 mi. N. of Jenner	•	•	•		•				•		•	•		•		•		•	•	•		
Eckert Acquisition	Hwy. 1, 8 mi. N. of Jenner	•	•	•			•			•					•		•			•	•		
Russian Gulch	Hwy. 1, 2-1/2 mi. N. of Jenner		•							•									•	•	•		
North Jenner Beaches	Hwy. 1, from Russian Gulch to Jenner		•							•												•	
Rivers End	Hwy. 1, Jenner	•	•	•		•								•	•						•		
Jenner Visitor Center	Hwy. 1, Jenner		•	•										•	•						•		
Vista Points	Hwy. 1, Jenner to Bridgehaven		•																			•	
Duncans Mills Campground	Hwy. 116, Duncans Mills	•	•	•		•	•	•						•	•		•			•	•		
Cassini Ranch Family Campground	Moscow Rd., 3/4 mi. E. of Hwy. 116, Duncans Mills	•	•	•		•	•	•					•	•	•	•	•		•	•	•		

STILLWATER COVE PARK: $1.50 day use fee, $5 camping fee for Sonoma County residents, $6 for others. A long stairway leads to the beach. Picnic tables, restrooms, and a path to the beach are wheelchair accessible. There is also another trail north of Stillwater Cove that leads to the beach and includes an observation deck. For information and reservations, call: (707) 847-3245.
Mass Transit: Mendocino Transit Authority (MTA) Coast Van.

TIMBER COVE CAMPGROUND: Privately owned. Day use fee $3/person, overnight camping $8/vehicle, $2 for electric hookup; use of hot tub included in fee. Boat rentals and sales, guided boat tours, boat launch, and scuba rentals and sales available; air station, fishing licenses, bait and tackle, and propane. Home and cabin rentals. 21350 Coast Highway 1, Jenner 95450; (707) 847-3278.
Mass Transit: MTA Coast Van.

KOLMER GULCH: Land is owned by Louisiana-Pacific. Future plans include a parking area, improved beach access, public campground, and a demonstration forest.
Mass Transit: MTA Coast Van.

FORT ROSS STATE HISTORIC PARK: An American outpost for Russian fur traders in the 19th century, currently being restored. Admission fee $2, open 8 AM-5 PM daily. Guided tours on weekends 11 AM-3 PM; museum. Picnic tables, hiking trails, and pocket beach. There is an offshore underwater park for divers adjacent to the park. For information, call: (707) 847-3286.
Mass Transit: MTA Coast Van.

ECKERT ACQUISITION: Fee for use $3/day, $5/night. Trails lead to a beach at Fort Ross in the north, and to two coves. The southern portion includes a trail to the beach at the bottom of Timber Gulch.
Mass Transit: MTA Coast Van.

RUSSIAN GULCH: Undeveloped state park land; trails lead to the beach. Parking along Highway 1.
Mass Transit: MTA Coast Van.

NORTH JENNER BEACHES: The state owns the land from Russian Gulch to the Russian River mouth at Jenner. Several beaches are reached by steep trails down eroding bluffs.
Mass Transit: MTA Coast Van.

RIVERS END: Privately owned. Day use, camping, and fishing. Facilities include boat launch and ramp, cabins, restaurant, and bar. For information, call: (707) 869-3252.
Mass Transit: MTA Coast Van.

JENNER VISITOR CENTER: The Visitor Center is under construction; scheduled to be completed summer 1983. A small boat launching ramp, picnic tables, and restrooms are currently available.
Mass Transit: MTA Coast Van.

VISTA POINTS: Several pull-offs along Highway 1 offer views of the Russian River mouth, Penny Island, and the coast.

DUNCANS MILLS CAMPGROUND: Privately owned campground on the Russian River. 80 tent sites, 45 trailer sites, all hookups. Fee for public day use. Fishing, boat rentals, picnic tables, and horse rentals. For information, call: (707) 865-2573.
Mass Transit: MTA Coast Van.

CASSINI RANCH FAMILY CAMPGROUND: Privately owned campground on the Russian River. Public day use allowed when the campground is not full. 160 tent sites, 214 trailer sites, all hookups. Fishing licenses, bait, tackle; boat launch, dock, and rentals; playground, picnic areas, recreation hall, and horseback riding. Information: Box 522, Monte Rio 95462; (707) 865-2255.
Mass Transit: MTA Coast Van.

Mouth of the Russian River

Seabirds

As their name implies, seabirds spend most of their time flying, feeding, or resting on the open ocean. Like many shorebirds and waterfowl, they migrate from summer nesting areas in the north to wintering grounds in milder climes.

There are three general categories of seabirds. The "nearshore" or "inshore" birds are those which are typically seen along the coast at beaches, bays, and rocky intertidal areas. Birds such as cormorants, grebes, loons, and scoters usually stay near land, feeding on organisms found in shallow water.

"Offshore" seabirds, such as shearwaters and common murres, usually stay out several miles from land and generally feed in deep water. These birds usually can be seen only from a boat or when they are nesting on offshore islands such as San Miguel or the Farallones. The third group, the "pelagic" or open ocean species, such as albatrosses, skuas, and Arctic terns, feed and rest in oceanic waters, often several miles from land.

The nesting and breeding activities of seabirds are related to the ocean currents. In the spring, nutrient-rich cooler waters upwell offshore, causing a phytoplankton bloom. This in turn causes a rise in the numbers of fish which provide a source of food for the seabirds.

In contrast to terrestrial birds, seabirds have evolved in an environment which is mainly free from competition. As a result, seabirds have long lifespans, low adult mortality rates, late sexual maturity, and small clutch sizes. Individual birds have been known to live for 20 to 30 years.

The Farallon and Channel Islands are important breeding areas for seabirds. The entire breeding populations of brown pelicans, black storm-petrels, and Xantus' murrelets nest on the Channel Islands, while large populations of several species of seabirds nest on the Farallones.

The Farallon Islands have long been a significant nesting site. In the 1850's the Farallon Egg Company was formed with the purpose of taking murre eggs from the islands for the booming population of San Francisco. This caused a massive drop in the murre population, and only recently have their numbers been increasing.

Seabirds generally eat fish of all sizes and types, although the anchovy is a favorite. Very few animals prey on the seabirds; however, recent evidence indicates that seabirds are very susceptible to oil spills and pesticides. Populations of many seabird species have begun to decline because of these factors, and from human disturbance of nests.

Heerman's gull

California gull

Ring billed gull

Western gull

Pelagic cormorant

Brown pelican

Western grebe

NAME	LOCATION	Entrance/Parking Fee	Parking	Restrooms	Lifeguard	Campground	Showers	Firepits	Stairs to Beach	Path to Beach	Bike Path	Hiking Trail	Facilities for Disabled	Boating Facilities	Fishing	Equestrian Trail	Sandy Beach	Dunes	Rocky Shore	Upland from Beach	Stream Corridor	Bluff	Wetland
Sonoma Coast State Beaches	Hwy. 1, Russian River to Bodega Head		•	•		•		•		•			•		•		•	•	•		•	•	
Goat Rock	Goat Rock Rd., off Hwy. 1		•	•				•		•			•				•	•		•			
Wright Beach	Hwy. 1, 6 mi. N. of Bodega Bay		•	•		•		•		•			•				•						
Duncans Landing	Hwy. 1, 5 mi. N. of Bodega Bay		•	•						•									•	•		•	
Gleasons Beach	Hwy. 1, 4 mi. N. of Bodega Bay		•	•						•							•						
Salmon Creek Beach	Hwy. 1, 2-1/2 mi. N. of Bodega Bay; or off Bean Ave.		•	•				•	•				•				•				•		
Bodega Dunes Campground	Hwy. 1, 1/2 mi. N. of Bodega Bay	•	•	•		•	•	•	•			•	•		•		•	•		•			

FACILITIES   **ENVIRONMENT**

SONOMA COAST STATE BEACHES: A series of beaches stretching from the Russian River to Bodega Head. Two camping areas are included: Wright Beach and Bodega Dunes. The park office is at Salmon Creek Lagoon: (707) 875-3483. A ranger leads walks each Sunday during the summer. An offshore underwater park for divers extends the length of the beaches.

Sonoma Coast State Beaches includes Willow Creek, upland from the Russian River, and Penny Island, near the mouth of the Russian River. The other beach units are: Goat Rock, Blind Beach, Shell Beach, Wright Beach, Duncans Landing, Duncans Cove, Gleasons Beach, Portuguese Beach, Schoolhouse Beach, Carmet Beach, Marshall Gulch, Arched Rock Beach, Colemans Beach, Miwok Beach, North Salmon Creek Beach, South Salmon Creek Beach, Bodega Dunes Campground, and Bodega Head.

All beaches have extremely unsafe currents and waves; even the surf area is unsafe. No lifeguards are provided. Each beach has parking and a path leading to the beach. Many have restrooms. Duncans Cove, Portuguese Beach, Schoolhouse Beach, Carmet Beach, and Colemans Beach all have especially steep trails to the beach. Beaches with other facilities are listed below.

GOAT ROCK: Open grassy peninsula between the Russian River and the ocean. Access to beaches on both the river and the ocean. Picnic tables. Restrooms are wheelchair accessible; the parking lot is adjacent to the beaches.

WRIGHT BEACH: Camping; 30 sites, $6/night. Picnic tables. Both the restrooms and the beach are wheelchair accessible.

DUNCANS LANDING: Used in the 1860's and 1870's for loading timber from Duncans Sawmill on the Russian River to ships anchored in the cove on the south side of the point. There is a small beach at this cove accessible by a steep trail.

GLEASONS BEACH: The state maintains a trail to the beach; all other paths are across private lands. Do not trespass.

SALMON CREEK BEACH: Both northern and southern accessways lead to large, popular sandy beaches. Salmon Creek channel crosses the beach; shallow swimming area and waterfowl habitat. A trail leading south to Bodega Head is scheduled to be completed by summer 1983; stay on the designated trail.

BODEGA DUNES CAMPGROUND: 98 campsites, $6/night. Day use fee $2. Trailer sanitation station, campfire center, picnic tables, horseback riding, and hiking trails. A boardwalk path leads over the dunes to the beach. Call: (707) 875-3483.

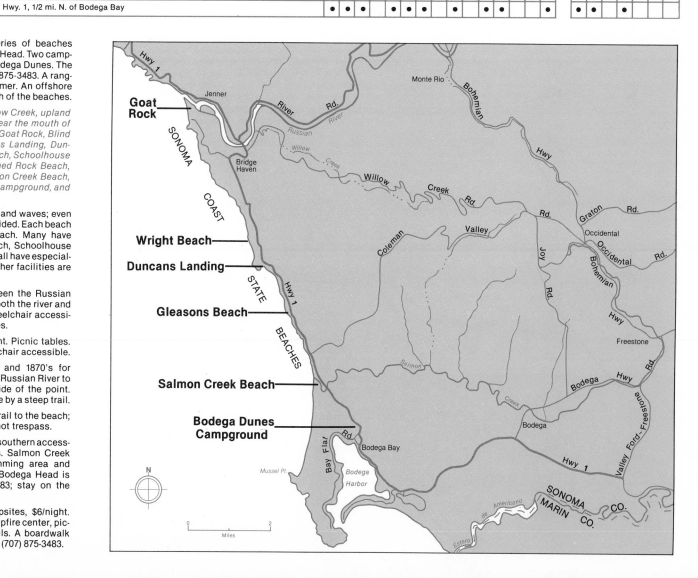

Shorebirds and Waterfowl

Shorebirds and waterfowl are a familiar sight on almost any lake, beach, or coastal bay. Shorebirds are found along the shore or in shallow ponds; they use their narrow, pointed bills to probe intertidal areas for small crustaceans, mollusks, worms, and other invertebrates. Waterfowl, such as ducks and geese, are more often seen in open water areas, diving for fish or submergent vegetation.

Almost all shorebirds and waterfowl found in California migrate during the spring and fall, either going south in the fall from summer breeding grounds in Canada or Alaska, or going north in the summer from wintering habitat in California, Mexico, or Central America. These birds follow the same routes every year, which are part of the Pacific Flyway. The Pacific Flyway covers the western part of North America and parts of the Arctic in eastern Asia, and is one of four major migration routes across North America. Migration along the coastline is very important for shorebirds in California, but less so for waterfowl, most of which fly through California's Central Valley.

Coastal wetlands provide food and resting areas during the fall and winter months for migrating birds. Most waterfowl are not confined to any one area, but move between the wetlands and bays along the coast, and between the coast and more inland areas. These movements are in response to changes in the season and weather, water conditions, and food availability.

Shorebirds are differentiated largely by their feeding habits. Different species have different bill lengths or shapes, and can effectively feed in different water levels. Black turnstones, for example, are usually found on rocky shores; snowy plovers and sanderlings on sandy flats; and avocets, western sandpipers, and long-billed dowitchers on mudflats. Willets, in contrast, can feed in a variety of habitats.

Waterfowl are categorized by their feeding habitat; dabbling, or puddle, ducks such as the mallard feed in marshes or nearby grain fields and rest on adjacent open water, while diving ducks such as the canvasback prefer bays, lagoons, or lakes and feed on aquatic vegetation or marine animals. Sea ducks such as the scoters seem comfortable in a variety of habitats and, as their name implies, feed primarily on marine invertebrates.

Habitat destruction and disturbance caused by people have been primary factors in population losses of these birds. The brant, for example, once numerous along the coast, has been reduced to low numbers due to the elimination of large areas of eel grass, their preferred food source, as a result of dredging and filling around bays.

Willet

Pintail duck

Great blue heron

Snowy egret

Sanderling

Avocet

Canvasback duck

Sonoma County

BODEGA BAY

NAME	LOCATION	Entrance/Parking Fee	Parking	Restrooms	Lifeguard	Campground	Showers	Firepits	Stairs to Beach	Path to Beach	Bike Path	Hiking Trail	Facilities for Disabled	Boating Facilities	Fishing	Equestrian Trail	Sandy Beach	Dunes	Rocky Shore	Upland from Beach	Stream Corridor	Bluff	Wetland
Masons Marina	1820 Westside Rd., Bodega Bay		•	•										•			•						
Westside County Park	Westside Rd. off Hwy. 1, Bodega Bay	•	•	•		•	•	•					•	•	•		•						
Bodega Marine Laboratory	Off Westside Rd., Bodega Bay		•	•													•	•	•				
Bodega Head	End of Westside Rd., Bodega Bay		•	•						•		•					•	•	•			•	
Porto Bodega	1500 Bay Flat Rd., Bodega Bay		•	•		•	•							•			•						
Tides Motel Wharf	Hwy. 1 in Bodega Bay		•	•										•	•		•						
Bodega Bay Harbor	Off Hwy. 1 and Bay Flat Rd., Bodega Bay													•	•		•						
Pinnacle Gulch Trail	Mockingbird Dr., Bodega Harbor		•							•							•			•	•		
Doran County Park	Doran Beach Rd., Bodega Bay	•	•	•		•		•						•	•	•	•	•					

MASONS MARINA: Private marina with berths, hoist, docks, fuel, and marine supplies. 1820 Westshore Rd., Bodega Bay 94923, (707) 875-3811.

WESTSIDE COUNTY PARK: Day use boating area with launch ramp. Camping $5/night for Sonoma County residents, $6/night for others, $1 walk-in. Picnic tables, trailer sanitation facility. (707) 875-3540.

BODEGA MARINE LABORATORY: University of California research facility, which includes a major aquaculture program. Open to the public Friday 2 PM-4 PM; a film, aquariums, and lobsters can be seen on the tour. Information: (707) 875-2211.

BODEGA HEAD: Unit of Sonoma Coast State Beaches. Fenced off area was the site of a proposed nuclear power plant. Hiking trails criss-cross the park; spectacular views of Marin and Sonoma coasts. Winter whale watching. A trail leading north to Salmon Creek Beach is scheduled to be completed by summer 1983; stay on the designated trail.

PORTO BODEGA: Private; boat dock and launch, 95 berths, bait and tackle. Accommodations available. 31 spaces for trailer camping with electric and water hookups; $10/night. 1500 Bay Flat Road, Bodega Bay 94923, (707) 875-2354.

TIDES MOTEL WHARF: Private accommodations, charter boats, docks, fuel, and food available. Box 547, Bodega Bay 94923, (707) 875-3595 or 875-3553.

BODEGA BAY HARBOR: Busiest harbor between San Francisco and Fort Bragg. Numerous parks and privately operated boating facilities. Fisherman's Festival is in April. For information: (707) 875-3422. A new marina is planned for Spud Point on the west side of the bay. Intended mainly for commercial fishing boats, the marina will also have slips for recreational boats, boat repair yards, fuel dock, utilities, parking areas, restrooms, coffee shop, and offices.

PINNACLE GULCH TRAIL: Take the Harbour Way exit off Highway 1, turn left on Heron Dr. and left on Mockingbird Dr.; the parking lot is on the left at the top of the hill. A steep trail starting across the street follows a narrow canyon to the sandy beach.

DORAN COUNTY PARK: Take Highway 1 to Smith Brothers Lane to Doran Beach Road. Day use fee: $1.50 for Sonoma County residents, $2 for others. 138 camping spaces; $5/night for Sonoma residents, $6/night for others, bike and hike-in $1/night. Picnic tables, boat launch, trailer sanitation station, fish cleaning station, and ocean fishing pier. Information: (707) 875-3540.

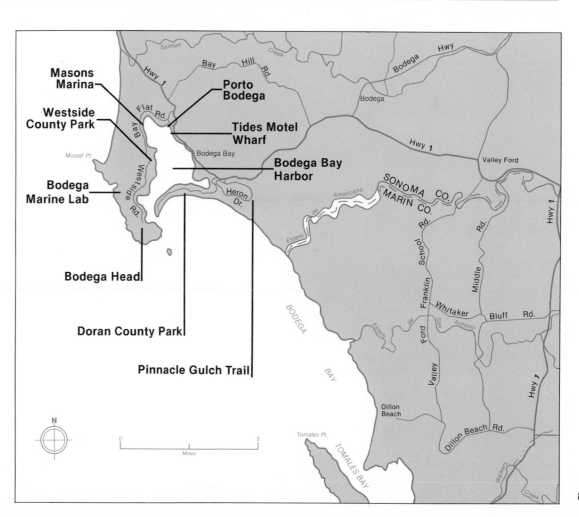

Golden Gate National Recreation Area, Rodeo Beach

Marin County

North of the Golden Gate, steep headlands form the Marin County coast, with grassy ridges and forested ravines dividing the numerous coastal bluffs. At Bolinas Lagoon the coastline arcs north-westward, creating the crescent-shaped Drakes Bay along the southern shore of the Point Reyes peninsula. The long, straight Point Reyes and McClures Beaches, which are frequently buffeted by strong winds and waves, stretch north from the western tip of this peninsula.

The rocky Marin coast, with its frequent fog, has a long history of shipwrecks; over 100 ships are known to have been wrecked here since the first recorded shipwreck in 1595, of the *San Augustin* from Manila. Two lighthouses were built in the late 1800's, one at Point Bonita and one at Point Reyes, to help ships navigate; today, electronic navigation equipment is also used. The Point Reyes Lighthouse, open to the public, is a popular spot to watch the migrating gray whales.

A primary force in the formation of the Marin County coast has been the San Andreas Fault, whose movements have created the southwest trending rift zone which contains the Olema Valley, Tomales Bay, and Bolinas Lagoon. This rift zone geologically separates the Point Reyes peninsula from the rest of the county, and roughly outlines the eastern boundary of the 64,000-acre Point Reyes National Seashore, one of only seven national seashores in the United States.

The sixteen-mile long Tomales Bay supports a thriving commercial shellfish industry which began in the late 1800's. Giant Pacific oyster seeds were imported from Japan and are the most significant commercial oyster type harvested in California. Drakes Estero, on the Point Reyes peninsula, produces 20% of California's commercial crop. Oyster beds can also be seen on the east side of Tomales Bay near Millerton Point. The southern end of the bay is a wildlife refuge for migrating waterfowl, while silver salmon and steelhead trout spawn in adjacent White House Pool.

The Miwok Indians were the native settlers of Point Reyes; it is estimated that they inhabited more than one hundred villages on the peninsula at the time of the English explorer Sir Francis Drake's supposed visit in 1579. The Miwok thrived on the bay and ocean shores until the Spanish missionaries arrived in 1820. Subsequent Spanish settlement of the coast led to the eventual destruction of the Miwok culture, primarily due to Spanish changes in land tenures and the introduction of European diseases.

The remoteness of Point Reyes, and the presence of heavy fog and strong winds have been major factors in preserving the rural character of the area. For over 60 years the main industries on the peninsula have been dairy and cattle ranching; in 1962, after long debate with developers, dairymen, and concerned citizens, Congress and President John F. Kennedy passed legislation creating the Point Reyes National Seashore, which formally preserved the land while allowing ranching to continue. Today, Point Reyes National Seashore is part of the federally owned Golden Gate National Recreation Area (GGNRA), established in 1972.

The grassy Marin Headlands, just across the Golden Gate from San Francisco, have also remained undeveloped; the Army maintained these lands for defense purposes until very recently. Now almost all the Army land in the Headlands, including the decaying bunkers, housing barracks, and an old balloon hangar, are part of GGNRA.

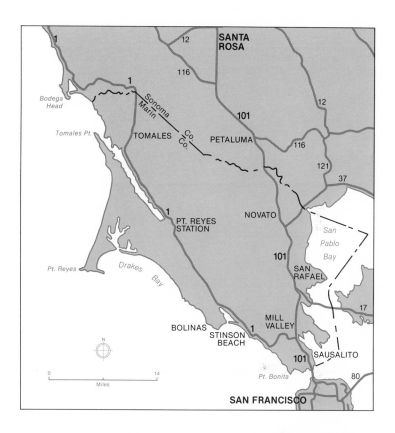

For additional information on the Marin County coast, write or call the Marin Coast Chamber of Commerce, P.O. Box 94, Olema 94950, (415) 663-1244, or the Marin County Chamber of Commerce and Visitors Bureau, 30 N. San Pedro Rd., Suite 150, San Rafael 94903, (415) 472-7470. For transit information, call Golden Gate Transit: (415) 453-2100 or 332-6600; and San Francisco's MUNI: (415) 673-MUNI.

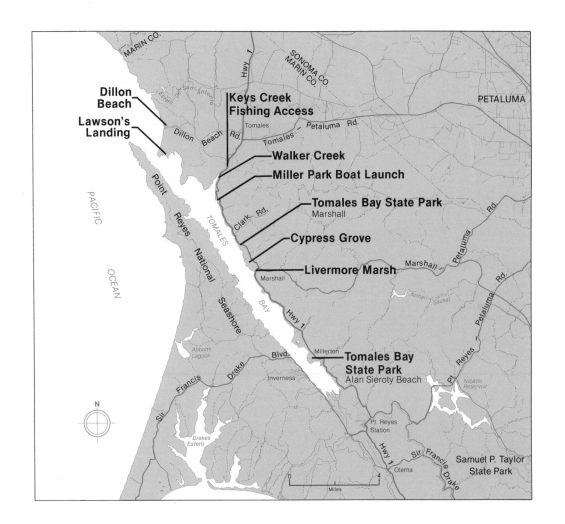

Dillon Beach

Lawson's Landing

Keys Creek Fishing Access

Walker Creek

Miller Park Boat Launch

Tomales Bay State Park
Marshall

Cypress Grove

Livermore Marsh

Tomales Bay State Park
Alan Sieroty Beach

MARIN CO.

SONOMA CO
MARIN CO.

PETALUMA

PACIFIC

OCEAN

Point Reyes National Seashore

TOMALES BAY

Hwy 1

Petaluma Rd.

Tomales

Tomales Rd.

Dillon Beach Rd.

Clark Rd.

Marshall

Arroyo Sausal

Petaluma Rd.

Pt. Reyes

Nicasio Reservoir

Abbotts Lagoon

Blvd.

Millerton

Inverness

Sir Francis Drake

Drakes Estero

Pt. Reyes Station

Samuel P. Taylor State Park

Sir Francis Drake

Hwy 1

Olema

N

0   4
Miles

Dillon Beach

Marin County
TOMALES BAY EAST

NAME	LOCATION	Entrance/Parking Fee	Parking	Restrooms	Lifeguard	Campground	Showers	Firepits	Stairs to Beach	Path to Beach	Bike Path	Hiking Trail	Facilities for Disabled	Boating Facilities	Fishing	Equestrian Trail	Sandy Beach	Dunes	Rocky Shore	Upland from Beach	Stream Corridor	Bluff	Wetland
Dillon Beach	Dillon Beach Rd., off Hwy. 1	•	•	•								•	•				•	•					
Lawson's Landing	5 mi. W. of Tomales, off Hwy. 1, S.W. of Dillon Beach	•	•	•		•						•	•				•	•					
Keys Creek Public Fishing Area	Hwy. 1, 1 mi. S.W. of Tomales		•	•											•						•		
Walker Creek	Delta area 2 mi. S. of Tomales, W. of Hwy. 1																				•		
Miller Park Boat Launch	Hwy. 1, 3 mi. N. of Marshall		•	•										•	•		•		•				
Tomales Bay State Park–Marshall	Hwy. 1, 1-1/4 mi. N. of Marshall																			•	•		
Cypress Grove	Hwy. 1, 1 mi. N. of Marshall-Petaluma Rd.						•															•	
Livermore Marsh	Marshall-Petaluma Rd., Hwy. 1 intersection																				•	•	•
Tomales Bay State Park–Alan Sieroty Beach	At Millerton, 4-1/2 mi. N. of Point Reyes Station		•	•			•			•		•	•		•		•					•	•

Tomales Bay State Park, Alan Sieroty Beach

DILLON BEACH: Privately owned beach. Day use parking fee $2, bicycles $1. Picnic tables on the wide, sandy beach.

LAWSON'S LANDING: Take the toll road from Dillon beach; $2/car day use fee, $5/car camping fee. Popular area for hang gliding and gaper clamming. Trailer camping and 46 campsites. Boat launch (by truck) and fuel dock; both open 7 AM-5 PM. Other facilities include pier, moorings, dry storage, boat and motor rentals, charters March-December, fishing licenses, bait and tackle. For information, call: (707) 878-2443.

KEYS CREEK PUBLIC FISHING AREA: Scheduled to be completed July 1983. A trail leads from the parking lot down to and along the shore of Keys Creek; facilities include picnic tables and chemical toilets. For information, call: (415) 924-4600.

WALKER CREEK: This Audubon Canyon Ranch land is administered by four cooperating Audubon chapters which maintain marshlands in Tomales and Bolinas Bays. Walker Creek and other Audubon Canyon Ranch lands on Tomales Bay are sensitive marsh areas and important migratory waterfowl habitats. Access is reserved primarily for educational and scientific purposes. For appointment, call: (415) 383-1644.

MILLER PARK BOAT LAUNCH: Open sunrise to sunset. Picnic tables.

TOMALES BAY STATE PARK-MARSHALL: The land at Marshall is presently undeveloped.

CYPRESS GROVE: Audubon Canyon Ranch land is undeveloped; visit by appointment only. (415) 383-1644.

LIVERMORE MARSH: Undeveloped Audubon Canyon Ranch land; visit by appointment only. (415) 383-1644.

TOMALES BAY STATE PARK-ALAN SIEROTY BEACH: This 180-acre state park unit at Millerton Point has a day use area with picnic tables and grills; restrooms are wheelchair accessible. There are two environmental campsites planned; for more information, call: (415) 669-1140.

Camping

There are many campgrounds within state and national parks, as well as hundreds of private campgrounds, located near the coast. Campsites can be found in redwood forests, along streams, in grassy fields, or even right on the sand.

A typical campsite in a developed park provides a place to park your car or recreational vehicle, a picnic table, room to pitch a tent, a fire ring or grill, and nearby water; restrooms serve a cluster of campsites. At some campgrounds there may be cupboards at each site, firewood for sale, hot showers, R.V. hookups and sanitation station, groceries and other concessions. There is a fee charged at all drive-in campgrounds.

There are also walk-in campsites for backpackers and bicyclists often available within large campgrounds, or at parks which are otherwise only for day use, such as Tomales Bay State Park in Marin County and Enderts Beach within Redwood National Park in Del Norte County. A nominal fee is usually charged for use of these sites.

Environmental and en route campsites are now also available in certain state parks.

During the summer and on holiday weekends campgrounds fill quickly, often by mid-day. If you do not have reservations, start early! Your stay is often limited to a few nights; in the off-season, however, the limit of stay is extended, and campgrounds are rarely full. Especially in northern California where there is persistent summer fog, spring and fall can be the best times to camp.

Most state campgrounds allow pets for a small fee; they must be kept on a leash during the day and in your vehicle at night. Always check the campground policy ahead of time. Permits are required in order to camp and to build fires at some national parks; check at the headquarters of the area.

State parks are now on a reservation system. Reservations can be made only at Ticketron outlets throughout the state, or by sending a Reservation Request Form, with payment, to: Ticketron, P.O. Box 26430, San Francisco 94126. There is a $2.00 reservation fee, in addition to the appropriate camping fee. Request forms may be obtained at most state parks and Ticketron outlets. Request forms, as well as a list of state campgrounds, can also be acquired from:

California Department of Parks and Recreation
P.O. Box 2390
Sacramento, CA 95811   (916) 323-2988

For Ticketron outlet locations, call:

San Francisco Area: (415) 393-6914
Sacramento: (916) 445-8828
Los Angeles Area: (213) 642-3888
San Diego Area: (619) 565-9947

For other reservation information, call toll free (in California only): (800) 952-5580.

NAME	LOCATION	Entrance/Parking Fee	Parking	Restrooms	Lifeguard	Campground	Showers	Firepits	Stairs to Beach	Path to Beach	Bike Path	Hiking Trail	Facilities for Disabled	Boating Facilities	Fishing	Equestrian Trail	Sandy Beach	Dunes	Rocky Shore	Upland from Beach	Stream Corridor	Bluff	Wetland
Marshall Beach	Access Rd. off Pierce Point Rd., 5-1/2 mi. N. of Inverness		•	•						•							•						
Tomales Bay State Park	2 mi. N. of Inverness on Pierce Point Rd.	•	•	•		•	•	•	•	•	•	•					•		•		•		
Chicken Ranch Beach	Sir Francis Drake Blvd., 1/2 mi. N. of Inverness		•							•							•				•		
Path to Beach	Sir Francis Drake Blvd., 1/4 mi. N. of Inverness		•							•							•						
Tomales Bay State Park-Inverness Ridge	Sir Francis Drake Blvd., 1 mi. S. of Inverness											•							•				
Shields Marsh	Sir Francis Drake Blvd., 1 mi. S. of Inverness		•																•	•			•
Tomales Bay Ecological Reserve	Southern portion of Tomales Bay		•												•				•	•			•

MARSHALL BEACH: Part of Point Reyes National Seashore; a steep trail leads to the beach, which is on Tomales Bay.

TOMALES BAY STATE PARK: A paved road leads to Heart's Desire Beach; Indian Beach and Pebble Beach are accessible by trail only. Shell Beach can be reached by a .3-mile long path from the end of Camino Del Mar (outside the park) where there is a small parking lot. A trail leads to Indian, Heart's Desire, and Pebble Beaches. Miwok Indian relics and a forest of ancient Bishop pines are within the park. Camping facilities for hike and bike-in only. Restrooms, parking, and picnic tables for the disabled. (415) 669-1140.

CHICKEN RANCH BEACH: A small creek must be crossed to reach this sandy beach on Tomales Bay. Limited street parking.

PATH TO BEACH: There is an unpaved path to a small beach on the bay, accessible from Sir Francis Drake Blvd. at the foot of Rannoch Way. Adjacent private property; do not trespass.

TOMALES BAY STATE PARK-INVERNESS RIDGE: An undeveloped unit of the park. There are some hiking trails; check at the main park for more information: (415) 669-1140.

SHIELDS MARSH: Audubon Canyon Ranch land. A trail leads into the marsh with a view of Tomales Bay. Small informational display upland.

TOMALES BAY ECOLOGICAL RESERVE: 500-acre reserve for migrating wildfowl and other wildlife. Many viewpoints from Highway 1 and Sir Francis Drake Blvd. on either side of Tomales Bay. Entering the marsh is not encouraged due to sensitive resources. Land area closed March 1 to June 30.

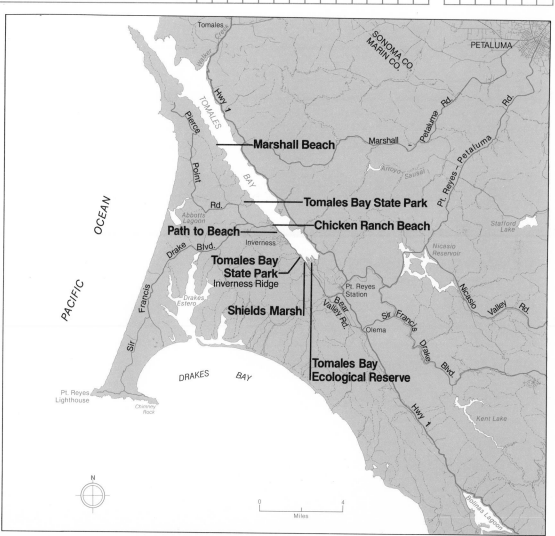

Point Reyes Lighthouse

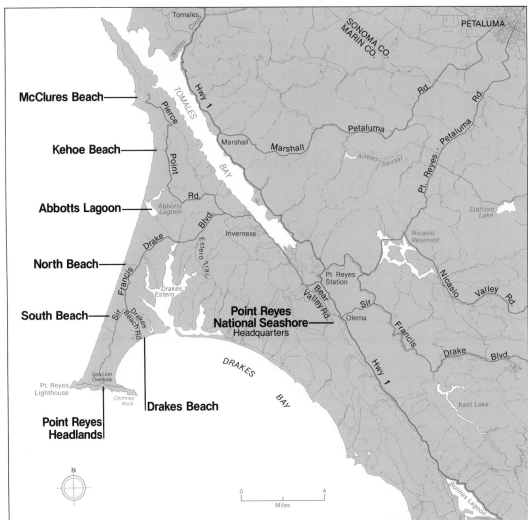

McClures Beach

Kehoe Beach

Abbotts Lagoon

North Beach

South Beach

Point Reyes
National Seashore
Headquarters

Drakes Beach

Point Reyes
Headlands

Marin County

POINT REYES WEST

NAME	LOCATION	Entrance/Parking Fee	Parking	Restrooms	Lifeguard	Campground	Showers	Firepits	Stairs to Beach	Path to Beach	Bike Path	Hiking Trail	Facilities for Disabled	Boating Facilities	Fishing	Equestrian Trail	Sandy Beach	Dunes	Rocky Shore	Upland from Beach	Stream Corridor	Bluff	Wetland
Point Reyes National Seashore	Headquarters on Bear Valley Rd., 1/4 mi. N.W. of Olema	●	●	●		●			●			●					●		●	●			
McClures Beach	End of Pierce Point Rd.	●	●						●			●					●	●					
Kehoe Beach	Trail off Pierce Point Rd., S. of McClures Beach	●	●							●							●						
Abbotts Lagoon	Trail from Pierce Point Rd.	●	●							●													●
North Beach	Off Sir Francis Drake Blvd.	●	●														●						
South Beach	Off Sir Francis Drake Blvd.	●	●										●				●						
Point Reyes Headlands	End of Sir Francis Drake Blvd.	●	●																●			●	
Drakes Beach	Drakes Beach Rd. off Sir Francis Drake Blvd.	●	●				●	●					●				●					●	

POINT REYES NATIONAL SEASHORE: Headquarters for the seashore are on Bear Valley Rd.; information and bookstore. Interpretive programs include a Miwok village, earthquake trail, and a Morgan horse farm. Trailhead for over 100 miles of trails, many of which lead to beaches; many species of birds and mammals in the area. Camping is permitted at four walk-in camps by reservation only. Reservations and information: (415) 663-1092. Point Reyes Field Seminars offers natural history courses at the seashore year-round. For information: Point Reyes Field Seminars, Point Reyes 94956; (415) 663-1200.
Mass Transit: Golden Gate Transit (GGT) #64, weekends and holidays only.

The following are within the Point Reyes National Seashore: Marshall Beach, McClures Beach, Kehoe Beach, Abbotts Lagoon, North Beach, South Beach, Point Reyes Headlands, and Drakes Beach.

McCLURES BEACH: A steep trail leads to the beach and tidepools; seals may be seen on the rocks. The strong surf makes swimming extremely unsafe. Pierce Point Trail leads north from the parking lot about four miles to Tomales Point at the tip of the peninsula. Avalis Beach is a small beach on Tomales Bay, just south of the point.

KEHOE BEACH: A stile at the road marks an unmaintained trail to the beach.

ABBOTTS LAGOON: Canoeing permitted; migratory waterfowl habitat.

NORTH BEACH AND SOUTH BEACH: A long windy strand with two main access areas. Picnic tables; dogs and campfires allowed on the beach. Unsafe swimming. Restrooms at South Beach are wheelchair accessible.

POINT REYES HEADLANDS: There are two overlook points: Chimney Rock and Sea Lion. Information is available at Sea Lion overlook; a long stairway leads to the Point Reyes Lighthouse. View of the offshore reserve and sea lions; gray whale migration is December-February.

DRAKES BEACH: A popular broad, sandy beach with chalk white cliffs. Information center, snack bar, and picnic tables. Fires allowed on the beach; swimming. Restrooms are wheelchair accessible.

Drakes Beach

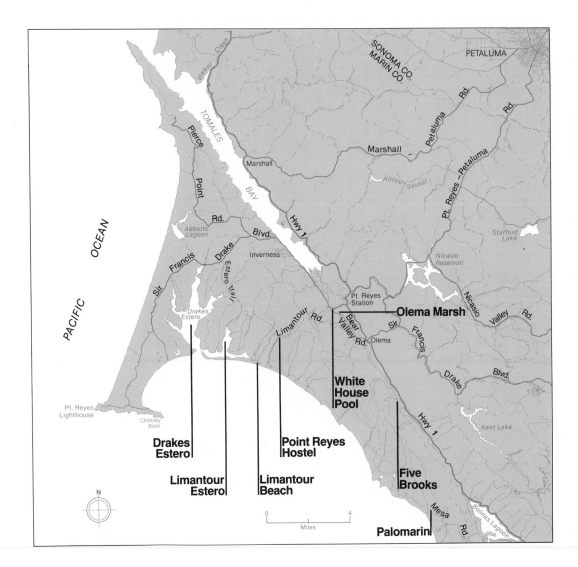

PACIFIC OCEAN

PACIFIC OCEAN

SONOMA CO.
MARIN CO.

PETALUMA

TOMALES BAY

Walker Creek

Pierce

Point

Rd.

Abbotts
Lagoon

Sir

Francis

Drake

Blvd.

Inverness

Estero Trail

Drakes
Estero

Marshall

Hwy 1

Marshall

Arroyo Sausal

Pt. Reyes – Petaluma Rd.

Rd.

Stafford
Lake

Nicasio
Reservoir

Nicasio

Valley

Rd.

Pt. Reyes
Station

Limantour Rd.

Bear Valley Rd.

Olema Marsh

Olema

Sir

Francis

Drake

Blvd.

Kent Lake

Hwy 1

**White
House
Pool**

**Five
Brooks**

Mesa

Rd.

Bolinas Lagoon

Pt. Reyes
Lighthouse

Chimney
Rock

**Drakes
Estero**

**Limantour
Estero**

**Limantour
Beach**

**Point Reyes
Hostel**

Palomarin

N

0   4
Miles

Five Brooks Trailhead

White House Pool

Marin County
POINT REYES SOUTH

NAME	LOCATION	Entrance/Parking Fee	Parking	Restrooms	Lifeguard	Campground	Showers	Firepits	Stairs to Beach	Path to Beach	Bike Path	Hiking Trail	Facilities for Disabled	Boating Facilities	Fishing	Equestrian Trail	Sandy Beach	Dunes	Rocky Shore	Upland from Beach	Stream Corridor	Bluff	Wetland
Drakes Estero	Estero Trail off Sir Francis Drake Blvd.		•	•						•		•										•	
Limantour Estero	End of Limantour Rd.		•	•								•										•	
Limantour Beach	End of Limantour Rd.		•	•					•						•		•	•					
Point Reyes Hostel	Off Limantour Rd., 5 mi. from Bear Valley Rd.	•	•	•			•	•				•								•			
White House Pool	Sir Francis Drake Blvd. and Bear Valley Rd. intersection, N.E. corner		•	•											•						•		
Olema Marsh	Sir Francis Drake Blvd. and Bear Valley Rd. intersection, S.E. corner		•	•																			•
Five Brooks Trailhead	Hwy. 1, 3 mi. S. of Olema		•	•								•			•					•			
Palomarin Trailhead	Mesa Rd., 4 mi. from Bolinas		•	•								•							•			•	

The following are within the Point Reyes National Seashore: Drakes Estero, Limantour Estero, Limantour Beach, Point Reyes Hostel, Five Brooks Trailhead, and Palomarin Trailhead.

DRAKES ESTERO: There is a monument to Sir Francis Drake's landing in 1579 at the southwest point of the estero. Oysters are available commercially; take a left turn off Sir Francis Drake Blvd. west of Estero Trail.

LIMANTOUR ESTERO: Marine reserve; permission is required from the Department of Fish and Game to remove any marine life.

LIMANTOUR BEACH: Long sandy spit with grassy dunes between the ocean and the estero. Free shuttle bus from Point Reyes Headquarters during the summer on weekends and holidays. Currently, Limantour Rd. is temporarily closed due to storm damage and visitors must hike to the beach. Information: (415) 663-1092.

POINT REYES HOSTEL: Five miles from Point Reyes Headquarters by road, or hike in via Balboa Ave. and Drakes Summit Rd. off Sir Francis Drake Boulevard. $4.50/night for members, $6.50/night for non-members; 40 beds. The hostel is temporarily open only to groups until Limantour Rd. is repaired; should re-open by fall 1983. For reservations and information, call (415) 669-7414 or write P.O. Box 247, Point Reyes Station 94956.
Mass Transit: Golden Gate Transit (GGT) #64 to Headquarters; Limantour shuttle bus stops nearby (summer only).

WHITE HOUSE POOL: Steelhead and salmon fishing stream; season is November-February. Benches and pedestrian bridge provide views of Tomales Bay and reserve. Good birding.

OLEMA MARSH: Undeveloped Audubon Canyon Ranch land; visit by appointment only. For information, call: (415) 383-1644.

FIVE BROOKS TRAILHEAD: A network of trails begins here for the southern part of Point Reyes; many lead over wooded Inverness Ridge to beaches (approximately three miles). Horse rentals available, call: (415) 663-8297.

PALOMARIN TRAILHEAD: Southernmost trailhead to Point Reyes. A network of trails leads along bluffs, past Bass, Pelican, Crystal, Ocean, and Wildcat Lakes, and to beaches (approximately five miles).

Drakes Estero

California Gray Whale

The gray whales (*Eschrichtius robustus*) are the most frequently seen whales along the California coast. They have a lengthy migration which takes them from their summer feeding grounds off Alaska in the Bering Sea and Arctic Ocean to the winter breeding lagoons along Baja California. During this migration, thousands of Californians head for the coast to witness the passing of 11,000 gray whales.

The gray whale is a bottom-feeder who lives on small amphipods. The whales are 15 feet long at birth, 25 feet at one year, 35 feet at sexual maturity (eight years), and 45 feet at physical maturity (30-40 years). A mature adult weighs about 50 tons, and has a series of ridges along its back (instead of a dorsal fin) called a caudal peduncle. Gray whales display their 10-foot wide flukes at the onset of deep dives and their blow usually has a single plume, reaching a height of 10 feet.

In winter, from November through February, the gray whale travels south along the coast, staying only about one-half mile offshore. The whales swim in small groups, with the pregnant females heading south first, followed by the other females and immature young, then the males. The whales swim about 20 hours a day at an average speed of four knots an hour. This migration is an eight month, 13,000-mile round trip – one of the longest migrations of any mammal. There is little evidence that the whales feed during the migration period, and their body weight drops about 20 percent.

The lagoons of Baja host the gray whales during winter. Here, the females give birth and nurse their young. Non-pregnant females often assist in the births. Gestation is 13 months, and females produce one calf every two years at most.

After the young are born the whales head for the northern waters. Newly pregnant females are the first to leave, followed by the adult males, then the mothers with calves.

The California gray whale once had a population estimated at 30,000. Whaling off California and Baja during the late 1800's reduced their numbers greatly. With few whales left, whalers no longer found it profitable to hunt the gray whale, and left them alone until the 1920's and 1930's. Hunting was resumed at that time until the whale population was again reduced. In 1938, an international treaty gave the gray whale complete protection. Since then, the population has steadily grown.

Whale watching has become quite an attraction along the coast during the gray whale's migration. The whales can be seen from many points along the coast, such as the Point Reyes Lighthouse, but many enthusiasts head offshore in powerboats. Organized whale watching expeditions leave from several points along the coast including Mission, San Diego, and Monterey Bays, San Pedro, and Redondo Beach.

Further information on whale watching expeditions can be obtained from the Oceanic Society:

San Francisco Chapter
Building E, Fort Mason
San Francisco, CA 94123   (415) 441-5970

Los Angeles Chapter
18034 Medley
Encino, CA 91316   (213) 987-3293

or the American Cetacean Society:
National Headquarters
P.O. Box 4416
San Pedro, CA 90731   (213) 548-6279

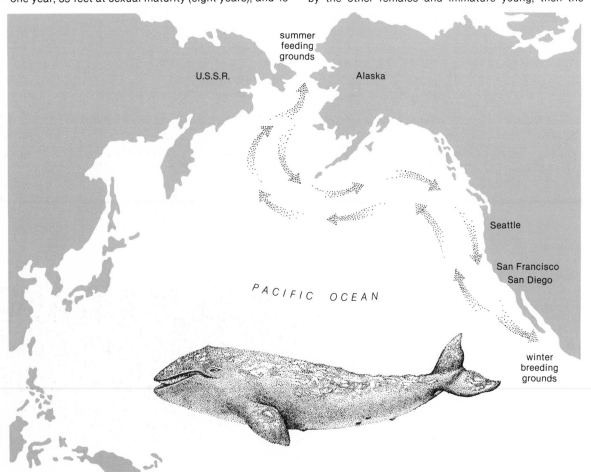

summer feeding grounds

U.S.S.R.

Alaska

Seattle

San Francisco
San Diego

PACIFIC OCEAN

winter breeding grounds

Marin County
BOLINAS

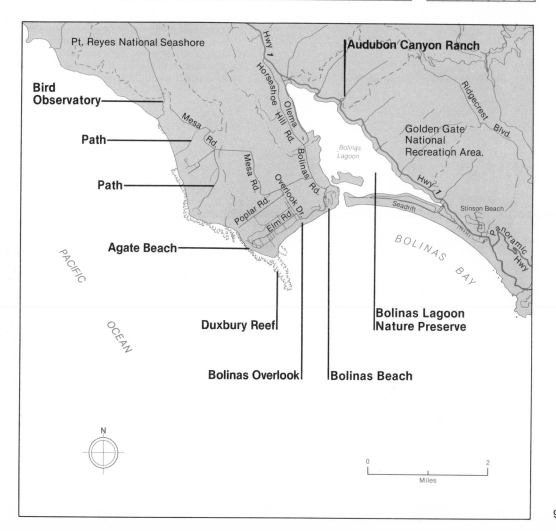

NAME	LOCATION	Entrance/Parking Fee	Parking	Restrooms	Lifeguard	Campground	Showers	Firepits	Stairs to Beach	Path to Beach	Bike Path	Hiking Trail	Facilities for Disabled	Boating Facilities	Fishing	Equestrian Trail	Sandy Beach	Dunes	Rocky Shore	Upland from Beach	Stream Corridor	Bluff	Wetland
Point Reyes Bird Observatory	Mesa Rd., 4-1/2 mi. N. of Bolinas	•										•							•				
Paths to Beach	Mesa Rd., 2-1/2 mi. N. of Bolinas							•					•				•		•	•	•		
Agate Beach	End of Elm Rd., Bolinas	•	•							•							•		•				
Duxbury Reef	S.W. perimeter of Bolinas Mesa	•	•							•					•								
Bolinas Overlook	End of Overlook Dr., Bolinas	•																	•				
Bolinas Beach	Ends of Brighton and Wharf Aves., Bolinas	•								•									•				
Bolinas Lagoon Nature Preserve	Between Hwy. 1 and Olema-Bolinas Rd., Bolinas	•																					•
Audubon Canyon Ranch	Hwy. 1, 3 mi. N. of Stinson Beach	•	•									•							•				•

POINT REYES BIRD OBSERVATORY: The only full time ornithological research station in the United States. Open every day April 1 through the summer, otherwise open Wednesdays and weekends only. Bird banding occurs early in the morning; sunrise to noon is the best time to visit. Special tours for groups can be arranged in advance; call (415) 868-1221. Year-round natural history trips are also offered.

PATHS TO BEACH: Two trails lead to a sandy beach. The southern trail is a signed dirt road across grassy uplands. The northern trail, 1/4 mile north, follows a creek ravine down to the beach. The National Park Service prefers that the public not use the southern trail due to sensitive resources.

AGATE BEACH: Small beach at the end of Elm Road. Check directions in town as the road is periodically washed away.

DUXBURY REEF: Nature reserve. Access is from Agate Beach. Permission is required from the Department of Fish and Game to take marine life from the reef. Limited public fishing; tidepools.

BOLINAS OVERLOOK: Spectacular view from Duxbury Reef south.

BOLINAS BEACH: A concrete ramp from the end of Brighton Ave. leads to a pebbly beach which is covered at high tide. The beach extends around the mesa to Bolinas Lagoon; access from the end of Wharf Avenue. Parking is limited at each entrance. Horses are allowed on the beach.

BOLINAS LAGOON NATURE PRESERVE: Viewing from either Highway 1 on the eastern side, or Olema-Bolinas Road on the western side. Migratory waterfowl habitat.

AUDUBON CANYON RANCH: Private nature reserve and educational center. Day use only weekends and holidays March through July 4. Great blue heron and egret nesting sites. Picnic area; information center. A trail leads to an upland viewing platform. Donation requested. (415) 383-1644.
Mass Transit: GGT #63.

Sharks

Sharks are among the oldest creatures on earth. Sharks first appeared nearly 400 million years ago during the Devonian period of the Paleozoic era, and today there are approximately 350 species of sharks in the world. About 30 species are known to inhabit California's bays and coastal waters; some common species include the sevengill, leopard, soupfin, and blue shark.

Sharks belong to the *Chondrichthyes* class of fishes, and the *Elasmobranchii* subclass, which includes sharks, rays, and skates. Unlike other fishes, elasmobranchs have no true bones; their skeletal system consists of cartilage.

Sharks vary considerably in size. The devil shark, found in deep water off the coast of Japan, reaches a length of about one foot, while an adult whale shark, found worldwide in warm seas, averages 45 feet long. Some sharks lay eggs; the majority, however, give birth to live pups. Only three species of sharks are known to feed primarily on plankton, while the rest are carnivores. A typical shark's diet consists of fish, mollusks, and crustaceans. Some of the larger sharks, notably the great white, sometimes feed on marine mammals such as seals, sea lions, and sea otters.

One characteristic common to virtually all sharks is a lifetime supply of teeth. The teeth are aligned in rows, with the outermost row being the oldest. When a tooth is lost, a tooth in the next row moves in to replace it. Some sharks can grow a new set of teeth in a little more than a week.

For centuries, sharks have been eaten in the Orient, Europe, Africa, and Mexico; however, the Japanese are probably the world's leaders in using sharks for food. Shark meat contains very little oil, fat, or cholesterol, is low in calories, and high in protein. As well as being used for food, sharks are processed for use in commercial products. For example, shark liver oil is used as a base in cosmetics, and the skeleton is processed into fertilizer and feed.

In recent years, the great white shark has been characterized as a vicious, human-eating beast, largely through highly publicized fictional and factual accounts of shark attacks. Many people have applied this reputation to all sharks. Actually, no shark normally feeds on humans, the vast majority of sharks would rather retreat than challenge an object as large as a human, and shark attacks by the great white or any other species of shark are quite rare.

The first known unprovoked shark attack in California occurred in 1924 in San Francisco Bay; since then, 49 known attacks have occurred off the California coast, with only four fatalities resulting from these attacks. According to shark researchers at the California Department of Fish and Game, most unprovoked shark attacks on humans can be classed as a search for food or an investigation of an object thought by a shark to be a food item. Other researchers believe that some shark attacks may also be a shark's response to a perceived threat.

Recently, shark attacks along the California coast have increased. This may be explained by the growing populations of prey, such as sea otters, seals, and sea lions, which may be bringing in more sharks as predators. California attacks have ranged from Imperial Beach in San Diego County to the Klamath River area in Del Norte County, with about one-half of the attacks occurring between Año Nuevo Island and Bodega Bay. The persons attacked most often were divers.

The Department of Fish and Game suggests a few common sense approaches to reduce the already rare chances of being attacked by a shark: Avoid areas of higher attack incidence; do not provoke any shark, regardless of its size; if bumped or harassed by a shark, get out of the water or into a kelp bed as soon as possible (there have been no reported attacks in kelp beds); keep speared fish aboard a float, not tied to your leg; and keep your wetsuit on if you are cut. Always report the time and location of a shark attack to local authorities and to the Department of Fish and Game.

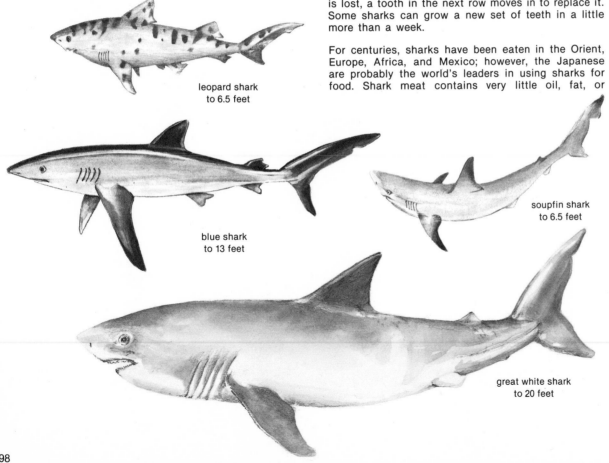

leopard shark
to 6.5 feet

blue shark
to 13 feet

soupfin shark
to 6.5 feet

great white shark
to 20 feet

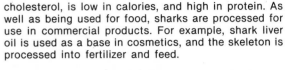

Marin County
STINSON BEACH/MOUNT TAMALPAIS

NAME	LOCATION	Entrance/Parking Fee	Parking	Restrooms	Lifeguard	Campground	Showers	Firepits	Stairs to Beach	Path to Beach	Bike Path	Hiking Trail	Facilities for Disabled	Boating Facilities	Fishing	Equestrian Trail	Sandy Beach	Dunes	Rocky Shore	Upland from Beach	Stream Corridor	Bluff	Wetland
		FACILITIES															**ENVIRONMENT**						
Stinson Beach	W. of Hwy. 1, N. of Panoramic Hwy., Stinson Beach	●	●	●		●	●						●				●	●					
Red Rock Beach	Hwy. 1, 1-1/2 mi. S. of Stinson Beach	●								●							●	●					
Steep Ravine Beach	Hwy. 1, 2 mi. S. of Stinson Beach	●				●				●							●	●					
Slide Ranch	Hwy. 1, 1-1/2 mi. N. of Muir Beach	●	●							●		●					●						
Muir Woods Hostel	Muir Woods Rd., 1 mi. N. of Muir Beach	●	●	●		●						●	●								●		
Mt. Tamalpais State Park	Off Panoramic Hwy.	●	●			●														●			

The following are within the Golden Gate National Recreation Area, which is administered by the National Park Service: Stinson Beach, Slide Ranch, and Muir Woods Hostel.

STINSON BEACH: Popular broad, sandy beach. Lifeguards from May to mid-September. Picnic area and food service. A roll-out boardwalk is available for wheelchair access from the parking lot to hard packed sand. Call to confirm its availability. Restrooms are also wheelchair accessible. Ranger station: (415) 868-0942.
Mass Transit: Golden Gate Transit (GGT) #63.

RED ROCK BEACH: Within Mount Tamalpais State Park. Big dirt pull out; a steep trail leads down to the small popular clothing optional beach.

STEEP RAVINE BEACH: Within Mount Tamalpais State Park. Day use parking lot off Highway 1; hike one mile to the beach. There is a locked gate at the entrance to the road that leads to the beach; only campers with reservations (available through Ticketron) for the environmental campsites or restored cabins used as rustic shelters may drive down to the beach. Campers must go to Pan Toll Station to receive the combination for the lock. For information, call: (415) 456-1286.

SLIDE RANCH: Down an unmarked gravel driveway, located one mile north of the vista point sign along Highway 1. Open for day use only; limited parking. Environmental education programs available for groups; call (415) 383-0358.

MUIR WOODS HOSTEL: This new AYH 28 bed hostel is scheduled to open in June 1983 for use Friday and Saturday nights, or for groups anytime. Fully equipped kitchen. $4.50/members, $6.50/non-members. Check-in 4:30 PM-9:30 PM. The redwood shingled buildings are located in Kent Canyon, one mile south of Muir Woods National Monument and one mile north of the intersection of Muir Woods Rd. and Highway 1. For more information, call the AYH Golden Gate Council: (415) 771-4647.
Mass Transit: GGT #61 stops at Muir Beach and Muir Woods.

MOUNT TAMALPAIS STATE PARK: 6,204-acre park including Muir Woods National Monument, beaches, and a popular trail system. The three main trails to the coast are the Steep Ravine and Matt Davis Trails from Pan Toll Ranger Station, and the Dipsea Trail from Muir Woods. All three trails end up near Stinson Beach. Walk-in primitive campsites at Pan Toll; camping fee $6/night; no reservations. En route campsites are located six miles west of Mill Valley on the Panoramic Highway. Reservations are required for Alice Eastwood group camp and Redwood Creek backpack camp. For reservations and more information, call: (415) 388-2070 or 456-1286.
Mass Transit: GGT #60, #61, and #63 all stop in the park.

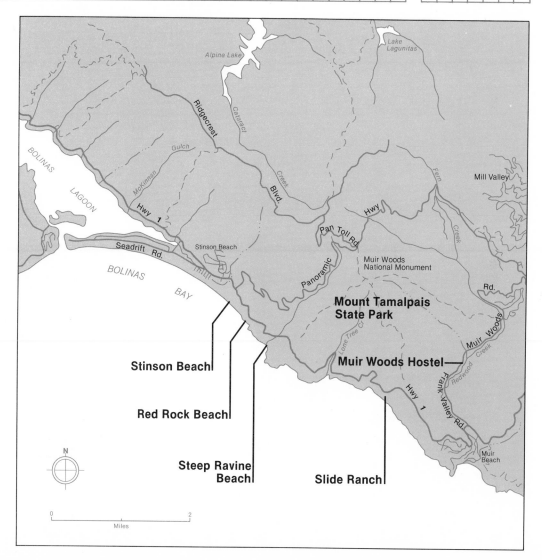

Muir Overlook

View of Muir Beach from Overlook

Rodeo Lagoon

NAME	LOCATION	Entrance/Parking Fee	Parking	Restrooms	Lifeguard	Campground	Showers	Firepits	Stairs to Beach	Path to Beach	Bike Path	Hiking Trail	Facilities for Disabled	Boating Facilities	Fishing	Equestrian Trail	Sandy Beach	Dunes	Rocky Shore	Upland from Beach	Stream Corridor	Bluff	Wetland
Muir Overlook	Off Hwy. 1, 1 mi. N. of Muir Beach		•	•																	•		
Muir Beach	Hwy. 1 at Muir Beach Junction		•	•			•		•			•			•		•		•				
Coastal Trail	Headlands between Golden Gate Bridge and Muir Beach		•	•						•		•			•				•	•	•		
Marin Headlands	Off Hwy. 101, N. of Golden Gate Bridge		•	•	•			•	•	•	•	•			•		•		•	•			
Tennessee Valley	Tennessee Valley Rd. off Hwy. 1 in Mill Valley		•	•								•			•					•			
Rodeo Beach	Bunker Rd. off Hwy. 101 (Alexander Avenue exit)		•	•					•	•		•			•		•			•			
Golden Gate Hostel	Off Bunker Rd., near Rodeo Lagoon	•	•				•	•		•	•	•			•					•			
Kirby Cove	Conzelman Rd. off Hwy. 101 (Alexander Avenue exit)		•		•	•		•		•		•	•		•		•	•					

The following are within the Golden Gate National Recreation Area: Muir Overlook, Muir Beach, Coastal Trail, Marin Headlands, Tennessee Valley, Rodeo Beach, Golden Gate Hostel, and Kirby Cove.

MUIR OVERLOOK: Spectacular views of the rocky coastline; picnic tables in a sheltered area.

MUIR BEACH: A popular local beach. Monarch butterflies rest in pine trees near the beach during the winter.

COASTAL TRAIL: It is possible to hike now from the Golden Gate Bridge to the tip of Point Reyes. While the trails within the Point Reyes National Seashore are well known, the trails along the Marin Headlands are less so. There is a steep but scenic 4-1/2 mile portion of the trail between Muir Beach and Tennessee Valley. Another popular section runs between Tennessee Valley and Rodeo Beach. Parts of the trails are not clearly marked. For more information about the trail system in the Headlands, call the ranger station at Rodeo Beach: (415) 331-1541.

MARIN HEADLANDS: A series of grassy hills and valleys; former military lands, now part of the Golden Gate National Recreation Area. The Headlands include beaches, campgrounds, and spectacular views of the coast and bay areas. Ranger station: (415) 331-1541.

TENNESSEE VALLEY: Gently sloping valley; hiking trails lead north and south in the headlands area and to Tennessee Cove.
Mass Transit: Golden Gate Transit (GGT) #61 and #63; ask to get off at Tennessee Valley Rd.

RODEO BEACH: Information center, guided walks: (415) 331-1541. Former bunkers house several environmental education programs, as well as the California Marine Mammals Center.
Mass Transit: Muni #76 weekends and holidays.

GOLDEN GATE HOSTEL: 60 beds, $4.50/night for members, $6.50/night for non-members; bicycle storage room and horse stables nearby. Operated by the AYH. For information, write or call: Building 941, Fort Barry, Sausalito 94965; (415) 331-2777.

KIRBY COVE: Follow Conzelman Rd. from Hwy. 101 1/2 mile to locked gate; walk to the beach at the foot of the dirt road. Picnic facilities and firepits. Overnight camping for groups in the summer by reservation only: (415) 331-1541. Facilities for disabled include modified picnic tables and a bridge to the beach. Check with the Marin Headlands ranger station for road conditions,

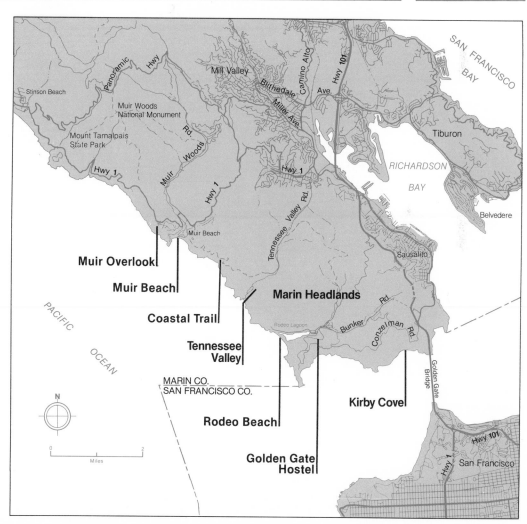

Ocean Beach

San Francisco County

The ocean coastline of San Francisco, from the Golden Gate Bridge to Burton Beach at the San Mateo border, is almost all public land. The Golden Gate National Recreation Area (GGNRA) encompasses this nearly eight-mile long coast, stretching from the former military outpost at Fort Point in the north to the sandy bluffs at Fort Funston in the south, and including coves and cliffs, forested blufftops, and sandy beaches.

Only one beach in San Francisco is safe for swimming, China Beach; all others have rip currents and large waves. However, there are other activities which draw visitors to the coast. A trail along the bluffs from the Golden Gate Bridge to the Cliff House offers spectacular views of the Marin Headlands, the Golden Gate, and the San Francisco shore. At Fort Funston, spectators watch hang-gliders soar over the ocean. Even on foggy days, Steller sea lions can be heard barking on the rocks offshore from the Cliff House, San Francisco's first seaside resort which has been a beach landmark for over one hundred years.

Ocean Beach, which stretches for about four miles from the Cliff House to Fort Funston, is the largest beach in the Bay Area. It is backed by sand dunes, and a seawall and walkway extend along the northern end. The old Beach Chalet along the Great Highway, currently under renovation, features WPA murals on the walls. Golden Gate Park, a popular tourist spot near the beach, encompasses more than 1,000 landscaped acres.

The fog which frequently covers the shore kept many early explorers from discovering San Francisco Bay. In 1769, Sergeant José Francisco de Ortega of Portolá's expedition was probably the first European to see San Francisco Bay from the area now called Sweeney Ridge. In 1775, Lieutenant Juan Manuel de Ayala sailed into San Francisco Bay, and a year later Mission Dolores and the Presidio of San Francisco were established.

Under Spanish and Mexican rule, San Francisco was a small port; with the gold strikes in 1848, San Francisco became the main port for travel to the foothills. Its population jumped from 500 residents in 1848 to 40,000 entering the city in 1849. The transcontinental railroad was completed in 1869, creating a land link with the rest of the United States. San Francisco currently has a population of nearly 700,000.

Despite its rapid population growth, San Francisco has retained much of its shoreline as publicly owned open space. Adolf Sutro, one of the city's more flamboyant citizens, bought the area at Lands End and the decaying Cliff House in the early 1880's. After extensive gardening, he opened the Lands End area as a park. Subsequently, he rebuilt the Cliff House and added the Sutro Baths on the cliffs next to it. These baths, which were housed in a glass building and warmed by the sun, used salt water funneled from the beach below into pools. The pools are now in ruins, although the Park Service is rehabilitating the area so it will be safe for visitors.

Within San Francisco Bay, access to the shore is under the jurisdiction of the San Francisco Bay Conservation and Development Commission (BCDC). For more information, and to obtain a copy of their four-part guide to access around the Bay, *Bay Edges,* write or call: S.F. Bay Conservation and Development Commission, 30 Van Ness, San Francisco 94102; (415) 557-3686. Each section of *Bay Edges* costs $1.00.

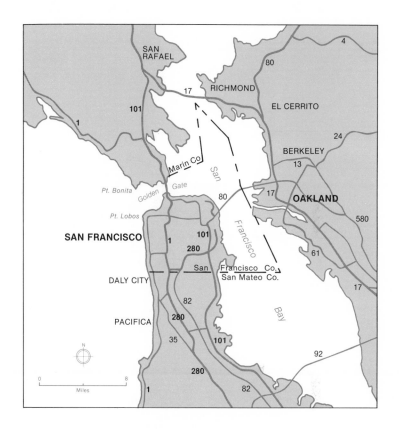

For more information about San Francisco, write or call the Convention and Visitors Bureau, 201 3rd Street, Suite 900, San Francisco 94103, (415) 974-6900. For information on transportation within the city, call MUNI: (415) 673-MUNI. Golden Gate Transit connects San Francisco with Marin and Sonoma Counties: (415) 332-6600; SAMTRANS buses travel to southern San Francisco and to San Mateo County: (415) 761-7000.

Over the next four years, construction of the San Francisco Sewer Project may hinder access to Ocean Beach between the Cliff House and the Zoo. Check with GGNRA for current access routes in the area; call: (415) 556-0560.

Fog

During the summer months, beachgoers leaving clear, warm inland areas are often surprised when they arrive at the beach and find fog or overcast skies. Generally, coastal fog is a result of the differences in temperature and moisture content between marine air and the air over land masses.

During the summer, a high atmospheric pressure cell over the Pacific Ocean induces the steady flow of air from the northwest that helps drive the California current off the coast. The location of this warm current is slightly offshore and can cause the cold waters found below the ocean's surface to rise to the surface. This upwelling process produces a band of cold water immediately offshore. As relatively warm moist air passes over the band of cold water, condensation occurs and a fog bank is formed. The prevailing northwest winds then move the fog inland to envelop the shoreline areas.

Inland climate also plays a role in the development of a foggy coastline. During the summer, as the inland valleys increase in temperature, the air there rises. Subsequently, fog is pulled inland with the cooler marine air that comes off the ocean to replace the rising warm air. This process is demonstrated dramatically in the San Francisco Bay area as fog funnels through the Golden Gate and spreads across the bay and the surrounding lowland areas.

Usually, as the day progresses, air temperatures above the land masses increase to the point where the fog vaporizes, or recedes away from the coastline ("burns off") by late morning or early afternoon. On some days, however, the fog lifts but does not completely burn off, resulting in partly cloudy or overcast skies. Although the cloud cover may appear to block out most of the sunshine, the sun's ultraviolet light waves (the portion of the spectrum responsible for tanning and sunburn) penetrate through the clouds. Beach users should keep this in mind when visiting the beach on overcast days.

San Francisco County

FORT POINT TO LANDS END

NAME	LOCATION	Entrance/Parking Fee	Parking	Restrooms	Lifeguard	Campground	Showers	Firepits	Stairs to Beach	Path to Beach	Bike Path	Hiking Trail	Facilities for Disabled	Boating Facilities	Fishing	Equestrian Trail	Sandy Beach	Dunes	Rocky Shore	Upland from Beach	Stream Corridor	Bluff	Wetland
San Francisco International Hostel	Bldg. 240, Fort Mason, San Francisco	•	•	•						•	•	•								•			
Coastal Trail	Fort Point to the Cliff House, San Francisco		•	•						•		•							•			•	
Baker Beach	W. of Lincoln Blvd., off 25th Ave., San Francisco		•	•				•		•					•		•						
China Beach	Seacliff Ave. and El Camino Del Mar, San Francisco		•	•	•		•		•						•		•						
Lands End	Pt. Lobos Ave. and 48th Ave., San Francisco	•	•							•		•			•		•		•	•		•	

The following are within Golden Gate National Recreation Area, which is administered by the National Park Service: San Francisco International Hostel, Coastal Trail, Baker Beach, China Beach, Lands End, Ocean Beach, Fort Funston, Burton Beach. Headquarters for GGNRA is at Fort Mason.

SAN FRANCISCO INTERNATIONAL HOSTEL: At Fort Mason; entrance to the Fort is at Bay and Franklin Streets. 130 Guests: $6/night for members, $8/night for non-members; laundry facilities. Views of San Francisco Bay. Reservations and information: Bldg. 240, Fort Mason, San Francisco 94123. (415) 771-7277.
Mass Transit: Muni #28, #30, #42, #47; any # Golden Gate Transit (GGT) to San Francisco.

COASTAL TRAIL: Extends from the Golden Gate Bridge to the Cliff House, and connects portions of the Golden Gate National Recreation Area. The trail begins above Fort Point National Historic Site; take the dirt road above Fort Point which goes under the bridge just where it leaves the toll plaza. Follow the paved path around the west side of the bridge to the signed trailhead. The trail follows steep coastal cliffs, and also portions of Lincoln Blvd. and El Camino Del Mar. Park at Fort Point, at the Vista Point on the southeast side of the Golden Gate Bridge, or in the gravel lot off Lincoln Boulevard. For more information, call (415) 556-8371.
Mass Transit: Muni #28, GGT #64 to Fort Point area; Muni #5, #18, and #38 to the Cliff House.

BAKER BEACH: Parking off Lincoln Boulevard. Grills and picnic tables in a cypress tree grove. Dangerous surf. Dogs allowed. Weekend tours of adjacent Battery Chamberlin. Information: (415) 556-8371.
Mass Transit: Muni #29, GGT #64.

CHINA BEACH: Parking off El Camino Del Mar; steep path to the beach. Lifeguard April to October. Changing rooms, showers, sundeck, picnic facilities. Lifeguard station: (415) 556-7894.
Mass Transit: Muni #29.

LANDS END: Parking off El Camino Del Mar, and at West Fort Miley and the Cliff House. Trail system along the bluffs; a steep trail leads to a small beach. Dogs allowed. Dangerous cliffs off trails. Landslides periodically close certain trails; call Fort Miley for information. Picnic area at West Fort Miley. Public Golf Course at adjacent Lincoln Park, (415) 221-9911. The historic Cliff House, San Francisco's first seaside resort, has Musee Mechanique, Camera Obscura, food service. The Cliff House Visitor Information Center features a collection of historic photographs and information about the Cliff House, and can also provide information on seals, whales, and tide pools; call (415) 556-8642, 8643. West Fort Miley Ranger Station: (415) 556-8371.
Mass Transit: Muni #1, #18, #29, #38.

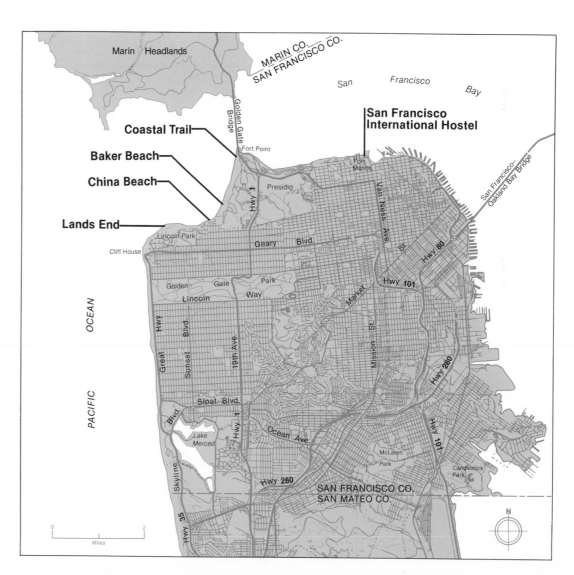

Ocean Beach, Cliff House

Fort Funston

Fort Funston, hang gliding observation deck

San Francisco County

OCEAN BEACH TO FORT FUNSTON

<table>
<thead>
<tr><th rowspan="2">NAME</th><th rowspan="2">LOCATION</th><th colspan="15">FACILITIES</th><th colspan="7">ENVIRONMENT</th></tr>
<tr><th>Entrance/Parking Fee</th><th>Parking</th><th>Restrooms</th><th>Lifeguard</th><th>Campground</th><th>Showers</th><th>Firepits</th><th>Stairs to Beach</th><th>Path to Beach</th><th>Bike Path</th><th>Hiking Trail</th><th>Facilities for Disabled</th><th>Boating Facilities</th><th>Fishing</th><th>Equestrian Trail</th><th>Sandy Beach</th><th>Dunes</th><th>Rocky Shore</th><th>Upland from Beach</th><th>Stream Corridor</th><th>Bluff</th><th>Wetland</th></tr>
</thead>
<tbody>
<tr><td>Ocean Beach</td><td>W. of the Great Highway, San Francisco</td><td></td><td>•</td><td>•</td><td></td><td></td><td></td><td>•</td><td>•</td><td></td><td>•</td><td></td><td></td><td></td><td>•</td><td></td><td>•</td><td>•</td><td></td><td></td><td></td><td></td><td></td></tr>
<tr><td>Golden Gate Park</td><td>E. of the Great Highway, between Lincoln Way and Fulton St., San Francisco</td><td></td><td>•</td><td>•</td><td></td><td></td><td>•</td><td></td><td></td><td>•</td><td>•</td><td>•</td><td>•</td><td>•</td><td>•</td><td></td><td></td><td></td><td></td><td>•</td><td></td><td></td><td></td></tr>
<tr><td>San Francisco Zoological Gardens</td><td>Sloat Blvd. and Skyline Blvd., San Francisco</td><td>•</td><td>•</td><td>•</td><td></td><td></td><td></td><td></td><td></td><td></td><td></td><td></td><td></td><td></td><td></td><td></td><td></td><td></td><td>•</td><td></td><td></td><td></td><td></td></tr>
<tr><td>Lake Merced/Harding Park</td><td>E. of Skyline Blvd. and the Great Highway, San Francisco</td><td></td><td>•</td><td>•</td><td></td><td></td><td></td><td></td><td></td><td></td><td>•</td><td></td><td>•</td><td>•</td><td></td><td></td><td></td><td></td><td>•</td><td></td><td></td><td>•</td></tr>
<tr><td>Fort Funston</td><td>W. of the Great Highway at Skyline Blvd., San Francisco</td><td>•</td><td>•</td><td></td><td></td><td></td><td>•</td><td></td><td>•</td><td>•</td><td>•</td><td></td><td>•</td><td></td><td>•</td><td></td><td>•</td><td>•</td><td></td><td>•</td><td></td><td></td><td></td></tr>
<tr><td>Phillip Burton Memorial Beach</td><td>S. of Fort Funston, San Francisco</td><td></td><td></td><td></td><td></td><td></td><td>•</td><td></td><td></td><td></td><td></td><td></td><td></td><td></td><td>•</td><td></td><td>•</td><td>•</td><td></td><td>•</td><td></td><td></td><td></td></tr>
</tbody>
</table>

OCEAN BEACH: Four-mile strand from the Cliff House to San Francisco Zoo. Stairs lead from the road to the beach. Path for bicycles, pedestrians, and skaters along the seawall. Pedestrian underpasses and restrooms are beneath the Great Highway at Geary, Judah, Taraval, and Wawona Streets. Horses allowed south of Golden Gate Park (Lincoln Way) on uncrowded days. Unsafe swimming. Ocean Beach will be under construction until 1986; accessways may be temporarily closed.
Mass Transit: Muni #5, #31, #38, #71, N-Judah and L-Taraval; #16x (peak hours only).

GOLDEN GATE PARK: John McLaren converted more than 1,000 acres of sand dunes into an urban park designed by William Hammond Hall, which now includes lakes for boating and fishing, de Young Art Museum, Asian Art Museum, Steinhart Aquarium, Morrison Planetarium, Strybing Arboretum, Conservatory of Flowers, playgrounds, sports facilities, and horse stables; free concerts on Sundays. Windmills near the beach once pumped water for irrigation into the park and are currently being restored. Information: (415) 558-3706.
Mass Transit: Muni #5, #7, #18, #21, #28, #29, #44, and #71; #16x and #72 (peak hours only).

SAN FRANCISCO ZOOLOGICAL GARDENS: Open 10 AM-5 PM daily; adjacent to Ocean Beach. Includes Storyland and Childrens Zoo. Information: (415) 661-4844. Nearby is the Recreation Center for the Handicapped, 207 Skyline Blvd., (415) 665-4100.
Mass Transit: Muni #10, #18, L-Taraval. Golden Gate Transit (GGT) #64. Use Muni transfers for a Zoo admission discount.

LAKE MERCED/HARDING PARK: Parking off Sunset Blvd. and Harding Park Road. Lake Merced area has a boat launch and rowboat rentals, fishing, benches, paths around the lake, par course, and food service: (415) 566-0300. Harding Park Golf Course information: (415) 566-3727. Broderick-Terry duelling site is at the southeast end of the park.
Mass Transit: Muni #18 and #29; #72 (peak hours only).

FORT FUNSTON: Parking at the southern end of the park, off Skyline Boulevard. Picnic area, hang-gliding observation deck. A steep unmarked trail leads to the beach; Sunset Trail is accessible for the disabled. Hang-gliding club facilities; environmental education/day camp.
Mass Transit: Muni #10, #18, L-Taraval.

PHILLIP BURTON MEMORIAL BEACH: Access from Fort Funston or Thornton State Beach in San Mateo County.

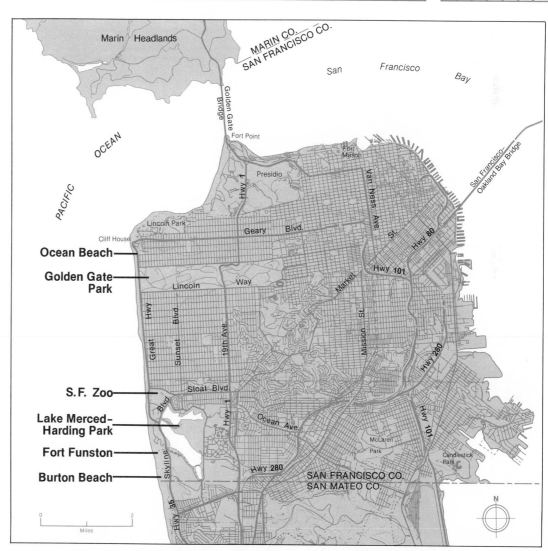

Pigeon Point Lighthouse

San Mateo County

San Mateo County has 55 miles of Pacific coastline; south of Montara Mountain, the towns of Half Moon Bay, Princeton, Moss Beach, San Gregorio, and Pescadero still retain the character of small coastside farming and fishing communities, in contrast to the suburban areas of Pacifica and Daly City to the north. The south county coast, largely undeveloped and bordering the base of the scenic Santa Cruz and San Gregorio Mountains, provides easily accessible beaches to the neighboring metropolises of San Jose and San Francisco.

Spectacular sea cliffs are characteristic of the county's coastline, rising to steep heights above the shore in the Daly City and Devils Slide areas. South of Devils Slide, the rich soils of the coastal terraces above the sea cliffs support abundant agriculture; Half Moon Bay is renowned for its fields of autumn pumpkins and harvests of artichokes and Brussels sprouts.

Although generally too cold and hazardous for swimming, San Mateo's beaches are popular for tidepooling, picnicking, marine mammal watching, and pier and shore fishing. Cabezon and lingcod are typical catches off the rocky shore of the south coast, while the north coast is noted for summertime striped bass and surfperch. Mussels are also popular, but are quarantined annually, usually between May and October.

Marine mammals can be observed at Año Nuevo State Reserve, one of the few areas where visitors are permitted to view northern elephant seals close-up during their breeding season. Año Nuevo is also noted as one of the first San Mateo County landmarks to be sighted by a Spanish explorer; Don Sebastián Vizcaíno named it Punta del Año Nuevo, New Year's Point, because it was the first landmark he sighted in the new year of 1603. The inhabitants of the region at that time were the Ohlone Indians; their shell middens are still visible at Año Nuevo. The Ohlone culture was eventually destroyed following Spanish settlement in the late 1790's.

Juan Gaspar de Portolá was among the first Spanish explorers to actually visit San Mateo; two plaques commemorate beaches where Portolá's expedition camped in 1769 — one at San Gregorio State Beach and the other across Highway 1 at the San Pedro Beach Rest Area. It was from the San Pedro Beach that Portolá's expedition climbed Sweeney Ridge on November 4, 1769 and first sighted the San Francisco Bay.

The rocky shore and heavy fogs of San Mateo's coastline have caused numerous shipwrecks throughout the county's history. Pigeon Point owes its name to the wreck of the Boston Clipper ship *Carrier Pigeon* off its rocky point in 1853; the lighthouse was later built in 1872. In 1896, the *Columbia* ran aground off Año Nuevo; Pescadero's residents salvaged the cargo of white paint, used it liberally on the town's buildings, and have since maintained the tradition of painting the houses white.

The steep sea cliffs of Devils Slide and Thornton State Beach were once the planned site of the 1905 Ocean Shore Railroad, intended to take passengers along the coast between San Francisco and Santa Cruz. The railroad was never completed, but remnants of the road cuts are still visible near the base of Devils Slide. Thornton State Beach to the north is where the San Andreas fault, one of the most active geologic faults in California, enters the sea. A movement of this fault in 1957 triggered a landslide, destroying the segment of Highway 1 which had previously run here along the coast.

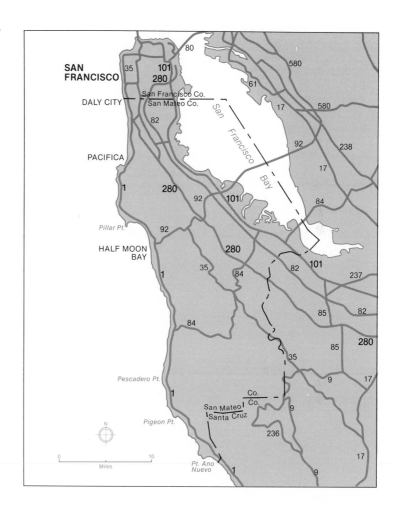

For additional information on San Mateo's coast, contact the Pacifica Chamber of Commerce, 80 Eureka Square, Suite 117, Pacifica 94044, (415) 355-4122 or the Half Moon Bay Chamber of Commerce, 225 Cabrillo Highway, the Caboose (P.O. Box 188), (415) 726-5202. For transit information: SAMTRANS, 400 S. El Camino Real, Suite 400, San Mateo 94402, (415) 871-2200 if calling from north San Mateo coast; 726-5541 from Half Moon Bay/Coastside; or 761-7000 from San Francisco.

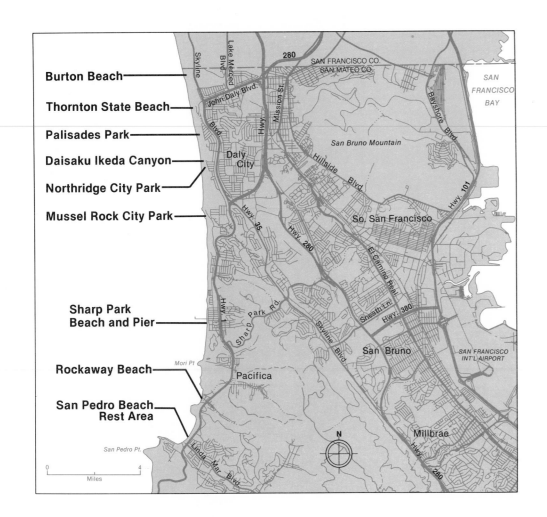

Burton Beach

Thornton State Beach

Palisades Park

Daisaku Ikeda Canyon

Northridge City Park

Mussel Rock City Park

**Sharp Park
Beach and Pier**

Rockaway Beach

**San Pedro Beach
Rest Area**

Burton Beach

San Mateo County

DALY CITY/PACIFICA

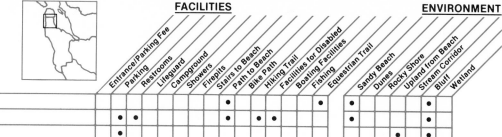

NAME	LOCATION	FACILITIES														ENVIRONMENT						
		Entrance/Parking Fee	Parking	Restrooms	Lifeguard	Campground	Showers	Firepits	Stairs to Beach	Path to Beach	Bike Path	Hiking Trail	Facilities for Disabled	Boating Facilities	Fishing	Equestrian Trail	Sandy Beach	Dunes	Rocky Shore	Upland from Beach	Stream Corridor	Bluff	Wetland
Phillip Burton Memorial Beach	1/2 mi. N. of Thornton State Beach, Daly City							●							●		●					●	
Thornton State Beach	Foot of Thornton Beach Rd., Daly City	●	●					●		●	●						●					●	
Palisades Park	Along Palisades Dr. at Westridge Ave., Daly City	●																	●			●	
Daisaku Ikeda Canyon	N. end of Northridge Dr., Daly City	●																	●	●	●	●	
Northridge City Park	Along Northridge Dr. at Carmel Ave., Daly City	●																	●			●	
Mussel Rock City Park	End of Westline Dr., off Skyline Dr., Daly City	●					●	●		●		●				●	●	●			●	
Sharp Park Beach and Pier	Beach Blvd. and Santa Rosa Ave., Pacifica	●	●											●		●							
Rockaway Beach	Foot of Rockaway Beach Ave. at San Mario Way, Pacifica						●							●		●							
San Pedro Beach Rest Area	Hwy. 1 between Crespi Dr. and Linda Mar Blvd., Pacifica	●	●							●						●							

PHILLIP BURTON MEMORIAL BEACH: Access from Fort Funston in San Francisco County or Thornton State Beach to the south.

THORNTON STATE BEACH: Panoramic coastal views from the picnic tables at the west end of the parking lot. Steep pathway to the beach; hiking trail along bluffs to the north. Popular kite and model glider area. Storm damage in 1982 has temporarily closed the upland area; best beach access is from Mussel Rock City Park to the south. Information: (415) 726-6238.
Mass Transit: SAMTRANS Route 1A to John Daly Blvd. and Dorchester Drive. Five block walk to Thornton Beach Rd.

PALISADES AND NORTHRIDGE CITY PARKS: Both parks overlook the ocean and contain municipal playgrounds.
Mass Transit: SAMTRANS. For Palisades Park: Route 1A to Skyline Dr. and Westridge Avenue. For Northridge Park: Route 1A to Skyline Dr. and Menlo Ave.; walk six blocks north.

DAISAKU IKEDA CANYON: Two vista points, which overlook Daisaku Ikeda Canyon and the ocean, are off the west and north ends of the parking lot, adjacent to Northridge City Park. Erosion of the bluffs and canyon prevents safe access to the beach; best beach access is from Mussel Rock City Park. The Nichiren Soshu Academy adjacent to the parking lot is private; do not trespass.
Mass Transit: SAMTRANS Route 1A to Skyline Dr. and Westmoor Ave.; walk one block south to Northridge Ave.

MUSSEL ROCK CITY PARK: A path and stairs lead from the overlook at the west end of the parking lot to the top of a seawall; beach access is at the north and south ends of the seawall. There is additional blufftop access at the north end of the parking lot. Unmarked wheelchair-accessible vista points are located along the perimeter of the parking lot.
Mass Transit: SAMTRANS Route 1A to Crenshaw and Skyline Drives; 1/2-mile walk to the park.

SHARP PARK BEACH AND PIER: Shoreline access is along Beach Boulevard. Facilities include a municipal fishing pier 200 yards long, concessions, and bait shop. Open all year.
Mass Transit: SAMTRANS Route 1A to Oceana Blvd. and Eureka Drive. 1/2-mile walk to the pier.

ROCKAWAY BEACH: Narrow, sandy beach, accessible except at highest tides from the short stairway just north of the end of Rockaway Beach Avenue. Popular fishing area.
Mass Transit: SAMTRANS Route 1A to Fassler Ave.

SAN PEDRO BEACH REST AREA: Popular beach for surfing, although it can be hazardous due to rip currents. Outdoor showers are at the restroom facilities.
Mass Transit: SAMTRANS Route 1A to Hwy. 1 and Linda Mar Blvd.

Mussel Rock

Mussel Rock City Park

111

Montara Lighthouse Hostel

Montara State Beach

James Fitzgerald Marine Reserve

San Mateo County

MONTARA/MOSS BEACH

NAME	LOCATION	Entrance/Parking Fee	Parking	Restrooms	Lifeguard	Campground	Showers	Firepits	Stairs to Beach	Path to Beach	Bike Path	Hiking Trail	Facilities for Disabled	Boating Facilities	Fishing	Equestrian Trail	Sandy Beach	Dunes	Rocky Shore	Upland from Beach	Stream Corridor	Bluff	Wetland
Gray Whale Cove State Beach	Hwy. 1, 1/2 mi. S. of Devils Slide, Montara	●	●	●				●	●								●					●	
Montara State Beach	Hwy. 1 and 2nd St., Montara		●	●				●	●				●				●					●	
Montara Lighthouse Hostel	Hwy. 1 and 16th St., Montara	●	●	●		●			●								●	●					
James Fitzgerald Marine Reserve	Off California Ave. at N. Lake St. and Nevada Ave., Moss Beach		●	●				●	●		●						●		●	●	●		

GRAY WHALE COVE STATE BEACH: Privately managed state beach, accessible by a steep trail and stairway west of Highway 1. Entrance fee $2/car. The parking lot is east of Highway 1; dangerous pedestrian crossing to get to the stairway. A grassy picnic area is above the beach along the bluffs. Popular sunbathing beach; clothing optional. Hazardous surf. No dogs, cameras, or binoculars permitted.
Mass Transit: SAMTRANS Route 1A.

MONTARA STATE BEACH: 1/2-mile long sandy beach. Hazardous surf. Across from the west end of Second St. is a steep path to the beach. Public parking is available at the small dirt lot at the top of the path, and during daylight hours until 5 PM at the Chart House Restaurant directly north. The stairs and path to the beach seaward of the Chart House are also for public use.
Mass Transit: SAMTRANS Route 1A to Highway 1 and 2nd St.

MONTARA LIGHTHOUSE HOSTEL: 30 beds, plus kitchen, laundry, and bike facilities, located in an old Victorian style house at the base of a historic Coast Guard operated lighthouse. Day use facilities for nonprofit groups; daily bike rentals available. Check-in hours are 4:30 PM-9:30 PM daily. Office also open 7:30 AM-9:30 AM. Overnight fee: members $4.50/night, non-members $6.50/night. Children accompanied by parents pay half price. Information and reservations: P.O. Box 737, Montara 94037; (415) 728-7177.
Mass Transit: SAMTRANS Route 1A to Highway 1 and 14th St.

JAMES FITZGERALD MARINE RESERVE: Three miles long, noted for its diverse marine life. Tidepool walks occasionally given by rangers at low tides; there is usually a walk given on Saturdays. Groups may make reservations for walks at other times. It is illegal to remove or disturb marine life or habitat. Tidepool rocks are slippery. Picnic tables are east of the parking lot in a sheltered cypress grove; hiking trails along grassy bluffs to the south. Information and reservations: (415) 728-3584 or 573-2595.
Mass Transit: SAMTRANS Route 1A to Etheldore St. and California Ave.

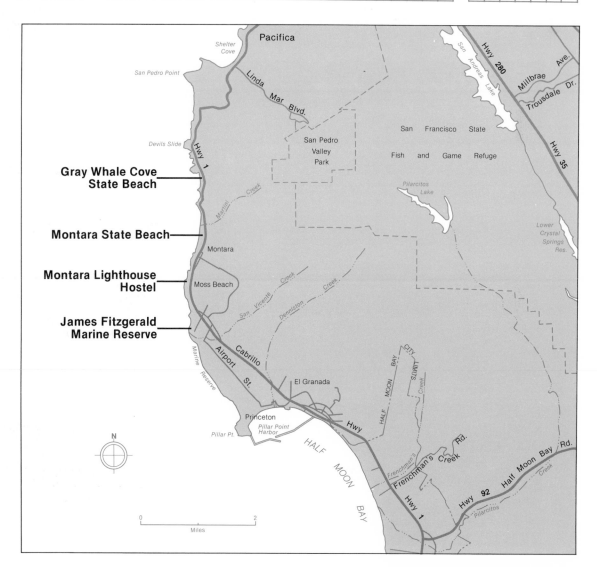

Pillar Point Harbor

Francis Beach

El Granada Beach

San Mateo County
PRINCETON/HALF MOON BAY

NAME	LOCATION	Entrance/Parking Fee	Parking	Restrooms	Lifeguard	Campground	Showers	Firepits	Stairs to Beach	Path to Beach	Bike Path	Hiking Trail	Facilities for Disabled	Boating Facilities	Fishing	Equestrian Trail	Sandy Beach	Dunes	Rocky Shore	Upland from Beach	Stream Corridor	Bluff	Wetland
Pillar Point Harbor (Johnson Pier)	W. of Hwy. 1 and Capistrano Rd., Princeton		•	•						•			•	•	•		•						
East Breakwater	W. of Hwy. 1, S. of Capistrano Rd., Half Moon Bay		•	•	•										•		•						
El Granada Beach	Between East Breakwater and Mirada Rd., Half Moon Bay		•												•		•						
Dunes Beach	Foot of Young Ave., Half Moon Bay		•	•					•							•	•	•				•	
Venice Beach	Foot of Venice Blvd., Half Moon Bay		•	•					•							•	•	•				•	
Francis Beach	Foot of Kelly Ave., Half Moon Bay	•	•	•		•		•		•			•		•	•	•					•	
Overlook	S. of Francis Beach, Half Moon Bay		•														•		•			•	
Pelican Point R.V. Park	End of Miramontes Point Rd., Half Moon Bay	•	•	•		•							•				•	•	•	•		•	

FACILITIES · ENVIRONMENT

PILLAR POINT HARBOR (JOHNSON PIER): This is the only small boat harbor between San Francisco and Santa Cruz. Contains a popular municipal fishing pier. Facilities include a boat ramp ($5 launching fee) and dinghy hoist (2,000 lb. cap., $1.85 launching fee), charter boats, picnic area, and food services. 200 moorings; some available for transient use. Open all year, 24 hours a day. For information, call: (415) 726-4382.
Mass Transit: SAMTRANS Route 1A to Capistrano Rd. and Carmel Ave.

EAST BREAKWATER: Popular fishing access. The dirt parking lot at the breakwater provides overnight camping for self-contained recreational vehicles. 14 day limit; $5/night. (415) 726-4382.
Mass Transit: SAMTRANS Route 1A to Capistrano Rd. and Carmel Ave.

EL GRANADA BEACH: Wide, sandy beach beneath the seawall along Highway 1. Restrooms and parking available at East Breakwater.
Mass Transit: SAMTRANS Route 1A to Capistrano Rd. and Carmel Ave.

The following are within the Half Moon Bay State Beach system and are administered by the California State Department of Parks and Recreation: Dunes Beach, Venice Beach, and Francis Beach. For information, contact the ranger station at 95 Kelly Ave., Half Moon Bay 94019; (415) 726-6238.

DUNES BEACH AND VENICE BEACH: Rough dirt road access. An equestrian trail is east of the parking lots and runs from Dunes Beach south to Francis Beach. Horse rentals are available at the two stables just off Highway 1 between Young Ave. and Venice Blvd.; (415) 726-9871 or 726-2362.
Mass Transit: SAMTRANS Route 1A to Highway 1 and Frenchmans Creek Road. 1/2-mile walk north to Young Ave.; one block walk south to Venice Blvd.

FRANCIS BEACH: 51 campsites for tent and R.V. camping; reservations through Ticketron recommended. There are also en route campsites available. $6 overnight fee, $2 day use fee. Picnic sites on the bluffs overlooking the ocean. Beach and restrooms are wheelchair accessible.
Mass Transit: SAMTRANS Route 1A to Kelly Ave. and Johnston St.

OVERLOOK: Undeveloped blufftop overlook is accessible from the dirt roads at the ends of Grove and Poplar Streets. Bluffs are highly eroded. Beach access is from Francis Beach to the north.

PELICAN POINT R.V. PARK: 75 recreational vehicle campsites located just upland of the ocean. Laundry and storage facilities, small store, and meeting room. Overnight fee $14 (includes hookups). No tent camping. Information and reservations: P.O. Box 65, Half Moon Bay 94019, (415) 726-9100.

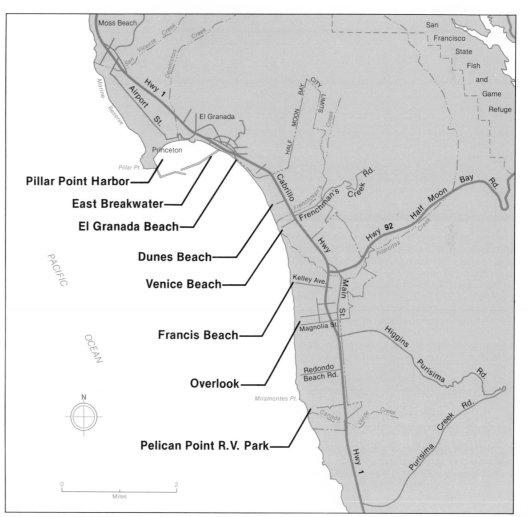

Agriculture

Over the last 200 years, California's coastal agriculture has grown from scattered subsistence farming to a strip of farm land that produces a diverse variety of high yield, high value specialty crops, and contains some of the best grazing lands in the State.

Native Californians were primarily hunter-gatherers and did not engage in agriculture until the establishment of the Spanish missions. Among the earliest coastal farms were those begun in 1812 by the Russians at Fort Ross in Sonoma County to sustain themselves as they conducted their fur seal and sea otter trade. The Spanish settlers to the south had only relatively small gardens, concentrating on raising cattle on their large *ranchos*. Farming and ranching were major contributors to the growth of early settlements along the coast, and the sea was often important in the commerce of agricultural products.

The stern-wheeler *Vaquero*, for example, made regular trips up and down Elkhorn Slough to take grain and potatoes from Watsonville to Moss Landing and on to San Francisco. Other schooners plied the coastline, loading lumber in the north and cattle in the south.

Since these times, vast areas of productive land have been lost to parcelization, accelerating land costs, and outright conversion to urbanization. In the 1960's alone,

one out of twelve acres of coastal cropland were covered by urban expansion. The remaining lands, however, are an important resource. Particular combinations of coastal soil and climate create special conditions of high agricultural productivity. The moderating marine influences provide timing and yield advantages for national markets, reduce the dangers of large scale crop loss from freezing, and extend the growing season, enabling farmers to raise and market multiple harvests in a single year.

Certain specialty crops, such as artichokes, avocados, broccoli, Brussels sprouts, celery, flowers, strawberries, tomatoes, and greenhouse products, do especially well under these conditions. However, in the event of need, the coastal zone's rich soil resources could also be converted to staple crops such as wheat, oats, and other basic cereals and vegetables.

Grazing lands, which cover more than 350,000 acres from Santa Barbara north, allow cattle and sheep to efficiently convert sun and rain into milk, meat, wool, and other products without depending on increasingly expensive feeds.

Soils in the coastal river valleys from Monterey County south are some of the most important agricultural lands in California. The deep alluvial and flood plain soils are highly suited for irrigation crops such as vegetables, citrus fruits, and avocados. Terraces along the southern California coast are also conducive to specialty crop production.

The specific climate and soil conditions along the San Mateo County coast are ideal for a number of valuable vegetable and flower crops, most of which are grown on deep, fertile, low-elevation marine terraces and alluvial soils between Pillar Point and Año Nuevo Point. The average daily temperature here varies less than ten degrees from summer to winter, and the growing season averages more than 300 days per year. During the summer months, fog covers much of the County's coastal strip and this foggy environment contributes to high yields of Brussels sprouts, artichokes, and cut flowers; a large percentage of the country's Brussels sprouts come from San Mateo County.

Mushrooms are also a successful crop along the San Mateo coast due to the high humidity and low evaporation; other crops include broccoli, cauliflower, peas, radishes, chard, and spinach. From late summer to fall, pumpkins become a prominent part of the County's landscape; the Half Moon Bay Pumpkin Festival, held in October, is a popular cultural event that celebrates the harvest of pumpkins and other crops.

Many of California's coastal crop and grazing lands extend virtually to the water's edge. It is very important that beach visitors respect the farmers' and ranchers' efforts to keep their lands in production. Please do not interfere with agriculture operations. Only access trails dedicated for public use should be used to reach the beach; do not walk across cultivated fields to obtain beach access.

San Mateo County

MID-COAST

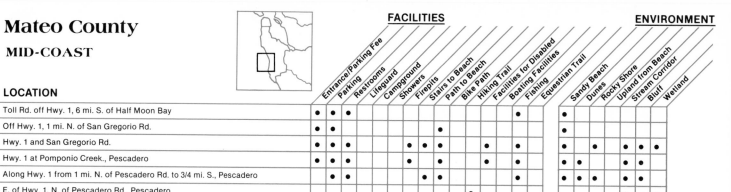

NAME	LOCATION	Entrance/Parking Fee	Parking	Restrooms	Lifeguard	Campground	Showers	Firepits	Stairs to Beach	Path to Beach	Bike Path	Hiking Trail	Facilities for Disabled	Boating Facilities	Fishing	Equestrian Trail	Sandy Beach	Dunes	Rocky Shore	Upland from Beach	Stream Corridor	Bluff	Wetland
Martin's Beach	Toll Rd. off Hwy. 1, 6 mi. S. of Half Moon Bay	•	•	•											•		•						
San Gregorio Private Beach	Off Hwy. 1, 1 mi. N. of San Gregorio Rd.	•	•						•								•						
San Gregorio State Beach	Hwy. 1 and San Gregorio Rd.	•	•	•				•	•			•			•		•		•			•	•
Pomponio State Beach	Hwy. 1 at Pomponio Creek., Pescadero	•	•	•				•		•					•		•	•				•	•
Pescadero State Beach	Along Hwy. 1 from 1 mi. N. of Pescadero Rd. to 3/4 mi. S., Pescadero		•	•				•							•		•	•	•			•	•
Pescadero Marsh Natural Preserve	E. of Hwy. 1, N. of Pescadero Rd., Pescadero											•										•	•

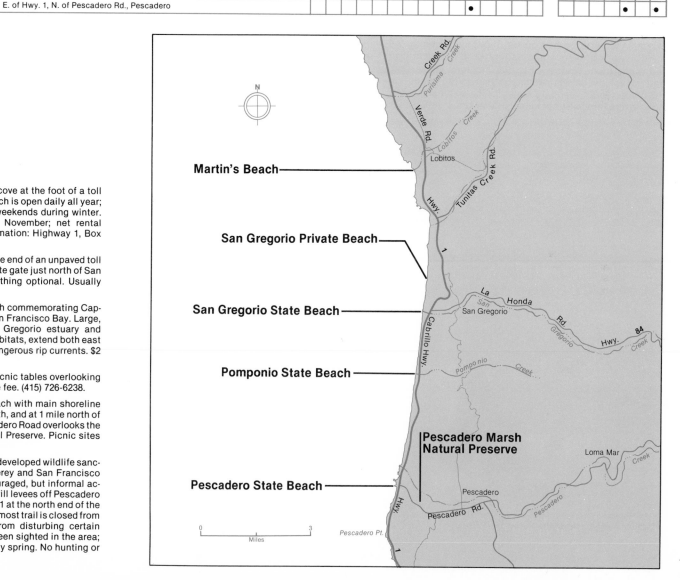

MARTIN'S BEACH: Privately developed fishing cove at the foot of a toll road off Highway 1; entrance fee $2/car. The beach is open daily all year; the store is open daily during summer and on weekends during winter. Popular for surf smelt fishing from April to November; net rental available. Picnic tables are on the beach. Information: Highway 1, Box 343, Half Moon Bay 94019; (415) 726-9943.

SAN GREGORIO PRIVATE BEACH: Located at the end of an unpaved toll road off Highway 1; it can be identified by its white gate just north of San Gregorio Road. Entrance fee $1.50/person. Clothing optional. Usually open on weekends, depending on the weather.

SAN GREGORIO STATE BEACH: Memorial beach commemorating Captain Portolá's 1769 Spanish expedition to the San Francisco Bay. Large, sandy cove directly off Highway 1. The San Gregorio estuary and freshwater marsh, noted as migratory wildlife habitats, extend both east and west of Highway 1. Highly eroded bluffs; dangerous rip currents. $2 day use fee. (415) 726-6238.

POMPONIO STATE BEACH: Facilities include picnic tables overlooking the ocean and day use cooking grills. $2 day use fee. (415) 726-6238.

PESCADERO STATE BEACH: One-mile long beach with main shoreline access points at Pescadero Road, at .2 miles north, and at 1 mile north of Pescadero Road. A vista point just north of Pescadero Road overlooks the Pacific Ocean and the Pescadero Marsh Natural Preserve. Picnic sites are located throughout the beach area.

PESCADERO MARSH NATURAL PRESERVE: Undeveloped wildlife sanctuary; the largest coastal marsh between Monterey and San Francisco Bays. Sensitive area. Heavy visitor use is discouraged, but informal access for birdwatching is permitted along the dirt fill levees off Pescadero Rd., and along the interpretive trails off Highway 1 at the north end of the preserve and near Pescadero Creek. The northernmost trail is closed from March 15 to September 1 to prevent hikers from disturbing certain breeding birds. Over 160 species of birds have been sighted in the area; best bird watching is during the late fall and early spring. No hunting or pets allowed. (415) 726-6238.

Northern Elephant Seal

The northern elephant seal *(Mirounga angustirostris)* is the largest of all pinnipeds (seals and sea lions) found in this hemisphere. Adult males reach a length of 14-16 feet with a weight of nearly three tons; they have a distinctive inflatable nasal sac which hangs down almost into their mouths when they rear their heads back. This proboscis gives them the name elephant seals. The females are smaller, reaching 10-12 feet in length and 1,200-2,000 lbs.

Despite their size, both sexes can move swiftly along the sand. Elephant seals come ashore only to breed, give birth, and molt. Their normal diet includes squid, fish, and occasional small sharks, but they do not eat during the three month breeding season. The elephant seals' only natural enemies are killer whales and sharks.

The breeding season begins in early December when the males begin arriving at the breeding site, called a rookery, and establish a dominance hierarchy through brief but violent battles; the bulls at the top of the rank will do most of the breeding. In late December, the females arrive and give birth within six days; pups weigh 75 lbs. at birth and increase to 300-400 lbs. within a month. Mothers nurse their young for 27-29 days.

Mating takes place about 24 days after the birth of the pups and the gestation period lasts eight months; a natural delay causes the fertilized egg to implant in the uterus wall three months later so that the young will be born at the same time the following year, not at sea. By mid-March the adults leave the rookery and head back to sea, leaving the young to follow within a few days.

Año Nuevo State Reserve in San Mateo County, home of a growing colony of northern elephant seals, hosts over 50,000 visitors each winter. The reserve encompasses over 700 acres of coastal bluffs, sand dunes, and beaches, as well as a 13-acre island one half mile off-shore. A rapid increase in the elephant seal population at Año Nuevo led to a corresponding increase of visitors in the winter of 1973-74; as a result the California Department of Parks and Recreation, in conjunction with U.C. Santa Cruz, developed an outstanding interpretive program at Año Nuevo, making it one of the most popular central coast parks.

During breeding season, visiting the elephant seal breeding grounds is restricted to guided tours, provided seven days a week from December through March by the State Parks Department. Tour reservations are available beginning in November and weekend spots usually fill immediately; call Año Nuevo State Reserve beginning in September for ticket information; (415) 879-0227. Tour reservations are available through Ticketron, (415) 393-6914, or SAMTRANS, (415) 348-SEAL. Santa Cruz Metropolitan Transit District (SCMTD) provides limited coupons on the 40 Davenport route which are redeemable for tour reservations; call (408) 425-8600. Tours take about 2-1/2 hours and cover about 3 miles along blufftops and sand dunes.

Northern elephant seal, Año Nuevo State Reserve

Northern elephant seal, Año Nuevo State Reserve

San Mateo County
SOUTHERN SAN MATEO COAST

NAME	LOCATION	Entrance/Parking Fee	Parking	Restrooms	Lifeguard	Campground	Showers	Firepits	Stairs to Beach	Path to Beach	Bike Path	Hiking Trail	Facilities for Disabled	Boating Facilities	Fishing	Equestrian Trail	Sandy Beach	Dunes	Rocky Shore	Upland from Beach	Stream Corridor	Bluff	Wetland
Pebble Beach	Hwy. 1, between Hill Rd. and Artichoke Rd., Pescadero		●	●				●									●		●			●	
Bean Hollow State Beach	Along Hwy. 1 from Artichoke Rd. to Bean Hollow Rd., Pescadero		●	●				●									●		●				
Butano State Park	Cloverdale Rd., 5 mi. S. of Pescadero and 3 mi. E. of Hwy. 1	●	●	●		●						●	●							●	●		
Pigeon Point Lighthouse Hostel	Pigeon Point Rd., W. of Hwy. 1, Pescadero	●	●	●			●				●				●		●		●	●		●	
Overlooks	Along Hwy. 1 from Pigeon Point Rd. to .4 mi. S., Pescadero		●												●				●			●	
Gazos Creek State Beach	Hwy. 1, N. of Gazos Creek Rd., Pescadero		●	●						●					●		●		●		●	●	
Año Nuevo State Reserve	From Franklin Point south to New Years Creek	●	●	●					●			●			●		●	●	●			●	

PEBBLE BEACH: In a small cove surrounded by protective bluffs. Noted for the beach's unique pebble composition; removal of pebbles is illegal.

BEAN HOLLOW STATE BEACH: Paved parking area and picnic tables are right off Highway 1 and located just above the beach. Rocky surf and hazardous rip currents. (415) 726-6238.

BUTANO STATE PARK: 2,200-acre redwood park, three miles inland from the coast. Hiking trails with scenic views of Año Nuevo Island. 21 drive-in and 19 walk-in campsites. $6 overnight fee and $2 day use fee. 50¢/person for special bicycle and hiker group camping. Open all year. Summertime nature walks and campfire programs available. (415) 879-0173.

PIGEON POINT LIGHTHOUSE HOSTEL: Located adjacent to the second tallest lighthouse in the United States. Facilities include 40 beds, kitchen, and bike storage. Day use facilities for nonprofit groups available. Daily check-in hours are 4:30 PM-9:30 PM. Office also open 7:30 AM-9:30 AM. Overnight fee: members $4.50/night, non-members $6.50/night. For information and reservations: Pigeon Point Rd., Pescadero 94060; (415) 879-0633.

OVERLOOKS: Undeveloped blufftop overlooks at .1 and .4 miles south of the crossing of Pigeon Point Rd. and Highway 1. Bluffs are highly eroded. Private land is adjacent to the south; do not trespass.

GAZOS CREEK STATE BEACH: Paved parking lot; a short pathway leads to the beach. Provides the only access to Franklin Point to the south, a popular fishing area; stay below the mean high tide line between Gazos Creek and Franklin Point. (415) 879-0227.

AÑO NUEVO STATE RESERVE: 1,500 acres; the site of some of the few remaining active dune fields on the California coast, and a protected breeding ground for northern elephant seals. The reserve is also noted for California gray whale sighting in January and March, spring and fall migratory bird-watching, and hiking May through November. The reserve's main entrance, parking lot, and office are on New Years Creek Road. The reserve north of Cascade Creek is accessible by three paths, marked with state park signs, off Highway 1 at 2.7, 3.2, and 3.3 miles north of New Years Creek Road. No parking on Highway 1 shoulders.

From December 1 to April 30, when the elephant seals are breeding, the reserve south of Cascade Creek is open only to guided tours available by reservation. Also during this time, it is illegal to enter any of the reserve's intertidal areas between Franklin Point and New Years Creek. The guided tours are three miles long and take 2-1/2 hours; $2.50/person. $2/car day use fee May-November. Hours year-round: 8 AM-sunset. No dogs allowed. A wheelchair-accessible path and viewing platform will be available soon; call Año Nuevo for information: (415) 879-0227. Guided tour reservations are available only through Ticketron, (415) 393-6914. Call Año Nuevo beginning in September for ticket information.

Mass Transit: SAMTRANS from the Hillsdale shopping center in San Mateo; $7.00/person, includes tour fee. Reservations: (415) 348-SEAL. Also SAMTRANS Route 90C operates from Half Moon Bay to Año Nuevo weekdays only. Santa Cruz Metropolitan Transit District (SCMTD) 40 Davenport route; (408) 425-8600. SAMTRANS and SCMTD buses to Año Nuevo operate December-March only.

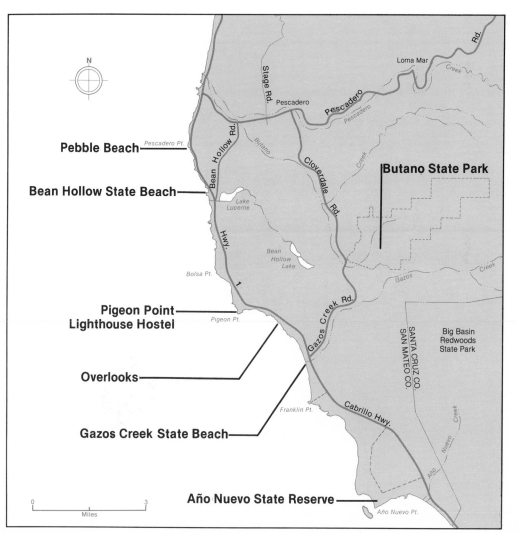

Santa Cruz Beach

Santa Cruz County

South of Año Nuevo Point, the varied coastline of Santa Cruz County begins, extending for 42 miles from the north county coastal terraces beneath the Santa Cruz Mountains to the productive farmlands of the Pajaro Valley in the south. Narrow, sandy beaches backed by steep bluffs are characteristic of the coast north of the City of Santa Cruz, in contrast to the wide, sheltered swimming beaches found along the north shore of Monterey Bay.

Agriculture is prevalent along most of the county's coast, providing fields of crops and open space adjacent to the shoreline sea cliffs and Highway 1. The fertile coastal terraces of the north coast produce 30 percent of California's Brussels sprouts, while the more inland Pajaro Valley near Watsonville is noted for crops of lettuce, strawberries, artichokes, and cut flowers.

The rugged Santa Cruz Mountains, which border the coastline north of Monterey Bay, contain beautiful upland forests of coastal redwoods (*Sequoia sempervirens*). These forests have been logged for over 115 years, but because of the establishment in 1902 of the Big Basin Redwoods State Park within the watershed of Waddell Creek, many old-growth redwood groves still remain. A popular hiking trail through redwood groves in Big Basin Redwoods State Park is the scenic 38-mile long Skyline-to-Sea Trail which begins at Castle Rock State Park near Saratoga Gap and ends at the ocean at Waddell Creek Beach.

Point Santa Cruz, seaward of the City of Santa Cruz, marks the northern limit of Monterey Bay. In 1602, the Spanish explorer Don Sebastián Vizcaíno visited the bay and described it in his ship's log in such enthusiastic terms that the Spanish government sent Juan Gaspar de Portolá on a coastal land expedition in 1769 to find and settle Monterey Bay for Spain. Although Portolá's expedition camped alongside the bay twice, and found San Francisco Bay, it wasn't until a second expedition in 1770 that Portolá recognized it as the same Monterey Bay in which Vizcaíno had originally anchored.

Portolá's expedition also raised the first Catholic cross on the bank of the San Lorenzo River, marking the site of the City of Santa Cruz (Spanish for "Holy Cross"). In 1791 the Santa Cruz Mission was founded by Father Fermín Francisco de Lasuén, and by 1840 a small town had been settled. Today, the City of Santa Cruz is a popular tourist town, with its warm weather, sandy beaches for swimming, surfing, and fishing, and the famous boardwalk amusement park, the last of its kind still open on the California coast. The boardwalk attracts numerous visitors each weekend, and offers food, rides, an arcade, and a mile-long protected sandy beach which stretches in front of it.

Prior to Spanish settlement, the Santa Cruz coast was inhabited by Costanoan Indians, whose diet was dependent upon the abundant shellfish found here. Shell middens left by the Costanoans were enormous; the volume of discarded shells was so great near some abandoned Indian camps that the material was used in the 1900's for road pavement and by farmers as a dietary supplement for their poultry.

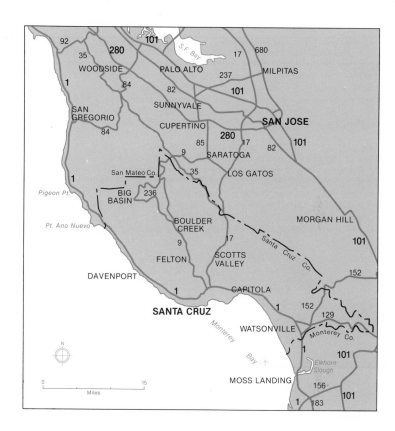

For further information on the Santa Cruz County coast, contact the Santa Cruz County Convention and Visitors Bureau, at Church Street and Center Avenue (inside the Civic Auditorium), P.O. Box 1476, Santa Cruz 95061, (408) 423-6927, or the Capitola Chamber of Commerce, 410 Capitola Avenue, Capitola 95010, (408) 475-6522. For transit information, write or call the Santa Cruz Metropolitan Transit District (SCMTD), 230 Walnut Avenue, Santa Cruz 95060, (408) 425-8600 or 688-8600.

Coastal Vegetation

A plant community is a naturally occurring group of different plants inhabiting a common environment. These plants often share certain characteristics which help to adapt them to their habitat. For example, the tough, leathery leaves of many chaparral plants allow them to survive in an arid environment. Plant communities are not always clearly defined, since they frequently merge into each other. Several plant communities are recognizable along the California coast.

The plants found on the sandy beaches and dunes adjacent to the ocean belong to the coastal strand community. Plants in the strand community are generally short, growing relatively close to the ground as herbs, vines, or low shrubs. Most of the species which grow here are specially adapted to the high amounts of dissolved salts found in the soils bordering the shoreline.

Characteristic features of coastal strand and other salt-tolerant vegetation are succulent, leathery leaves and stems which retain high amounts of water and resist water loss through evaporation. One of the most common strand plants is ice plant; these low growing succulents were introduced from South America and South Africa. Other plants in this community include the sand verbena, beach primrose, and beach morning glory.

Salt marsh and fresh water marsh plant communities are also located near the water's edge, especially where the slope is very shallow, but unlike coastal strand vegetation, they are frequently inundated by the tides or by floods. Because the high amount of water reduces the availability of oxygen, these plants have adaptations to increase the amount of oxygen available to the plant roots.

Salt marsh plants, like coastal strand plants, are adapted to salt stress. Many of these plants, such as pickleweed or glasswort, are succulents, which can hold water to reduce the drying effect of the salt. Other species, such as salt grass, exude the salt from small glands on their leaves. Generally, salt marshes tend to be characterized by low, shrubby vegetation, often growing in clumps separated by nonvegetated salt or mud flats. Fresh water marshes, on the other hand, are typified by fairly tall (four to ten feet) plants such as cattails or bulrushes.

Above the high water level, coastal sage scrub is the predominant vegetation type along the southern California coast. An association of woody shrubs ranging in height from one to five feet, it is typified by California sagebrush, white and black sage, California buckwheat, and lemonade-berry. Plants in this community are adapted to arid coastal climates from about sea level to 3,000 feet. The leaves are usually small and leathery, adapted to resist water loss through evaporation.

Similar to the coastal sage scrub, but ranging roughly from Monterey to the Oregon border, is the northern coastal scrub community. Characterized by coyote bush, California blackberry, and bush monkeyflower, northern coastal scrub is found at elevations below 500 feet on often steep hillsides. The picturesque Monterey cypress, which grows along the blufftops of the central coast, is also found in this community. Most of the species in this community, however, rarely grow over six feet in height and are often intermixed with extensive areas of grass.

Chaparral is a common plant community on the hill and mountain sides of coastal California, usually growing at higher elevations than the coastal sage scrub association. This vegetation type is typically found growing in dense, almost impenetrable stands with individual plants from three to ten feet tall. Most of the plants are well adapted to the harsh climate on these dry slopes; the leaves are often small and covered with a gray fuzz to reflect the sun's rays, and frequently have strong spines. Typical chaparral plants are chamise, manzanita, mountain lilac, toyon or Christmas holly, and scrub oak.

Plants which grow along coastal rivers and streams belong to the riparian community. Riparian habitat, because of the relatively high amount of water present, is some of the most valuable habitat for wildlife in California. The riparian plant community is dominated in the south by trees such as the big-leaf maple, canyon sycamore, willow, and alder. From San Francisco north, the creek bottoms are often dominated by redwoods and attendant species such as madrone and Douglas fir.

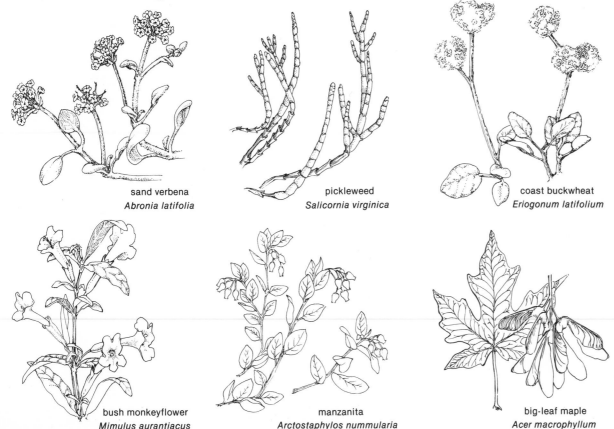

sand verbena
Abronia latifolia

pickleweed
Salicornia virginica

coast buckwheat
Eriogonum latifolium

bush monkeyflower
Mimulus aurantiacus

manzanita
Arctostaphylos nummularia

big-leaf maple
Acer macrophyllum

Santa Cruz County

NORTHERN SANTA CRUZ COAST

NAME	LOCATION	Entrance/Parking Fee	Parking	Restrooms	Lifeguard	Campground	Showers	Firepits	Stairs to Beach	Path to Beach	Bike Path	Hiking Trail	Facilities for Disabled	Boating Facilities	Fishing	Equestrian Trail	Sandy Beach	Dunes	Rocky Shore	Upland from Beach	Stream Corridor	Bluff	Wetland
Waddell Creek Beach (Unit of Big Basin Redwoods State Park)	Hwy. 1, 1 mi. S. of San Mateo County line		•	•											•		•	•		•	•	•	
Big Basin Redwoods State Park	14 mi. N. of Santa Cruz on Hwy. 9, 7 miles N.W. on access rd.	•	•	•		•	•	•				•			•					•			
Greyhound Rock Fishing Access	Hwy. 1 and Swanton Rd., 4 mi. S. of Año Nuevo		•					•	•			•			•		•	•	•		•		
Bonny Doon Beach	Hwy. 1 and Bonny Doon Rd., 12 mi. N. of Santa Cruz		•							•							•	•	•			•	
Red, White and Blue Beach	5021 Hwy. 1, 5-1/2 mi. N. of Santa Cruz	•	•	•		•		•							•		•	•	•		•	•	
Four Mile Beach (Part of Wilder Ranch State Park)	Off Hwy. 1, 4 mi. N. of Santa Cruz		•							•							•	•				•	•

WADDELL CREEK BEACH: Located at the southwest corner of Big Basin Redwoods State Park. Harbor seal rookery offshore south of the beach. Theodore J. Hoover Natural Preserve, which includes Waddell Marsh, is located at the mouth of Waddell Creek. Waddell Bluffs to the north has also been acquired by State Parks as part of Big Basin.
Mass Transit: Santa Cruz Metropolitan Transit District (SCMTD) Route 40, Davenport.

BIG BASIN REDWOODS STATE PARK: More than 14,000 acres. Located in the Santa Cruz Mountains. Acquired in 1902; the oldest park in the California State Park System. Park Headquarters and Nature Lodge museum are 9-1/2 miles west of Boulder Creek, on the Opal Creek flatlands. Over 40 miles of hiking trails, an equestrian trail, picnic sites, 236 campsites, numerous waterfalls, and a variety of wildlife within the park. No trailer hookups; trailer sanitation station at Huckleberry Campground. Camping fee $6, day use fee $2. Open all year. (408) 338-6132.
Mass Transit: SCMTD Route 37. Two round trips a day to Park Headquarters.

GREYHOUND ROCK FISHING ACCESS: Popular rock fishing spot. Developed by the Wildlife Conservation Board and the Department of Fish and Game. A steep trail and stairs lead down to the beach.
Mass Transit: SCMTD Route 40, Davenport.

BONNY DOON BEACH: Steep climb up to the Southern Pacific railroad tracks, then down the bluff to the beach. Sheltered cove. Extent of public and private rights is undetermined; subject to further investigation.
Mass Transit: SCMTD Route 40, Davenport.

RED, WHITE AND BLUE BEACH: Private fee beach, clothing optional. Look for the red, white, and blue mailbox 4.2 miles south of Davenport on the west side of Highway 1; turn onto Scaroni Rd. and cross the Southern Pacific railroad tracks. Day use and camping; must be 21, married, or with parents to attend beach. Picnic tables available; no cameras or dogs allowed.
Mass Transit: SCMTD Route 40, Davenport.

FOUR MILE BEACH: Part of Wilder Ranch State Park, which is owned by the Department of Parks and Recreation; not yet open for public use. Proposed developments include a Dairy Museum, upland camping, and beach facilities. Although pesticides are in use and pose a possible health hazard, Four Mile Beach is currently used by surfers and hikers. A dirt path which leads to the beach begins above the rough, dirt parking area along Highway 1.
Mass Transit: SCMTD Route 40, Davenport.

Santa Cruz Boardwalk

Mark Abbott Memorial Lighthouse

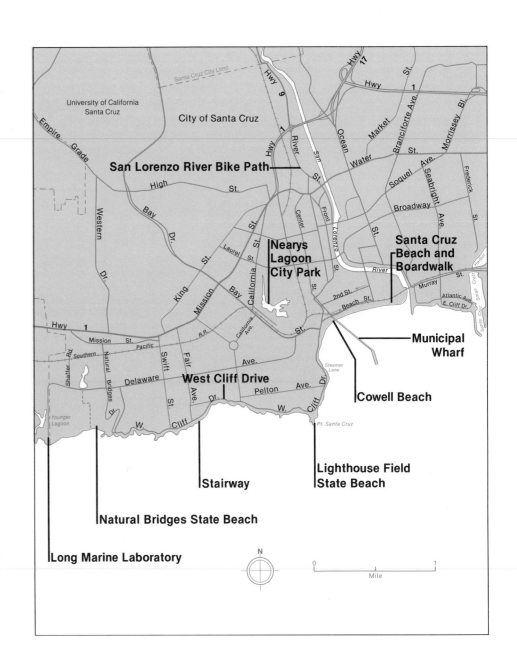

University of California
Santa Cruz

City of Santa Cruz

Santa Cruz City Limit

Hwy 9

Hwy 17

Hwy 1

San Lorenzo River Bike Path

High St.

Empire Grade

Bay Dr.

Western Dr.

King St.

Laurel St.

Mission St.

Bay

California St.

Nearys Lagoon City Park

Ocean St.

Water St.

Market St.

Branciforte Ave.

Morrissey Bl.

Soquel Ave.

Seabright Ave.

Frederick St.

Broadway

Santa Cruz Beach and Boardwalk

River St.

San Lorenzo River

Center St.

Front St.

2nd St.

Beach St.

Murray St.

Atlantic Ave.

E. Cliff Dr.

Santa Cruz Small Craft Harbor

Hwy 1

Mission St.

Pacific Ave.

R.R.

California Ave.

Swift St.

Fair Ave.

Delaware Ave.

Dr.

Pelton Ave.

W. Cliff Dr.

Steamer Lane

Natural Bridges Dr.

Shaffer Rd.

Southern

West Cliff Drive

W. Cliff

Pt. Santa Cruz

Municipal Wharf

Cowell Beach

Younger Lagoon

Lighthouse Field State Beach

Stairway

Natural Bridges State Beach

Long Marine Laboratory

N

0   1
Mile

Santa Cruz County
CITY OF SANTA CRUZ

NAME	LOCATION	Entrance/Parking Fee	Parking	Restrooms	Lifeguard	Campground	Showers	Firepits	Stairs to Beach	Path to Beach	Bike Path	Hiking Trail	Facilities for Disabled	Boating Facilities	Fishing	Equestrian Trail	Sandy Beach	Dunes	Rocky Shore	Upland from Beach	Stream Corridor	Bluff	Wetland
Long Marine Laboratory	Corner of Delaware Ave. and Shaffer Rd., Santa Cruz		•																•				
Natural Bridges State Beach	2531 W. Cliff Dr., Santa Cruz	•	•	•			•		•	•	•	•			•		•		•	•	•		
West Cliff Drive	Runs from Natural Bridges to Cowell Beach, Santa Cruz		•								•								•	•			
Stairway to Beach	W. Cliff Dr., between Fair Ave. and De La Costa Ave., Santa Cruz		•						•										•	•			
Santa Cruz Hostel	Call (408) 423-8304 or 298-0670	•																	•				
Nearys Lagoon City Park	Off California St., N. of Bay Dr., Santa Cruz		•	•				•				•	•						•				•
Lighthouse Field State Beach	Along W. Cliff Dr. at Pt. Santa Cruz		•												•				•	•		•	
Cowell Beach	W. Cliff Dr. and Bay St., Santa Cruz	•	•	•											•		•		•				
Santa Cruz Municipal Wharf	Foot of Washington St. and Beach St., Santa Cruz		•	•										•	•								
Santa Cruz Beach and Boardwalk	E. of Municipal Wharf, Santa Cruz		•	•	•										•		•		•				
San Lorenzo River Bike Path	Along San Lorenzo River, Santa Cruz										•								•	•			

LONG MARINE LABORATORY: A research facility of U.C. Santa Cruz. The aquarium is open to the public 1 PM-4 PM daily except Monday; call (408) 429-2883 for information. The aquarium includes fish and invertebrate tanks, a shell collection, and fossil exhibit; docents on duty.

NATURAL BRIDGES STATE BEACH: 54 acres. Scenic overlook with 20-minute free parking above natural bridge rock formations; sandy beach and tidepools below. Wheelchair–accessible restroom near the beach. Picnic sites are at the rear of the park near the creek amid eucalyptus trees. $2 day use fee. Noted for butterfly study area; annual migration of the Monarch butterfly is from September through December. (408) 423-4609 or 688-3241. The De Anza walkway is a paved walkway leading from Delaware Ave. through the mobile home park to the sandy beach. Shoreline access to Natural Bridges via the sandy beach, tidepools, and blufftop.
Mass Transit: Santa Cruz Metropolitan Transit District (SCMTD) Route 3C, Mission.

WEST CLIFF DRIVE: Panoramic views of the Pacific Ocean and Monterey Bay. Numerous scenic overlooks with parking and benches; bicycle/pedestrian path is seaward of the road.

STAIRWAY TO BEACH: Coastal bluffs highly eroded; tidal rocks are slippery when wet.
Mass Transit: SCMTD Route 3C, Mission.

SANTA CRUZ HOSTEL: Operated during summer months only. No permanent facility. For information, contact Santa Cruz Hostel Project: P.O. Box 1241, Santa Cruz 95061, (408) 423-8304; or call the AYH Central California Council: (408) 298-0670.

NEARYS LAGOON CITY PARK: Nature refuge. Facilities include wildlife sanctuary, picnic area, tennis courts, and children's playground. Paved roadway to parking lot and lagoon; a floating platform extends into the lagoon for wildlife viewing. No dogs, hunting, or bathing permitted.
Mass Transit: SCMTD Route 3A, 3B, and 3C, Mission.

LIGHTHOUSE FIELD STATE BEACH: 40 acres, including undeveloped uplands and a scenic viewpoint with picnic table and benches; cliffs are highly eroded. Mark Abbott Memorial Lighthouse at Point Santa Cruz overlooks Monterey Bay and the Pacific Ocean; the Lighthouse is not open to the public.
Mass Transit: SCMTD Route 7, Beach.

COWELL BEACH: Volleyball standards and nets provided during summer months. Steamer Lane, one of the most famous surfing spots on the coast, is just offshore. A paved ramp near the foot of Manor Ave. leads to a restroom; the stairway to the beach is deteriorated, and has been replaced by a concrete stairway at the foot of Monterey Ave. just north.
Mass Transit: SCMTD Route 7, Beach.

SANTA CRUZ MUNICIPAL WHARF: Accommodates both cars and pedestrians. Over one-half mile long. Ramp, small boat hoist, boat and motor rentals, shops, restaurants, fishing licenses and equipment available. Open all year. For information on boat rentals, call: (408) 423-1739.
Mass Transit: SCMTD Route 7, Beach.

SANTA CRUZ BEACH AND BOARDWALK: Public access points at the western end of the beach, foot of Municipal Wharf; further east adjacent to the Coconut Grove terminus of the boardwalk; and at the eastern end of the beach near the mouth of the San Lorenzo River, across the railroad bridge (pedestrian sidewalk section). Popular swimming beach. Santa Cruz Seaside Company owns and operates the boardwalk and ten stairways down to the beach. Boardwalk offers food, rides, and other amusements.
Mass Transit: SCMTD Route 7, Beach.

SAN LORENZO RIVER BIKE PATH: A bike path runs along both sides of the San Lorenzo River levee from Highway 9 (River St.) to the river mouth at the Santa Cruz Beach. The path goes under the bridge at Laurel St.

Tidepool, Natural Bridges State Beach

Waves and Surf

The breakers that crash upon California's beaches originate hundreds of miles offshore as a result of winds blowing across the ocean's surface and creating ripples; as the wind continues to blow, ripples turn into progressively larger waves. The size of waves generated by the wind is proportional to wind velocity and duration, and the extent of the open ocean across which the winds blow.

As waves move away from the generating center they become rounded, lower, and symmetrical and move in groups of similar height and period (i.e., the time it takes for two successive waves to pass a point). These groups of waves, called swell or ground swell, move in this form until they approach coastal areas.

Waves start to break once they reach a water depth less than half of their wavelength (i.e., the distance between successive wave crests). As the wave continues to move toward the beach, its height increases until the wave topples over and breaks, resulting in the surf visible along the shoreline.

The action of the waves in the nearshore zone is responsible for shaping beaches. In the winter, when storm centers are often relatively near the shoreline, steep, short period waves can attack a beach and remove much of the sand, leaving a narrow, steep beach. During calmer times of the year, longer period waves bring sand back onshore and reshape the beach to form a wider, flatter shoreline. This seasonal fluctuation of beach width and shape caused by waves is a process known as on/offshore sediment transport.

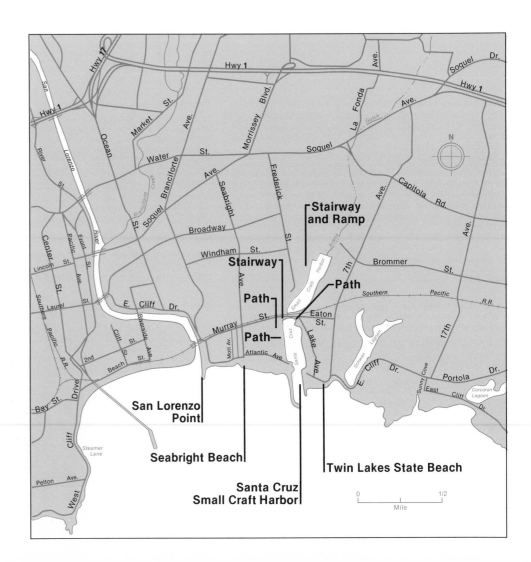

Santa Cruz County

SANTA CRUZ HARBOR AREA

NAME	LOCATION	Entrance/Parking Fee	Parking	Restrooms	Lifeguard	Campground	Showers	Firepits	Stairs to Beach	Path to Beach	Bike Path	Hiking Trail	Facilities for Disabled	Boating Facilities	Fishing	Equestrian Trail	Sandy Beach	Dunes	Rocky Shore	Upland from Beach	Stream Corridor	Bluff	Wetland
San Lorenzo Point	Foot of E. Cliff Drive off Murray St., Santa Cruz		●																●	●	●		
Seabright Beach (Unit of Twin Lakes State Beach)	E. Cliff Drive, San Lorenzo Point to Seabright Ave., Santa Cruz		●	●			●		●		●						●					●	
Santa Cruz Small Craft Harbor	Eaton St. at Lake Ave., Santa Cruz	●	●	●						●				●	●								
Bike and Footpath	Around Harbor, Santa Cruz										●												
Stairway to Harbor	W. side of Harbor, S. side of Murray St., Santa Cruz								●														
Stairway and Ramp to Harbor	Upper Harbor at Frederick Street Park, Santa Cruz									●												●	
Path to Harbor	E. side of Harbor and Eaton St., Santa Cruz													●	●								
Path to Harbor	At Coast Guard Station on Fairview Pl., Lower Harbor, Santa Cruz														●								
Twin Lakes State Beach	7th Ave. at E. Cliff Drive		●	●	●		●							●	●	●	●			●		●	

SAN LORENZO POINT: The long, narrow promontory which projects into Monterey Bay, to the east of the San Lorenzo River; part of Twin Lakes State Beach. Accessible via E. Cliff Drive and a path which leads to the end of the promontory. Limited parking on E. Cliff Drive.
Mass Transit: Santa Cruz Metropolitan Transit District (SCMTD) Route 6, Seabright, to the corner of Seabright Ave. and Murray St.; 1/4-mile walk.

SEABRIGHT BEACH: Also called Castle Beach. Safe access at E. Cliff Drive at the foot of Mott and Cypress Avenues and, at the eastern end, via the end of Atlantic Ave. and a pathway to the beach. Restrooms are wheelchair accessible. Limited on-street parking only. Call: (408) 688-3241. The Santa Cruz Museum nearby on E. Cliff Drive has natural science and history exhibits; open 10 AM–5 PM Tues.-Sat. and 1 PM–5 PM Sun.; Museum: (408) 429-3773.
Mass Transit: SCMTD Route 6, Seabright, to the corner of Seabright Ave. and Murray St.; 1/4-mile walk to the beach.

SANTA CRUZ SMALL CRAFT HARBOR: Upper and Lower Harbors are separated by Murray/Eaton Streets; there is a pedestrian/bike path around the perimeter of the harbor. Upper Harbor provides 526 boat berths; Lower Harbor has 398. Berths to 60 feet. Ramp is four-lanes, concrete, open 24 hours. Two hoists: cap. 1-ton and 40 tons, open 8 AM–5 PM. Fuel dock open 5:30 AM–5:00 PM. Fishing boat rentals and supplies available; restaurant and shops. Open all year. Transient vessels report to the harbor office at the southeast corner of the harbor for berth assignments. (408) 475-6161.
Mass Transit: SCMTD Route 6, Seabright, to the corner of Lake Ave. and E. Cliff Drive. Also 7N, 67, and 68.

STAIRWAY TO HARBOR: At Murray St.; wooden stairway with rail. Near U.C. Santa Cruz sailing facility.
Mass Transit: SCMTD Routes 6, 7N, 67, and 68.

PATH TO HARBOR: At Eaton St.; paved path serves bicycles and pedestrians.
Mass Transit: SCMTD Routes 6, 7N, 67, and 68.

PATH TO HARBOR: At the Coast Guard Station; access via Seabright Ave. to Marine Parade to Fairview Place.

TWIN LAKES STATE BEACH: On both sides of the harbor; 86 acres. Volleyball nets and standards, picnic area, jettyfishing. Schwanns Lagoon is a wildfowl refuge. Call: (408) 688-3241.
Mass Transit: SCMTD Routes 6, 7N, 67, and 68.

San Lorenzo Point

Littoral Current

Longshore sediment transport is a type of sand movement in the nearshore zone. Longshore transport is caused by the littoral current, which is established when waves move toward the shoreline at an oblique angle. Littoral current is a predominant characteristic along most of the California coast because the prevailing wave direction for much of the state is at an angle to the shoreline. The sand that is lifted by breaking waves is carried in the direction of the littoral current until it is stopped by a natural feature such as a headland or an artificial structure such as a breakwater.

The direction of littoral current can be determined simply by observing which direction a floating object just offshore moves with respect to a fixed point on shore. Although the force of the littoral current may not be noticeable to people in the water, bathers who find themselves leaving the water up or down coast from where they entered were probably moved there by the littoral current.

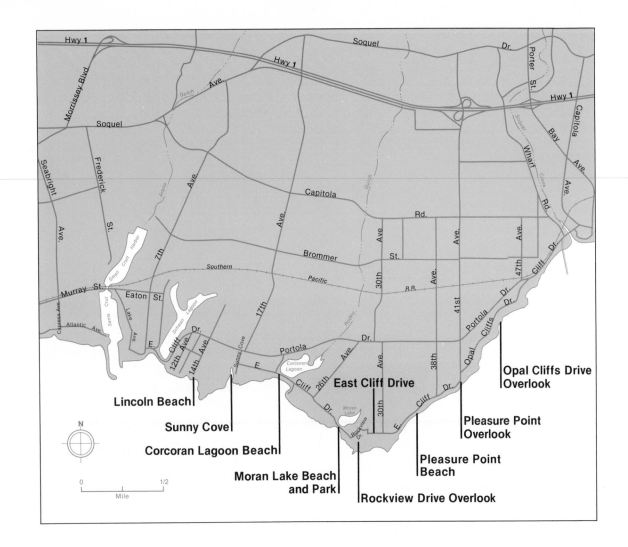

Santa Cruz County

LIVE OAK

NAME	LOCATION	Entrance/Parking Fee	Parking	Restrooms	Lifeguard	Campground	Showers	Firepits	Stairs to Beach	Path to Beach	Bike Path	Hiking Trail	Facilities for Disabled	Boating Facilities	Fishing	Equestrian Trail	Sandy Beach	Dunes	Rocky Shore	Upland from Beach	Stream Corridor	Bluff	Wetland
East Cliff Drive	Runs from Twin Lakes to 41st Ave.	•							•										•			•	
Lincoln Beach (Unit of Twin Lakes State Beach)	Foot of 14th Ave., Live Oak		•					•									•					•	•
Sunny Cove	Foot of Sunny Cove, Live Oak								•								•		•			•	
Corcoran Lagoon Beach	E. of 21st Ave. and E. Cliff Drive, Live Oak								•								•				•	•	
Moran Lake Beach	2700 block of E. Cliff Drive, Live Oak														•		•					•	
Moran Lake Park	N. of Moran Lake Beach, Live Oak	•	•										•							•			•
Rockview Drive Overlook	Foot of Rockview Dr., Live Oak	•							•										•			•	
Pleasure Point Overlook	E. Cliff Drive at 41st Ave., Live Oak	•																	•			•	
Pleasure Point Beach	E. Cliff Drive, 34th-36th Avenues, Live Oak	•													•		•		•			•	
Overlook on Opal Cliffs Drive	4500 block of Opal Cliffs Dr., Live Oak	•																	•			•	

EAST CLIFF DRIVE: Numerous scenic overlooks and parking pull-outs; bike lane. A bike path runs along both sides of 17th Ave. from Soquel Ave. to E. Cliff Drive and connects with the E. Cliff Drive bike lane.

LINCOLN BEACH: Wide, sandy beach; accessible to pedestrians via the end of 14th Ave., and via a stairway at the end of 12th Street. Bonita Lagoon, a small wetland, supports some wildfowl.
Mass Transit: Santa Cruz Metropolitan Transit District (SCMTD) Routes 67, 68, Live Oak.

SUNNY COVE: Pocket beach, accessible via the foot of Sunny Cove or Johans Beach Drive. Extent of public and private rights is undetermined; subject to further investigation.

CORCORAN LAGOON BEACH: The beach is seaward of E. Cliff Drive and the lagoon; a public walkway leads from the road to a sandy ocean beach and tidepools.
Mass Transit: SCMTD Routes 67, 68, Live Oak.

MORAN LAKE BEACH: Wide, sandy beach south of Moran Lake.
Mass Transit: SCMTD Routes 67, 68, Live Oak.

MORAN LAKE PARK: Nature trail on the northwest side of the lake.
Mass Transit: SCMTD Routes 67, 68, Live Oak.

ROCKVIEW DRIVE OVERLOOK: Excellent ocean view; popular spot to watch surfers. A stairway leads down to the shore.
Mass Transit: SCMTD Routes 67, 68, Live Oak.

PLEASURE POINT OVERLOOK: Another popular spot to watch surfers. Hazardous cliffs.
Mass Transit: SCMTD Routes 67, 68, Live Oak.

PLEASURE POINT BEACH: The stairway at 35th St. has been closed due to erosion; no safe vertical access to the beach. Pocket beaches are covered at high tide. Popular surfing spot; tidepools.
Mass Transit: SCMTD Routes 67, 68, Live Oak.

OVERLOOK AT OPAL CLIFFS DRIVE: Only six parking spaces available. Cliff highly eroded and hazardous; the stairway is partially destroyed and unusable. Private property on either side of the overlook; do not trespass.

Pleasure Point Overlook

Tides

The gradual rise and fall of sea level along the world's shorelines is caused by a long period wave commonly called the tide. Tides are generated by the sun's and moon's gravitational "pull" on the earth. As the sun and moon change positions relative to the earth, the ocean waters form a bulge that tends to face the moon as the earth rotates under it. The bulge traveling around the earth translates into the rise and fall in sea level. Generally, on the California coast the tide cycles from a high to low water level approximately twice a day. However, there is a difference between the two highs and lows, so that there is one high-low tide, one high-high tide, and one low-low and one low-high tide almost every day.

The tides go through a cycle of maximum and minimum differences in height every 14 days, so that there are two periods of extreme tides every lunar month. In regions where these tides coincide with the full and new moons, these extreme tides are called springs; the tides of minimum range, associated with the quarters of the moon, are called neaps. However, on the California coast the tides are more properly known as tropic and equatorial or declinational tides, because the periods of maximum and minimum ranges coincide more closely with the height of the moon in relation to the celestial equator than with the moon's phases.

Because the position of the earth with respect to the sun and moon can be determined for any period of time, the times and magnitudes of high and low tides can be predicted. Knowledge of the times of the tides is a useful aid to beach visitors. For example, those interested in tidepool study need to know when low tide occurs so they can view the exposed rock formations that make up the pools. Conversely, surf fishers should be aware of the high tide period because this is when fish come closest to shore in search of food.

Those visiting pocket beaches (i.e., small cove areas) or narrow beaches should also be aware of the tide cycles. Without such knowledge, a beachgoer at a pocket beach, for example, may find unexpectedly that as the tide rises, the access route out of the cove is cut off by breaking waves, and he or she may become trapped in a continually narrowing beach. Most newspapers that serve coastal communities publish tide tables for the local coastal area; it is recommended that these tide tables be consulted before visiting the beach. However, because tide predictions are derived by computer and cannot take into account those variable effects of wind and waves, these predictions are not always accurate.

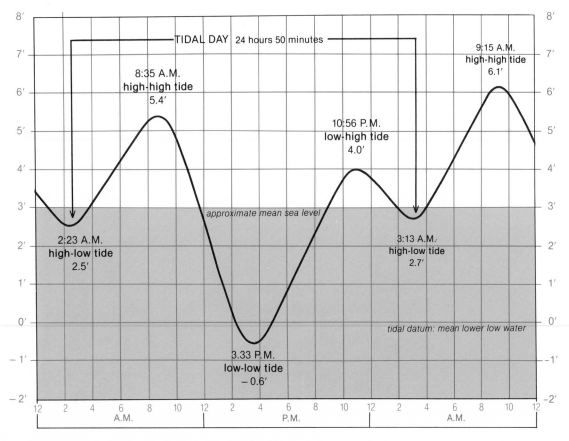

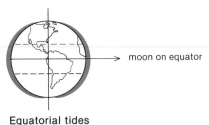

Declinational Tides

Tropic tides
tide cycle of greater range
(highest high and lowest low tides)

Equatorial tides
tide cycle of lesser range
(intermediate tides)

The times and heights of the tides shown here are only for illustrative purposes.

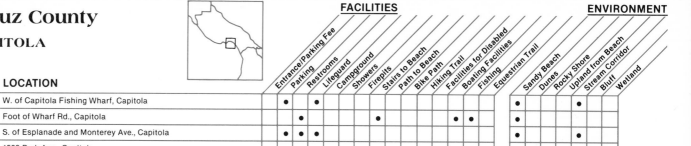

NAME	LOCATION	Entrance/Parking Fee	Parking	Restrooms	Lifeguard	Campground	Showers	Firepits	Stairs to Beach	Path to Beach	Bike Path	Hiking Trail	Facilities for Disabled	Boating Facilities	Fishing	Equestrian Trail	Sandy Beach	Dunes	Rocky Shore	Upland from Beach	Stream Corridor	Bluff	Wetland
Hooper Beach	W. of Capitola Fishing Wharf, Capitola	•		•													•		•				
Capitola Fishing Wharf	Foot of Wharf Rd., Capitola		•						•					•	•		•						
Capitola City Beach	S. of Esplanade and Monterey Ave., Capitola		•	•	•												•		•				
New Brighton State Beach	1500 Park Ave., Capitola	•	•	•	•	•	•	•	•	•		•	•		•		•			•		•	

HOOPER BEACH: Sandy beach adjacent to the Capitola Wharf.
Mass Transit: Santa Cruz Metropolitan Transit District (SCMTD) Routes 56, Depot Hill, and 58, Park Avenue.

CAPITOLA FISHING WHARF: Free public fishing access. Boat rentals; bait and tackle shop. A wooden stairway leads from the base of the pier to the beach.
Mass Transit: SCMTD Routes 56, Depot Hill, and 58, Park Avenue.

CAPITOLA CITY BEACH: Seaward of the Esplanade, which offers shops, restaurants, and galleries. The beach has volleyball standards and nets; benches line the sidewalk behind the beach. Popular swimming area.
Mass Transit: SCMTD Routes 56, Depot Hill, and 58, Park Avenue.

NEW BRIGHTON STATE BEACH: Four miles south of Santa Cruz on Highway 1 to Park Avenue exit. 68 acres. 115 campsites, sanitary station, and bicycle camping available; no trailer hookups; $6 camping fee. Restrooms are wheelchair accessible. Shoreline access via a stairway from the beach parking lot and also down a trail from the campground, which is upland. View of Monterey Bay. Interpretive nature trails; many species of wild birds. A small grunion run occurs spring to late summer. The beach is open all year; day use fee $2. En route camping $6. For Information, call: (408) 475-4850 or 688-3241.
Mass Transit: SCMTD Route 58, Park Avenue.

Capitola City Beach

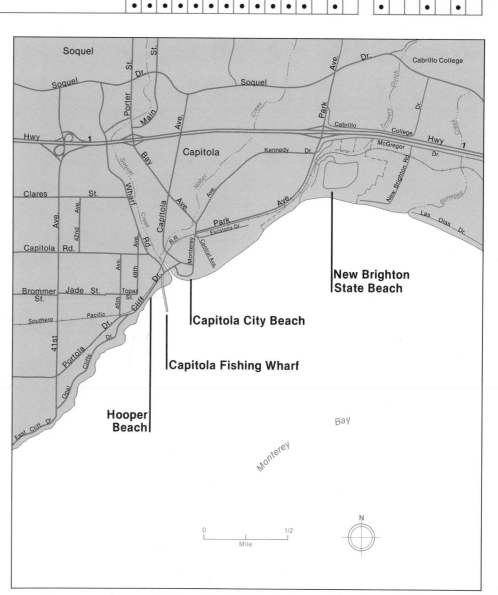

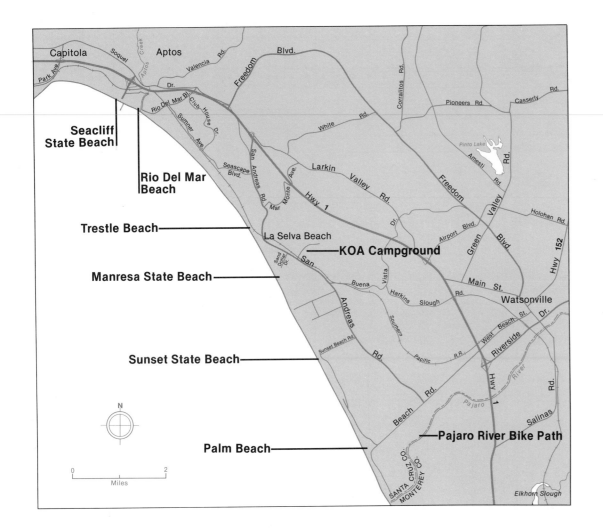

Seacliff State Beach

Rio Del Mar Beach

Trestle Beach

Manresa State Beach

Sunset State Beach

Palm Beach

KOA Campground

Pajaro River Bike Path

Capitola
Aptos

N

0   2
Miles

Seacliff State Beach

Santa Cruz County

CAPITOLA TO THE PAJARO RIVER

NAME	LOCATION	FACILITIES — Entrance/Parking Fee	Parking	Restrooms	Lifeguard	Campground	Showers	Firepits	Stairs to Beach	Path to Beach	Bike Path	Hiking Trail	Facilities for Disabled	Boating Facilities	Fishing	Equestrian Trail	ENVIRONMENT — Sandy Beach	Dunes	Rocky Shore	Upland from Beach	Stream Corridor	Bluff	Wetland
Seacliff State Beach and Pier	Foot of State Park Dr., Capitola	•	•	•	•	•	•	•	•				•	•	•		•				•	•	
Rio Del Mar Beach (Unit of Seacliff State Beach)	End of Rio Del Mar Blvd.		•	•					•		•						•				•	•	
Trestle Beach	N. of Manresa State Beach														•		•					•	
Santa Cruz KOA Campground	1186 San Andreas Rd., Watsonville	•	•	•		•	•	•												•			
Manresa State Beach	W. of San Andreas Rd. at Southern Pacific track, Watsonville	•	•	•				•	•						•		•					•	
Sunset State Beach	201 Sunset Beach Rd., Watsonville	•	•	•	•	•	•	•							•		•			•		•	
Palm Beach (Unit of Sunset State Beach)	Foot of Beach Rd., Watsonville		•	•					•	•	•						•	•					
Pajaro River Bike Path	Runs from corner of Holohan Rd. and Hwy. 152 to mouth of river										•									•			

SEACLIFF STATE BEACH: Take Highway 1 to Aptos-Seacliff exit. 85 acres, 26 campsites, trailer hookups right on the sand; camping fee $9. En route campsites $6. Large picnic area, shaded tables; day use fee $2. Northern limit of the Pismo clam. The fishing pier leads to a 435-foot concrete supply ship, the Palo Alto, which was built during WWI; formerly an amusement pier with a dance floor on deck. The ship is now closed; the fishing pier is open all year. The pier and the restrooms are wheelchair accessible. (408) 688-3222 or 688-3241.
Mass Transit: Santa Cruz Metropolitan Transit District (SCMTD) Route 54, Aptos/La Selva Beach.

RIO DEL MAR BEACH: Southern end of Seacliff State Beach; a pedestrian/bike path leads to Seacliff.
Mass Transit: SCMTD Route 54, Aptos/La Selva Beach.

TRESTLE BEACH: The beach directly north of Manresa State Beach is La Selva Beach, which is private; Trestle Beach is north of that. No access to the public beach from San Andreas Rd.; walk from Manresa below the mean high tide line.
Mass Transit: SCMTD Route 54, Aptos/La Selva Beach.

SANTA CRUZ KOA CAMPGROUND: Take Mar Monte exit off Highway 1, then take San Andreas Road. Private campground with laundry, snack bar, store, tennis, pool, hot tubs, etc. Open all year; $11.75/tentsite; $13.75/two-person vehicle with water and electricity April-September, $10.75 otherwise. $2 extra for sewer hookup. 238 sites; pets on leash allowed. Call: (408) 722-0551 or 722-2377.
Mass Transit: SCMTD Route 54, Aptos/La Selva Beach.

MANRESA STATE BEACH: Take Highway 1 to Mar Monte exit; take Mar Monte Ave. to San Andreas Road. There is access to the beach down the bluff via a stairway and path from the main parking lot at the north end, and via Sand Dollar Dr. to Sand Dollar Lane and through the gate to pathways between condominiums (walk through only). A new paved accessway off Sand Dollar Dr. leads to a parking lot, restroom, and stairway to the beach. The beach is famous for its Pismo clams, September through April. Unsafe swimming; good surfing. $2 day use fee. (408) 688-3241.
Mass Transit: SCMTD Route 54, Aptos/La Selva Beach to La Selva Beach; 1.5-mile walk to Manresa.

SUNSET STATE BEACH: South of Santa Cruz on Highway 1 to Mar Monte exit; take San Andreas Rd. to Sunset Beach Road. 218 acres, 90 campsites, no trailer hookups. Camping fee $6; day use fee $2. En route campsites also $6. Picnic area on the bluff behind the beach; in March and April poppies and bush lupine bloom in the surrounding meadows. Popular fishing spot. Pismo clams September-April. Seven miles of beachfront (including Palm Beach); unsafe swimming. Open all year. (408) 724-1266 or 688-3241.

PALM BEACH: South of Santa Cruz on Highway 1 to Watsonville 129 exit; take Beach Rd. west. The beach runs to the Pajaro River mouth. Picnic area, fitness trail. Open all year.

PAJARO RIVER BIKE PATH: The bike path, which runs for nearly nine miles, begins at the intersection of Holohan Rd. and Highway 152 and runs southwest to the mouth of the Pajaro River, paralleling the river for about six miles.

Rio Del Mar Beach

Big Sur Coast

Monterey County

Monterey County's coastline is one of the most beautiful in the State, stretching from the flat coastal plain around Monterey Bay in the north, through the steep hills of the Monterey Peninsula, to the magnificent, rugged Big Sur Coast.

Monterey Bay was sighted in 1542 by Juan Rodríguez Cabrillo, and visited again sixty years later by Sebastián Vizcaíno, who named it in honor of his Mexican viceroy, the Count of Monte Rey. In 1770 Gaspar de Portolá and Padre Junípero Serra established the Presidio and the second California mission. The settlement was immediately successful largely because of abundant timber, fertile soil, and mild weather.

Prior to Spanish settlement the Monterey Bay area was inhabited by the Costanoan Indians, who were hunter-gatherers, shellfish being their primary food source. During the Spanish occupation the Indians were concentrated in the missions, but following the secularization of the missions by the Mexicans, the Indians were dispersed, and eventually disappeared. By 1920, there were only 56 surviving Costanoans.

Moss Landing, the northernmost coastal town in Monterey, was established in the 1860's by Captain Charles Moss, and soon became a bustling harbor and whaling station. Now it's a pleasure and fishing boat harbor, with antique shops, flea markets, and restaurants.

Monterey Peninsula, at the southwest end of Monterey Bay, is the focal point of the county, with its towns of Monterey, Pacific Grove, Pebble Beach, and Carmel. Historically, the City of Monterey was the capital of Alta California under both Spanish and Mexican rule. Today, the "Path of History" meanders through the city and passes many historic buildings and sites. Cannery Row, made famous by John Steinbeck's novel, *Cannery Row,* was the site of flourishing sardine canneries in the 1940's until the sardines suddenly vanished. Today only one cannery still operates, but Cannery Row is a tourist attraction with shops, restaurants, and galleries.

Pacific Grove, on the north side of the peninsula, is noted for its beautiful flowering ice plant, *Mesembryanthemum,* and the millions of Monarch butterflies which winter in the trees. 17-Mile Drive winds through the forested hills and along the rocky coast of the Del Monte Forest and Pebble Beach. Carmel-by-the-Sea, at the southwest edge of the peninsula, is a Mediterranean-like village which has become a mecca for both artists and tourists with its shops on the hill, sailboats in the water, and clean, white sandy beach on Carmel Bay.

South of Carmel is Point Lobos State Reserve, a magnificent headland with trails leading through Monterey cypress groves and along the shore, tidepools rich in aquatic life, and sea lions and otters in the offshore kelp beds.

South of Point Lobos, Highway 1 narrows and winds along the Big Sur Coast between the steep Santa Lucia Mountains and the sparkling Pacific Ocean. There are many pull-offs with spectacular vistas, and several public picnic areas and beaches along Highway 1; Los Padres National Forest and the Ventana Wilderness begin at the coast and stretch inland for miles, providing numerous hiking trails and campsites. The original inhabitants of the Big Sur Coast were the Esselen Indians, who lived from Point Sur to Lucia; the Salinans, who lived south of Lucia; and the Costanoans, who lived along the coast from the Palo Colorado Canyon to the Big Sur River mouth.

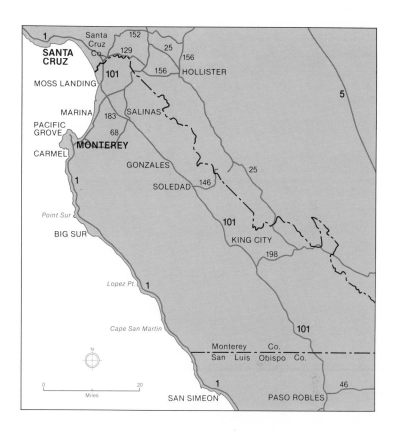

For more information on Monterey County's coast, write or call: Monterey Peninsula Chamber of Commerce, 380 Alvarado (P.O. Box 1770), Monterey 93940, (408) 649-3200; Pacific Grove Chamber of Commerce on Forest and Central Avenues (P.O. Box 167), Pacific Grove 93950, (408) 373-3304; or Carmel Business Association on San Carlos and 7th Avenue (P.O. Box 4444), Carmel 93922, (408) 624-2522.

For transit information, contact Monterey-Salinas Transit: One Ryan Ranch Road, Monterey 93940, (408) 899-2555 or 424-7695, or Coastlines Bus Service: (408) 649-4700.

Wetlands

Wetlands are areas where the land meets the water in a gradual transition, characterized by wet soils or by plants adapted to a wet environment; a variety of coastal areas are categorized as wetlands, including salt marshes, freshwater or brackish water marshes, shallow-water lagoons, tidal mudflats, salt flats, and fens.

Coastal wetlands are usually created by the flow of sediments into a bay, river mouth, or other shallow area, forming a delta. This delta gradually builds up to an elevation above low tide level; at that point, plants such as cordgrass and other salt marsh species move in. These plants slow the currents and trap more sediments, causing the wetlands to expand further. As more sediment becomes trapped on the delta, upland plant species take over, converting prior wetlands to uplands. Thus, like most natural landforms, wetlands are continuously subject to periodic creation and destruction.

Up until 500 years ago, wetlands covered over 300,000 acres of California's coastal areas, not including the San Francisco Bay area. Only 70,000 acres of coastal wetlands remain today. Diking and filling of wetlands for development projects account for much of this loss. In addition, soil erosion from hillsides has tripled the rate of sedimentation of wetlands during the last hundred years. If wetland sedimentation continues at this level, many remaining wetlands will be lost as well.

Ecologists have found that coastal wetlands are essential habitats for certain fish, birds, and mammals; in addition, many migratory ducks, geese, and shorebirds depend on wetlands for feeding and nesting. San Diego Bay wetlands, for example, seasonally support more than 180 species of birds, 50 species of mammals, 43 species of fish, and thousands of smaller organisms such as crabs, mussels, and ghost shrimp. Elkhorn Slough in Monterey County contains similar numbers of species, including more than 90,000 gaper clams, one of the species sought by clammers.

Of the ten species of birds and mammals listed by the Department of Fish and Game as endangered in California, eight are either directly dependent on or somehow associated with wetlands, such as the salt marsh harvest mouse, the California clapper rail, and the California least tern.

Wetlands also provide a number of direct and indirect benefits to humans. They help stabilize shorelines; they can be used to absorb flood waters, lessening the need for costly flood control measures; and they purify coastal waters through natural sewage treatment, trapping sediments which would otherwise fill navigation channels. Wetlands are also significant recreation resources and provide opportunities for fishing and bird watching, as well as for nature study and scientific research.

Since wetlands are so valuable from both an economic and biologic standpoint, the California Coastal Act, and many other federal and state statutes and regulations, mandate governmental regulation in these areas to protect and restore California's wetlands.

Elkhorn Slough, Near Kirby Park Fishing Access

Monterey County
MOSS LANDING/ELKHORN SLOUGH

NAME	LOCATION	Entrance/Parking Fee	Parking	Restrooms	Lifeguard	Campground	Showers	Firepits	Stairs to Beach	Path to Beach	Bike Path	Hiking Trail	Facilities for Disabled	Boating Facilities	Fishing	Equestrian Trail	Sandy Beach	Dunes	Rocky Shore	Upland from Beach	Stream Corridor	Bluff	Wetland
Zmudowski State Beach	Foot of Giberson Rd., Moss Landing		•						•					•	•		•	•		•			•
Moss Landing State Beach	Hwy. 1 at Jetty Rd., Moss Landing		•	•										•	•		•	•					•
Moss Landing Harbor	Sandholdt Rd., W. of Hwy. 1, Moss Landing	•	•	•										•	•					•			•
Moss Landing Marine Laboratory	W. of Sandholdt Rd., Moss Landing		•												•		•	•					
Elkhorn Slough	E. of Hwy. 1 at Moss Landing		•											•	•								•
Kirby Park	Kirby Rd., W. of Elkhorn Rd., Moss Landing		•											•	•								•
Royal Oaks County Park	537 Maher Rd., N. of Prunedale	•	•	•			•					•	•		•					•			
Salinas River State Beach	W. of Hwy. 1 at Potrero Rd., Moss Landing		•	•											•		•	•		•			•

ZMUDOWSKI STATE BEACH: 177 acres. Private agricultural lands are adjacent to Giberson Rd., which leads to the beach; do not trespass. McClusky Slough is to the east. Climb steep, vegetated dunes to the sandy beach; surfing and clamming. Horses are permitted. Information: (408) 688-3241.

MOSS LANDING STATE BEACH: Also known as Jetty Beach; 55 acres. Bennett Slough is at the northeast end. The jetty extends into the ocean; view of the harbor. Surfing and clamming. Information: (408) 688-3241.

MOSS LANDING HARBOR: Take Highway 1 to Moss Landing Rd. to Sandholdt Road. T-shaped harbor considered to be an extremely safe refuge; commercial fishing and pleasure boating. Guest slips are available from the Harbormaster, whose office is near the inner turning basin.

Facilities include slips and dry storage; fuel dock and boat ramp in the South Harbor; hoist: cap. 50 tons, open 8 AM-5 PM; pumpout station; yacht club, restaurants, and shops. Supplies, fishing licenses, bait and tackle available. New two-lane boat ramp under construction in the north harbor area. Harbor: Box 102, Moss Landing 95039; (408) 633-2461. Skipper's, off Highway 1 north of the Sandholdt Bridge, is private and has boat and fishing docks, and a large parking lot; fee.

MOSS LANDING MARINE LABORATORY: A research and educational institution; public access to the shore is across the dunes adjacent to the marine laboratory building; fishing and surfing.

ELKHORN SLOUGH: Tidal slough used extensively for research and education. Small fishing and pleasure boats can be taken from the harbor into the slough at low tides; small boat launch at Kirby Park. Two endangered bird species, the California brown pelican and the California clapper rail, are found here; the peregrine falcon and golden eagle have also been spotted.

The Elkhorn Slough Estuarine Sanctuary presently encompasses about 1,250 acres of wetlands and uplands adjacent to the slough; not yet open to the public. Planned facilities include a visitor center with interpretive displays, parking areas, and trails. For information, call (408) 728-0560.

KIRBY PARK: 10-acre public fishing access at the northeast end of Elkhorn Slough; operated by the Moss Landing Harbor District. Popular shore fishing area. Small boat launching ramp available; however, it is underwater at seasonal high tides, and during lowest tides is totally out of the water.

ROYAL OAKS COUNTY PARK: The only developed park in the north county; 122 acres including several picnic areas with barbecues and tables, modified restrooms for the disabled, tennis courts, a softball field, a meeting room, and hiking trails. Day use fee.

SALINAS RIVER STATE BEACH: 246 acres. There are two entrances, one at the end of Potrero Rd. off Highway 1, the other at the end of Monterey Dunes Way off Molera Rd., both with small parking lots. Steep dunes; broad, sandy beach. Fishing, clamming, and hiking. Information: (408) 688-3241. The Salinas Wildlife Area, 518 acres owned by the U.S. Fish and Wildlife Service as a wildlife refuge and managed by the State Department of Fish and Game, is just south of the State Beach; no facilities other than trails and a small parking lot.

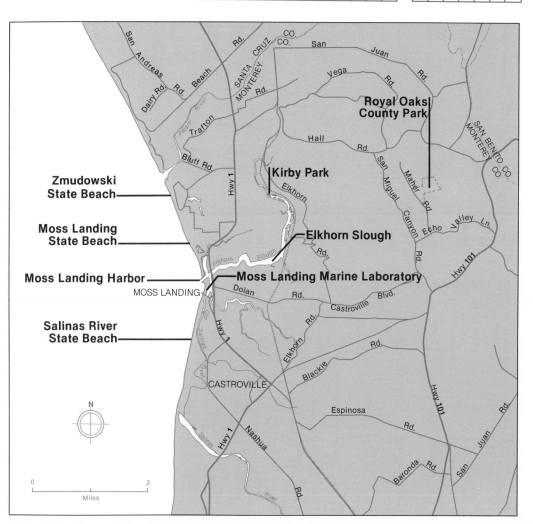

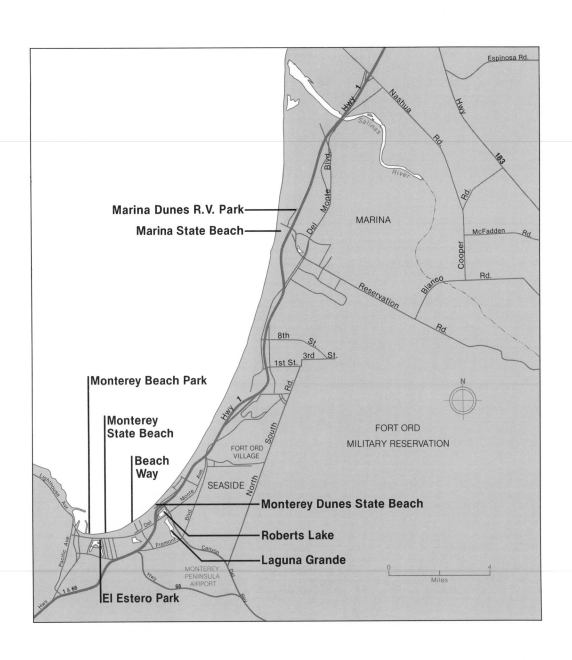

Marina State Beach

Monterey County
MARINA/SEASIDE/MONTEREY

NAME	LOCATION	FACILITIES															ENVIRONMENT						
		Entrance/Parking Fee	Parking	Restrooms	Lifeguard	Campground	Showers	Firepits	Stairs to Beach	Path to Beach	Bike Path	Hiking Trail	Facilities for Disabled	Boating Facilities	Fishing	Equestrian Trail	Sandy Beach	Dunes	Rocky Shore	Upland from Beach	Stream Corridor	Bluff	Wetland
Marina Dunes R.V. Park	3330 Dunes Dr., Marina	●	●	●		●	●										●			●			
Marina State Beach	Foot of Reservation Rd., Marina		●	●						●					●		●	●				●	
Monterey Dunes State Beach	Foot of Sand Dunes Dr., Monterey		●	●													●	●					
Roberts Lake	Roberts Ave. and Canyon Del Rey, Seaside		●																	●			●
Laguna Grande Accessway	Del Monte Ave. and Canyon Del Rey, Seaside													●						●			●
Beach Way Access	Beach Way and Tide Ave., Monterey		●	●													●	●					
Monterey State Beach	Foot of Park Ave., off Del Monte Ave., Monterey		●												●		●						
El Estero Park	Del Monte Ave. and Camino El Estero, Monterey		●	●				●						●							●		●
Monterey Beach Park	E. of Municipal Wharf, Monterey		●	●	●												●						
Monterey Peninsula Hostel	Call (408) 373-4166	●																					

MARINA DUNES R.V. PARK: Take the Reservation Rd. exit off Highway 1, turn right, then right again on Dunes Drive. Private R. V. campground with 33 sites and all hookups; $15/two-person vehicle during summer. Open all year; pets on leash allowed. Reservations required. Beach access is via Marina State Beach to the west. Information: (408) 384-6914.
Mass Transit: Monterey-Salinas Transit (MST) Routes 7, 12, and 20.

MARINA STATE BEACH: 131 acres. The parking lot, restrooms, and ranger's residence are at the main entrance at the foot of Reservation Rd.; there is also pedestrian access to the southern part of the beach through a gate on the west side of Lake Court, then via a steep, sandy trail across the dunes. The beach closes at sunset. Popular for hang-gliding and fishing; swimming is unsafe due to dangerous surf and rip currents. Information: (408) 649-2836. Do not trespass onto the Fort Ord Military Reservation shoreline to the south, which is adjacent to the rifle range.
Mass Transit: MST Routes 7, 12, and 20; walk west on Reservation Rd.

MONTEREY DUNES STATE BEACH: 22 acres; sandy beach and dunes. Undeveloped access via Sand Dollar Drive. Chemical toilets available. There is a wooden cross commemorating the landing of Portolá in the 1700's. The gate is locked at night.
Mass Transit: MST Routes 7, 12, and 20.

ROBERTS LAKE: Currently undeveloped; used for model boat racing and duck feeding. Parking along Roberts Avenue. Planned improvements include more parking, landscaping, a walkway, picnic tables, restrooms, and a model boat staging area. A portion will be designated as a waterfowl protection area.
Mass Transit: MST Routes 7, 12, and 20.

LAGUNA GRANDE ACCESSWAY: Undeveloped wetland area; used for jogging and picnicking. The proposed regional park, currently under construction, will include restrooms, parking, non-power boating facilities, a group picnic area, play area, pedestrian trail, bicycle path, and a natural preserve.
Mass Transit: MST Routes 7, 8, 12, and 20.

BEACH WAY ACCESS: Small parking area and sloping sandy beach at the end of Beach Way.
Mass Transit: MST Routes 7, 12, and 20.

MONTEREY STATE BEACH: Narrow, sandy, 14-acre beach; hazardous surf. Dogs are permitted if leashed. Limited on-street parking. There is access also from Monterey Beach Park to the west. Information: (408) 649-2836.
Mass Transit: MST Routes 7, 12, and 20.

EL ESTERO PARK: Alongside El Estero Lake; popular for duck feeding. Facilities include benches, picnic tables, par course, snack bar, and canoe, kayak, and paddleboat rentals. Dennis the Menace Play Area across the lake was designed by Hank Ketcham, creator of the comic strip; open 10 AM-sundown, and contains a Southern Pacific steam locomotive, wading pools, and other unusual play equipment. Monterey Tennis Center at Jacks Ball Park, two blocks west on Franklin and Figueroa Streets, has four tennis courts which are lit at night.
Mass Transit: MST Routes 7, 12, 20, and 21. No service on Route 21 Sundays and holidays.

MONTEREY BEACH PARK: Wide, sandy beach just east of the Municipal Wharf; parking at the wharf lot. Lifeguard near the wharf only during the summer.
Mass Transit: MST Routes 7, 12, and 20.

MONTEREY PENINSULA HOSTEL: Open summers only. Currently no permanent facility. Call the YMCA for hostel location and information: (408) 373-4166.

Monterey Dunes State Beach

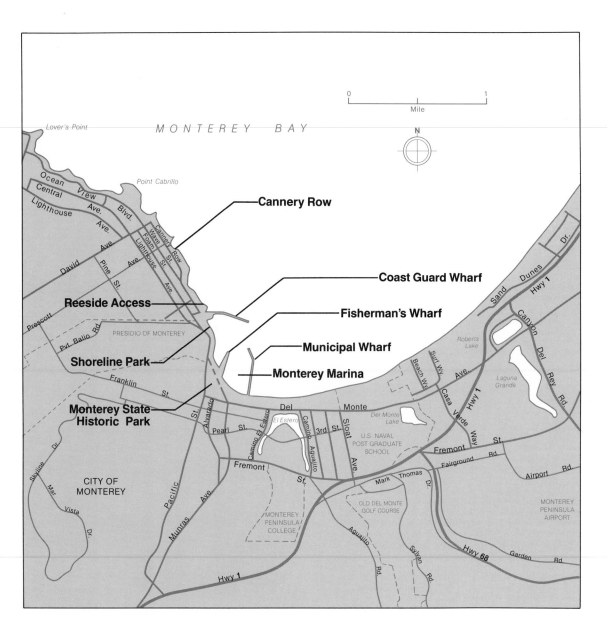

MONTEREY BAY

Lover's Point

Point Cabrillo

0   1
Mile

N

Cannery Row

Coast Guard Wharf

Reeside Access

Fisherman's Wharf

Municipal Wharf

Shoreline Park

Monterey Marina

**Monterey State
Historic Park**

Ocean View Blvd.
Central Ave.
Lighthouse Ave.
David Ave.
Pine St.
Lighthouse Ave.
Prescott Ave.
Pvt. Ballo Rd.
PRESIDIO OF MONTEREY
Franklin St.
Del Monte
El Estero
Camino El Estero
Camino Aguajito
3rd St.
Sloat Ave.
Pearl St.
Fremont St.
Alvarado St.
Del St.
Skyline Dr.
Mar Vista Dr.
CITY OF
MONTEREY
Pacific St.
Munras Ave.
MONTEREY
PENINSULA
COLLEGE
U.S. NAVAL
POST GRADUATE
SCHOOL
Del Monte
Lake
Mark Thomas Dr.
OLD DEL MONTE
GOLF COURSE
Aguajito Rd.
Sylvan Rd.
Hwy 68
Garden Rd.
Hwy 1
Fremont St.
Fairground Rd.
Airport Rd.
MONTEREY
PENINSULA
AIRPORT
Laguna
Grande
Roberts
Lake
Surf Wy.
Beach Wy.
Casa Verde Way
Hwy 1
Sand Dunes
Canyon Del Rey Rd.
Dr.

Monterey Marina, Fisherman's Wharf

Monterey County

CITY OF MONTEREY

NAME	LOCATION	Entrance/Parking Fee	Parking	Restrooms	Lifeguard	Campground	Showers	Firepits	Stairs to Beach	Path to Beach	Bike Path	Hiking Trail	Facilities for Disabled	Boating Facilities	Fishing	Equestrian Trail	Sandy Beach	Dunes	Rocky Shore	Upland from Beach	Stream Corridor	Bluff	Wetland
Municipal Wharf	Wharf #2, foot of Figueroa St., Monterey	●	●	●										●	●								
Monterey Marina	Del Monte Ave. and Figueroa St., Monterey	●	●	●										●									
Fisherman's Wharf	Foot of Olivier St., Monterey	●	●																				
Monterey State Historic Park	Headquarters at 210 Olivier St., Monterey		●	●																●			
Shoreline Park	Lighthouse Curve and Foam Ave., Monterey										●									●			
Coast Guard Wharf	S.E. end of Wave St., Monterey		●	●					●						●		●		●				
Reeside Access	Foot of Reeside Ave., Monterey									●									●				
Cannery Row	Cannery Row, Monterey	●	●												●		●		●				

MUNICIPAL WHARF: Located in Monterey Harbor; built in 1926. Used by commercial fishermen to unload their boats and clean their fish; includes a snack bar, supplies, bait and tackle, and a boat hoist: cap. 2 tons, open all year. Boat hoist: (408) 372-9547. Metered parking 9 AM-9 PM daily. A pedestrian walkway extends along the harbor between the Municipal Wharf and Fisherman's Wharf.
Mass Transit: Monterey-Salinas Transit (MST) Routes 7, 12, and 20.

MONTEREY MARINA: Just west of the Municipal Wharf; open all year. The office is located in the trailer between Wharf #1 and #2. Facilities include two public ramps, each two-lanes concrete, open 24 hours, a hoist, and a fuel dock open 8 AM-5 PM, closed Sunday. Slips, moorings, boat and motor rentals, marine supplies, charter boats, fishing licenses, bait and tackle available. No fishing in the marina. Metered parking. (408) 646-3950.
Mass Transit: MST Routes 7, 12, and 20.

FISHERMAN'S WHARF: Adjacent to the marina; picturesque tourist spot with fish markets, restaurants, shops, galleries, the Wharf Theatre, and the Sea Garden Diving Bell. Sea lions are frequently seen in the bay, begging for food. Metered parking in the lot 9 AM-9 PM daily.
Mass Transit: MST Routes 1, 2, 7, 12, and 20.

MONTEREY STATE HISTORIC PARK: Park Headquarters and restrooms are at 210 Olivier Street. The park consists of ten historic buildings and sites in old Monterey, including the Custom House at Custom House Plaza; Casa Del Oro at Scott and Olivier Streets, which exhibits trade items of early Monterey; California's First Theatre at Scott and Pacific Streets, open as a monument 9 AM-5 PM Tues.-Sun., with 19th century plays presented weekly; Pacific House at Custom House Plaza, which houses a museum of California history and a collection of Indian artifacts; and Larkin House at Jefferson St. and Calle Principal, which was designed and built by Thomas Larkin in the 1830's and became the pattern for the "Monterey" style of architecture. Guide maps and brochures are available at Park Headquarters; for information, call: (408) 649-2836.
Mass Transit: MST Routes 1, 2, 7, 12, and 20 to Park Headquarters.

Pacific House, Monterey State Historic Park

SHORELINE PARK: Narrow, grassy strip along Monterey Bay, with a walkway, benches, and bike path. The Presidio of Monterey is on the hillside just west of the park overlooking the harbor.
Mass Transit: MST Routes 1 and 2. No service on Route 2 Sundays and holidays.

COAST GUARD WHARF: Two Coast Guard cutters are moored here; a parking lot and boat launch are south of the wharf. Popular area for diving; there is access from the wharf via a stairway to San Carlos Beach. Private property is adjacent to the beach; do not trespass. The public may walk out onto the wharf; a rocky outcropping at the end of the wharf is a haul-out for seals and sea lions.
Mass Transit: MST Routes 1 and 2. No service on Route 2 Sundays and holidays.

REESIDE ACCESS: At the City of Monterey Pumping Plant; access over the rocks to San Carlos Beach just south.
Mass Transit: MST Routes 1 and 2. No service on Route 2 Sundays and holidays.

Custom House, Monterey State Historic Park

CANNERY ROW: Formerly the site of a flourishing sardine canning industry in the first part of the century until the sardines mysteriously vanished from Monterey Bay in 1946; the street was immortalized by Nobel and Pulitzer prizewinning author John Steinbeck. Cannery Row is now a tourist attraction with shops, restaurants, and galleries. The new Monterey Bay Aquarium at David Ave. is currently under construction, and will include numerous tanks (one more than two stories high), exhibits, galleries, and will offer tours and programs; scheduled for completion November 1984.

Public access to Macabee Beach between McClellan and Prescott Avenues is next to the Casa Maria Restaurant, and from the parking lot at the northern end of the beach. Access to the rocky promontory at the end of the Chart House Restaurant is via a walkway under the building.
Mass Transit: MST Routes 1 and 2. No service on Route 2 Sundays and holidays.

Monarch Butterfly

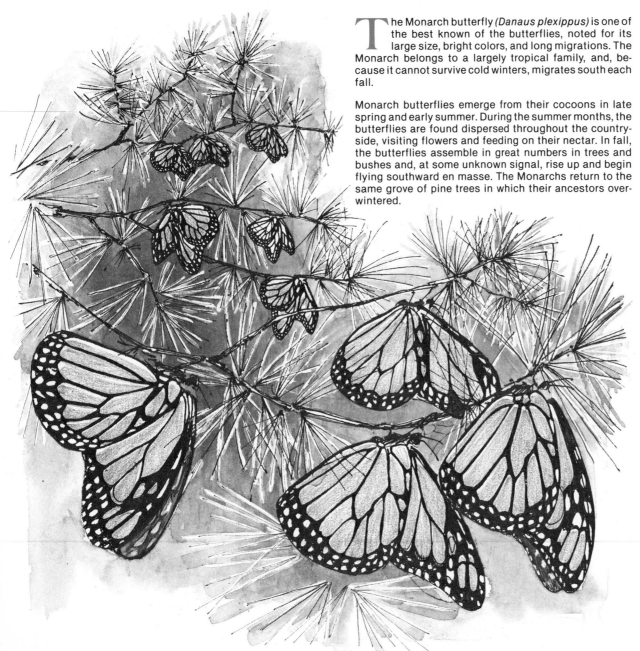

The Monarch butterfly *(Danaus plexippus)* is one of the best known of the butterflies, noted for its large size, bright colors, and long migrations. The Monarch belongs to a largely tropical family, and, because it cannot survive cold winters, migrates south each fall.

Monarch butterflies emerge from their cocoons in late spring and early summer. During the summer months, the butterflies are found dispersed throughout the countryside, visiting flowers and feeding on their nectar. In fall, the butterflies assemble in great numbers in trees and bushes and, at some unknown signal, rise up and begin flying southward en masse. The Monarchs return to the same grove of pine trees in which their ancestors overwintered.

At their wintering grounds they pack themselves tightly together in the trees, and remain there in a state of semi-dormancy until spring. The evergreen pines may be so filled with butterflies that the trees appear orange. When spring arrives, the Monarchs fly northward individually, not as a band.

The life expectancy of a Monarch is about a year, and not all adults survive the entire journey back north. Some fly part way, lay their eggs and die; their progeny then continue north, even as far as Canada. The butterflies that return south the following fall are the descendants of those that migrated north in the spring.

There are two major populations of Monarchs in the United States. Members of the eastern population migrate as far as 3,000 miles to overwintering spots in central Mexico. The western population returns to wintering grounds along the California coast. Monarchs overwinter in many places along our coast, but the best known spot is Pacific Grove, where thousands of Monarchs may be seen during the winter months in "butterfly trees" throughout the town. Monarchs are protected by law in Pacific Grove, and anyone disturbing them may receive a fine or a jail sentence.

Monarch butterflies are somewhat protected from predation because they feed on milkweed, a poisonous plant which makes the Monarchs themselves inedible to birds. A bird which has tasted one Monarch and become sick learns not to eat other Monarchs. The Monarch's bright, highly visible "warning coloration" serves to remind potential predators of the butterfly's toxicity. The Viceroy butterfly *(Limenitis archippus)* possesses coloration and habits almost identical to those of the Monarch, and enjoys a certain degree of protection from predation because of this "protective mimicry." Potential predators mistake the edible Viceroy for the unpalatable Monarch, and therefore avoid the Viceroy.

The Monarch, like other butterflies, passes through four stages of development, in a process called metamorphosis. The female Monarch lays her eggs on the underside of a leaf, usually of a milkweed plant. The striped caterpillar that emerges three to twelve days later immediately starts feeding on the milkweed. After several molts, the full-grown larva finds a sheltered spot and sheds its skin once again, revealing a pale green pupa, or chrysalis. This is a resting stage during which the insect reorganizes physiologically to form a butterfly. After about two weeks the adult Monarch emerges from the chrysalis. The process from egg to adult takes about five weeks.

Monterey County

PACIFIC GROVE

NAME	LOCATION	Entrance/Parking Fee	Parking	Restrooms	Lifeguard	Campground	Showers	Firepits	Stairs to Beach	Path to Beach	Bike Path	Hiking Trail	Facilities for Disabled	Boating Facilities	Fishing	Equestrian Trail	Sandy Beach	Dunes	Rocky Shore	Upland from Beach	Stream Corridor	Bluff	Wetland
Shoreline Park	Along Ocean View Blvd., between Pt. Cabrillo and Lover's Pt., Pacific Grove		•														•		•			•	
Berwick Park	Ocean View Blvd. and Monterey Ave., Pacific Grove		•					•									•		•			•	
Lover's Point	17th St. and Ocean View Blvd., Pacific Grove	•	•	•			•	•				•	•	•			•		•			•	
Perkins Park	Along Ocean View Blvd., N.W. of Lover's Point, Pacific Grove		•				•	•	•								•		•			•	
Point Pinos Lighthouse Reservation	End of Lighthouse Ave., W. of Asilomar Ave., Pacific Grove		•															•	•				
Asilomar State Beach and Conference Grounds	Pico Ave. at Sunset Dr., Pacific Grove		•												•		•	•	•			•	

SHORELINE PARK: Runs along the blufftops above the shore, and provides paths, benches, and a view of the bay. Access to several pocket beaches is via steep paths or by climbing over rip-rap; hazardous surf. Vivid pink and lavender ice plant blooms from April through August along the bluffs. Street parking.
Mass Transit: Monterey-Salinas Transit (MST) Routes 1 and 2. No service on Route 2 Sundays and holidays.

BERWICK PARK: Narrow, grassy park south of the railroad tracks, with benches and a path; street parking only. Nearby Andy Jacobsen Park at the foot of 7th St. and Ocean View Blvd. is a small landscaped park on a slope. Greenwood Park at the foot of 13th St. and Ocean View Blvd. is a grassy park with a foot bridge which crosses a small creek running through the center of the park; view of the bay.
Mass Transit: MST Routes 1 and 2. No service on Route 2 Sundays and holidays.

LOVER'S POINT: Grassy blufftop area with benches, paths, picnic tables and grills, plus a fishing pier and three small protected sandy beaches accessible by stairways. Wheelchair access to the pier and to the beach south of the pier. Popular diving and surfing spot; no dogs allowed. Glass-bottomed boat rides available in the summer for viewing underwater marine life. Metered parking lot.

The Pacific Grove Marine Gardens Fish Refuge is offshore; it is illegal to take any marine or plant life without a permit. The Pacific Grove Museum of Natural History at Forest and Central Avenues is free and is open 10 AM-5 PM Tues.-Sun.; exhibits include displays of birds, shells, butterflies, fish, marine mammals, and Indian artifacts. Museum: (408) 372-4212.
Mass Transit: MST Route 2. No service Sundays and holidays.

PERKINS PARK: Blufftop park with benches and a spectacular view of the bay; paths wind through the ice plant. There is a small parking lot at the foot of Beach St., and another at the foot of Asilomar Ave., where there are picnic tables and grills overlooking the shore. Four stairways provide access to small pocket beaches. Undeveloped Esplanade Park is at Esplanade and Ocean View Blvd.
Mass Transit: MST Route 2. No service Sundays and holidays.

POINT PINOS LIGHTHOUSE RESERVATION: The lighthouse was built in 1855 of 18-inch thick granite quarried on site; now the oldest operating lighthouse on the west coast. Open to the public Sat. and Sun. 1 PM-4 PM; small Coast Guard historical museum. The Reservation is a preserve for plants and wildlife, such as the rare Tidestrom's lupine, deer, sea otters, and pelicans. No pets allowed.

The Pacific Grove Municipal Golf Course is east of the Reservation; tiny Crespi Pond is a bird sanctuary. Golf Course: (408) 375-3456 or 373-3063.
Mass Transit: MST Route 2. No service Sundays and holidays.

ASILOMAR STATE BEACH AND CONFERENCE GROUNDS: Rugged rocky shore with dunes, tidepools, and sandy beach areas; ice plant lines the road. Diving area. Unsafe swimming; hazardous rip currents. Dogs on leash only. Parking along Sunset Drive. The nonprofit Conference Grounds, in a beautifully wooded and landscaped setting, provide conference space and lodging. Conference Center: 800 Asilomar Avenue, Pacific Grove 93950; call (408) 372-8016.
Mass Transit: MST Route 1.

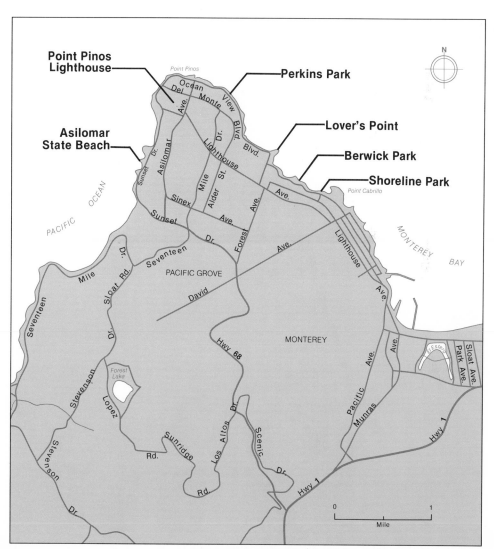

Monterey Pine and Monterey Cypress

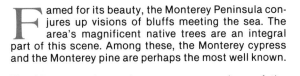

Famed for its beauty, the Monterey Peninsula conjures up visions of bluffs meeting the sea. The area's magnificent native trees are an integral part of this scene. Among these, the Monterey cypress and the Monterey pine are perhaps the most well known.

The Monterey pine and cypress are members of the 'closed cone pine forest' plant community – they are evergreen, conebearing plants growing on or near the coast from sea level to about 1,000 feet. Both occur in relatively cool climates with much fog, and reach a height of about 100 feet. Although each starts as a symmetrical tree, with age they both become flat-topped and frequently take on a characteristic windblown appearance.

Monterey pine *(Pinus radiata)* is quite easy to distinguish from a cypress by its needle-like leaves which occur in clusters. There are only four native stands in the world; the only mainland stands are on Año Nuevo Point in Santa Cruz County, on the Monterey Peninsula, and in Cambria in San Luis Obispo County. The fourth is located on islands off Baja California. This tree has been planted outside its native range and has, in fact, become the most important cultivated timber tree in the Southern Hemisphere even though its use in California, where it is vulnerable to natural 'pests' and diseases, is severely limited.

The Monterey cypress *(Cupressus macrocarpa)* is restricted to two native stands. Both are on the Monterey Peninsula immediately adjacent to the sea. The larger is at Pebble Beach, the second in Point Lobos State Reserve. Monterey cypress has been extensively planted along the coast as an ornamental and windbreak.

Monterey pine *Pinus radiata*

Monterey cypress *Cupressus macrocarpa*

Monterey County
17-MILE DRIVE/CARMEL

NAME	LOCATION	Entrance/Parking Fee	Parking	Restrooms	Lifeguard	Campground	Showers	Firepits	Stairs to Beach	Path to Beach	Bike Path	Hiking Trail	Facilities for Disabled	Boating Facilities	Fishing	Equestrian Trail	Sandy Beach	Dunes	Rocky Shore	Upland from Beach	Stream Corridor	Bluff	Wetland
17-Mile Drive	Between Pacific Grove and Carmel, Del Monte Forest	•	•	•											•	•	•	•	•	•		•	
Seal and Bird Rocks	Bird Rock Rd., 17-Mile Drive		•	•															•				
Fanshell Beach	Signal Hill Rd., 17-Mile Drive		•												•		•						
Cypress Point Lookout	W. of the foot of Portola Rd., 17-Mile Drive		•																•				
The Lone Cypress	S.E. of Cypress Point, 17-Mile Drive		•																•				
Pescadero Point	1 mi. S.E. of Cypress Point, 17-Mile Drive		•																•	•		•	
Carmel City Beach	Foot of Ocean Ave., Carmel		•	•			•	•							•		•		•			•	
Carmel River State Beach	Scenic Rd. at Carmelo St., Carmel		•	•					•	•					•		•	•			•	•	•
Point Lobos State Reserve	W. of Hwy. 1 at Riley Ranch Rd., Carmel	•	•	•						•		•			•		•		•	•		•	•

FACILITIES **ENVIRONMENT**

17-MILE DRIVE: Famous scenic drive which winds along the coast and through pine forests and Monterey cypress groves in the Del Monte Forest, including spectacular views, picnic areas, equestrian trails, abundant wildlife, and several golf courses open to the public. There are four entrances with toll gates; pay $4/car, refundable if you dine or stay at the Pebble Beach Lodge. Bicyclists need to get a permit at the gate. No plant or animal life may be disturbed. All roads in Del Monte Forest are privately owned and the right to pass is by permission and is revocable.

The following areas are along 17-Mile Drive: Seal and Bird Rocks, Fanshell Beach, Cypress Point Lookout, the Lone Cypress, and Pescadero Point.

SEAL AND BIRD ROCKS: Picnic tables; coin-operated telescopes for viewing birds on Bird Rock, and sea lions and leopard and harbor seals on Seal Rock offshore.

FANSHELL BEACH: White sand cove used for picnicking, fishing, and swimming.

CYPRESS POINT LOOKOUT: Magnificent view of the coast; coin-operated telescopes for viewing sea lions, seals, and sea otters offshore. Tidepools.

THE LONE CYPRESS: A walkway leads down to the famous Lone Cypress tree growing on nearly bare rock overlooking the ocean at Midway Point.

PESCADERO POINT: Roadside parking only; blufftop overlook with rocky shore and tidepools below. Outstanding view of Carmel Bay.

CARMEL CITY BEACH: Fine, white sand beach bordered by cypress trees; hazardous surf. Parking along Ocean Ave.; crowded on weekends. Fire rings on the beach. **Mass Transit:** Monterey-Salinas Transit (MST) Routes 4, 5, and 22.

CARMEL RIVER STATE BEACH: 106-acre sandy beach with a marsh at the north end and a lagoon near the river mouth. Popular for diving; hazardous surf. Access to the north part of the beach is from the parking lot on Scenic Road. Access to the east side of the marsh, which is a bird sanctuary, is from a path at the foot of Monte Verde Ave.; no powerboats or dogs allowed. The portion of the beach south of the river is accessible from Ribera Road. The southernmost part of the beach, known as San Jose Creek Beach or Monastery Beach, is accessible from Hwy. 1. Information: (408) 649-2836. The undersea Carmel Bay Ecological Reserve is adjacent to the beach. **Mass Transit:** MST Route 5 to the north end; Route 22 to the south end (Memorial Day weekend and June 7-Sept. 1 only).

POINT LOBOS STATE RESERVE: 1,276 acres of headland with spectacular views of the coast, sandy coves and beaches, tidepools, Monterey cypress groves, more than 300 plant and 250 bird and animal species, trails, and picnic areas. Swimming in China Cove. Admission fee; guided tours in the summer. Numerous sea lions can be seen on the rocks offshore at Sea Lion Point; Bird Island is a sanctuary for thousands of birds. Sea otters can frequently be seen from the bluffs. Diving access is only from Whaler's Cove parking lot; diving allowed only in Whaler's and Bluefish Coves with a permit. No fires; pets not permitted on trails or beaches, and must be leashed elsewhere.

It is illegal to disturb or take any plant or marine life within the reserve or within the adjoining underwater Ecological Reserve. For information, write: Point Lobos State Reserve, Route 1, Box 62, Carmel 93923; or call (408) 624-4909. **Mass Transit:** MST Route 22 (limited service) or Coastlines Bus Service.

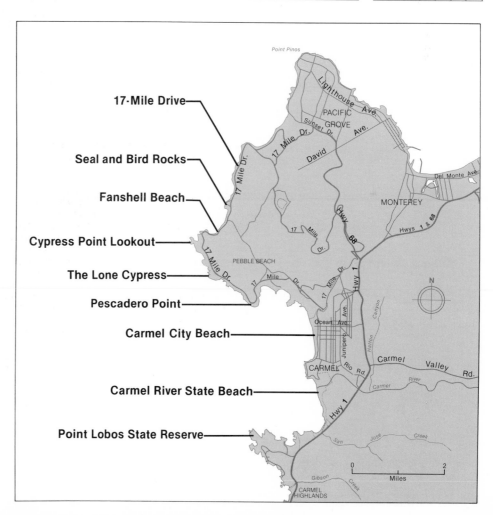

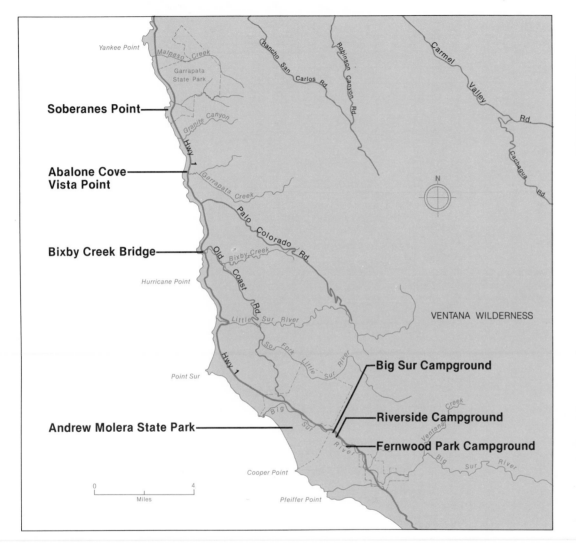

Yankee Point

Malpaso Creek

Garrapata State Park

Rancho San Carlos Rd.

Robinson Canyon Rd.

Carmel Valley Rd.

Cachagua Rd.

Soberanes Point

Granite Canyon

Hwy 1

Abalone Cove Vista Point

Garrapata Creek

Palo Colorado Rd.

N

Bixby Creek Bridge

Old Coast Rd.

Bixby Creek

Hurricane Point

Little Sur River

VENTANA WILDERNESS

So. Fork Little Sur River

Big Sur Campground

Point Sur

Hwy 1

Ventana Creek

Riverside Campground

Andrew Molera State Park

Big Sur River

Fernwood Park Campground

Big Sur River

0   4
Miles

Cooper Point

Pfeiffer Point

Bixby Bridge

Monterey County
NORTHERN BIG SUR

NAME	LOCATION	Entrance/Parking Fee	Parking	Restrooms	Lifeguard	Campground	Showers	Firepits	Stairs to Beach	Path to Beach	Bike Path	Hiking Trail	Facilities for Disabled	Boating Facilities	Fishing	Equestrian Trail	Sandy Beach	Dunes	Rocky Shore	Upland from Beach	Stream Corridor	Bluff	Wetland
Soberanes Point (Unit of Garrapata State Beach)	Hwy. 1, 2 mi. S. of Malpaso Creek, Big Sur		•	•						•							•		•	•		•	
Abalone Cove Vista Point	Hwy. 1, 1.4 mi. N. of Palo Colorado Rd., Big Sur		•																•			•	
Bixby Creek Bridge	Hwy. 1, N. end of Old Coast Rd., Big Sur		•																•			•	
Andrew Molera State Park	W. of Hwy. 1, S. end of Old Coast Rd., Big Sur		•	•		•		•		•		•			•		•		•	•	•	•	
Big Sur Campground	Hwy. 1, 1.7 mi. N. of Pfeiffer Big Sur State Park, Big Sur	•	•	•		•	•	•							•					•	•		
Riverside Campground	Hwy. 1, 1.6 mi. N. of Pfeiffer Big Sur State Park, Big Sur	•	•	•		•	•	•				•			•					•	•		
Fernwood Park Campground	Hwy. 1, .7 mi. N. of Pfeiffer Big Sur State Park, Big Sur	•	•	•		•	•	•							•					•	•		

Andrew Molera State Park

SOBERANES POINT: Scenic 1.2-mile trail winds along the steep bluff; spectacular view of the coast. Whales and sea otters can be seen offshore. Hazardous cliffs; tidepools below. Chemical toilets; roadside parking only. First phase of development of Garrapata State Beach. Call: (408) 667-2315. The California Sea Otter Game Refuge offshore extends along the entire Big Sur Coast south into San Luis Obispo County; do not disturb the otters.
Mass Transit: Monterey-Salinas Transit (MST) Route 22 (June-Sept. only) or Coastlines Bus Service.

ABALONE COVE VISTA POINT: Paved highway pull-off with a view of Abalone Cove and Kasler Point.
Mass Transit: MST Route 22 (limited Service) or Coastlines Bus Service.

BIXBY CREEK BRIDGE: A major landmark of the Big Sur Coast; one of the world's longest concrete arch span bridges, 260 feet high and over 700 feet long, with highway pull-offs on both sides and observation alcoves on the bridge itself; spectacular view.
Mass Transit: MST Route 22 (limited service) or Coastlines Bus Service.

ANDREW MOLERA STATE PARK: 2,154 acres of flatland, meadows, mountains, and sandy beach west of Highway 1. Day use areas and walk-in campground .3 mile from the dirt parking lot; 50 campsites with firepits, chemical toilets, and a tank trailer which provides water. Camping fee 50¢/night, $1/dog; three night limit. The Big Sur River flows through the park and empties into the ocean, forming a shallow lagoon which is a bird sanctuary; hiking trails lead to the beach adjacent to the lagoon. Information: (408) 667-2315.

The Point Sur Lighthouse, three miles north of the park, was built in 1889 on an enormous volcanic rock 350 feet above the sea. Closed to the public.
Mass Transit: MST Route 22 (limited service) or Coastlines Bus Service.

BIG SUR CAMPGROUND: Privately owned, with sites in the redwoods and along the Big Sur River; cabins, tent rentals, water and electric hookups, picnic tables, laundry, store, and playground. Campsites $10/two-person car, $2/electric hookup. Day use fee $3/person. Open all year, reservations accepted. Highway 1, Big Sur 93920, (408) 667-2322.
Mass Transit: MST Route 22 (limited service) or Coastlines Bus Service.

RIVERSIDE CAMPGROUND: Privately owned, with 46 campsites in the redwoods and along the Big Sur River; cabins, picnic tables, playground, hiking trails, laundry, and a swinging footbridge over the river. Tent rentals and firewood available. Campsites $9/two-person car, $2/electric hookup. P.O. Box 3, Big Sur 93920, (408) 667-2414.
Mass Transit: MST Route 22 (limited service) or Coastlines Bus Service.

FERNWOOD PARK CAMPGROUND: Privately owned, with sites in the redwoods and along the Big Sur River; campsites $8/two-person car, $2/electric hookup. Firewood for sale. Day use until 5 PM $2/car. Restaurant, bar, gas station, motel, and grocery store. Call (408) 667-2422.
Mass Transit: MST Route 22 (limited service) or Coastlines Bus Service.

Pfeiffer-Big Sur State Park

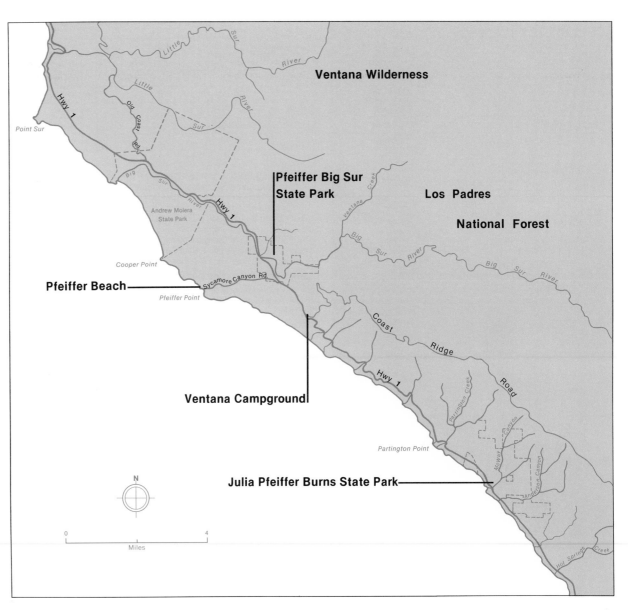

Ventana Wilderness

Point Sur

Hwy 1

Little River

Little River

Old Coast Rd.

Sur River

Big Sur River

Andrew Molera State Park

Hwy 1

Pfeiffer Big Sur
State Park

Los Padres

National Forest

Cooper Point

Ventana Creek

Big Sur River

Big Sur River

Pfeiffer Beach

Sycamore Canyon Rd.

Pfeiffer Point

Coast Ridge

Hwy 1

Road

Ventana Campground

Partington Creek

McWay Canyon

Anderson Canyon

Partington Point

Julia Pfeiffer Burns State Park

N

0   4
Miles

Hot Springs Creek

FACILITIES   **ENVIRONMENT**

NAME	LOCATION	Entrance/Parking Fee	Parking	Restrooms	Lifeguard	Campground	Showers	Firepits	Stairs to Beach	Path to Beach	Bike Path	Hiking Trail	Facilities for Disabled	Boating Facilities	Fishing	Equestrian Trail	Sandy Beach	Dunes	Rocky Shore	Upland from Beach	Stream Corridor	Bluff	Wetland
Pfeiffer Big Sur State Park	E. of Hwy. 1, 26 mi. S. of Carmel, Big Sur	•	•	•		•	•	•			•	•		•	•				•	•			
Los Padres National Forest/Ventana Wilderness	Big Sur Coast		•	•		•		•		•	•	•		•	•		•		•	•	•	•	•
Pfeiffer Beach	W. of Hwy. 1, end of Sycamore Canyon Rd., Big Sur		•	•						•							•	•	•	•		•	
Ventana Campground	Hwy. 1, 2.4 mi. S. of Pfeiffer Big Sur State Park, Big Sur	•	•	•		•	•	•											•	•			
Julia Pfeiffer Burns State Park	E. and W. of Hwy. 1, 11 mi. S. of Pfeiffer Big Sur State Park, Big Sur	•	•	•		•				•		•			•				•	•	•	•	

Pfeiffer Beach

PFEIFFER BIG SUR STATE PARK: 821 acres in the redwoods and along the Big Sur River. Facilities include 218 campsites (each with a stove, locker, and picnic table), a bicycle camp area, group camp, hiking trails, store, and laundry; no trailer hookups. Some campsites are wheelchair accessible. Swimming and fishing in the river; abundant wildlife. Popular spots along the trails include Pfeiffer Falls and the Gorge. Guided walks and campfire programs in the summer.

The park is open all year; reservations accepted year-round, through Ticketron only. Seven-day camping limit June 1-Sept. 30. $6/campsite, $2 day use fee. Information: (408) 667-2315. The Big Sur Lodge has rooms and cabins, swimming pool and sauna, restaurant, and gift shop. Write: Big Sur Lodge, Big Sur 93920 or call (408) 667-2171.
Mass Transit: Monterey-Salinas Transit (MST) Route 22 (June-Sept.) or Coastlines Bus Service.

LOS PADRES NATIONAL FOREST / VENTANA WILDERNESS: The National Forest, which consists of two sections, comprises almost two million acres and extends into five counties, with 1,750 miles of recreation trails. The smaller section is in Monterey County, and includes part of the Big Sur Coast and the Santa Lucia Mountains. For general information on the National Forest, call: (805) 968-1578.

The 150,000-acre Ventana Wilderness within the forest has a system of trails through the woodlands and canyons. Permits are required to enter the Ventana Wilderness, and to camp within the National Forest if you camp anywhere other than in a designated campsite. Permits and information can be obtained from the Monterey District Ranger's Office: U.S. Forest Service, 406 S. Mildred St., King City 93930; call (408) 385-5434.

There are two Forest Service stations along the coast where information, maps, and permits can be obtained, and where trails begin which lead into the National Forest. The Big Sur Station is located off Highway 1, .7 mile south of Pfeiffer Big Sur State Park, and Pacific Valley Station is 33 miles south of the Big Sur Valley; permits can also be obtained at Bottcher's Gap.

PFEIFFER BEACH: A unit of Los Padres National Forest. A hard-to-find but beautiful white sandy beach at the end of Sycamore Canyon Rd., which is the second right-hand turn off Highway 1 south of Pfeiffer Big Sur State Park. The turn-off, which is one

mile from the State Park entrance, is a sharp right turn downhill. The two-mile road to the beach is very narrow and winding. Private property is adjacent; do not trespass.

The beach is at the end of a sandy trail leading from the parking lot through cypress trees, and is surrounded by steep cliffs, sea stacks, and sea caves; spectacular waves crash through natural arches in the rocks. Sycamore Creek empties onto the beach into a small lagoon. Hazardous surf; gusty winds. Fires are prohibited. Beach open 6 AM-sundown. Call: (408) 385-5434.
Mass Transit: MST Route 22 (limited service) or Coastlines Bus Service.

VENTANA CAMPGROUND: Privately owned campground in the redwoods; $8/site. Restaurant, bar, and store up the hill at the Ventana Inn. (408) 667-2331.
Mass Transit: MST Route 22 (limited service) or Coastlines Bus Service.

JULIA PFEIFFER BURNS STATE PARK: 1,800 acres with wooded hiking trails and picnic tables; the restrooms are wheelchair modified. A paved footpath leads to a spectacular overlook of McWay Waterfall cascading 50 feet into the ocean near Saddle Rock; another trail leads to a picnic area near McWay Creek. Partington Cove is accessible by a trail on the west side of Highway 1, 1.8 miles north of the park entrance; look for an iron gate. The trail leads across Partington Creek on a wooden footbridge and through a 200-foot long tunnel cut into the cliff. $2 day use fee; park closes at sunset. Environmental campsites available; $6 fee.

The area offshore has been designated an underwater park for divers; prior permission is required in order to drive down to the water. For information, call: (408) 667-2315.
Mass Transit: Coastlines Bus Service.

California Sea Otter

The California sea otter *(Enhydra lutris),* one of the most interesting of California's marine mammals, can be found off the coast between Santa Cruz and Avila Beach (in San Luis Obispo County). The sea otter is a member of the weasel family; adult males measure up to 4-1/2 feet long and weigh up to 85 lbs., while females are somewhat shorter and lighter. Otters have dense fur ranging in color from black to dark red, and short front paws used primarily for feeding and grooming; hind feet are webbed and used as flippers for swimming.

Like primates, otters use tools in their daily routines. For example, an otter will dive beneath the water's surface and, with its paws, use a rock to remove shellfish from the sea bottom; once it has surfaced, the otter floats on its back, positions its catch on its chest, and hammers the shell until edible portions are accessible.

The sea otters' diet varies according to environment and the length of time they have stayed in an area. Where kelp beds are present, otters will float in the beds and search for crabs and snails; in coastal areas with sandy beaches, otters will come ashore and forage for crabs and clams. When otters first move into an area, their preferred diet consists primarily of abalone, sea urchins, and crabs if the area is rocky, and clams and crabs in sandy locations. As the population increases and becomes established, abalone and sea urchins become less abundant, and crabs become the otters' chief food source; otters may also feed on other marine species such as squid, mussels, limpets, and starfish.

To compensate for the lack of blubber that insulates most marine mammals from the ocean, the average otter consumes up to 25% of its body weight daily. An otter consumes 2.5 tons of food during a single year; this large quantity of food fuels its metabolism and maintains proper body temperature. Although its fur is not a very efficient insulator in the water, the otter meticulously grooms it to provide maximum warming; part of the grooming process includes rolling vigorously in the water to trap air bubbles in the fur.

The otter's thick, attractive fur nearly resulted in the animal's extinction. Although native North Americans hunted the otter from Alaska to southern California for many years, large-scale hunting did not occur until the mid-18th century. Between 1741 and 1911, Russian, American, French, and British fur traders hunted marine mammals off the western coast of the United States and the otter population declined to a near extinct level. In 1911 the Fur Seal Treaty was signed and included provisions to protect the sea otters; subsequently, a number of state and national laws providing for marine mammal protection were enacted. Today, most of the California sea otters live within the California Sea Otter Game Refuge, a protected habitat area between the Carmel River in Monterey County and Santa Rosa Creek in San Luis Obispo County.

Spotting sea otters in offshore waters can be difficult because otters often remain in kelp beds, and the kelp bladders resemble otter heads. One of the best times to observe otters is during feeding times, usually in the early morning and late afternoon. Sea gulls hovering above kelp beds are a good indicator of an otter's presence, as gulls often wait above the beds to feed on scraps left by otters. With binoculars one can observe the otters feeding and grooming themselves and their young; at times it is even possible to hear otters pounding on shells with rocks and pups crying out for their mothers.

Sea otters are protected by state and federal law; it is illegal to take or even temporarily possess a sea otter. Any person finding a dead, sick, or wounded otter or an apparently abandoned otter pup should not touch the animal but immediately notify the California Department of Fish and Game. In the Monterey County area, call (408) 649-2870; in San Luis Obispo County, call (805) 772-3011.

NAME	LOCATION	Entrance/Parking Fee	Parking	Restrooms	Lifeguard	Campground	Showers	Firepits	Stairs to Beach	Path to Beach	Bike Path	Hiking Trail	Facilities for Disabled	Boating Facilities	Fishing	Equestrian Trail	Sandy Beach	Dunes	Rocky Shore	Upland from Beach	Stream Corridor	Bluff	Wetland
Esalen Institute	W. of Hwy. 1, 14.6 mi. S. of Pfeiffer Big Sur State Park, Big Sur	•	•	•																		•	
Limekiln Beach Redwoods Campground	Off Hwy. 1, 2 mi. S. of Lucia	•	•	•		•	•	•	•		•				•		•		•	•	•		
Kirk Creek Campground	W. of Hwy. 1, 4 mi. S. of Lucia	•	•	•		•	•	•	•		•				•		•		•	•		•	
Mill Creek Picnic Ground	W. of Hwy. 1, 5 mi. S. of Lucia		•	•				•		•			•		•				•	•		•	
Sand Dollar Picnic Area and Beach	W. of Hwy. 1, 11 mi. S. of Lucia		•	•				•		•	•		•		•		•		•	•		•	
Plaskett Creek Campground	E. of Hwy. 1, 11.7 mi. S. of Lucia	•	•	•		•		•												•		•	
Jade Cove	W. of Hwy. 1, 12.4 mi. S. of Lucia								•						•				•			•	
Willow Creek Picnic Ground	W. of Hwy. 1, 14 mi. S. of Lucia		•	•						•					•				•	•		•	

ESALEN INSTITUTE: Privately owned hot springs and facilities; hot springs open to the public 1 AM-5:30 AM, Mon.-Sat. mornings, $5/person. Call for information: (408) 667-2335. Workshops offered on all phases of human development; for a catalog, send $1 to: Esalen Institute, Big Sur 93920.
Mass Transit: Coastlines Bus Service.

LIMEKILN BEACH REDWOODS CAMPGROUND: Privately owned, with 60 sites in the redwoods and on the beach; waterfalls and historic limekilns. Supplies and sanitation station; no electricity. Campsites $9.50/two-person car, $2/additional person, day use $2/person. Open all year; for reservations, write: Limekiln Beach Redwoods, Big Sur 93920 or call (408) 667-2403. $1.50 charge for reservations.
Mass Transit: Coastlines Bus Service.

The following areas are units of the Los Padres National Forest: Pfeiffer Beach, Kirk Creek Campground, Mill Creek Picnic Ground, Sand Dollar Picnic Area and Beach, Plaskett Creek Campground, Jade Cove, and Willow Creek Picnic Ground.

KIRK CREEK CAMPGROUND: 33 campsites on the bluffs above a sandy beach; magnificent view of the coast. Two trails lead to the beach; diving area. $7/family campsite; $10/double site; bicycle camp area $1/person. Free day use picnic area. Information: (408) 385-5434.
Mass Transit: Coastlines Bus Service.

MILL CREEK PICNIC GROUND: Picnic tables overlook the ocean; a path leads to the rocky shore; diving. Pets on leash only. The chemical toilets are wheelchair accessible. Information: (408) 385-5434.
Mass Transit: Coastlines Bus Service.

SAND DOLLAR PICNIC AREA AND BEACH: Picnic tables among the cypress trees; trails lead across the field to a crescent-shaped sandy beach. Pets must be leashed. Restrooms are wheelchair accessible. Popular hang-gliding area. Information: (408) 385-5434.
Mass Transit: Coastlines Bus Service.

PLASKETT CREEK CAMPGROUND: 44 sites with picnic tables and grills at the base of the Santa Lucia Mountains. $7/family site, $10/double site, $1 bike-in; group sites for up to 50 persons cost $25 and require reservations. Call (408) 385-5434.
Mass Transit: Coastlines Bus Service.

JADE COVE: Look for the Los Padres National Forest sign on Highway 1. Shoulder parking only; a steep trail leads down the bluff to several rocky coves. Diving area. Named after the nephrite jade found here. Information: (408) 385-5434.
Mass Transit: Coastlines Bus Service.

WILLOW CREEK PICNIC GROUND: Picnic area along the rocky shore near where Willow Creek flows into the ocean; view of Plaskett Rock offshore. Jade can sometimes be found on the beach. Information: (408) 385-5434.
Mass Transit: Coastlines Bus Service.

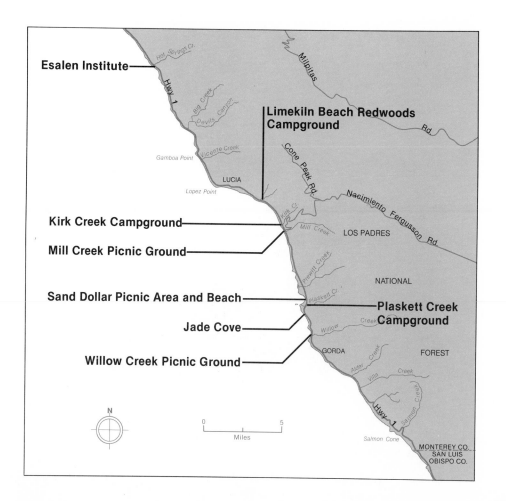

Morro Rock

San Luis Obispo County

Ranging from the rugged sea cliffs south of Big Sur to the extensive sand dune fields of Pismo Beach, San Luis Obispo's coast is a favorite among visitors. 96 miles long, the county's coast includes numerous wide, sandy beaches, sheltered bays, and many vista points offering scenic views of the Pacific Ocean.

San Luis Obispo County's topography and natural features are a result of the intense geologic activity which has taken place here. Complex folding and uplifting of the earth's crust five million years ago produced the Santa Lucia Mountain Range bordering the shoreline along the north coast, and the San Luis Mountains between Pismo Beach and Morro Bay. This folding formed the tilted strata at the base of the San Luis Mountains, which has since been eroded by the ocean into spectacular tidepool areas accessible from Montana de Oro State Park and the Shell Beach area.

Morro Rock and the six other volcanic peaks between Morro Bay and the City of San Luis Obispo were formed by volcanic activity over 20 million years ago. The Rock marks the narrow and once treacherous entrance to Morro Bay, sighted originally by the Spanish explorer Juan Cabrillo in 1542. Cabrillo never landed here, and it wasn't until Juan Gaspar de Portolá's expedition in 1769 that Europeans first explored the land and met the Chumash Indians, the native inhabitants of the region. Chumash villages and camps have been found at Los Osos Creek, and Montana de Oro and Morro Bay State Parks.

Today, Morro Bay is a heavily used fishing port and one of the largest bay wildlife habitats on California's coast. At low tide, 1,400 acres of mudflats are exposed, providing a vast feeding area for over 250 species of birds; the adjacent Morro Bay State Park is noted as one of the best sites for bay bird-watching.

Popular for clam digging and sand dune recreation, Pismo State Beach along the south county coast contains more than 2,000 acres of beach and windswept sand dunes. The beach and dunes are formed here because the effects of longshore drift are interrupted by Point San Luis to the north; longshore drift is a coastal process which, along this part of the coast, would ordinarily carry sediments south. Consequently, sands are deposited here, instead of being transported away, and widespread sand dune fields have resulted.

In contrast to the Pismo dunes and beach in the south are the grassy coastal terraces and steep sea cliffs in the north county. Above these terraces overlooking the Pacific Ocean, William R. Hearst, in collaboration with the renowned architect Julia Morgan, built his enormous private castle from 1920 until his death in 1951. In 1958, the Hearst family donated the castle and immediate grounds to the State Department of Parks and Recreation; it has since become one of the most popular visitor attractions in California.

For more information on the San Luis Obispo coast, write or call: Cayucos Chamber of Commerce, P.O. Box 141, Cayucos 93430, (805) 995-1200; Morro Bay Chamber of Commerce, P.O. Box 876, Morro Bay 93442, (805) 772-4467; and the Pismo Beach Chamber of Commerce, 581 Dolliver Street, Pismo Beach 93449, (805) 773-4382.

For transit information, call Coastlines Bus Service, (408) 649-4700; San Luis Obispo County Area Transit (SLOCAT), (805) 549-5252; North Coastal Transit, (805) 544-6454; and South County Area Transit (SCAT), (805) 489-5400. Buses for all systems can be boarded at regular stops or flagged at any corner or safe location.

Hearst Castle

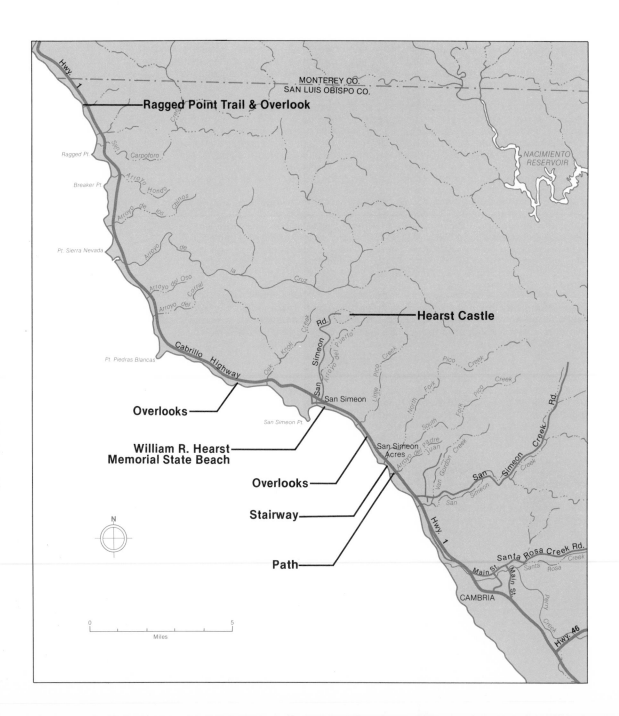

MONTEREY CO.
SAN LUIS OBISPO CO.

Ragged Point Trail & Overlook

Hwy. 1

Ragged Pt.

San Carpoforo Creek

Breaker Pt.

Arroyo Hondo

Arroyo de los Chinos

Pt. Sierra Nevada

Arroyo de la Cruz

Arroyo del Oso

Arroyo del Corral

Arroyo del

Hearst Castle

San Simeon Rd.

Oak Knoll Creek

Arroyo del Puerto

Cabrillo Highway

Pt. Piedras Blancas

San Simeon

Overlooks

San Simeon Pt.

Little Pico Creek

North Fork

Pico Creek

Pico Creek

South Fork

**William R. Hearst
Memorial State Beach**

San Simeon Acres

Arroyo del padre Juan

Van Gordon Creek

Overlooks

San Simeon Creek

San Simeon Creek

Stairway

San Simeon

San Simeon Creek Rd.

Hwy. 1

Path

Santa Rosa Creek Rd.

Santa Rosa Creek

NACIMIENTO
RESERVOIR

Main St.

Main St.

Santa Rosa

Perry Creek

N

CAMBRIA

Hwy. 46

0   5
Miles

NAME	LOCATION	Entrance/Parking Fee	Parking	Restrooms	Lifeguard	Campground	Showers	Firepits	Stairs to Beach	Path to Beach	Bike Path	Hiking Trail	Facilities for Disabled	Boating Facilities	Fishing	Equestrian Trail	Sandy Beach	Dunes	Rocky Shore	Upland from Beach	Stream Corridor	Bluff	Wetland
Ragged Point Trail and Overlook	W. of Hwy. 1, 15 mi. N. of San Simeon		•	•						•							•		•	•	•		
Overlooks	2.9 and 3.5 mi. N. of San Simeon Rd. along Hwy. 1		•																•		•		
Hearst Castle	E. of Hwy. 1 on San Simeon Rd., San Simeon	•	•	•									•							•			
William R. Hearst Memorial State Beach	W. of Hwy. 1 on San Simeon Rd., San Simeon	•	•	•			•		•						•		•				•		
Overlooks	.3, 1, and 2 mi. S. of San Simeon Rd. along Hwy. 1		•																•		•		
Stairway to Beach	W. end of Pico Ave., San Simeon Acres		•						•								•		•	•	•		
Path to Beach	Corner of Cliff Dr. and San Simeon Ave., San Simeon Acres		•							•							•		•	•	•		

William R. Hearst Memorial State Beach

RAGGED POINT TRAIL AND OVERLOOK: Seaward of the Ragged Point Inn, located north of the Ragged Point peninsula, is a grassy area and overlook on a high blufftop terrace above the ocean. Scenic views of the Big Sur Coast to the north. A steep switchbacked trail leads past a waterfall to the small sandy beach and rocky shore. Taking of abalone not permitted. The trail and overlook are privately managed.
Mass Transit: Coastlines Bus Service.

OVERLOOKS: Two parking areas on Highway 1 north of San Simeon provide views of the ocean.
Mass Transit: Coastlines Bus Service.

HEARST CASTLE: Formerly William R. Hearst's private estate, now open to the public as a 123-acre State Park Historical Monument located within the 235,000 acres of private Hearst Ranch holdings; tours leave from 8:20 AM-3:20 PM daily except on Thanksgiving and Christmas Days; extended hours during the summer. Constructed between 1920 and 1950, Hearst's architecturally renowned mansion and grounds still contain portions of his famous art collection and unique herds of exotic animals; the estate provides numerous scenic views of San Simeon Bay and the San Luis Obispo coast.

Three different tours run continuously every 20 minutes, leaving by shuttle bus from the visitor parking lot just off Highway 1. Tour 1 views the gardens, pools, a guest house, and the main floor of the castle; recommended as an introductory tour. Tour 2 visits the castle's upper floors and bedrooms. Tour 3 views the north wing, gardens, pools, and a guest house. Each tour takes 2-1/2 hours and involves considerable walking; tour 1 (150 steps) is recommended as easier than tours 2 and 3 (300 steps each). A fourth tour runs from April through early fall, and visits the formal gardens, wine cellar, unfinished bowling alley, and the lower level of a guest house.

Smoking is restricted. Wheelchair access requires use of personal vehicle; contact the park office one week prior to visit. Entrance fee: $8/adult, $4/child under 12. $1 reservation fee. Reservations for tours, available only through Ticketron, are highly recommended. For information, contact Ticketron or Hearst—San Simeon State Historical Park, P.O. Box 8, San Simeon 93452. (805) 927-4621.
Mass Transit: Coastlines Bus Service. Hearst Castle tickets, guaranteeing admittance, may be purchased on the bus.

WILLIAM R. HEARST MEMORIAL STATE BEACH: Excellent swimming area; protected from heavy surf and wind by scenic San Simeon Point. 1,000-foot long pier, fishing equipment rentals, and boat charter service are located at the west end of the main parking lot. Picnic tables are in the eucalyptus grove just north of the pier and in the grassy area near the park entrance. Additional parking lot adjacent to the beach is north of the eucalyptus grove. $2/car day use fee. Hours 8 AM (earlier in summer) to sunset. For information, call: (805) 927-4621.
Mass Transit: Coastlines Bus Service.

OVERLOOKS: Three parking lots along Highway 1 between San Simeon and San Simeon Acres overlook the ocean south of San Simeon Bay.
Mass Transit: Coastlines Bus Service.

STAIRWAY TO BEACH: At the end of the Pico Ave. cul-de-sac, just south of Pico Creek, is an overlook with benches and a short stairway leading to a sandy beach. Parking on Pico Ave.
Mass Transit: Coastlines Bus Service.

PATH TO BEACH: A public path along the north bank of Arroyo del Padre Juan Creek leads to a sandy ocean beach. The path is located directly south of the Cavalier Inn, west of Highway 1 and Hearst Avenue. On-street parking.
Mass Transit: Coastlines Bus Service.

Native Americans of the Coast

At one time, as many as 300,000 Native Americans inhabited what is now California. Of the more than 50 different native groups that occupied California, 16 lived, hunted, and fished along the shoreline and on offshore islands.

Most California Native Americans were hunter-gatherers; that is, they exploited naturally occurring plant and animal life for food, clothing, and tools, rather than planting crops and maintaining livestock. Along the coast, many Native American groups relied heavily on the sea for sustenance. For example, the Chumash, who inhabited the coast from San Luis Obispo to Los Angeles Counties, plied the coastal waters in planked canoes, called tomols, and hunted sea otters, fished for albacore, and harvested shellfish such as clams, abalone, and mussels; the Chumash also used the tomols to travel to offshore islands and trade with other Native American groups.

The societal structure and specific lifestyle of coastal Native American groups varied from place to place. In general, the members of a particular tribe inhabited small villages; in some cases their villages were governed by a larger, centrally located one. Villages usually consisted of a number of domiciles, a ceremonial structure or area, storehouses, and a burial ground; buildings were often constructed of wooden poles woven with grasses. Many tribes had distinct hunting, collecting, and fishing areas.

Trade with inland tribes was also a major characteristic of the coastal Native Americans. Artifacts made by various coastal tribes include baskets, wood trays and boxes (often inlaid with shells or coral), water pots and cookware, and obsidian projectile points; some tribes used shells for dishes and pieces of jewelry.

The San Luis Obispo area was occupied by the Obispeño group of the Chumash tribe. The Chumash in general had one of the most highly developed societal structures of all California Native Americans; they evolved from a simple hunter-gatherer culture to a society based on diverse subsistence activities and an extensive trade network.

The Chumash's ability to exploit ocean resources such as sea otters, fish, and shellfish contributed to their affluence relative to other Native American groups in California. The abundance of food resources and the favorable coastal climate allowed the Obispeño Chumash to enjoy a peaceful existence.

Native Americans in California lived according to their own lifestyles and customs until the effects of the Spanish missions set in. Native American attitudes toward missionization varied. The Ipai tribe, from the San Diego area, was very hostile and rebellious toward the Spanish missionaries; the Chumash, however, typically were friendly and, for example, even taught the Spanish how to use asphaltum to make watertight roofs and bowls. The establishment of the missions resulted in the introduction of European diseases and a displacement of Native American culture; Euro-American influences virtually exterminated the Native American population along much of coastal California by the early 1900's. Today, place names such as Malibu, Hueneme, Pismo, Sinkyone, and Talawa remain as evidence of Native American existence along the California coast.

San Luis Obispo County

SAN SIMEON/CAMBRIA

NAME	LOCATION	Entrance/Parking Fee	Parking	Restrooms	Lifeguard	Campground	Showers	Firepits	Stairs to Beach	Path to Beach	Bike Path	Hiking Trail	Facilities for Disabled	Boating Facilities	Fishing	Equestrian Trail	Sandy Beach	Dunes	Rocky Shore	Upland from Beach	Stream Corridor	Bluff	Wetland
San Simeon State Beach	Between San Simeon Creek and Santa Rosa Creek	•	•	•		•				•							•		•			•	
San Simeon Creek Access	W. of Hwy. 1 at San Simeon Creek		•							•							•		•				
Moonstone Beach Drive Vista Point	N. end of Moonstone Beach Dr. and Hwy. 1, Cambria		•						•										•	•		•	
Leffingwell Landing	Moonstone Beach Dr., 1/4 mile S. of intersection with Hwy. 1, Cambria		•	•				•	•	•	•	•							•	•		•	
Santa Rosa Creek Access	W. of Hwy. 1, near S. end of Moonstone Beach Dr., Cambria		•						•								•					•	•
Shamel County Park	Windsor Blvd. and Nottingham Dr., Cambria		•	•			•		•								•		•				
Overlooks	W. of Nottingham Dr. at Plymouth and Lancaster Streets., Cambria		•																	•		•	
Cambria Pines Beach	Along Sherwood Dr., between Wedgewood and Lampton Streets., Cambria Pines Manor		•							•							•		•				

The following are administered by the State Department of Parks and Recreation as part of San Simeon State Beach: San Simeon Creek Access, Moonstone Beach Drive Vista Point, Leffingwell Landing, and Santa Rosa Creek Access. For information: (805) 927-4509.

SAN SIMEON STATE BEACH: Runs from San Simeon Creek to Santa Rosa Creek, west of Highway 1 and Moonstone Beach Drive. 500-acre campground is east of Highway 1 off San Simeon Creek Rd.; includes 139 campsites, a bicycle and hiker group site, a trailer sanitation station, and an overflow trailer camp area south of San Simeon Creek. An environmental campground is planned.

A short path to the beach is at the southwest corner of the campground underneath the Highway 1 San Simeon Creek overpass. Creek riparian area is accessible by short trails from the lower campground; there is a foot bridge at the east end of the creek. $3 overnight fee; reservations through Ticketron recommended during the summer. For information: (805) 927-4509.
Mass Transit: Coastlines Bus Service.

SAN SIMEON CREEK ACCESS: Adjacent to the south bank of San Simeon Creek. The parking area off Highway 1 provides access to San Simeon State Beach.
Mass Transit: Coastlines Bus Service.

MOONSTONE BEACH DRIVE VISTA POINT: Overlooks the Moonstone Beach area of San Simeon State Beach; named after the moonstone agates occasionally seen here. Beach access is from San Simeon Creek to the north. Highly eroded bluffs; hiking trails along the edge are south of the parking area.
Mass Transit: Coastlines Bus Service.

LEFFINGWELL LANDING: Facilities include picnic tables east of the parking lot in a sheltered cypress grove, and a ramp for car-top boat launching. Hiking trails along blufftops to the north connect to the Moonstone Beach Drive Vista Point. Noted as a good spot for watching sea otters, which are frequently seen resting on the rocky tidepool areas offshore and to the south. Tidepool and offshore areas are part of the California Sea Otter Game Refuge; do not disturb the otters.

SANTA ROSA CREEK ACCESS: Parking area and benches are adjacent to the ocean; Santa Rosa Creek marshland is south of the parking lot. Hiking trails along blufftops to the north overlook the rocky shore and tidepool areas below.

SHAMEL COUNTY PARK: Parking and access to the beach is along the southern edge of the park; the park contains a playground area, grassy playing field, and a swimming pool which is open May through September.
Mass Transit: San Luis Obispo County Area Transit (SLOCAT), Morro Bay-Cambria route.

CAMBRIA PINES BEACH: Access down low bluffs to the sandy beach and rocky shore is along Sherwood Dr. at the ends of Wedgewood St., Castle St., Harvey St., Lampton St., and south of Lampton Street. To reach Sherwood Dr., take Ardath Dr. off Highway 1; Drake St. off Ardath Dr. leads to Sherwood Dr.

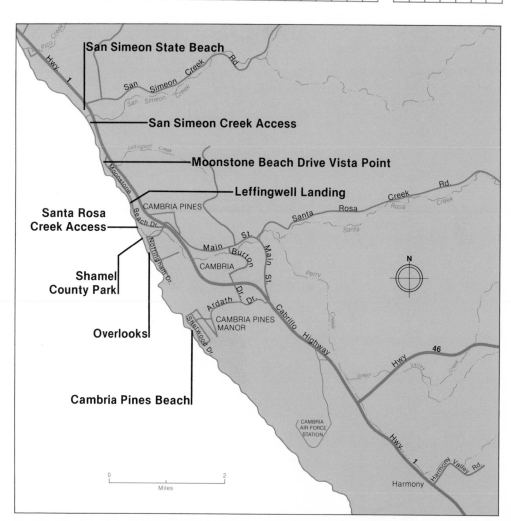

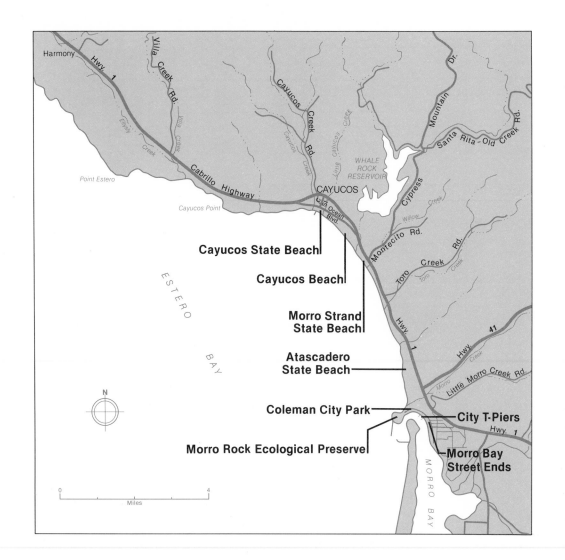

Cayucos State Beach

Cayucos Beach

Morro Strand State Beach

Atascadero State Beach

Coleman City Park

Morro Rock Ecological Preserve

City T-Piers

Morro Bay Street Ends

Atascadero State Beach

San Luis Obispo County
CAYUCOS/NORTH MORRO BAY

NAME	LOCATION	Entrance/Parking Fee	Parking	Restrooms	Lifeguard	Campground	Showers	Firepits	Stairs to Beach	Path to Beach	Bike Path	Hiking Trail	Facilities for Disabled	Boating Facilities	Fishing	Equestrian Trail	Sandy Beach	Dunes	Rocky Shore	Upland from Beach	Stream Corridor	Bluff	Wetland
Cayucos State Beach	W. of North Ocean Dr. between Cayucos Rd. and E St., Cayucos		•	•	•		•	•					•		•		•						
Cayucos Beach	Along Pacific Ave. between 1st and 22nd Streets, Cayucos		•						•								•		•			•	
Morro Strand State Beach	Along Studio Dr. between 24th St. and Cody Ave., Cayucos		•	•			•	•									•			•	•		
Atascadero State Beach	W. of Hwy. 1 between Yerba Buena Ave. and Atascadero Rd., Morro Bay	•	•	•		•	•		•				•				•	•			•		
Coleman City Park	W. of Coleman Dr. and the Embarcadero, Morro Bay		•	•													•	•					
Morro Rock Ecological Preserve	W. end of Coleman Dr., Morro Bay		•	•											•		•		•				
City T-Piers	W. end of the Embarcadero, seaward of the power plant, Morro Bay		•	•									•	•	•								
Morro Bay Street Ends	Along the Embarcadero, between Beach St. and Anchor St., Morro Bay		•												•								•

CAYUCOS STATE BEACH: Facilities include a popular fishing pier which is lit at night and wheelchair accessible, and group barbeque and picnic facilities in the patio area adjacent to the Veterans Memorial building. Parking is along Ocean Front Rd., and in the lot adjacent to the patio area. For reservations of the group facilities or buildings, contact: County General Services Department, (805) 549-5930.
Mass Transit: Coastlines Bus Service or San Luis Obispo County Area Transit (SLOCAT), Morro Bay-Cambria route.

CAYUCOS BEACH: There are nine stairways along Pacific Ave. between 1st and 22nd Streets which lead to the sandy beach below; all stairways are marked "Public Beachwalk"; private property adjoins both sides. Do not trespass.
Mass Transit: Coastlines Bus Service or SLOCAT, Morro Bay-Cambria route.

MORRO STRAND STATE BEACH: Extends from 24th St. to the south end of Studio Drive. Paved parking lot, restrooms, and picnic tables are at the end of 24th St., with an additional unpaved parking area at the north end of Studio Drive. Stairs and paths to the beach are along Studio Dr. 200 feet north of Juanita Ave., and at the ends of Coronado, Mayer, Mannix, and Cody Avenues. For information, call: (805) 543-2161.
Mass Transit: Coastlines Bus Service or SLOCAT, Morro Bay-Cambria route.

ATASCADERO STATE BEACH: 1.7 miles long; runs from the creek at the north end of Beachcomber Dr. to the mouth of Morro Creek south of Atascadero Road. 104-site campground is at the west end of Yerba Buena Dr., with pedestrian access at the west end of Hatteras St. and through the tunnel at the end of Orcas St.; $6 overnight fee. No fee for beach day use. Clam digging not permitted between Azure St. and Morro Rock. Facilities include dressing rooms and outdoor showers. Additional beach access is at the end of Easter St. and at the end of Atascadero Rd., as well as through the "Cloisters Parcel," which is now state property, located west of Sandalwood Ave. and between Sienha and Azure Streets. For information, call: (805) 772-8812 (summer only) or 772-2560.
Mass Transit: Coastlines Bus Service or SLOCAT, Morro Bay-Cambria route.

COLEMAN CITY PARK: Contains playground equipment and picnic tables; access to the dunes area and Atascadero Beach directly north. South of the park and the Embarcadero is a protected sandy beach within Morro Bay.

MORRO ROCK ECOLOGICAL PRESERVE: Morro Rock is 576 feet high; the northernmost of the volcanic peaks running from San Luis Obispo City to Morro Bay. Protected state preserve for the nesting of the endangered peregrine falcon; entry or climbing is prohibited. However, fishing, hiking, and parking around the base of the rock are permitted; a large parking area and restrooms are northeast of the rock. The breakwater on the southwest side can be hazardous during heavy surf.

CITY T-PIERS: Both the North and South T-Piers are used primarily for fishing and commercial boat docking. Public parking at both piers, west of the Embarcadero; restrooms, restaurant, bait and tackle shop, and fish loading facilities at the North T-Pier. Two U.S. Coast Guard cutters berth at the North T-Pier and are usually open for tours weekdays 4 PM-6 PM and weekends and holidays 12 PM-4 PM; call (805) 772-1293. For Morro Bay boating information, contact the Harbormaster office at the base of the pier: (805) 772-1214.
Mass Transit: SLOCAT, Morro Bay-Cambria route. North Coastal Transit to Harbor St. and Morro Bay Blvd., Mon.-Sat. only.

MORRO BAY STREET ENDS: All the street ends along the Embarcadero between Beach St. and Anchor St. lead to the bay and provide public access for viewing and fishing; limited on-street parking. There are shops and restaurants along the Embarcadero.
Mass Transit: SLOCAT, Morro Bay-Cambria route. North Coastal Transit to Harbor St. and Morro Bay Blvd., Mon.-Sat. only.

Morro Bay, City T-Pier

Clams

A variety of clams are found along the California coast; bent-nosed, geoduck, gaper, soft-shell, and Washington clams live in the mudflats of bays and lagoons which contain quiet waters with little oxygen content. Chione species and jackknife clams prefer the same environment, but their range is limited to south of Point Conception. Littleneck clams, or rock cockles, live in the gravel areas of bays.

Razor clams, considered the most delicious, are also the fastest burrowers and are found at gently sloping beaches with moderate surf, most commonly along the Del Norte and Humboldt County coasts. The Pismo clam is probably the most popular, and is found on beaches between Half Moon Bay (in San Mateo County) and Baja California, with the greatest population at Pismo State Beach.

Clams are filter feeders. To feed, they extend a double tubed siphon to the surface of the sand and draw water and food in one tube while expelling the waste through the second tube. Clams can often be located by searching for exposed siphon tubes. One clam, the large gaper, expels from its tube, at fairly regular intervals, jets of water two or three feet in the air, sometimes hitting those who attempt to disturb it.

Clams are potentially prolific reproducers. For example, a single, sexually mature Pismo clam will spawn about 15 million eggs. These eggs hatch into free-swimming larvae which must settle into the sand and attach themselves to grains of sand where they develop into young clams. During this free-swimming period a majority of the larvae succumb to predation and unfavorable environmental conditions.

Those clams which manage to establish themselves in the sand are subject to predation by shorebirds, gulls, surf fish, and people, who are the greatest predators; the California Department of Fish and Game reported that 150,000 people once removed 75,000 pounds of clams during a single weekend at Pismo State Beach. In fact, the Pismo clam, once so abundant it was commercially harvested at southern California beaches by the wagonload, is now usually found only at low tide by clam diggers who are willing to wade out into sometimes hazardous surf.

common littleneck clam
1.5"-2"

160

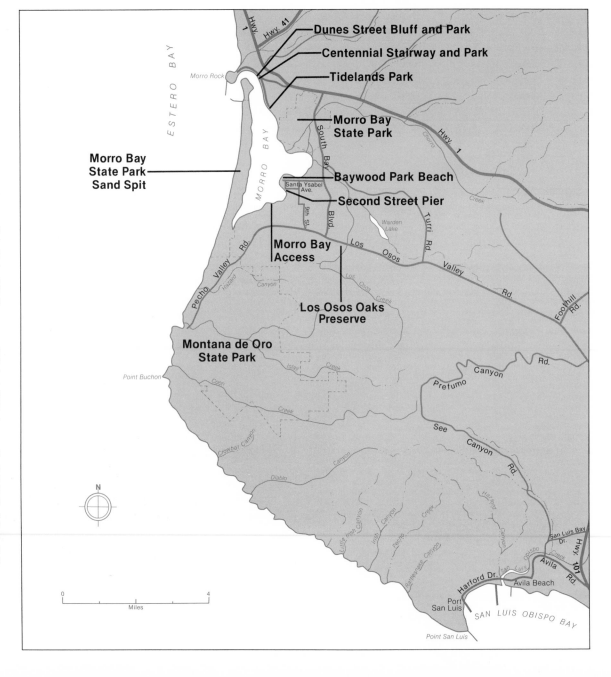

San Luis Obispo County

SOUTH MORRO BAY

NAME	LOCATION	FACILITIES															ENVIRONMENT						
		Entrance/Parking Fee	Parking	Restrooms	Lifeguard	Campground	Showers	Firepits	Stairs to Beach	Path to Beach	Bike Path	Hiking Trail	Facilities for Disabled	Boating Facilities	Fishing	Equestrian Trail	Sandy Beach	Dunes	Rocky Shore	Upland from Beach	Stream Corridor	Bluff	Wetland
Dunes Street Bluff and Park	W. of Dunes St., 1 block N. of Harbor St. on the Embarcadero, Morro Bay													•	•					•		•	
Centennial Stairway and Park	W. of Morro Bay Blvd., at Front St. and the Embarcadero, Morro Bay			•													•						
Tidelands Park	S. end of the Embarcadero, Morro Bay		•	•										•	•								
Morro Bay State Park	S.W. of Hwy. 1 at S. Bay Blvd., Morro Bay	•	•	•		•	•	•		•		•	•	•	•		•						•
Baywood Park Beach	W. of Pasadena Dr. between Santa Ysabel Ave. and Baywood Way, Baywood Park		•							•							•						
Second Street Pier	S. end of Second St., Baywood Park		•														•						
Morro Bay Access	N. end of Doris Ave., N. of Mitchell Dr., Cuesta By the Sea		•														•						
Morro Bay State Park Sand Spit	W. of Morro Bay											•			•		•	•					
Los Osos Oaks Preserve	S. of Los Osos Valley Rd. at Palamino Dr., Los Osos		•									•								•			
Montana de Oro State Park	S. end of Pecho Valley Rd.	•	•	•		•		•		•		•		•	•		•		•	•	•	•	

DUNES STREET BLUFF AND PARK: There is a vista point with a public bench at the end of Dunes St. above the Embarcadero. West of the Embarcadero is a small grassy park with benches and tables adjacent to Morro Bay. There is also a small boat dock with slips and a fishing and viewing deck.
Mass Transit: San Luis Obispo County Area Transit (SLOCAT), Morro Bay-Cambria route. North Coastal Transit, Mon.-Sat. only.

CENTENNIAL STAIRWAY AND PARK: A stairway leads from the west end of Morro Bay Blvd. down to a small park which contains benches, a shuffleboard court, and a giant chessboard. Restrooms are west of the Embarcadero at the end of Front Street. For information, call: (805) 772-1214.
Mass Transit: SLOCAT, Morro Bay-Cambria route. North Coastal Transit to Harbor St. and Morro Bay Blvd., Mon.-Sat. only.

TIDELANDS PARK: Two-lane boat ramp with two docks is adjacent to a small picnic area at the south end of the parking lot. No mooring of boats is allowed at the ramps or buoys. Fish cleaning station near the ramps; parking spaces for boat trailers. For information, call: (805) 772-1214.

MORRO BAY STATE PARK: Park entrances are one mile south of Highway 1 on South Bay Blvd., and at the south end of Main St. in Morro Bay. Most of the park overlooks Morro Bay and the southern mudflats at the mouth of Los Osos Creek; best vista points are at the peak of Black Mountain and from the Museum of Natural History at White Point. The Natural History Museum has exhibits of wildlife, ecology, and Native American history of Morro Bay; open daily 10 AM-5 PM; $.50/adult, $.25/child entrance fee. The museum and some park restrooms are accessible to wheelchairs. Museum: (805) 772-2694.

The campground contains 135 units with tables and stoves; 20 sites have electric and water hookups. Laundry tubs available. $6 overnight fee, $9 with hookups; $2 day use fee for picnic sites. 50-person group campground is at Chorro Creek, east of South Bay Blvd.; reservations required. Some campsites are wheelchair accessible. En route campsites are also available for self-contained R.V.'s. An 18-hole public golf course is accessible from Black Mountain or Golf Course Roads. Park facilities include a small car-top boat launch ramp and a path to the beach north of the museum, and a dock with berths and restrooms to the south. Protected heron rookery is south of the park's west entrance;

visitors may observe from the road but may not enter or disturb the herons. Great blue herons nest in the eucalyptus treetops from January to August. For information, call: (805) 772-2560.
Mass Transit: North Coastal Transit to Quintana Rd. and South Bay Blvd., Mon.-Sat. only.

BAYWOOD PARK BEACH: A public path leads from the small parking area on Pasadena Dr. to a sandy beach with picnic tables and benches. The beach provides access to Morro Bay mudflats at low tides.
Mass Transit: North Coastal Transit, Mon.-Sat. only.

SECOND STREET PIER: 50-foot long T-pier, primarily used as a vista point. Benches are in a cypress grove to the east. A County street right-of-way at the south end of First St. also provides bay access.
Mass Transit: North Coastal Transit, Mon.-Sat. only.

MORRO BAY ACCESS: A 40-foot wide dirt accessway leads to Morro Bay; popular bird-watching area. Limited on-street parking. The extent of public and private rights is undetermined and is subject to further investigation.
Mass Transit: SLOCAT, Los Osos Route 2. North Coastal Transit, Mon.-Sat. only.

MORRO BAY STATE PARK SAND SPIT: Undeveloped; popular for bird-watching and clamming. Best access is by private boat or by rental boat available at the foot of Pacific Ave. off of the Embarca-

dero. Dirt road access for four-wheel drive vehicles begins off Pecho Valley Rd., 1/2 mile south of the junction with Los Osos Rd.

LOS OSOS OAKS PRESERVE: Two miles of marked trails lead through undisturbed groves of scenic old-growth coast live oak; the preserve contains vista points overlooking the Los Osos Valley and the Santa Lucia Mountains. Fragile environment; do not leave main trails. Poison oak is prevalent. Dogs are prohibited.
Mass Transit: SLOCAT, Los Osos Route 4.

MONTANA DE ORO STATE PARK: 6,956 acres and 1.5 miles of coastline south of the Morro Bay Sand Spit. 50 campsites with tables and stoves are east of the ranger's office above the Spooners Cove beach and day use parking area; $3 overnight fee. There are also four environmental campsites. The park contains 50 miles of trails, some of which are open to equestrian use. Hazard Canyon Trail is 1.5 miles south of the park entrance on the west side of Pecho Valley Rd.; the 1/4-mile long path leads through eucalyptus groves used by the Monarch butterflies for nesting October through March. Several trails to blufftop overlooks begin along the road between the park office and Coon Creek to the south. Special equestrian camp area is 1/4 mile south of the park entrance on Pecho Valley Rd., and contains two camps, each with a 25-horse and 12-vehicle limit. Camping fee: $4/night, plus $1/horse. Dogs prohibited on trails. Equestrian camps available by reservation only: Morro Bay State Park, Lower State Park Rd., Morro Bay 93442. Call: (805) 528-0513 (summer only) or 772-2560.

gaper clam
6"-8"

razor clam
4"-6"

Pismo clam
4.5"-5"

Clamming

The Pismo clam is the most sought-after clam along the central California coast. Adapted to an environment of well-oxygenated surf, Pismo clams burrow no more than six inches deep and are usually found in areas of one to three feet of water at low tide.

To dig for Pismo clams, use a clam fork with 8 to 10 inch tines. Attach a "C" type clamming gauge with a 4-1/2 inch span to the handle and use this gauge to measure every clam removed. Clams less than 4-1/2 inches across their greatest width must be reburied on their edge, with the points of their shells toward the ocean and the small dark buttons near the hinges pointing upwards.

To locate clams, work in a line parallel to the edge of the ocean, probing with a clam fork about every two inches until a clam is found. Always face the breaking surf in order to anticipate large waves; rip currents are extremely dangerous. Never clam in water deeper than waist high, or deeper than knee high if wearing waders; large waves can fill them and pull you down. Clam bags should be easily detachable so that they do not become dangerous weights.

Pismo clams may be taken anywhere along the coast except in the following preserves in San Luis Obispo County: along Atascadero State Beach between Azure Street and Morro Rock; along Montano de Oro State Park between the southern tip of Morro Bay and Hazard Canyon; along Pismo State Beach between the Grand Avenue vehicle ramp and .3 mile north, and from the mouth of Oso Flaco Creek to the county line at the Santa Maria River.

Preserve areas alternate approximately every five years; contact the California Department of Fish and Game for the most up-to-date information.

Many other species of clams grow in the mud and gravel of bays, estuaries, and river mouths. These clams live eight inches to three feet below the surface, depending on the species and age of the clam. Along mudflats at low tide, clam diggers with shovels, clam forks, or trowels are frequently seen digging clams out of their burrows.

Clams may be taken only between one-half hour before sunrise to one-half hour after sunset. Licenses are required. For bag limits, seasons, and size restrictions, refer to the current California Sport Fishing Regulations, available at sporting goods stores or from the Department of Fish and Game.

NAME	LOCATION	Entrance/Parking Fee	Parking	Restrooms	Lifeguard	Campground	Showers	Firepits	Stairs to Beach	Path to Beach	Bike Path	Hiking Trail	Facilities for Disabled	Boating Facilities	Fishing	Equestrian Trail	Sandy Beach	Dunes	Rocky Shore	Upland from Beach	Stream Corridor	Bluff	Wetland
Port San Luis	W. end of Harford Dr., Avila Beach	●	●											●	●								
Port San Luis Beach	Along Harford Dr., W. of Avila State Beach, Avila Beach								●								●						
Avila State Beach	S. of Front St., between Harford Dr. and San Rafael St., Avila Beach	●	●	●			●		●						●		●						
Spyglass City Park	S.W. intersection of Spyglass Dr. and Solano Rd., Shell Beach	●							●										●			●	
Seacliff City Park	Along seaward edge of Seacliff Dr., Shell Beach	●																	●	●		●	
Vista Point	S.W. corner of Naomi Ave. and Seacliff Dr., Shell Beach	●																	●			●	
Ocean City Park	Along Ocean Blvd. between Vista Del Mar and Capistrano Aves., Shell Beach	●							●										●			●	
Margo Dodd City Park	Along Ocean Blvd. from Windward to Cliff Aves. and just S. of Cliff Ave., Shell Beach	●							●										●	●		●	
Elmer Ross Beach	S. of intersection of Mattie Rd. and Shell Beach Rd., Shell Beach	●							●										●			●	

PORT SAN LUIS: Vehicles are allowed to drive onto the 1,320-foot long pier which is lit at night. Boating facilities include: 500-lb. capacity small boat hoist; 15,000-lb. capacity trailer boat hoist (open 5 AM-7 PM); 50-ton capacity mobile hoist (open 7 AM-3:30 PM); diesel fuel dock at the pier end; gasoline and diesel dock for shallow draft boats, located east of the pier; trailer boat parking; boat storage; and limited visitor moorings (two week limit). Launching and storage fees. For information: Box 249, Pier 3, Avila Beach 93424. (805) 595-2381.

PORT SAN LUIS BEACH: Sandy beach at the foot of the seawall along Harford Dr., between Port San Luis and the Union Oil Pier; two stairways lead to the beach.

AVILA STATE BEACH: Playground equipment and volleyball standards are along the beach west of the public fishing pier; fish cleaning facilities at the pier. Lifeguards on duty during the summer.

SPYGLASS CITY PARK: Grassy bluffs at the west end of the parking lot; a dirt pathway leads to the rocky shore and tidepools below. Bluffs are highly eroded. Additional access to the bluffs is from the pathway at the northwest corner of Seacliff Dr.; private property is on either side of the path. Do not trespass.
Mass Transit: South County Area Transit (SCAT), Express route.

SEACLIFF CITY PARK: Grassy blufftop overlook with benches for viewing.
Mass Transit: SCAT, Express route.

VISTA POINT: Narrow, gravel pathway begins at the southwest corner of Naomi Ave. and Seacliff Dr. and leads to a public walkway ending at a blufftop viewing pavilion with benches. The concrete walkway above the gravel path and the property on both sides of the accessway are private; do not trespass.

OCEAN CITY PARK: Grassy park on the bluffs overlooking the ocean; facilities include benches, bike storage racks, a short concrete walkway, and picnic tables. Stairways leading to the sandy beach and tidepools below are located at the end of Vista Del Mar Ave., between Cuyama and Morro Avenues, and at the ends of Morro and Palomar Avenues.
Mass Transit: SCAT, Express route.

MARGO DODD CITY PARK: Grassy blufftop park; dirt parking areas are west of Seaview Ave. and south of Cliff Avenue. A stairway to a rocky beach is at the end of Pier Avenue. Bluffs are highly eroded.
Mass Transit: SCAT, Express route.

ELMER ROSS BEACH: Rocky pocket beach adjacent to the Shore Cliff Lodge and Motel. Beach and metal circular stairway are public; access to the stairs is through the wooden gate at the parking lot. Lodge facilities other than the accessway are private. Do not trespass.
Mass Transit: SCAT, Express route.

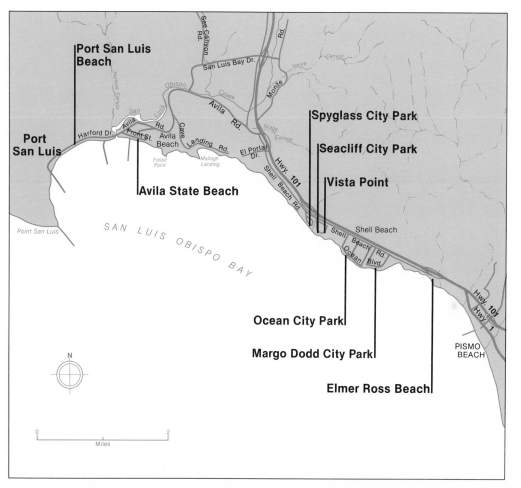

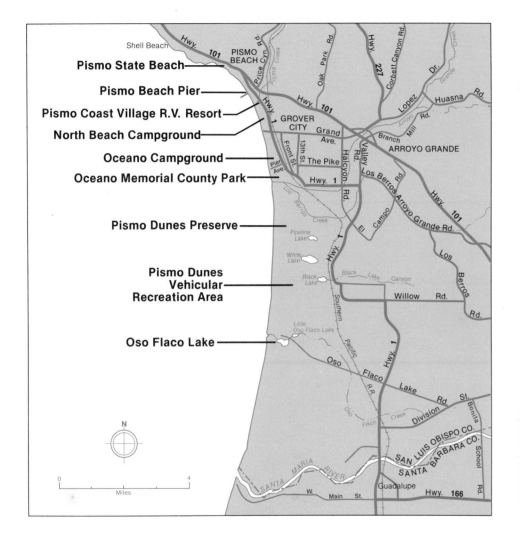

Pismo State Beach

Pismo Beach Pier

Pismo Coast Village R.V. Resort

North Beach Campground

Oceano Campground

Oceano Memorial County Park

Pismo Dunes Preserve

Pismo Dunes
Vehicular
Recreation Area

Oso Flaco Lake

Pismo State Beach

Oso Flaco Lake

NAME	LOCATION	Entrance/Parking Fee	Parking	Restrooms	Lifeguard	Campground	Showers	Firepits	Stairs to Beach	Path to Beach	Bike Path	Hiking Trail	Facilities for Disabled	Boating Facilities	Fishing	Equestrian Trail	Sandy Beach	Dunes	Rocky Shore	Upland from Beach	Stream Corridor	Bluff	Wetland
Pismo State Beach	Runs from Wilmar Ave. to the county line		•						•	•					•		•	•					
Pismo Beach Pier	End of Pomeroy and Hinds Aves., Pismo Beach		•	•					•	•			•		•		•						
Pismo Coast Village R.V. Resort	1615 S. Dolliver St. (Hwy. 1), Pismo Beach	•	•	•		•	•	•									•						
Pismo State Beach North Beach Campground	S. Dolliver St. (Hwy. 1), S. of Addie St., Pismo Beach	•	•	•		•	•			•							•	•					•
Pismo State Beach Oceano Campground	Roosevelt Dr., E. of Pier Ave., Oceano City	•	•	•		•	•			•							•	•		•	•		
Oceano Memorial County Park	Along Pier Ave. and Mendel Dr., Oceano City	•	•	•		•	•	•												•			•
Pismo Dunes Preserve	S. of Arroyo Grande Creek											•					•	•					
Pismo Dunes Vehicular Recreation Area	W. of Hwy. 1, S. of Oceano City	•															•	•					
Oso Flaco Lake	W. end of Oso Flaco Lake Rd.		•				•											•		•			•

Pismo State Beach runs from the foot of Wilmar St. to the county line at the Santa Maria River. The area north of Pismo Creek is administered by the City of Pismo Beach; the area south of the creek is administered by the State Department of Parks and Recreation. For information: (805) 489-2684.

PISMO STATE BEACH: The following street ends have paths and/or stairways leading to Pismo State Beach: Wilmar St., Wadsworth Ave., Main St., Stimson Ave., Ocean View Ave., Park Ave., Addie St., La Sage Dr., Grand Ave., Pier Ave., McCarthy St., Juanita St., Gray St., Surf St., York St., and Utah St.
Mass Transit: South County Area Transit (SCAT), Local and Express routes, and South County Express (SCE).

PISMO BEACH PIER: 950 feet long, lit at night, with wheelchair access. Stairs to a wide, sandy beach are at the north end of the parking lot. Concession stand, bait sales, and fishing equipment rentals. Surfing allowed south of the pier only.
Mass Transit: SCAT, Local and Express routes, and SCE.

PISMO COAST VILLAGE R.V. RESORT: 400 R.V. sites with full hookups, located adjacent to Pismo State Beach. Laundry, store, and pool. Camping fee $14/night (summer), $10.50/night (non-summer months). Information and reservations: 1615 S. Dolliver St., Pismo Beach 93449, (805) 773-1811.
Mass Transit: SCAT, Local and Express routes.

PISMO STATE BEACH NORTH BEACH CAMPGROUND: 300 yards from the ocean, separated by sand dunes and eucalyptus groves. Contains 103 campsites with stoves and tables; $6 overnight fee. Meadow Creek is along the south boundary of the campground; a trail to the beach which extends along the creek begins off Dolliver St. and passes through a Monarch butterfly preserve. Trailer sanitation station is near the entry kiosk. Information: (805) 489-2684. Pismo Beach Golf Course, which is open to the public, is south of the campground off La Sage Drive. Golf Course: (805) 489-9939.
Mass Transit: SCAT, Local and Express routes.

PISMO STATE BEACH OCEANO CAMPGROUND: Adjoins the Oceano Lagoon to the east and Pismo Beach to the west; short hike to the ocean. 82 campsites with stoves and tables; 42 have trailer hookups. $6 overnight fee, $9 with hookups. Hiking trail around the lagoon begins along the eastern side of the campground. 500 additional primitive campsites primarily for trailers are along the beach beginning 3/4 mile south of Arroyo Grande Creek; $3 fee. For information: (805) 489-2684.
Mass Transit: SCAT, Local route.

OCEANO MEMORIAL COUNTY PARK: Overnight camping area is southwest of Mendel Dr. and Pier Ave.; 64 campsites, some with trailer hookups. Overnight fee $6, $3/additional vehicle. Discount for 7, 14, and 30 day visits between October 15 and March 15. No reservations accepted. Day use grassy park is west of Norswing Dr. and north of Mendel Dr.; contains picnic sites, playground, and the Oceano Lagoon. Information: County General Services Department, (805) 549-5930.
Mass Transit: SCAT, Local route.

PISMO DUNES PRESERVE: The area of the dunes adjacent to the ocean, from Arroyo Grande Creek to approximately 1.5 miles south and 1 mile inland, is restricted from vehicular use. Unique, undeveloped areas of large dunes; popular with hikers.

PISMO DUNES VEHICULAR RECREATION AREA: 850 acres of dunes and hard, sandy beach open to vehicular use. Vehicle access to the beach at non-high tides is from the ramps at the ends of Grand and Pier Avenues. Street-legal vehicles are permitted between Meadow Creek and the Sand Highway. Off-highway vehicles are allowed only between the Sand Highway and Oso Flaco Creek, and in designated dune areas. Fee for O.H.V. day use; reservations through Ticketron required.

Vehicles driven in the dunes must conform to the Pismo Beach off-highway vehicle regulations: vehicles must have a flag 10 feet tall, and are prohibited within the dune preserve and any vegetated areas or private property; vehicles with more than three wheels must have a roll bar or cage; drivers must be licensed or be accompanied by a licensed driver. Regulations may change; drivers are responsible for knowing all rules. For current information, or maps defining staging areas and boundaries of the O.H.V. area, contact the ranger at the Pismo State Beach Oceano Campground: (805) 489-2684, or the State Department of Parks and Recreation in San Luis Obispo: (805) 543-2161.

OSO FLACO LAKE: 3.6 miles west of Highway 1; 75-acre lake and marshland area located within the Pismo Dunes. Limited trailer camping permitted along the roadside near the lake.

Jalama Beach County Park

Santa Barbara County

South of the San Luis Obispo County line, the vast sand dunes of Guadalupe give way to the undeveloped Casmalia and Solomon Hills, which border the rugged coastline between Point Sal and Point Conception in Santa Barbara County. The steep hillsides here abut the shoreline, creating narrow, sandy beaches which are secluded because of their distance from Highway 101.

At Point Conception, the shoreline curves abruptly east, providing an unusually long stretch of coast which faces south and is sheltered from large waves by the northern Channel Islands, located offshore 20 to 30 miles south. The sandy beaches here, known for good swimming, are situated beneath the bluffs of the narrow coastal terrace which extends from Point Conception to the south county line. Bordering this terrace to the north are the scenic mountains of the Santa Ynez range, characterized by steep-walled canyons and sharp peaks which vary in elevation from 1,500 to 4,000 feet.

Between the south county shoreline and the Channel Islands is the Santa Barbara Channel, noted as a productive fishery resource. The Chumash Indians, who settled in large villages along the Santa Barbara and Ventura County coasts, caught such great quantities of swordfish, marlin, tuna, sardines, and other fish in the channel that some early Spanish explorers were prompted to believe that the fishing industry alone could support all future settlers.

Beneath the Santa Ynez Mountains and adjacent to the Santa Barbara Channel is the City of Santa Barbara. The city, with its numerous Spanish style buildings, was once the site of one of the larger coastal Chumash villages. It was here that Captain José Francisco Ortega, accompanied by Father Junípero Serra, founded a military presidio in 1782 to protect the Spanish-claimed coast from Russian explorers. In 1786, the Spanish established the Santa Barbara Mission for the purpose of converting the neighboring Indians to Christianity; this had devastating effects on the Chumash culture.

After secularization of the Mission in 1834, officers of the presidio were given large and very profitable land grant ranches along the Santa Barbara coast. Among these was Rancho Lompoc, which, after the ranch's subdivision in 1874, eventually became the city of Lompoc, now noted as one of the largest commercial flower-growing areas on the west coast. Directly north of Lompoc is the vast Vandenberg Air Force Base, established by the military in 1949 for coastal defense. Point Sal State Beach is on the northern boundary of the Vandenberg base, and is one of the most secluded beaches in the county.

The Southern Pacific Railroad line runs along three quarters of the county's coast directly above the shoreline, from the Ventura County boundary to six miles south of Point Sal, before heading inland. Amtrak's Coast Starlight passenger train runs this route daily, providing one of the most scenic railroad trips available on the California coast.

Santa Barbara County includes four of the offshore islands within the Channel Islands National Park. Described as America's Galapagos, the isolated islands support many unique species of flora and fauna not found on the mainland. Several of the islands are open to public access; visiting permits are usually required.

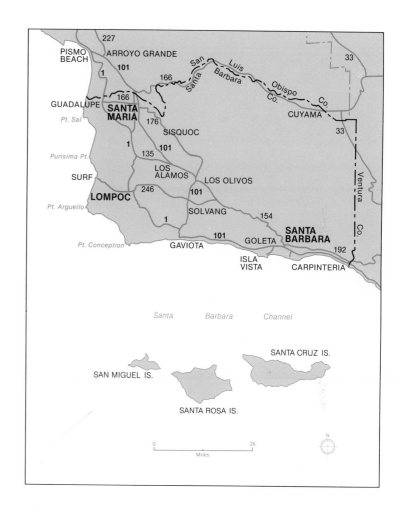

For more information on Santa Barbara County's coast, contact the Santa Barbara City Chamber of Commerce, P.O. Box 299, Santa Barbara 93102, (805) 965-3021, or the Carpinteria Chamber of Commerce, P.O. Box 956, Carpinteria 93013, (805) 684-5479. For transit information, write or call the Santa Barbara Metropolitan Transit District (MTD), P.O. Box 355, Santa Barbara 93102, (805) 962-7682.

Sand Dunes

Sand dunes are a prominent landscape feature found at numerous locations along the California coast. Sand dunes are likely to develop in areas where an abundant sand supply restricted to a limited portion of coastline is combined with strong onshore winds, a gently sloping beach, relatively low precipitation and humidity, and large differences between high and low tide levels.

Typical dune formation occurs when onshore winds transport loose, dry sand across wide stretches of low-lying beach areas. The sand accumulates around vegetation, driftwood, or other elements that inhibit air flow. Eventually, the stockpiled sand forms continuous ridges perpendicular to the prevailing winds.

Examples of areas in California with large coastal dune fields include Pelican Bay, north of Crescent City; the Humboldt Bay area; Inglenook Fen/MacKerricher State Beach, north of Fort Bragg; Ocean Beach, San Francisco; Monterey Bay; and Pismo and Guadalupe Dunes, west of Santa Maria.

Coastal dune systems naturally protect low-lying inland areas from ocean storms. The dunes provide a large buffer of sand that absorbs wave energy and prevents storm waves from eroding areas farther inland. Portions of a dune field may be obliterated by a single winter storm. However, during calmer periods, the dune system will rebuild.

Although sand dunes can provide valuable protection from the erosive power of ocean waves, the dune field itself is a very delicate system. A healthy, stable dune system consists of a series of dune ridges stabilized by salt tolerant grasses and other vegetation such as hottentot fig, sand verbena, and salt bush. The vegetative cover can be removed by natural causes such as storms or, as is often the case, as a result of paths made by vehicles and people.

A loss of this protective cover can destroy dune stability and cause the eventual loss of a dune system. As dunes lose stability, sand migrates inland with the prevailing wind and covers highways, houses, and inland vegetation, creating an expensive and hazardous maintenance problem. In addition, sand blown inland is no longer available for natural beach replenishment.

Visitors are encouraged to enjoy the beauty of the sand dunes, but are asked to respect the fragile nature of the system; stay on marked trails, avoid trampling dune vegetation, and watch for warning or use information signs.

Evening primrose *Oenothera cheiranthifolia*   Hottentot fig *Mesembryanthemum edule*   Beach morning glory *Convolvulus soldanella*   Salt bush *Atriplex semibaccata*

Santa Barbara County
NORTHERN SANTA BARBARA COAST

NAME	LOCATION	Entrance/Parking Fee	Parking	Restrooms	Lifeguard	Campground	Showers	Firepits	Stairs to Beach	Path to Beach	Bike Path	Hiking Trail	Facilities for Disabled	Boating Facilities	Fishing	Equestrian Trail	Sandy Beach	Dunes	Rocky Shore	Upland from Beach	Stream Corridor	Bluff	Wetland
Rancho Guadalupe County Park	W. end of Main St., Guadalupe		●												●		●	●		●			●
Point Sal State Beach	End of Brown and Point Sal Roads, W. of Guadalupe		●							●					●		●	●	●			●	
Vandenberg Air Force Base Blufftop Access	From Purisima Point to 3-1/2 mi. S. of the Point		●							●					●		●		●			●	
Ocean Beach County Park	Ocean Park Rd., 10 mi. W. of Hwy. 1, Surf		●	●				●		●					●		●	●					●
Vandenberg Air Force Base Beach Access	From 1-1/2 mi. N. to 3-1/2 mi. S. of Ocean Beach County Park														●		●					●	
Jalama Beach County Park	Jalama Beach Rd., 20 mi. S. of Lompoc	●	●	●		●		●				●	●		●		●		●			●	●

RANCHO GUADALUPE COUNTY PARK: 26-acre unimproved park located within the Guadalupe dunes just south of the Santa Maria River. The dunes provide habitat for several endangered bird species such as the California least tern and California brown pelican, and endangered plants such as the surf thistle *(Cirsium rhothophilum)*. Popular area for fishing. The park is the site of the highest sand dune on the west coast, Mussel Rock at 450 feet. There is a wetland area at the Santa Maria River mouth. Wind-blown sand frequently closes the parking lot and entrance road. For information, call: (805) 937-1302.

POINT SAL STATE BEACH: Secluded, undeveloped beach nine miles west of Highway 1 at the foot of the Casmalia Hills; access is via the long, rough, dirt Point Sal Road. The road is unmaintained, often impassable, and subject to closure during the winter or during missile launchings at Vandenberg Air Force Base. Steep paths lead to the beach from the dirt parking area. Point Sal, which is a harbor seal haul-out and seabird roosting area, is within walking distance. For information, call: (805) 733-3713.

VANDENBERG AIR FORCE BASE BLUFFTOP ACCESS: Limited public access along the blufftop from Purisima Point south for 3-1/2 miles; trails lead down the steep bluffs to pocket beaches. No swimming or diving; fishing and abalone gathering are permitted. Visitors must first obtain a pass from the Game Warden at Building 13401 on the Base; the pass contains information on which roads to use and where to park. Access is limited to 50 persons per day, weekends and holidays only. Game Warden: (805) 866-6804.

OCEAN BEACH COUNTY PARK: Take Highway 246 to Ocean Park Road. 28-acre park contains a broad beach area and lagoon at the mouth of the Santa Ynez River. The area is a habitat for several endangered species such as the California brown pelican, the California least tern, and salt marsh bird's beak plant *(Cordylanthus maritimus maritimus)*. Picnic tables and barbecue pits are available. A 1/4-mile long path beneath the railroad trestle leads to the beach. Certain portions of the sand dunes may be closed to public use in order to protect nesting least terns from April to September. Information: (805) 736-0443.

VANDENBERG AIR FORCE BASE BEACH ACCESS: Unlimited public beach access is available from 1-1/2 miles north of Ocean Beach County Park to 3-1/2 miles south of Ocean Beach. No swimming or diving; fishing is permitted. Use the parking and restroom facilities at Ocean Beach.

JALAMA BEACH COUNTY PARK: 28 acres; broad beach area with coastal bluffs north of Point Conception. Facilities include 120 campsites, store, and snack stand. $5 camping fee, $2 day use fee. Restrooms are accessible to wheelchairs. The drainage of Jalama Creek creates a small wetland habitat frequented by the endangered California brown pelican. The beach is popular for surfing and surf fishing. Hazardous rip currents. For information: (805) 734-1446. For campsite reservations, call: (805) 963-7108. Vandenberg Air Force Base also provides one mile of unlimited beach access north of Jalama Beach.

Amtrak Coast Starlight

The Amtrak Coast Starlight, a passenger train that runs daily between Seattle, Washington and Los Angeles, California, provides panoramic views of much of the California coast between Monterey and Ventura counties. Some portions of the coast along the train's route are not readily accessible by any other means. Points of interest along the Coast Starlight's route include Elkhorn Slough, the sand dunes along the San Luis Obispo and Santa Barbara County coasts, Vandenberg Air Force Base, and the Santa Barbara Channel coast. For the best views of the coast, passengers should sit in the upper deck of one of the Starlight's observation cars.

Approximately one hour out of the San Jose station going south (about 10 minutes out of Salinas going north), the Coast Starlight begins its run close to the Monterey County coast at the Elkhorn Slough estuary, one of the richest wildlife habitats in California. The origin of the slough is not completely certain. One theory is that during the Pleistocene period (10,000 to 3 million years ago), the slough was the point where runoff from the Sacramento and San Joaquin valleys emptied into the Pacific Ocean. Elkhorn Slough was fed regularly with flows from the Salinas River until the early 1900's, when a new river mouth was formed by extensive flooding caused by heavy storms; the old river channel that ran to the slough was subsequently diked.

Today the slough provides valuable habitat for harbor seals, sea otters, and more than 70 species of fish and 90 species of birds; as many as 20,000 birds may be seen nesting and feeding in the slough at one time. Elkhorn Slough meets Monterey Bay at Moss Landing, which is the location of a Pacific Gas and Electric Company electric power generating station. The power plant's twin smokestacks can be seen rising above the horizon beyond the slough. The agricultural fields seen along the slough are used primarily for growing strawberries.

After leaving Salinas, the Coast Starlight travels south through the Salinas River Valley on the train's way to the City of San Luis Obispo. As the Starlight descends the Cuesta Pass into San Luis Obispo, a string of eroded, conical-shaped peaks come into view. These peaks, or volcanic plugs, are the remnants of volcanic activity that occurred 11-25 million years ago. The peaks lie in a line from the City of San Luis Obispo to Morro Bay. The westernmost peak (not visible from the train), which is 576 feet high, is Morro Rock, at the mouth of Morro Bay. Bus transportation to Hearst Castle, which is located on the coast at San Simeon, north of Morro Bay, is available to passengers disembarking in the City of San Luis Obispo.

About 15 minutes out of San Luis Obispo going south (two hours and 15 minutes out of the Santa Barbara station going north), the Starlight reaches the coastline at Pismo Beach, long known as a summer seaside resort and famous for Pismo clams. Pismo Beach is the northern end of a 40-mile stretch of coast that is characterized by extensive sand dunes. The Coast Starlight travels along the inland side of the dune fields; at times the shoreline is visible beyond the expanse of bare and vegetated dunes.

Thirty minutes out of San Luis Obispo going south (two hours out of the Santa Barbara station going north), the Coast Starlight crosses the Santa Maria River and enters Santa Barbara County at Guadalupe, a small town that serves as a shipping point for agricultural products from the fertile Santa Maria Valley. Twenty minutes beyond Guadalupe (one hour out of the Santa Barbara station going north), the Starlight enters Vandenberg Air Force Base. Vandenberg has been used as a launch site for satellites and missile tests, and is the west coast launch site for NASA's Space Shuttle; train passengers can see launch pad towers scattered throughout the dunes of the 35-mile long base.

Point Conception, about 1-1/2 hours out of San Luis Obispo going south (50 minutes out of Santa Barbara going north), marks the point where the coastline changes from a north-south orientation and continues to Santa Barbara along a west-to-east line parallel to the Channel Islands. This shoreline orientation, combined with the prevailing wave direction, makes this portion of the coast one of the world's best surfing spots.

Petroleum deposits lie beneath the ocean floor within the Santa Barbara Channel; a number of offshore oil platforms, and the Channel Islands beyond them, are visible from the Coast Starlight. Continuing south to the City of Santa Barbara, the Starlight passes a number of oil storage stations, pumping facilities, and other shoreside facilities that support offshore oil operations.

The Coast Starlight crosses the Santa Barbara-Ventura County line 20 minutes out of Santa Barbara (30 minutes out of Oxnard going north) at Rincon Point, a popular surfing area. The Starlight parallels the Old U.S. Highway 101 from the Rincon area into Ventura; during periods when waves are high, spray from waves breaking on the rocky shoreline may carry over the highway to the railroad tracks.

After crossing the Ventura River, about 30 minutes out of Santa Barbara, the Starlight crosses to the inland side of Highway 101. The masts of boats in the Ventura Marina are the last bit of coastal scenery one can see from the Coast Starlight before it leaves the farms of the Oxnard Plain for the Los Angeles metropolitan area.

For reservations, scheduling, fares, or other information on the Coast Starlight, look for the Amtrak listing in the white pages of your telephone directory.

Santa Barbara County

POINT CONCEPTION TO NAPLES

NAME	LOCATION	Entrance/Parking Fee	Parking	Restrooms	Lifeguard	Campground	Showers	Firepits	Stairs to Beach	Path to Beach	Bike Path	Hiking Trail	Facilities for Disabled	Boating Facilities	Fishing	Equestrian Trail	Sandy Beach	Dunes	Rocky Shore	Upland from Beach	Stream Corridor	Bluff	Wetland
Gaviota Rest Area	U.S. 101, .5 mi. S. of Gaviota Pass		•	•		•														•			
Gaviota State Park	U.S. 101 at Gaviota Beach Rd., Gaviota	•	•	•	•	•	•			•		•	•	•	•		•				•		
Refugio State Beach	S. of U.S. 101 at Refugio Rd., 15 mi. N. of Goleta	•	•	•	•	•	•		•	•	•				•		•		•		•		
Bike Path and Ramp to Beach	Between Refugio and El Capitan State Beaches, Goleta								•	•	•	•	•		•		•		•	•	•		
El Capitan State Beach	S. of U.S. 101, 12 mi. N. of Goleta	•	•	•	•	•	•			•	•	•	•		•		•		•	•			
El Capitan Ranch Park	11560 Calle Real, N. of El Capitan State Beach, Goleta	•	•	•		•	•	•				•								•			

GAVIOTA REST AREA: The rest area is one-half mile from the entrance to Gaviota State Park and is situated in a narrow canyon with a scenic view of the coast. Both the north and south bound stops have 30 parking spaces, restrooms, public telephones, and picnic tables.

GAVIOTA STATE PARK: 2,776 acres. The park has 39 trailer sites, 20 tent sites, and a store at the campground; no hookups or sanitary station. There are also environmental campsites available, and 20 en route campsites for self-contained R.V.'s; $6 camping fee, $3 day use fee. The park extends on both sides of U.S. 101 with primary access at the campground near the ocean. There is a day use picnic area and a fishing pier with a three-ton boat launch; fishing licenses, bait and tackle available. Lifeguards on duty during the summer. Access to the upland wilderness area is via Highway 1 toward Lompoc; turn right at the stop sign. Hiking trails lead from the dirt parking lot to a small hot spring (approximately body temperature) and the Los Padres National Forest; no overnight parking permitted in the parking lot. For information, call: (805) 968-0019.

REFUGIO STATE BEACH: Narrow seasonal beach with rocky shore and tidepools; 90 acres. The campground has 85 campsites and a snack stand. Campground operated year-round. Lifeguards on duty during the summer. Day use parking, en route campsites, fishing licenses, and bait available. $6 camping fee, $3 day use fee. Call: (805) 968-1350 or 968-0019.

BIKE PATH AND RAMP TO BEACH: A bike path, which is also open to hikers, runs seaward of the railroad tracks and Highway 101 between Refugio and El Capitan State Beaches. A newly constructed ramp, located at the south end of the oil facilities tunnel leading to Las Flores Canyon, leads from the path to the two state beaches. The ramp is accessible to wheelchairs.

EL CAPITAN STATE BEACH: 133-acre narrow beach, popular for catching grunion. A hiking trail goes through a grassy picnic area. The campground includes 142 campsites and a snack stand; no hook-ups or sanitary station. Campground open year-round. Day use parking and en route campsites also available. $6 camping fee, $3 day use fee. El Capitan Point is a noted surfing area. Lifeguards on duty during the summer. For information, call: (805) 968-1411 or 968-0019.

EL CAPITAN RANCH PARK: Privately managed campground, located north of Highway 101. Facilities include 200 tent and trailer campsites, store, laundry, snack bar, and game arcade. $8/night (weekdays) and $10/night (weekends) minimum camping fee. Information and reservations: 11560 Calle Real, Goleta 93117; (805) 968-2214.

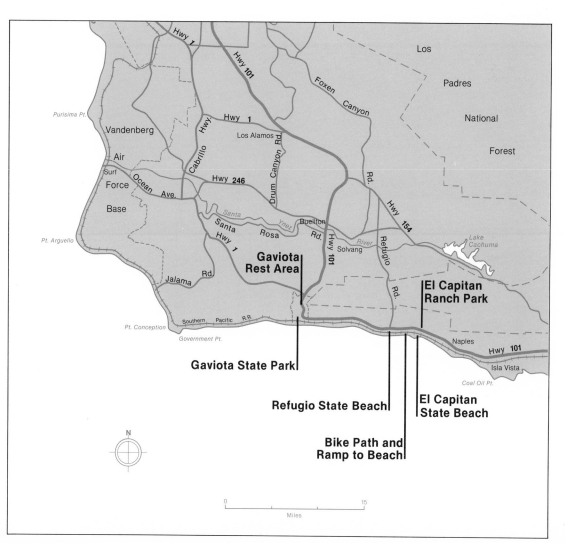

Map: Santa Barbara County coast — Point Conception to Naples. Labeled sites: Gaviota Rest Area, Gaviota State Park, Refugio State Beach, Bike Path and Ramp to Beach, El Capitan State Beach, El Capitan Ranch Park. Place names include Purisima Pt., Vandenberg Air Force Base, Pt. Arguello, Pt. Conception, Government Pt., Jalama Rd., Los Alamos, Buellton, Solvang, Lake Cachuma, Naples, Isla Vista, Coal Oil Pt., Los Padres National Forest; highways Hwy 1, Hwy 101, Hwy 246, Hwy 154; rivers/roads Santa Ynez River, Santa Rosa Rd., Foxen Canyon, Drum Canyon Rd., Refugio Rd., Cabrillo Hwy, Ocean Ave., Southern Pacific R.R.

0 — 15 Miles

171

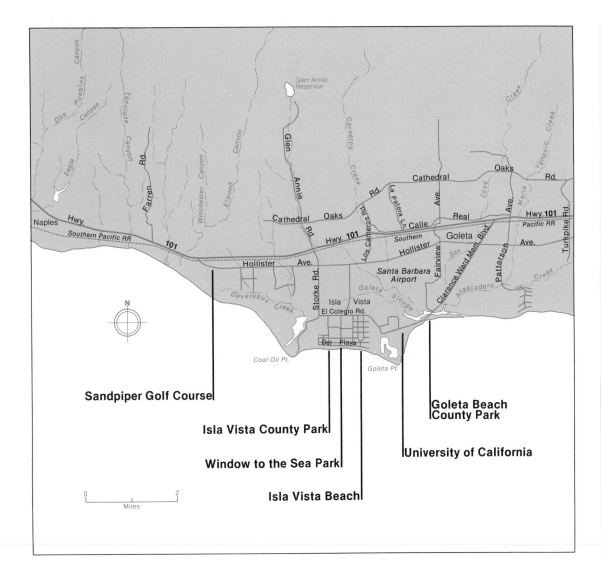

Sandpiper Golf Course

Isla Vista County Park

Window to the Sea Park

Isla Vista Beach

Goleta Beach County Park

University of California

0   2
    Miles

Isla Vista County Park

Santa Barbara County

ISLA VISTA/GOLETA

NAME	LOCATION	Entrance/Parking Fee	Parking	Restrooms	Lifeguard	Campground	Showers	Firepits	Stairs to Beach	Path to Beach	Bike Path	Hiking Trail	Facilities for Disabled	Boating Facilities	Fishing	Equestrian Trail	Sandy Beach	Dunes	Rocky Shore	Upland from Beach	Stream Corridor	Bluff	Wetland
Sandpiper Golf Course	8000 Hollister Ave., Goleta	●	●	●																●		●	
Isla Vista County Park	Del Playa Dr. at Camino Corto, Isla Vista		●						●	●			●			●				●		●	
Window to the Sea Park	Del Playa Dr., just S. of Camino del Sur		●																	●		●	
Isla Vista Beach	S. of Del Playa Dr., Isla Vista		●							●							●		●			●	●
University of California at Santa Barbara	Off Clarence Ward Memorial Blvd., Goleta, and on El Colegio Rd., Isla Vista	●	●	●					●	●	●						●		●	●	●	●	●
Goleta Beach County Park	5990 Sandspit Rd., Goleta		●	●	●		●						●	●	●	●	●		●	●		●	

SANDPIPER GOLF COURSE: Full 18-hole course located on a blufftop overlooking the Santa Barbara Channel. Privately owned, open to the public; the facility includes a pro shop and snack stand. Open weekdays at 7:30 AM and weekends at 6:30 AM. Entrance fee: $11.50 (weekdays) and $14.50 (weekends). (805) 968-1541.
Mass Transit: Santa Barbara Metropolitan Transit District (MTD) Route 6.

ISLA VISTA COUNTY PARK: 1.4-acre grassy blufftop park with picnic tables, blufftop benches, and a sand volleyball court. Overlooks the sandy Isla Vista Beach. A stairway to the beach is west of the grassy area. On-street parking only.
Mass Transit: MTD Route 11 to Sabado Tarde Rd.

WINDOW TO THE SEA PARK: Blufftop overlook; very small landscaped park with a swinging bench. No access to the beach. On-street parking only. (805) 968-2017.
Mass Transit: MTD Route 11 to Sabado Tarde Rd.

ISLA VISTA BEACH: Sandy beach and tidepools; there are stairways to the beach at the ends of Camino Majorca, Camino del Sur, and Camino Pescadero, and a paved ramp leading to the beach at the end of El Embarcadero. Blufftop overlooks are located at the ends of Camino Majorca, Camino Pescadero, and El Embarcadero. On-street parking only.
Mass Transit: MTD Route 11 to Sabado Tarde Rd.

UNIVERSITY OF CALIFORNIA: U.C. Santa Barbara includes the main campus at Goleta Point and the west campus at Coal Oil Point. Pedestrian and bicycle access is permitted through both campuses. Vehicle access through the west campus is limited primarily to those with university business. Visitors may drive on-to the main campus when parking is available; parking fee. Paths and stairs which lead to the beach adjacent to the main campus are located near the Santa Cruz dormitory, and near the south and east portions of the Campus Lagoon.

At the west campus, pedestrian access to the beaches at the Coal Oil Point Reserve is restricted to unposted areas; do not disturb vegetation or other resources. Posted areas are sensitive habitats and use is limited to official scientific study; do not trespass. Devereaux Lagoon, located at the reserve, is a habitat for numerous birds; bird watching is possible from the adjacent entrance road. Good surfing at Coal Oil Point. (805) 961-2311.
Mass Transit: MTD Routes 4 (no weekend service), 9, 11, and 24.

GOLETA BEACH COUNTY PARK: 29-acre park with a wide, sandy beach, a grassy picnic area, and a children's play area. Facilities include volleyball courts, a snack stand, and a recently lengthened fishing pier with a boat hoist (four-ton capacity; $8 fee). Fishing licenses, bait, tackle, and boat and motor rentals available. Restrooms are accessible to wheelchairs. The Goleta Slough wetland area is popular for bird watching. (805) 967-1300.
Mass Transit: MTD Routes 9 and 11.

Coal Oil Point Reserve

Devereaux Lagoon, Coal Oil Point Reserve

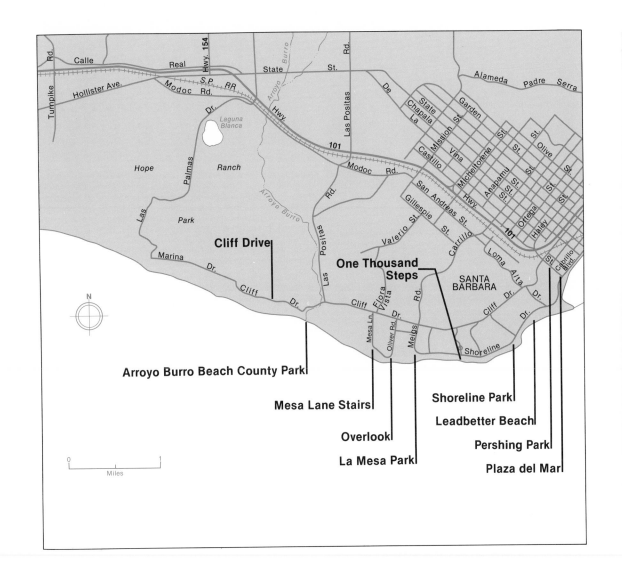

Cliff Drive

One Thousand
Steps

SANTA
BARBARA

Arroyo Burro Beach County Park

Mesa Lane Stairs

Overlook

La Mesa Park

Shoreline Park

Leadbetter Beach

Pershing Park

Plaza del Mar

One Thousand Steps

Santa Barbara County

CITY OF SANTA BARBARA

NAME	LOCATION	Entrance/Parking Fee	Parking	Restrooms	Lifeguard	Campground	Showers	Firepits	Stairs to Beach	Path to Beach	Bike Path	Hiking Trail	Facilities for Disabled	Boating Facilities	Fishing	Equestrian Trail	Sandy Beach	Dunes	Rocky Shore	Upland from Beach	Stream Corridor	Bluff	Wetland
Cliff Drive	W. of Arroyo Burro Beach to Marina Dr., Santa Barbara		•																			•	
Arroyo Burro Beach County Park	2981 Cliff Dr., Santa Barbara		•	•	•		•		•				•		•	•	•		•	•	•	•	
Mesa Lane Stairs	S. end of Mesa Lane, Santa Barbara		•						•								•					•	
Overlook	S. end of Oliver Rd., Santa Barbara		•																•			•	
La Mesa Park	Meigs Rd. at Shoreline Dr., Santa Barbara		•	•				•												•		•	
One Thousand Steps	S. end of Santa Cruz Blvd., Santa Barbara		•						•								•		•			•	
Shoreline Park	1200 Shoreline Dr., Santa Barbara		•	•					•	•							•		•			•	
Leadbetter Beach	1000 Shoreline Dr., Santa Barbara		•	•	•		•						•		•		•						
Pershing Park	200 Castillo St., Santa Barbara		•	•									•							•			
Plaza del Mar	Castillo St. at Cabrillo Blvd., Santa Barbara		•	•									•							•			

Leadbetter Beach

CLIFF DRIVE: Scenic drive with views of the Santa Barbara Channel and Channel Islands; there is a turnout near Yankee Farm Rd.
Mass Transit: Santa Barbara Metropolitan Transit District (MTD) Route 5.

ARROYO BURRO BEACH COUNTY PARK: Six acres. The park contains a natural stream habitat area and coastal bluffs. Facilities include a snack stand, grassy picnic area, and volleyball courts. The parking lot is often crowded on summer days. A short equestrian trail leads from Cliff Dr. to the sandy beach. Lifeguards on duty during the summer. (805) 687-3714.
Mass Transit: MTD Route 5.

MESA LANE STAIRS: A stairway descends a steep cliff to a beach which is popular with surfers and sunbathers. Limited on-street parking.
Mass Transit: MTD Route 5.

OVERLOOK: Undeveloped; provides views of the Channel Islands. Beach access from the overlook is hazardous; use the Mesa Lane Stairs just west.
Mass Transit: MTD Route 5 to Oliver Rd.

LA MESA PARK: Nine-acre neighborhood playground on the bluff above the beach, with picnic tables, barbecue, and play equipment. On-street parking.
Mass Transit: MTD Route 15 to Meigs Rd. and Shoreline Dr.

ONE THOUSAND STEPS: Overlook and stairway to the beach.
Mass Transit: MTD Route 15 to Santa Cruz Blvd. and Shoreline Dr.

SHORELINE PARK: 15-acre linear park with an extensive grassy picnic area, blufftop overlook of the Santa Barbara Harbor and Channel, and children's play area. The park is used for walking, kite flying, frisbee, and picnics. Stairs lead to the shore.
Mass Transit: MTD Route 15.

LEADBETTER BEACH: This popular wide, sandy beach is located along a shallow cove. Facilities include a landscaped picnic area and snack stand. The parking lot is shared with the harbor.
Mass Transit: MTD Route 15.

PERSHING PARK: Five-acre park with a lighted baseball diamond and two softball fields used for team sports. The Santa Barbara City College tennis courts are in the park and are open for public use on weekends.
Mass Transit: MTD Routes 15 and 21.

PLAZA DEL MAR: Five-acre park with a shaded, grassy picnic area and a view of the harbor. Summertime concerts are sometimes held at the band pavilion.
Mass Transit: MTD Routes 15 and 21.

Harbor Seals

The harbor seal *(Phoca vitulina)* differs significantly from the other marine mammals found in the waters off the California coast. The subspecies of harbor seal that inhabits the waters offshore the Santa Barbara and Ventura coasts has a black or brown coat with silver, white, or yellow spots; because of the spots, the harbor seal is sometimes called the leopard seal. As the name suggests, harbor seals are most often found in bays, harbors, and river mouths and are frequently seen hauling out on the sand in these areas. However, harbor seals have also been observed offshore on San Nicolas Island, one of the Channel Islands.

Unlike fur seals and sea lions, harbor seals are unable to turn their hind flippers forward for movement on land. Whereas fur seals and sea lions use their front flippers for swimming, harbor seals rely primarily on their hind flippers. The harbor seals' lack of external ears further distinguishes them from fur seals and sea lions. Male harbor seals average five to six feet in length, with a weight of 275 pounds when fully grown; females are somewhat smaller.

Harbor seals have an interesting diving technique. The seal floats vertically with only its head above the water surface; when it wants to dive, it drops straight down until totally submerged and then turns horizontal to swim.

Harbor seals feed on fish, squid, octopus, and some shellfish. These seals do not breed in colonies. Males do not have harems, which is characteristic of most pinniped species, but they do mate with more than one female. Pups are born from the end of May through July, usually on land.

Harbor seals are protected by state and federal laws.

Santa Barbara County
SANTA BARBARA HARBOR AREA

NAME	LOCATION	Entrance/Parking Fee	Parking	Restrooms	Lifeguard	Campground	Showers	Firepits	Stairs to Beach	Path to Beach	Bike Path	Hiking Trail	Facilities for Disabled	Boating Facilities	Fishing	Equestrian Trail	Sandy Beach	Dunes	Rocky Shore	Upland from Beach	Stream Corridor	Bluff	Wetland
Santa Barbara Harbor	Cabrillo Blvd. at Shoreline Dr., Santa Barbara		•	•			•							•	•								
Los Banos del Mar	400 block of Cabrillo Blvd., Santa Barbara		•	•			•						•						•				
Ambassador Park	100 Cabrillo Blvd., Santa Barbara		•																•				
West Beach Park	Seaward of Cabrillo Blvd., Santa Barbara		•		•					•					•		•						
Stearns Wharf	State St. at Cabrillo Blvd., Santa Barbara	•	•	•									•		•		•						
Palm Park	500 E. Cabrillo Blvd., Santa Barbara		•	•	•			•		•							•						

SANTA BARBARA HARBOR: Multi-use harbor and marina. Facilities include more than 1,000 boat slips, marine specialty shops, boat repair services, restaurants, sport fishing excursions, boat rentals, private floating dry dock, boat hoists (1,000 and 3,000 lb. cap., $2 fee), launching ramp ($4 fee), bait and tackle shop, and yacht club. Fuel dock open 8 AM-5 PM. Guest slips available through Harbormaster; phone (805) 963-1737. Scenic views from the walkway along the breakwater; good surfing conditions outside the harbor.
Mass Transit: Santa Barbara Metropolitan Transit District (MTD) Routes 15 and 21.

LOS BANOS DEL MAR: A municipal swimming pool located at West Beach; offers lessons, and competition and recreational swimming. Use harbor parking lots. For hours and fees, call: (805) 966-6119.
Mass Transit: MTD Route 21.

AMBASSADOR PARK: Grassy open area bordered by palm trees, located on the north side of Cabrillo Boulevard. The half-acre park, which is a State Historic Landmark, is the site of an old Indian village. Provides a view of the harbor.
Mass Transit: MTD Route 21.

WEST BEACH PARK: 11.5 acres; the broad, sandy beach located between Stearns Wharf and the harbor has a boardwalk for pedestrians, bicyclists, and roller skaters.
Mass Transit: MTD Route 21.

STEARNS WHARF: Originally constructed in 1872, Stearns Wharf historically served the City of Santa Barbara as a seaport for cargo, passenger, and fishing ships. Restoration of the wharf was completed in 1981; a major portion of the wharf is currently open to recreation such as fishing or viewing of the Santa Barbara coast. There are restaurants, shops, and a seafood market. Future plans may include chartered sailboat tours. Open 24 hours. Fee parking on the wharf; free parking is available in the city lots at Cabrillo Blvd. and Santa Barbara Street. Information: (805) 963-1979.

PALM PARK: Wide sandy beach and grassy park, lined with palm trees and picnic areas, located along East Cabrillo Boulevard. Community arts and craft show every Sunday. Palm Park Cultural Center is used for community meetings. Cultural Center or craft show information: (805) 963-0611 ext. 331.
Mass Transit: MTD Route 21.

Seals and Sea Lions

Pinnipedia is the Latin name for the group of marine mammals commonly known as seals and sea lions; pinnipedia means "feather feet," which describes the animals' flipper-like limbs. Like cetaceans (whales and dolphins), pinnipeds rely on fat, or blubber, to keep warm. Fur seals and sea lions belong to the Otariidae family of the pinnipeds. The characteristic features of this family include small external ears, hind flippers that turn forward for moving on land, and large fore flippers that are used chiefly for swimming.

A number of species of fur seals and sea lions have been observed off the California coast and some species have established breeding grounds, or rookeries, on the Channel Islands. Seals and sea lions may also be seen resting on many other offshore rocks and islands along the coast.

The Northern, or Alaska, fur seal *(Callorhinus ursinus)*, which has established rookeries in the Channel Islands (on San Miguel Island and just off the island on Castle Rock), almost became extinct as a result of extensive fur trading during the 18th and 19th centuries. The fur seals' breeding habits also aided in their near extinction. Northern fur seals usually return to breed at the same rookery where they were born, regardless of any harassment or danger posed by intruders; therefore, once hunters located a fur seal rookery, they were assured of finding seals there year after year. Fur seals and all other marine mammals are now protected by state and federal laws.

Male northern fur seals grow to up to eight feet in length and weigh up to 700 pounds. Mature females are much smaller; their average length is four to five feet, and they weigh approximately 125 pounds. Adult males have a dark brown coat, while females and pups are greyish. Along the California coast, the northern fur seal diet consists primarily of squid, anchovies, and hake (a non-commercial fish). Fur seals usually stay well offshore, except during the breeding season; they are known to spend months at a time in the water without coming ashore at all.

People throughout the world have probably seen the California sea lion *(Zalophus californianus)* more than any other pinniped, because this species is used almost exclusively in the trained seal acts of circuses and marine animal parks. The most likely place to observe them in a natural environment is off the Santa Barbara County coast. The California sea lion territory ranges from British Columbia to Baja California; most are located between San Francisco and Baja, with the largest rookeries on San Miguel and San Nicolas Islands.

Male California sea lions have a pronounced ridge running down the middle of their skulls, which distinguishes them from females and other species of sea lions. A characteristic that helps distinguish both sexes of this species from other species is their almost constant barking. The average California sea lion is comparable to the northern fur seal in size, although the largest of the male sea lions can weigh up to 1,000 pounds. Males have a dark brown color; females are lighter brown. The California sea lion diet consists primarily of octopus, squid, and many species of non-commercial fish.

The Steller, or northern, sea lion *(Eumetopias jubatus)* is one of the largest pinnipeds found in the waters off the California coast. Males measure up to 13 feet long and weigh as much as one ton; adult females average nine feet in length, with a weight of 600 pounds. The Steller sea lion's larger size and lighter color distinguishes it from the California sea lion. In addition, Steller sea lions do not bark as regularly as California sea lions.

Stellers breed during June and July. Rookeries are typically located on the rocky parts of islands; the largest Steller breeding colonies are on the Farallon and Año Nuevo Islands. Large numbers of Stellers also haul out, or rest, on Seal Rocks offshore from the Cliff House in San Francisco. However, a small percentage of the Steller sea lion population does breed as far south as the Channel Islands.

NAME	LOCATION	Entrance/Parking Fee	Parking	Restrooms	Lifeguard	Campground	Showers	Firepits	Stairs to Beach	Path to Beach	Bike Path	Hiking Trail	Facilities for Disabled	Boating Facilities	Fishing	Equestrian Trail	Sandy Beach	Dunes	Rocky Shore	Upland from Beach	Stream Corridor	Bluff	Wetland
Cabrillo Ball Field	Milpas St. at Punta Gorda St., Santa Barbara		●																	●			
East Beach	1100 E. Cabrillo Blvd., Santa Barbara		●	●	●		●			●	●		●			●	●						
Dwight Murphy Field	Ninos Dr. and Por La Mar, Santa Barbara		●	●			●	●												●			
A. Child's Estate Zoological Gardens	1300 E. Cabrillo Blvd., Santa Barbara	●	●	●									●							●			
Andree Clark Bird Refuge	E. Cabrillo Blvd. at U.S. 101, Santa Barbara		●								●									●			●
Stairways to Beach	Along Channel Dr., Montecito		●						●								●		●	●		●	
Trail and Ramp to Beach	End of Eucalyptus Lane, Montecito		●							●							●					●	

CABRILLO BALL FIELD: Five-acre field used for team sports. The field has a single softball diamond, bleachers, and lights. For group reservations of the field, call: (805) 963-0611.
Mass Transit: Santa Barbara Metropolitan Transit District (MTD) Route 21.

EAST BEACH: 44 acres. Wide, sandy beach with volleyball courts; annual state and local volleyball tournaments are held here. Grassy picnic area with barbecues. Cabrillo Arts Center offers art shows, lectures, and movies. For Arts Center information: (805) 962-8956.
Mass Transit: MTD Route 21.

DWIGHT MURPHY FIELD: 10.5-acre park used primarily for softball and soccer. Facilities include lighted fields, children's play area, picnic tables, and barbecues. Across from A. Child's Zoo. For group reservations of the field, call: (805) 963-0611.
Mass Transit: MTD Route 21.

A. CHILD'S ESTATE ZOOLOGICAL GARDENS: A beautifully landscaped 16-acre zoo and park. The gardens occupy a prominent knoll which overlooks East Beach and the harbor area. Facilities include a nature theater, children's train ride, play area, snack stand, and picnic area. Entrance fee. Phone: (805) 962-5339.
Mass Transit: MTD Routes 16 and 21.

ANDREE CLARK BIRD REFUGE: 42-acre refuge near the zoo and East Beach with an enclosed saltwater marsh. The refuge is a habitat for a variety of birds, including herons, egrets, cormorants, ducks, and geese. Popular bike path and grassy area are along the south and east shores. Limited parking available on Los Patos Way.
Mass Transit: MTD Routes 16 and 21.

STAIRWAYS TO BEACH: Three public stairways lead to the sandy beach south of Channel Drive. They are located at the end of Butterfly Lane, and along the boardwalk seaward of the Biltmore Hotel. Channel Dr. provides on-street parking and is a scenic route with views of the Santa Barbara Harbor and Channel.
Mass Transit: MTD Routes 16 and 21.

TRAIL AND RAMP TO BEACH: The ramp is paved but in poor condition; the narrow beach is shared with the adjacent hotel. Limited on-street parking available.
Mass Transit: MTD Route 14 to San Ysidro Rd.; walk south one-quarter mile.

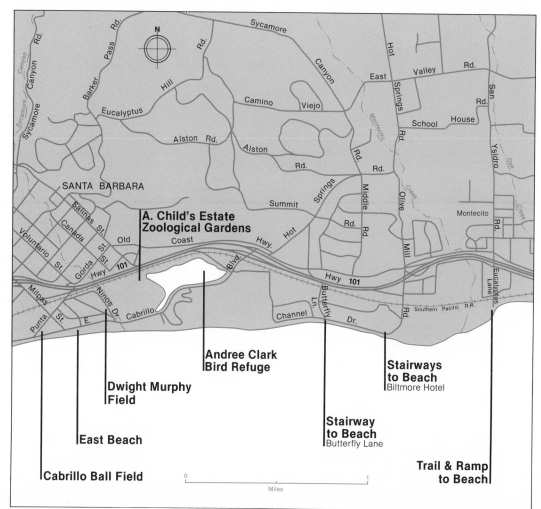

Coastal Crops

Moderate weather conditions, fertile coastal valleys and terraces, and a long growing season make California's coastal strip well suited to agriculture. Specialty crops such as artichokes and Brussels sprouts, as well as a number of other food and ornamental crops, may be seen growing in the cultivated fields along the coast.

The artichoke plant is a member of the thistle family; the portion of the plant that is harvested for eating is its unopened flower head. If allowed to mature, the head of the artichoke will develop into an attractive purple thistle flower. The lower portion of each "petal," which is in fact a bract, is edible, as is the fleshy heart, which is found near the flower's base, beneath the inedible "choke." Artichokes are usually prepared for eating by boiling or steaming them until the leaves are tender. Artichoke hearts can be pickled, deep fried, or used to make soup.

The coastal areas of San Mateo and Santa Cruz counties produce the majority of this country's Brussels sprouts. Brussels sprouts are members of the mustard family. The edible sprouts are small cabbage-like heads that grow on a vertical stem beneath the leafy portion of the plant. Raw Brussels sprouts are quite tough, but when cooked make a tasty and very nutritious side dish.

Citrus fruits, avocados, and kiwi fruit are lucrative crops produced in some coastal areas of Santa Barbara and Ventura counties. Since their establishment during California's mission period (1769-1833), lemons and oranges have been a major cash crop in Ventura County; in addition, citrus packing is a major industry for the area. The avocado (also known as the alligator pear) is a greenish, pear-shaped fruit which grows on trees; these trees are members of the laurel family. Avocados have become an increasingly popular food item in the west, and are used most often as an ingredient in salads, sandwiches, and dips. The number of acres in avocado production in California has tripled in less than ten years; in 1981 more than 486 million pounds of avocados were produced.

The kiwi fruit, introduced into California from New Zealand, is an egg-sized, fuzzy, brown-skinned fruit which grows on a vine. The edible portion of the fruit is the green, fleshy interior, which is similar in texture and taste to the strawberry. Six years ago, the amount of kiwi fruit grown in California was only 200 tons, but 1981 production amounted to 6,000 tons. Most of California's kiwi production is exported, but the fruit has been gaining popularity within the state, and in recent years many local markets have begun stocking kiwi fruit.

Other food crops grown in coastal areas include strawberries, raspberries, blackberries, tomatoes, and leafy vegetables such as lettuce, spinach, and cabbage. Several coastal areas also produce ornamental crops such as nursery stock and flowers. Lilies are grown on the Smith River coastal plain in Del Norte County, and other flowers are grown in San Mateo County near Half Moon Bay, in Santa Barbara and Ventura Counties between Carpinteria and Oxnard, and along the northern San Diego coast.

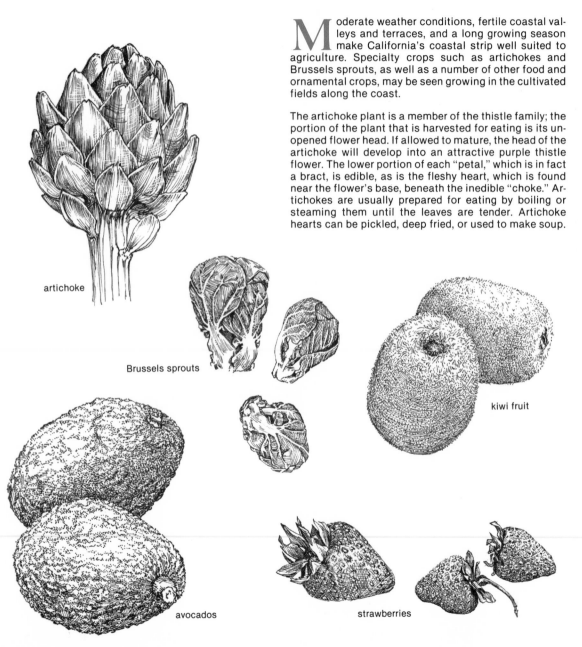

artichoke

Brussels sprouts

kiwi fruit

avocados

strawberries

Santa Barbara County
SUMMERLAND/CARPINTERIA

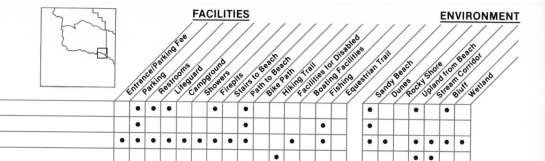

NAME	LOCATION	Entrance/Parking Fee	Parking	Restrooms	Lifeguard	Campground	Showers	Firepits	Stairs to Beach	Path to Beach	Bike Path	Hiking Trail	Facilities for Disabled	Boating Facilities	Fishing	Equestrian Trail	Sandy Beach	Dunes	Rocky Shore	Upland from Beach	Stream Corridor	Bluff	Wetland
Lookout County Park	Lookout Park Rd., Summerland		•	•	•		•			•							•		•			•	
Carpinteria City Beach	End of Linden Ave. and Ash Ave., Carpinteria		•							•					•		•						
Carpinteria State Beach	End of Palm Ave., Carpinteria	•	•	•	•	•	•	•	•	•			•		•		•	•		•		•	•
Santa Monica Creek Trail	Via Real to Foothill Rd., Carpinteria											•								•	•		
Rincon Beach County Park	Bates Rd. and U.S. 101, Carpinteria		•	•					•	•					•		•		•			•	

LOOKOUT COUNTY PARK: Small blufftop park with a grassy picnic area, volleyball court, and children's play area; a paved ramp leads to the beach. Lifeguards on duty weekends during the summer; service may be extended to weekdays. (805) 969-1720.
Mass Transit: Santa Barbara Metropolitan Transit District (MTD) Route 20 to Summerland Post Office; walk south on Evans Rd. to the park.

CARPINTERIA CITY BEACH: One-quarter mile of narrow, sandy beach. Limited parking at the ends of Ash, Holly, Elm, and Linden Avenues.
Mass Transit: MTD Route 20 to Linden Ave.; walk south one mile.

CARPINTERIA STATE BEACH: 50 acres. Narrow beach bordered by a dune area on the east side and by a bluff on the west; Chumash Indian interpretive display. Facilities include 101 tent and trailer campsites, 160 motor home sites, trailer sanitation station, grassy picnic area, and day use parking. Some campsites are wheelchair accessible. $6 camping fee ($9 with hookups), $3 day use fee. Lifeguards on duty during the summer. Known as the "safest beach on the coast" because of the shallow offshore shelf which prevents rip currents. A popular surfing area, called the "tarpits," is off the south end of the beach. (805) 684-2811.
Mass Transit: MTD Route 20 to Linden Ave.; walk one mile south to the beach.

SANTA MONICA CREEK TRAIL: Hiking trail along the east bank of the creek north of U.S. 101 between Via Real and Foothill Road. The graded trail follows a flood control easement and parallels the channelized creek.
Mass Transit: MTD Route 20.

RINCON BEACH COUNTY PARK: A new wooden stairway, located off the picnic area and paved parking lot north of Bates Rd., leads down the steep bluff to a sandy beach. Provides access to Rincon Point, one of the most popular surfing areas along the California coast. Additional parking and beach access is available south of Bates Rd. at Rincon Point Surfer Park in Ventura County.
Mass Transit: MTD Route 20.

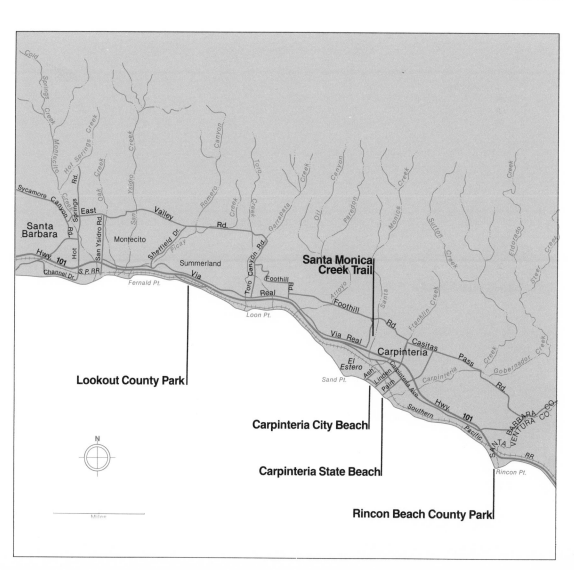

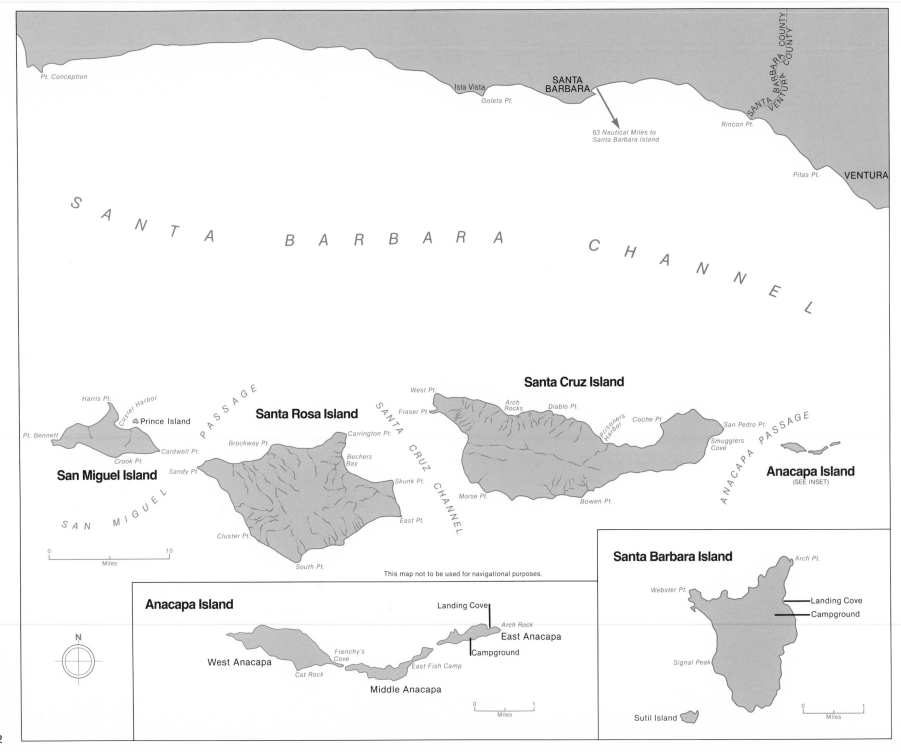

Pt. Conception

Isla Vista

SANTA
BARBARA

Goleta Pt.

SANTA BARBARA COUNTY
VENTURA COUNTY

Rincon Pt.

63 Nautical Miles to
Santa Barbara Island

Pitas Pt.   VENTURA

S A N T A   B A R B A R A   C H A N N E L

Harris Pt.

Cuyler Harbor

Prince Island

Pt. Bennett

Cardwell Pt.

Crook Pt.

Sandy Pt.

San Miguel Island

S A N   M I G U E L

PASSAGE

Santa Rosa Island

Brockway Pt.

Carrington Pt.

Bechers
Bay

Skunk Pt.

East Pt.

Cluster Pt.

South Pt.

SANTA CRUZ CHANNEL

West Pt.

Fraser Pt.

Arch
Rocks

Diablo Pt.

Santa Cruz Island

Prisoners
Harbor

Coche Pt.

San Pedro Pt.

Smugglers
Cove

Morse Pt.

Bowen Pt.

ANACAPA PASSAGE

Anacapa Island
(SEE INSET)

0   10
Miles

This map not to be used for navigational purposes.

N

Anacapa Island

West Anacapa

Cat Rock

Frenchy's
Cove

East Fish Camp

Middle Anacapa

Landing Cove

Arch Rock

East Anacapa

Campground

0   1
Miles

Santa Barbara Island

Webster Pt.

Arch Pt.

Landing Cove

Campground

Signal Peak

Sutil Island

0   1
Miles

NAME	LOCATION	Entrance/Parking Fee	Parking	Restrooms	Lifeguard	Campground	Showers	Firepits	Stairs to Beach	Path to Beach	Bike Path	Hiking Trail	Facilities for Disabled	Boating Facilities	Fishing	Equestrian Trail	Sandy Beach	Dunes	Rocky Shore	Upland from Beach	Stream Corridor	Bluff	Wetland
San Miguel Island	Offshore, 38 nautical miles S.W. of Santa Barbara														•			•	•				
Santa Rosa Island	Offshore, 28 nautical miles S. W. of Santa Barbara														•		•	•	•				
Santa Cruz Island	Offshore, 22 nautical miles S.W. of Santa Barbara	•													•		•	•	•				
Anacapa Island	Offshore, 32 nautical miles S.W. of Santa Barbara			•		•		•	•			•			•		•		•			•	
Santa Barbara Island	Offshore, 63 nautical miles S.W. of Santa Barbara			•		•			•			•			•				•			•	

The following comprise the Channel Islands National Park: San Miguel, Santa Rosa, Santa Cruz, Anacapa, and Santa Barbara Islands. Anacapa and Santa Barbara Islands are administered and managed by the National Park Service. San Miguel Island is administered by the U.S. Navy, but daily management is by the National Park Service. Santa Rosa and Santa Cruz Islands are privately owned. The Channel Islands National Marine Sanctuary extends for six nautical miles around all five islands; boating, diving, and fishing are regulated within these waters. For additional information on the park, the Marine Sanctuary, and island landing permits, contact Channel Islands National Park Headquarters, 1901 Spinnaker Drive, Ventura 93001; (805) 644-8157.

SAN MIGUEL ISLAND: 14,000 acres. Anchoring and landing by permit only, obtainable from the National Park Headquarters. Visitors are required to remain with the National Park ranger stationed on the island year-round. Day use only; no camping. 10-acre Prince Island is just outside of Cuyler Harbor.

SANTA ROSA ISLAND: Privately owned by Vail & Vickers, 123 West Padre, Santa Barbara 93105. Permits to visit must be obtained from the owners before landing.

SANTA CRUZ ISLAND: 62,000 acres. The western 90% of Santa Cruz Island is managed and controlled by the Santa Cruz Island Company. Permits to land on this portion of the island are strictly limited and must be obtained prior to landing from the Santa Cruz Island Company, 515 South Flower Street, Los Angeles 90071; (213) 485-9208. Permit applicants must have boats equipped with complete cooking and sleeping facilities aboard ship; landing permits are for day use only. Permit fee: $10 for 30 days or $40/year. The Nature Conservancy hosts fee day-trips for nonprofit groups and the general public to this end of the island. For information and applications: The Nature Conservancy, Santa Cruz Island Project, 735 State Street, Suite 201, Santa Barbara 93101; (805) 962-9111.

The small eastern tip of Santa Cruz Island is also privately owned. Visiting permits, limited to the beach at Scorpion Harbor, must be granted by the owners at least two weeks prior to a planned visit; send requests to Francis Gherini, 162 South "A" Street, Oxnard 93030, or Pier Gherini, Suite 230, 1114 State Street, Santa Barbara 93101. Requests should include complete information on the name and registration number of the vessel, and names and addresses of the vessel's owner and those planning on going ashore.

No hunting, fires, camping, use of firearms, or removal or disturbance of artifacts or property is allowed on any portion of Santa Cruz Island. Do not trespass or disturb any livestock. There are no facilities available on the island.

ANACAPA ISLAND: Three separate islets; 700 total acres. Islets cannot be reached from each other except by boat. Primitive campsites with firepits, tables, and outhouses are on the east island 1/4 mile from the ranger station. There is a steep stairway and 1/2-mile walk from the landing cove to the campsites; light packs are recommended. A 1.5-mile self-guided nature trail is on the east island; trail guides are available from the ranger station. Island is noted for Arch Rock, brown pelicans, seals and sea lions, and for the springtime blooming of the giant coreopsis (tree sunflower).

Excellent fishing and diving; several submerged shipwrecks still exist. Fishing allowed in designated areas only. Avoid the automated lighthouse on the east island; high intensity foghorn can permanently damage hearing. The west island is designated as protected for California brown pelican nesting; access is restricted and visitors must be accompanied by a National Park ranger. No public access is permitted to the west island during the pelican breeding season between March 1 and July 31.

SANTA BARBARA ISLAND: 640 acres. Primitive campsites and outhouses are above the northeast landing cove near the ranger's quarters; steep climb up the trail from the beach. California sea lions frequently haul out along the western rocky shore and elephant seals are sometimes seen on the northwest shore of Webster's Point. Disturbing the marine mammals is prohibited.

Numerous organizations lead trips to the islands; contact the Channel Islands National Park Headquarters for current listings and information.

San Buenaventura State Beach

Ventura County

Neighboring the large Los Angeles metropolis to the south, Ventura County's 43-mile long coastline offers numerous stretches of popular sandy beaches. In the north and south county areas, the coastal ranges of the Santa Ynez and Santa Monica Mountains border the shoreline, providing a scenic, rural mountain backdrop to the narrow beaches found here. Dividing these ranges in the central county is the large, flat Oxnard Plain, which contains the cities of Ventura, Oxnard, and Port Hueneme. The Oxnard Plain, the former delta area of the Santa Clara River, is noted for its agricultural fertility and the adjoining long stretches of wide, sandy beach which are characteristic of the county's central coast.

Offshore of Ventura, between 10 and 45 miles away, the Channel Islands National Park includes the islands of San Miguel, Santa Rosa, Santa Cruz, Santa Barbara, and Anacapa. Several of the islands are open to the public by permit, and provide excellent areas for hiking, diving, and fishing. Anacapa is the only island actually within Ventura County, while the other four are within Santa Barbara County. The Channel Islands National Park headquarters is located at the Ventura Harbor.

The northern Channel Islands off Ventura and Santa Barbara were formed approximately 14 million years ago by volcanic activity. Isolated from the mainland, many endemic species of flora and fauna have evolved and survived on the islands. Recent archaeological evidence suggests that one of the larger northern Channel Islands, Santa Rosa, may be one of the earliest sites of human occupation in the Americas.

Juan Cabrillo, during his exploration of the California coast for Spain, recorded in 1542 the first sighting of the Channel Islands, then inhabited by the Chumash Indians. Cabrillo died a year later from injuries sustained in a fall, and is believed to be buried on San Miguel Island.

The Chumash of the islands and mainland were decimated by diseases introduced by the European explorers and settlers. In the early 1800's, most of the remaining Chumash were inducted into the Spanish missions in the cities of Santa Barbara and Ventura, and later became local ranch hands. The deserted islands were subsequently inhabited by sea otter and seal hunters, who remained until the mid 1800's, when the islands were used for cattle and sheep ranching. Santa Rosa and Santa Cruz Islands, although within the Channel Islands National Park boundaries, are still private ranches. Anacapa and Santa Barbara Islands were proclaimed as a national monument by Franklin Roosevelt in 1938, and San Miguel was acquired by the military and at one time used as a bombing range and missile tracking station.

The military also owns the Point Mugu Lagoon along the south coast, one of Ventura County's most productive wildlife habitats. Although the lagoon is entirely within the Navy's Pacific Missile Test Center at Point Mugu, a majority of the wetlands can be observed from the Point Mugu Wildlife Sanctuary overlook on Highway 1 near Point Mugu Rock. A total of 191 species of birds have been sighted here; approximately 10,000 birds annually winter at the lagoon.

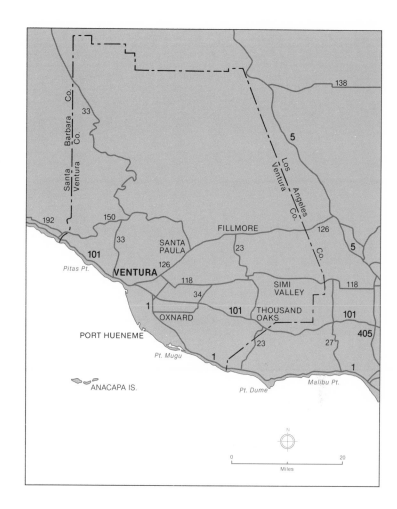

For additional information about Ventura County's coast, contact the Greater Ventura Chamber of Commerce, 785 S. Seaward Avenue, Ventura 93003, (805) 648-2875, or the Oxnard Chamber of Commerce, 228 S. "A" Street, Oxnard 93030, (805) 487-6305. For transit information, contact: South Coast Area Transit (SCAT), 301 E. 3rd Street, P.O. Box 1146, Oxnard 93032, (805) 643-3158 or 487-4222.

Offshore Oil

California is one the of the nation's leading producers of oil. While most of the oil comes from land within the state, approximately 15% of it comes from offshore. Oil has been removed from offshore wells in California since 1896, when over 400 wells were drilled from wooden piers extending into the ocean off the Santa Barbara coast. These wells were approximately 600 feet deep, and produced between one and two barrels of oil each day. Today, the wells in the Santa Barbara Channel are drilled in water up to 900 feet deep, 8,000-9,000 feet beneath the ocean floor, and produce an average of 2.3 million barrels a month.

In the 1950's, as the first leases for exploring and drilling on state-owned tidelands were issued, exploration and development of oil proceeded rapidly. In 1954 the first artificial offshore island for oil drilling was built, and in 1958 the first offshore platform, Hazel, was built off Summerland in Santa Barbara County. The federal government began leasing its offshore lands on the Outer Continental Shelf (those lands seaward of three nautical miles offshore) in 1966.

Santa Barbara Channel, Platform Hope

Offshore oil production is concentrated in Southern California; in 1981 about 39.3 million barrels of oil were produced in the San Pedro Bay and Santa Barbara Channel areas. The oil reserves are trapped in areas of subsurface irregularities, such as salt plugs or domes, buried reefs, faults, and folds, which create a trap in which oil accumulates. Various sources of data are used to determine where oil may lie; magnetic, electrical, seismic, and drilling information all help determine the relative amounts and locations of oil. The number of wells drilled and where the wells are located depends on the estimated boundaries of the field.

Exploratory wells are usually drilled from floating vessels such as drillships which are moored above the site, or anchored semisubmersibles which float above the sea bottom. Exploration of oil offshore continues until enough oil is found to be economically worthwhile to remove, or until a series of dry wells discourages further exploration. Exploratory activity may last several years after a lease sale. When economically recoverable reserves of oil are discovered, the oil company then locates and constructs offshore and onshore facilities.

Offshore oil production facilities include platforms and artificial islands. Each platform contains living quarters for the crew, work decks, a heliport, and a derrick, which is used to drill the oil wells. The derrick is the tower which stands above the platform and is the most visible portion of the platform from shore; on a clear day, the platforms can be seen 15-20 miles offshore. Artificial islands, such as those off Long Beach, have the same function as platforms; however, the islands have been camouflaged, soundproofed, and landscaped with trees and shrubs so that they resemble offshore high-rise developments.

Once the well is drilled, the flow of oil is controlled by a system of valves and gauges called a "christmas tree." Water, steam, or gas is injected into the well to maintain the pressure which forces the oil out. The oil is then transferred to shore for processing and refining. In California, oil is transferred ashore either by pipeline or by tanker. In most cases, it is more advantageous to pipe the oil to shore; using tankers to transfer the oil increases the chance of oil spills and can contribute to air pollution.

NAME	LOCATION	Entrance/Parking Fee	Parking	Restrooms	Lifeguard	Campground	Showers	Firepits	Stairs to Beach	Path to Beach	Bike Path	Hiking Trail	Facilities for Disabled	Boating Facilities	Fishing	Equestrian Trail	Sandy Beach	Dunes	Rocky Shore	Upland from Beach	Stream Corridor	Bluff	Wetland
Rincon Point Surfer Park	Off Hwy. 101, S. of Bates Rd.		•	•						•					•		•		•				
La Conchita Beach	Along Hwy. 101 between Rincon Point and Mussel Shoals														•		•						
Mussel Shoals Beach	W. of Old Pacific Coast Hwy., Mussel Shoals		•														•						
Oil Piers Beach	N. end of Old Pacific Coast Hwy., S. of Mussel Shoals		•														•						
Hobson County Park	Off old Pacific Coast Hwy., just S. of Seacliff	•	•	•		•	•	•							•				•				
Rincon Parkway North	Along old Pacific Coast Hwy., between Hobson and Faria County Parks	•	•	•		•				•					•		•						

RINCON POINT SURFER PARK: Parking lot is south of Rincon Beach County Park and adjacent to the Highway 101 southbound entrance ramp. Short, dirt pathway to the beach begins at the south end of the lot; restrooms are at the north end. Heavily used surfing area. Private beach property is adjacent to the north; do not trespass.

LA CONCHITA BEACH: Shoreline access is from the road shoulder down a rocky seawall, along Highway 101 from the sign indicating the end of the freeway, south to Mussel Shoals. Small sandy beach area is just north of Mussel Shoals. No parking or pedestrians allowed along the freeway shoulder to the north. The Mussel Shoals community is private; do not trespass.

MUSSEL SHOALS BEACH: Access to a sandy public beach fronting the Mussel Shoals community is at the north end of Breakers Way and at the west end of Ocean Avenue. Parking on the old Pacific Coast Highway. The extent of public and private rights is undetermined, and subject to further investigation, for the beach above the mean high tide line from the north side of the foot of Ocean Ave. to approximately 160 feet north.

OIL PIERS BEACH: Small sandy beach and rocky seawall adjacent to the Mobil Oil piers north of Seacliff. Primarily used for surfing. The piers are closed to the public. Main parking area is along the old Pacific Coast Highway east of Highway 101; do not block service access to the piers.

HOBSON COUNTY PARK: Small day use and overnight camping area next to the ocean. Picnic sites, barbecue pits, concession stand, and 29 trailer and tent campsites. $6 overnight fee; $7 May 15-October 15. The park is periodically closed during heavy storms. For information and reservations: (805) 654-3975.

RINCON PARKWAY NORTH: Roadside parking area along the seawall of the old Pacific Coast Highway. Overnight camping permitted in designated areas for self-contained recreational vehicles; $4 overnight fee, no reservations accepted. Rung ladders along the seawall provide beach access at low tide. For information: (805) 654-3975.

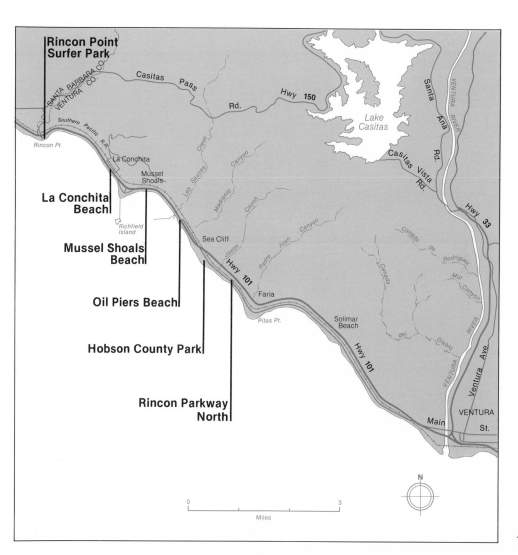

187

Seaside Wilderness Park

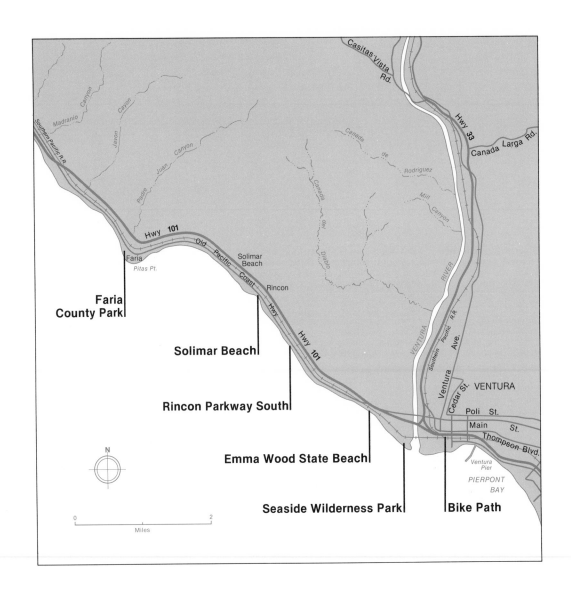

Faria
County Park

Solimar Beach

Rincon Parkway South

Emma Wood State Beach

Seaside Wilderness Park

Bike Path

NAME	LOCATION	FACILITIES															ENVIRONMENT						
---	---	Entrance/Parking Fee	Parking	Restrooms	Lifeguard	Campground	Showers	Firepits	Stairs to Beach	Path to Beach	Bike Path	Hiking Trail	Facilities for Disabled	Boating Facilities	Fishing	Equestrian Trail	Sandy Beach	Dunes	Rocky Shore	Upland from Beach	Stream Corridor	Bluff	Wetland
Faria County Park	Off old Pacific Coast Hwy. at Pitas Point	•	•	•		•	•	•							•				•				
Solimar Beach	W. of old Pacific Coast Hwy., Solimar Beach		•						•						•		•						
Rincon Parkway South	Along old Pacific Coast Hwy., N. and S. of Solimar Beach	•	•	•		•		•							•		•						
Emma Wood State Beach	S. end of old Pacific Coast Hwy., N. of West Main St., Ventura	•	•	•	•	•	•				•				•		•	•	•				
Seaside Wilderness Park	W. of Hwy. 101, N. of the Ventura River, Ventura									•					•		•	•		•	•		•
Bike Path	Along Main St. and the Ventura River, Ventura										•								•				

FARIA COUNTY PARK: Picnic sites, firepits, concession stand, and 37 tent and trailer campsites located adjacent to the ocean. $6 overnight fee, $7 May 15-October 15. Park may be closed during heavy storms. For information and reservations: (805) 654-3975.

SOLIMAR BEACH: A public sandy beach fronts the private community of Solimar Beach. The beach is accessible from paths located approximately 450 feet northwest and 75 feet southeast of the community. Day use only. Parking along the Rincon Parkway.

RINCON PARKWAY SOUTH: Roadside parking areas along the seawalls of the old Pacific Coast Highway. Day use areas are just north of Solimar Beach across from Dulah Rd., and just north of Emma Wood State Beach. Overnight camping for recreational vehicles is permitted south of Solimar Beach in designated areas; $4 overnight fee, no reservations accepted. Rung ladders along the seawall and a stairway south of Solimar Beach provide beach access at low tide. For information, call: (805) 654-3975.

EMMA WOOD STATE BEACH: 150 primitive campsites along a narrow roadway, primarily used by trailers; railroad tracks are adjacent to the east. $3 fee for day use or camping. En route campsites $6. Fishing, swimming, and surfing off the long rocky cobble and sand beach. Lifeguards on duty summer only. Bike path is east of the railroad tracks and begins at the southbound Highway 101 entrance ramp. Group campground area is at the south end of the park; $6 fee for 25-person site. Storm damage during early 1983 has temporarily closed the park. (805) 643-6037 or 654-4611.

SEASIDE WILDERNESS PARK: Only access is from Emma Wood State Beach to the north, along the beach and sand dunes west of the railroad tracks; 3/4-mile walk. Small, undeveloped park of Monterey pines and palm trees adjacent to the mouth of the Ventura River. Good bird watching area.

BIKE PATH: A bike path extends from Emma Wood State Beach to Promenade Park and San Buenaventura State Beach. The bike path runs along Main St., along the east side of the Ventura River, and seaward of the Ventura Fairgrounds.

Faria County Park

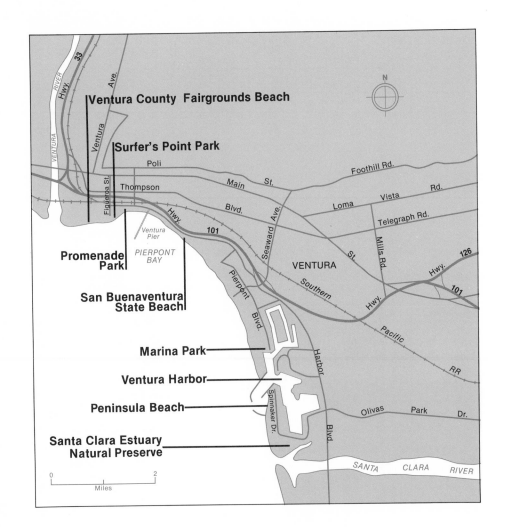

Ventura County Fairgrounds Beach

Surfer's Point Park

Promenade Park

San Buenaventura State Beach

Marina Park

Ventura Harbor

Peninsula Beach

Santa Clara Estuary Natural Preserve

0   2
Miles

Ventura County Fairgrounds Beach

NAME	LOCATION	FACILITIES															ENVIRONMENT						
		Entrance/Parking Fee	Parking	Restrooms	Lifeguard	Campground	Showers	Firepits	Stairs to Beach	Path to Beach	Bike Path	Hiking Trail	Facilities for Disabled	Boating Facilities	Fishing	Equestrian Trail	Sandy Beach	Dunes	Rocky Shore	Upland from Beach	Stream Corridor	Bluff	Wetland
Ventura County Fairgrounds Beach	Between the Ventura River and Surfer's Point Park, Ventura									●									●				
Surfer's Point Park	Foot of Figueroa St., Ventura		●							●									●				
Promenade Park	Extends from foot of Figueroa St. E. to San Buenaventura State Beach, Ventura		●	●						●	●						●						
San Buenaventura State Beach	From the Ventura Pier S. to Marina Park, Ventura	●	●	●	●		●			●	●				●		●						
Marina Park	S. end of Pierpont Blvd., Ventura		●	●						●	●			●			●	●					
Ventura Harbor	W. of Harbor Blvd. at Anchors Way Dr., Ventura		●	●						●			●	●	●								
Peninsula Beach	Along the W. end of Spinnaker Dr., Ventura		●	●										●	●		●						
Santa Clara Estuary Natural Preserve	S. of Spinnaker Dr. at the Santa Clara River, Ventura		●																				●

VENTURA COUNTY FAIRGROUNDS BEACH: Rocky cobble beach; access is from Surfer's Point Park to the south. The Ventura County Fair runs annually for approximately one week at the beginning of October. Other events are held almost every weekend. For information, call: (805) 648-3376.
Mass Transit: South Coast Area Transit (SCAT) Route 3, Ojai-Thompson Blvd., to Ventura Ave. and Thompson Blvd.

SURFER'S POINT PARK: Large, dirt parking lot above a rocky seawall and beach. Popular surfing area.
Mass Transit: SCAT Route 3, Ojai-Thompson Blvd., to Ventura Ave. and Thompson Blvd.

PROMENADE PARK: Long, narrow park with a concrete walkway and bike path along the edge of the beach. Facilities include benches, tables, playground equipment, volleyball standards, and wide ramps to the beach. Parking at Surfer's Point Park to the north or at the lot just west of the San Buenaventura State Beach pier.
Mass Transit: SCAT Route 3, Ojai-Thompson Blvd., to Ventura Ave. and Thompson Blvd.

SAN BUENAVENTURA STATE BEACH: Park headquarters, parking lot, main entrance, and facilities are off San Pedro St. at Pierpont Boulevard. Additional access is at the Ventura Pier area to the north, along Harbor Blvd. between park headquarters and the pier, and at 24 residential street ends between Marina Park and San Pedro Street. Public parking for cars and bicycles is available at the lot on the southeast corner of Seaward Ave. and Zephyr Court.

Wide, sandy beach protected by breakwaters is noted for good swimming; lifeguards on duty daily during the summer and on weekends in spring and fall. Facilities include a snack bar, outdoor showers, dressing rooms, picnic areas, beach equipment rentals, and volleyball standards. Park open 7 AM-sunset. 1,700-foot fishing pier at the north end of the park has a restaurant, bait shop, and snack bar, and is accessible to wheelchairs. Bike path begins at the park entrance and runs north along the edge of the beach. $3 parking fee at the main entrance. For information, call: (805) 654-4611 or 654-4616.
Mass Transit: SCAT Route 3, Ojai-Thompson Blvd.

MARINA PARK: Located in the sand dunes of the north peninsula of Ventura Harbor. Facilities include a short bike path, playground equipment, basketball court, sheltered picnic sites, ocean beach access, and a small boat dock. Sailing classes are available year-round from the Ventura City Parks and Recreation Department: (805) 654-7837.

VENTURA HARBOR: Extensive inland harbor with two marinas, boat charters, fuel dock, launching ramp (no fee), boat storage and repair, bait shop, and fishing equipment and small sailboat rentals (14 and 21 foot). Car and boat trailer parking off Anchors Way Dr. near the boat ramp.

Two public golf courses are east of Harbor Blvd. on Olivas Park Dr., (805) 642-4303 or 642-2231. The Ventura City Parks and Recreation Department runs periodic whale watching trips and Channel Islands tours: (805) 654-7837. For harbor information, call: 642-8538.

The Channel Islands National Park headquarters, located at the harbor at 1901 Spinnaker Dr., provides park information and contains exhibits of the islands' flora and fauna; call: (805) 644-8157.

PENINSULA BEACH: Municipal beach on the south peninsula of Ventura Harbor. Small Marina Cove play area, restroom facility, and limited paved parking are at the north end of Spinnaker Dr.; undeveloped parking area at the south end. Popular for surfing. The swimming area at Marina Cove is protected by breakwaters.

SANTA CLARA ESTUARY NATURAL PRESERVE: Marshland wildlife habitat at the mouth of the Santa Clara River; accessible from Peninsula Beach to the north or McGrath State Beach to the south. Sensitive area. Good bird watching; fenced wastewater lagoons north of the river along Spinnaker Dr. are migratory waterfowl habitats.

Ventura Harbor

191

Channel Islands Harbor

Ventura Harbor

Ventura

RIVER

SANTA CLARA

McGrath State Beach

Vineyard Ave.

Santa Clara Ave.

Blvd.

Hwy.

Rd.

101

Gonzales

McGrath Lake

Mandalay County Park

Harbor

Victoria Ave.

5th

Oxnard Rd.

Street

Ave.

Hwy. **34**

Blvd.

Wooley

Oxnard

Oxnard

Rd.

Oxnard Shores

Channel

Islands

Saviers Rd.

Blvd.

Rice Rd.

Rd.

Oxnard Blvd.

Valley

Peninsula Park

Hollywood Beach

U.S. Naval

Ventura Rd.

Bubbling Springs Park

Hwy. **1**

Channel Islands Harbor

Construction

Battalion Center

Pleasant

Silver Strand Beach

Port

Hueneme Rd.

Hueneme Pt.

Hueneme

Arnold Rd.

Point Mugu
Pacific Missile Range

N

Port Hueneme Beach Park

MUGU LAGOON

Ormond Beach

0   2
Miles

NAME	LOCATION	Entrance/Parking Fee	Parking	Restrooms	Lifeguard	Campground	Showers	Firepits	Stairs to Beach	Path to Beach	Bike Path	Hiking Trail	Facilities for Disabled	Boating Facilities	Fishing	Equestrian Trail	Sandy Beach	Dunes	Rocky Shore	Upland from Beach	Stream Corridor	Bluff	Wetland
McGrath State Beach	Along Harbor Blvd., 1.2 miles S. of Spinnaker Dr.	●	●	●	●	●	●	●		●		●	●		●		●	●		●		●	
Mandalay County Park	5th St. and Mandalay Beach Rd., Oxnard																●	●					
Oxnard Shores	Along Mandalay Beach Rd., Oxnard	●															●						
Hollywood Beach	Along Ocean Dr. between Channel Islands Blvd. and San Miguel Ave., Oxnard		●	●	●										●		●						
Peninsula Park	Near the S. end of Peninsula Rd., Oxnard		●	●			●				●			●									
Channel Islands Harbor	W. of Victoria Ave., S. of Channel Islands Blvd., Oxnard		●	●	●					●			●	●	●		●						
Silver Strand Beach	Along Ocean Dr. between San Nicholas Ave. and Sawtelle Ave., Port Hueneme		●	●	●								●		●		●						
Port Hueneme Beach Park	Along W. end of Surfside and Ocean View Drives, Port Hueneme	●	●	●	●					●	●		●		●		●						
Bubbling Springs Park	E. of Park Ave. and Ventura Rd., Port Hueneme		●	●			●				●		●							●	●		
Ormond Beach	Foot of Perkins Rd., S. of Port Hueneme		●							●							●	●					

McGRATH STATE BEACH: 295-acre park south of the Santa Clara River. 174 semi-private campsites with tables and stoves. A nature trail begins north of the entrance kiosk. Two miles of beach frontage; lifeguards on duty daily during summer and on weekends in spring and fall. McGrath Lake wildlife area is at the southern end of the park; public access to the lake is along the beach and dunes west of the Chevron Oil Company facilities. $6 overnight fee, $3 day use fee. For information, call: (805) 483-8034 or 654-4611. Restrooms are accessible to wheelchairs.

MANDALAY COUNTY PARK: 104 acres of undeveloped beach and dunes. Access is from 5th St. to the south. The power plant facility to the north is private; do not trespass.

OXNARD SHORES: Private subdivision; the only public access is at the ends of Breakers Way and Seabreeze Way, seaward of Capri Way, and at Neptune Square. A small park with playground equipment and picnic tables is at Neptune Square. Private property is to the north and south of all these accessways; do not trespass.

HOLLYWOOD BEACH: Access is at street ends along Ocean Drive. Restrooms with outdoor showers and a small parking lot are at the corner of Ocean Dr. and La Brea Street. Lifeguards on duty summer only. Volleyball standards and nets.

PENINSULA PARK: Municipal park. Children's sandy playground area, boat dock, and restrooms are at the west end. Two tennis courts are near the parking lot. Grassy picnic areas with day use cooking grills.

CHANNEL ISLANDS HARBOR: Harbor facilities include boat ramps, hoists, berths, fuel dock, and boat trailer parking. Channel Islands Harbor Park is along most of the inner perimeter of the harbor; features include grassy picnic sites, restrooms with outdoor showers, and a beach area with lifeguards (summer only) at the corner of Anacapa and Victoria Avenues. For information: Harbormaster Office, 3900 Pelican Way; (805) 985-5544.
Mass Transit: South Coast Area Transit (SCAT) Route 9, Pleasant Valley-Beach, to the south end of Victoria Avenue. No Sunday service.

SILVER STRAND BEACH: The beach is west of Ocean Dr.; main access and parking at the foot of San Nicholas Avenue. Lifeguards (summer only) and volleyball standards. En route camping available. At the south end of the beach, the rock-filled shipwreck of the *S.S. La Jenelle* is now a fishing jetty; access and parking at the end of Sawtelle Avenue. The jetty may be hazardous during heavy surf.
Mass Transit: SCAT Route 9, Pleasant Valley-Beach, to the south end of Victoria Ave.; walk south to San Nicholas Avenue. No Sunday service.

PORT HUENEME BEACH PARK: Large sandy beach with extensive parking areas; contains fishing pier, beach playground facilities, protected picnic sites, and snack bar. Bike path runs along the edge of the beach. Parking fee.
Mass Transit: SCAT Route 8, Port Hueneme-Village, to Hueneme Rd.

BUBBLING SPRINGS PARK: Grassy inland park with picnic tables, firepits, and a playground area. The park includes a 1-1/2 mile long bike path which runs along a landscaped drainage channel to Port Hueneme Beach Park. Parking lots are off Park Ave. at the Community Center, and at Ventura Rd. and Bard Road. The bike path passes Moranda Park, which contains tennis courts, a baseball field, and a playground.
Mass Transit: SCAT Route 8, Port Hueneme-Village, to Bard Rd.

ORMOND BEACH: Dunes and wide, sandy beach, most of which is publicly owned, within the area 3,000 feet south of Perkins Rd. to 1,000 feet north. A public path and footbridge lead from the car and bicycle parking lot at the end of Perkins Rd. to the beach. Extent of public and private rights undetermined; subject to further investigation.
Mass Transit: SCAT Route 8, Port Hueneme-Village, to Hueneme and Perkins Roads.

Santa Clara River Mouth, McGrath State Beach

Hiking and Backpacking

California's coastal mountain ranges provide a variety of opportunities for hiking and backpacking in wilderness areas, many of which are accessible from Highway 1. California's mild climate permits hiking and backpacking year-round; however, during the summer, early morning and late afternoon fog are prevalent near the coast, and during the rainy season (November through March), hikers should be prepared for cold, wet weather.

Wool clothing is best because it retains its insulating qualities even when wet. For really heavy rain, some sort of waterproof rain gear is necessary; Gore-tex fabrics, though expensive, provide the ultimate in rain protection. It's a good idea to carry rain gear even in summer months. Since the terrain is not particularly rugged in most parts of the coastal mountains, lightweight hiking boots are adequate footgear for hikers and backpackers. Blisters, the most common foot ailment on the trail, can usually be prevented by placing adhesive tape or moleskin over sensitive areas.

Essential items for any hike include water, food, a map, and a small first aid kit; these items, plus rain gear and some warm clothing, can be easily carried in a small pack. Backpackers will find a tent useful year-round as protection against rain in winter, and against insects in summer; backpackers should also bring a flashlight, rope, sunscreen, and insect repellent. Open fires are prohibited in most wilderness areas, so a lightweight backpackers' stove is an excellent investment.

The coastal mountains are administered by a variety of state and federal agencies, each of which has its own regulations regarding hiking and backpacking, as well as different times and dates of operation. A permit is required in order to backpack in most wilderness areas; check with the manager of the area when planning a trip. One regulation is common to *all* areas: DON'T LITTER! Please pack out all your refuse, stay on designated trails for your own safety and to prevent erosion, and avoid disturbing plants or wildlife.

Some of the more popular areas for hiking and backpacking near the coast are Del Norte Coast Redwoods State Park in Del Norte County, King Range Conservation Area in Humboldt County, Point Reyes National Seashore in Marin County, Ventana Wilderness in Monterey County, and Point Mugu State Park in Ventura County. Point Mugu provides access to the Santa Monica Mountains.

For information on California State Parks, write:

California Department of Parks
and Recreation
P.O. Box 2390
Sacramento, CA 95811   (916) 445-6477

For information on federal parks in California, write:

National Park Service
450 Golden Gate Avenue
San Francisco, CA 94102   (415) 556-4122

The California Office of Tourism publishes a brochure which provides names and addresses of public agencies to write to for information on hiking and camping facilities. For a copy, send a business-size, self-addressed stamped envelope to:

California Office of Tourism
1030-13th Street, Suite 200
Sacramento, CA 95814

Ventura County

SOUTHERN VENTURA COAST

NAME	LOCATION	Entrance/Parking Fee	Parking	Restrooms	Lifeguard	Campground	Showers	Firepits	Stairs to Beach	Path to Beach	Bike Path	Hiking Trail	Facilities for Disabled	Boating Facilities	Fishing	Equestrian Trail	Sandy Beach	Dunes	Rocky Shore	Upland from Beach	Stream Corridor	Bluff	Wetland
Mugu Lagoon	Pacific Missile Test Center, N. of Point Mugu Rock		•																				•
Point Mugu Beach	At Point Mugu Rock, S. of the Navy Firing Range		•														•	•			•		
La Jolla Valley (Unit of Point Mugu State Park)	E. of Hwy. 1 and La Jolla Beach	•	•	•		•	•			•										•	•		
La Jolla Beach (Unit of Point Mugu State Park)	W. of Hwy. 1, 1-1/2 miles N. of Sycamore Cove	•	•	•	•	•	•										•						
Sycamore Canyon Campground (Unit of Point Mugu State Park)	E. of Hwy. 1 and Sycamore Cove	•	•	•		•				•											•	•	
Sycamore Cove Beach (Unit of Point Mugu State Park)	9000 Pacific Coast Hwy.	•	•	•	•					•							•						
County Line Beach	W. of Hwy. 1 at Yerba Buena Rd., Malibu		•														•						
Leo Carrillo Beach North	40000 Pacific Coast Hwy., Malibu		•						•	•					•		•		•			•	•

MUGU LAGOON: 1,800 acres; largest coastal estuary-lagoon habitat between Morro Bay and San Diego County. Entirely within the Navy's Pacific Missile Test Center. Wildlife viewing possible from the small pavilion on Highway 1, 1/2 mile north of Point Mugu Rock. Public access within the lagoon is restricted to weekend group interpretive tours, available by reservation only, made at least one month in advance; groups must consist of 15 to 25 persons, adults only. Call the P.M.T.C. Public Affairs Office: (805) 982-8094.

POINT MUGU BEACH: There is blufftop off-road parking on the west side of Highway 1, both north and south of Point Mugu Rock. A small, sandy beach is below Highway 101 between Point Mugu Rock and the Navy Firing Range to the north. The Navy base and firing range are closed to the public.

The following are administered by the State Department of Parks and Recreation as part of the Point Mugu State Park: La Jolla Valley, La Jolla Beach, Sycamore Canyon Campground, and Sycamore Cove Beach. For information: 9000 Pacific Coast Highway, Malibu 90265. (805) 499-2112.

LA JOLLA VALLEY: Small walk-in campground and group camp east of Highway 1. Trailhead for access into the 13,000-acre Point Mugu State Park within the Santa Monica Mountains. The La Jolla Valley Natural Preserve is adjacent to this trailhead, and the Boney Mountain Wilderness area is inland; both are popular for hiking. Two mile walk to campsites; tap water and tables available. 12 campsites; 50¢ overnight fee. Trailer camping in the parking lot area. No open fires; the area may be closed during periods of high fire danger. The gates to the park close at sunset.

LA JOLLA BEACH: 102 unprotected trailer and tent campsites directly on the beach adjacent to Highway 1. Camping only, no day use. $3 overnight fee. Facilities include picnic tables, outdoor showers, sanitary tank disposal, and summertime lifeguards. The tent camping area is at the north end.

SYCAMORE CANYON CAMPGROUND: 55 primitive drive-in campsites at a trailhead for the Point Mugu State Park. $3 overnight fee. Tables and barbeque grills available. Special bicycle/hiker group campsite; 50¢ overnight fee.

SYCAMORE COVE BEACH: Developed park area contains picnic tables, grassy areas, outdoor showers, cooking grills, and summertime lifeguards. $3 day use fee. Headquarters of Point Mugu State Park.

COUNTY LINE BEACH: Undeveloped beach directly off Highway 1; popular surfing area.

LEO CARRILLO BEACH NORTH: Northernmost undeveloped portion of Leo Carrillo State Beach. Path and stairway access to the beach is from the public parking lot of the state park rangers' residence at 40000 Pacific Coast Highway, and at .2 miles and .5 miles south. No camping or open fires allowed. Several blufftop vista points. For information: (805) 499-2112 or (213) 706-1310.

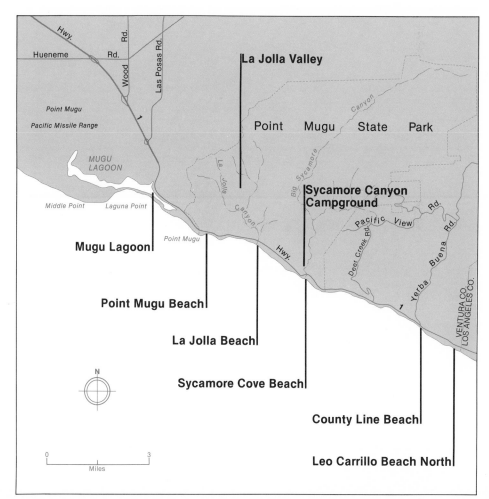

Marina del Rey

Los Angeles County

In the book *Two Years Before the Mast,* written in 1840, author Richard Henry Dana wrote of Los Angeles: "In the hands of an enterprising people, what a country this might be." Since that time, "enterprising people" have transformed Los Angeles County from an arid coastal basin inhabited by Chumash and Gabrieleño Indians to the nation's wealthiest agricultural county and, more recently, into one of the country's largest metropolitan regions, with industries ranging from motion pictures and television to oil refining and aerospace systems. Throughout this transformation, the county's 74 miles of coastline have been a significant attraction and source of recreation; today, the coast is visited more than 50 million times a year by tourists and the county's residents.

Los Angeles's Mediterranean climate has always been a major influence on the county's development. Coastal air and water temperatures are mild; summer air temperatures average in the low 70s, while water temperature is a comfortable 67 degrees. Night and early morning fog or low clouds are prevalent in many areas, but the overcast usually burns off by mid to late morning.

In the summer of 1769, a Spanish Missionary named Juan Crespi, one of the first non-natives to visit Los Angeles, described the area as a beautiful and perfect place for a settlement. Descriptions by subsequent visitors and entrepreneurs continued to praise the climate and other virtues of the Los Angeles area; railroad lines eventually connected east with west and spawned a series of development booms. The beach community of Venice, which was built in 1892 on the sand dunes and marshes at the mouth of Ballona Creek, was one of these boom developments; it was patterned after the Italian city of the same name, and included a series of interconnecting canals complete with gondolas. Today, only remnants of this turn-of-the-century coastal resort remain.

The topography of the county's coastline varies dramatically. The Santa Monica Mountains, at the northwest end of the county, drop sharply into the ocean at Malibu, resulting in a series of rocky coves, headlands, points, and sandy pocket beaches; the shore from Malibu to the west is the most rural portion of the coastline. Santa Monica Bay, which comprises most of the county's shoreline, consists of a string of wide, sandy beaches backed by urban development resting on a coastal plain called the Los Angeles Basin. Oil was discovered beneath this basin in 1891, and from the turn of the century to the present, oil derricks, well pumps, and refineries have been a noticeable landscape feature from Venice south.

The Palos Verdes Peninsula, 15 miles of rocky shoreline with tidepools and excellent diving and fishing spots, separates Santa Monica Bay from San Pedro Bay. Catalina Island, located 22 miles offshore, is visible from the south end of the peninsula at Point Fermin. The island is largely a rural area with rugged mountain terrain, and was a hideout for buccaneers during the 17th and 18th centuries; since the resort town of Avalon was developed in 1887, Catalina has become a popular visitor destination.

A little more than half of the county's coastline is in public ownership. The diverse shoreline topography and facilities available to the public allow people to enjoy virtually every type of beach recreation, including sun bathing, swimming, surfing, fishing, and diving. A number of communities along the coast have fishing piers, boat launches, and marinas; Marina Del Rey, located just south of Venice along the Ballona Creek, is the largest artificial small pleasurecraft harbor in the world.

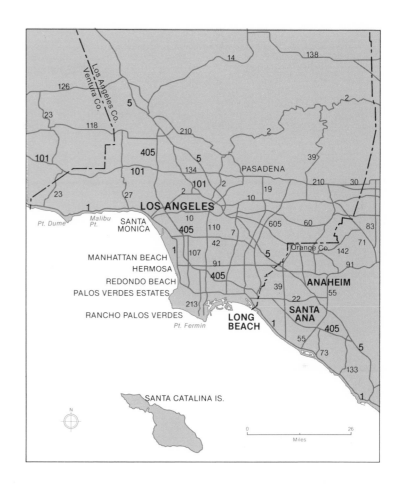

For more information on the Los Angeles County coast, call or write the Chamber of Commerce office in the area you plan to visit, or the Greater Los Angeles Visitors and Convention Bureau, Visitor Information Center, 505 S. Flower Street, Los Angeles 90071, (213) 628-3101. For transit information, call or write the Southern California Rapid Transit District (RTD), Customer Services, 425 S. Main Street, Los Angeles 90013, (213) 626-4455.

Other transit services within Los Angeles County include Santa Monica Municipal Bus Lines, (213) 451-5445; Torrance Transit System, (213) 328-7402; Long Beach Public Transit, (213) 591-2301; and the City of Hermosa Beach free bus, (213) 376-6984.

El Pescador State Beach

Leo Carrillo State Beach

El Matador State Beach

NAME	LOCATION	Entrance/Parking Fee	Parking	Restrooms	Lifeguard	Campground	Showers	Firepits	Stairs to Beach	Path to Beach	Bike Path	Hiking Trail	Facilities for Disabled	Boating Facilities	Fishing	Equestrian Trail	Sandy Beach	Dunes	Rocky Shore	Upland from Beach	Stream Corridor	Bluff	Wetland
Leo Carrillo State Beach	36000 block of Pacific Coast Hwy., Malibu	•	•	•	•	•	•	•	•			•			•		•		•	•	•	•	
Nicholas Canyon County Beach	Pacific Coast Hwy., about 1 mi. S. of Leo Carrillo, Malibu	•	•	•	•				•	•							•					•	
Charmlee County Park	Encinal Canyon Rd., N. of Pacific Coast Hwy., Malibu			•	•							•								•			
El Pescador State Beach	32900 Pacific Coast Hwy., Malibu	•	•	•	•					•			•				•		•			•	
La Piedra State Beach	32700 Pacific Coast Hwy., Malibu	•	•	•	•					•			•				•		•	•		•	
El Matador State Beach	32350 Pacific Coast Hwy., Malibu	•	•	•	•				•	•			•				•		•			•	

LEO CARRILLO STATE BEACH: 1,600-acre park at the west end of Malibu, named after L.A.-born actor Leo Carrillo, famous for his T.V. role as Pancho, Cisco Kid's sidekick. Good surfing, swimming, skin diving, and camping; nature trail, tidepools, and rock formations. $3 fee for day use parking and $6 fee for camping. The 6,600-foot beach is divided into two areas by Sequit Point, which contains sea caves and a natural tunnel. Lifeguards year-round. Migrating gray whales may be seen from the beach November-May.

The park has three campgrounds: the canyon campground, which has 138 campsites; the beach campground, which has 25 tent sites and 25 trailer sites accessible only to vehicles less than 8' in height; and the walk-in group campground (reservations required) which accommodates up to 75 people. For information, call: (213) 706-1310 or (805) 499-2112.

NICHOLAS CANYON COUNTY BEACH: Across Pacific Coast Highway from the Malibu Riding and Tennis Club. The parking lot is on the bluff; a stairway and path lead down to the 23-acre sandy beach. The beach is also accessible from Leo Carrillo to the west. Cliffs are highly eroded; surfing and diving at the beach. $3 parking fee. Call: (213) 457-9811.

CHARMLEE COUNTY PARK: 460-acre park in a natural setting with picnic tables and a view of the ocean. Planned future developments include a camping area, equestrian trail, and interpretive center.

EL PESCADOR STATE BEACH: 10 acres; facilities include a 20-car parking lot, wheelchair-accessible restrooms, and picnic tables on the bluff, and a pedestrian trail down the bluff to the narrow, sandy beach. $3 parking fee. Steep cliffs; stay on the trail. Private property is adjacent; do not trespass. Lifeguard during summer only. For information, call: (213) 706-1310.

LA PIEDRA STATE BEACH: Nine acres, with a 15-car parking lot, picnic tables, and wheelchair-accessible restrooms on the bluff, and a trail leading down the bluff to the beach; stay on the trail. $3 parking fee. Respect adjacent private property; do not trespass. Lifeguard during summer only. Call: (213) 706-1310.

EL MATADOR STATE BEACH: 18 acres; facilities include a 40-car parking lot, wheelchair-accessible restrooms, and picnic area. Beach access is via a trail and stairway down the bluff to the narrow, sandy, 1/4-mile long beach. $3 parking fee. Eroded cliffs; stay on the trail. Scenic sea stacks. Private property is adjacent; do not trespass. Lifeguard during summer only. For information, call: (213) 706-1310.

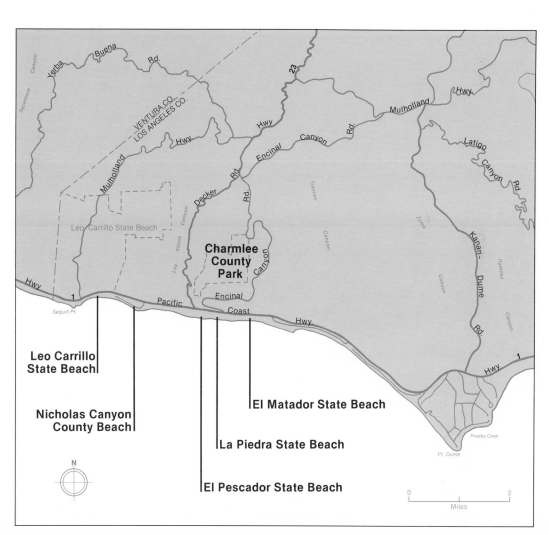

Rip Currents

A nearshore current called a rip current (commonly known as rip tide) is often formed along the coast and presents a potential hazard to the uninformed swimmer. When higher than average waves pass over an offshore sand bar and break on the beach in rapid succession, water is piled up in the surf zone faster than it can recede back to the open ocean. In order to recede, the water breaches the bar in various locations. Thus, rip channels are created and strong currents of water rush through the channels directly out to sea. After the volume of water passes beyond the sand bar, the current dissipates.

Rip currents move away from the shoreline faster than most people can swim. Therefore, ocean swimmers should look for rip current warnings and avoid swimming in these areas. Fortunately, rip currents are confined to narrow channels, so if a swimmer does get caught in the current, he or she can get out of it by swimming parallel to the shoreline for a short distance.

Westward Beach

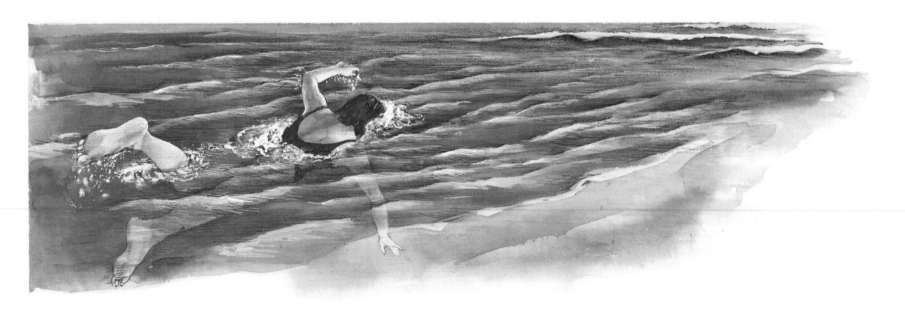

NAME	LOCATION	Entrance/Parking Fee	Parking	Restrooms	Lifeguard	Campground	Showers	Firepits	Stairs to Beach	Path to Beach	Bike Path	Hiking Trail	Facilities for Disabled	Boating Facilities	Fishing	Equestrian Trail	Sandy Beach	Dunes	Rocky Shore	Upland from Beach	Stream Corridor	Bluff	Wetland
Stairway to Beach	31300 block of Broad Beach Rd., Malibu								●								●						
Walkway and Steps to Beach	31200 block of Broad Beach Rd., Malibu								●								●						
Zuma Beach County Park	30000 block of Pacific Coast Hwy., Malibu	●	●	●	●										●		●		●				
Point Dume Whale Watch	Corner of Westward Beach Rd., Malibu																		●	●			
Westward Beach Point Dume State Beach	S. end of Westward Beach Rd., Malibu	●	●	●	●										●		●			●			

Los Angeles County-operated public accessways and beaches may be recognized by the yellow garbage cans located at accessway entrances or along the beaches themselves.

STAIRWAY TO BEACH: A public stairway leads to the beach from Broad Beach Rd.; private property on either side. Do not trespass.
Mass Transit: Southern California Rapid Transit District (RTD) Route 434 to the west end of Zuma Beach; walk west about one mile.

WALKWAY AND STEPS TO BEACH: A cement walkway and steps lead to the beach from Broad Beach Rd.; private property on either side. Do not trespass.
Mass Transit: RTD Route 434 to the west end of Zuma Beach; walk west about 3/4 mile.

ZUMA BEACH COUNTY PARK: Wide, sandy beach on the west side of Point Dume outside Santa Monica Bay; L.A.'s largest county-owned beach with playgrounds, food concessions, volleyball courts, and eight fee parking lots. $3 parking fee. Rough surf; surfing and diving. Zuma Lifeguard Headquarters: (213) 457-9891.
Mass Transit: RTD Route 434.

POINT DUME WHALE WATCH: A stairway from Westward Beach Rd. leads up to the whale watch; view of the ocean. Restaurant below the whale watch.
Mass Transit: RTD Route 434.

WESTWARD BEACH POINT DUME STATE BEACH: Good swimming, surfing, diving, and tidepools; sandstone cliffs. Beach closes at dark. Parking lot and restrooms at the southeast end of the beach; $3 parking fee. Access also from Zuma Beach to the northwest. The State Department of Fish and Game is currently developing 35 acres of Point Dume Headlands, including portions of Pirates Cove and Dume Cove, as an Ecological Reserve. There will be limited access, trails, and chemical toilets. (213) 457-9891.
Mass Transit: RTD Route 434.

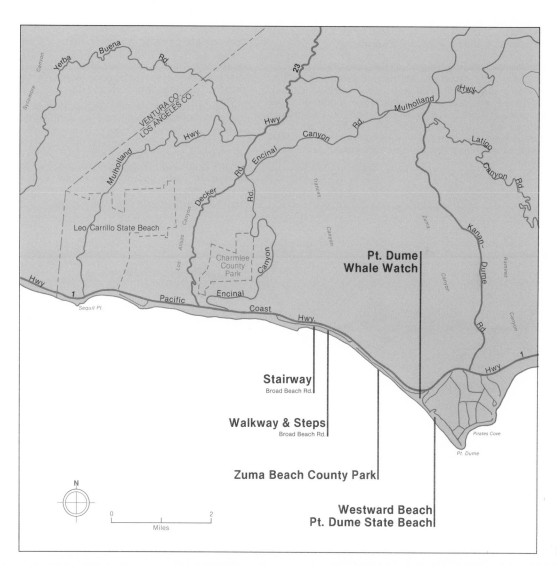

Fishing

There are many methods of fishing the California coast, such as pier fishing, poke-pole fishing in tidepools, fishing from shore, which includes surf casting and rock fishing, and trolling and deep sea fishing (bottomfishing) from party boats and skiffs offshore. The type of gear, bait, and method of fishing vary with the species of fish.

Steelhead trout, king salmon, and silver salmon, for example, are usually caught by trolling, while rockfish are caught by bottomfishing, surfperch by surf fishing, and monkeyface and rock eels by poke-poling.

Steelhead trout, king salmon, and silver salmon are three of the most important northern California species; striped bass and lingcod are also important. Bonito, yellowtail, and barracuda, which are found offshore around kelp beds, are significant southern California fish, as are Pacific mackerel, jack mackerel, albacore, bluefin tuna, and blue shark. Halibut, rockfish, and surfperch, other popular catches, are found along most of the coast.

A fishing license is required if you are 16 years of age or older in order to take any fish, mollusk, invertebrate, amphibian, or crustacean in California, except if you fish from a public pier along the coast. A California resident license costs $6.75 and a non-resident license is $26.50. A fishing license stamp which costs $4.00 is also required for trout, salmon and steelhead fishing, and an inland water license stamp is $2.75; these stamps must be permanently affixed to the licenses. These prices are current as of 1983 and are subject to change.

Licenses are good for one year; there are also special 10-day, 3-day, and 1-day licenses for non-residents and vacationers. Fishing licenses are available at most bait and tackle shops, sporting goods stores, diving shops, or from the Department of Fish and Game.

The *California Sport Fishing Regulations,* published annually by the Department of Fish and Game, includes such information as the type of bait which may be used for some of the common species, the type of gear permitted, seasons and hours when each species may be taken, and the legal limit per day for each species. Anglers are advised to keep up on annual law and regulation changes. You can get a copy of the current Sport Fishing Regulations where you buy your license.

Ocean Fishing Maps, produced by Fish and Game, are available for all coastal counties except Ventura and Santa Barbara. These maps indicate where various species may be found, and contain area descriptions and information on fishing techniques and the type of gear required. Ocean Fishing Maps, as well as California Sport Fishing Regulations, may be obtained from:

Publications Section
Office of Procurement
General Services
P.O. Box 1015
North Highlands, CA 95660   (916) 924-4800

An *Atlas of California Coastal Marine Resources,* also published by Fish and Game, contains information on fishing areas, gear, fishing piers, shellfish resources and spawning areas, artificial fishing reefs, marine mammals and birds, and other information pertaining to the coastal zone. Copies of the Atlas or individual maps can be purchased from:

Visual Graphics
2124 19th Street
Sacramento, CA 95818   (916) 443-6838

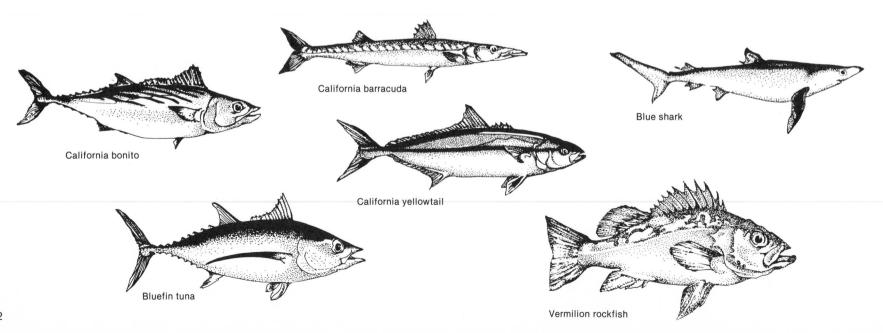

California barracuda

California bonito

Blue shark

California yellowtail

Bluefin tuna

Vermilion rockfish

Los Angeles County

MALIBU

NAME	LOCATION	Entrance/Parking Fee	Parking	Restrooms	Lifeguard	Campground	Showers	Firepits	Stairs to Beach	Path to Beach	Bike Path	Hiking Trail	Facilities for Disabled	Boating Facilities	Fishing	Equestrian Trail	Sandy Beach	Dunes	Rocky Shore	Upland from Beach	Stream Corridor	Bluff	Wetland
Paradise Cove	28128 Pacific Coast Hwy., Malibu	•	•	•										•	•		•					•	
Escondido Beach	27200 block of Pacific Coast Hwy., Malibu								•						•		•		•				
Corral State Beach	26000 block of Pacific Coast Hwy., Malibu		•	•	•										•		•						
Stairways to Beach	Along Malibu Rd., Malibu								•								•						
Malibu Bluffs State Park	Malibu Canyon Rd. and Pacific Coast Hwy., Malibu		•	•																•	•	•	

PARADISE COVE: Private fee beach and 400-foot fishing pier; $5/car, $1 walk-in. Open 6 AM-5 PM. Facilities include 1.5-ton boat hoist, boat and tackle rental, fishing boat charters, fishing licenses, bait and tackle, and a restaurant and snack bar. Scuba diving; water-skiing. (213) 457-2511.
Mass Transit: Rapid Transit District (RTD) Route 434.

ESCONDIDO BEACH: A stairway leads to the small sandy beach at the mouth of Escondido Creek; diving area.
Mass Transit: RTD Route 434.

CORRAL STATE BEACH: Also known as Solstice Beach. Narrow, sandy, beach with .7 mile of ocean frontage; scuba diving and surfing. Roadside parking only. For information, call: (213) 457-9891.
Mass Transit: RTD Route 434.

STAIRWAYS TO BEACH: Public stairways at the 25100, 24700, 24500, 24400, and 24300 blocks of Malibu Rd. lead to the beach; there is off-street parking for three cars at the 25100 block stairway. Private property adjoins each accessway; do not trespass.
Mass Transit: RTD Route 434.

MALIBU BLUFFS STATE PARK: An upland park with a grassy playing field, restrooms, day use parking, and trails leading south to Malibu Rd., where there is beach access via public stairways at the 25100, 24700, 24500, and 24300 blocks. Scheduled to be completed summer 1983.
Mass Transit: RTD Route 434.

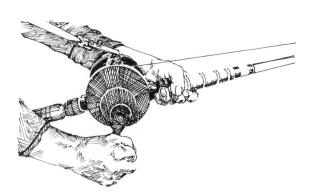

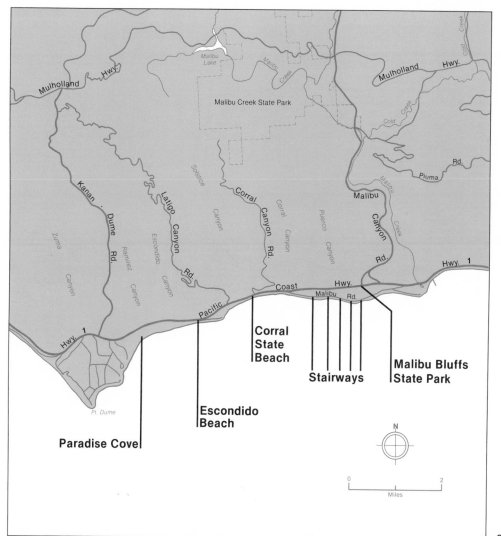

Wildfires

Numerous wildfires occur annually throughout California. Most of these fires are extinguished quickly, before causing much damage. However, almost every year there are uncontrollable wildfires that burn extensive areas, resulting in millions of dollars in damages to homes, property, and natural resources. Many of the largest wildfires occur in Southern California, where there are long arid summers, seasonal dry winds, and extensive areas of dry brushland and rugged terrain.

The most critical periods of wildfire danger occur when vegetation is dry, temperatures are hot, and relative humidities are low. In California, which has a Mediterranean climate, these conditions occur every summer and fall, primarily because of seasonal weather patterns that produce very little rainfall from May to November.

Wildfire conditions become extremely hazardous in the months following the hot, dry summer when strong winds blow from the east for several days at a time. These winds, called foehn winds (locally known in Southern California as Santa Ana winds), occur when a strong high-pressure system forms in the Great Basin with the development of a corresponding low-pressure system off the Southern California coast. The low-pressure system draws desert air over the Southern California mountains, creating hot dry winds with speeds of up to 60 to 90 miles per hour. Under these conditions, wildfires are extremely difficult to contain; most of the devastating fires in Southern California burn during periods of Santa Ana winds.

The areas near the coast in Southern California that are most susceptible to large wildfires are the vast coastal sage scrub and chaparral brushlands. Over the past 100,000 years, fires started by lightning or possibly by Native Americans have periodically burned through chaparral areas. Many chaparral species are remarkably well adapted to deal with these recurring fires; shrubs can sprout from burned-over stumps, and some chaparral seeds, which are capable of remaining dormant for long periods of time between fires, are resistant to heat and may in fact even require heat to germinate.

In the early 1900's, the U.S. Forest Service and the California Department of Forestry adopted policies of prohibiting fires on certain designated public and private lands. However, the practice of complete fire exclusion has allowed some brushlands to reach over-maturity, creating conditions where historically unburned areas contain high amounts of very old dead and dry brush. Fires occurring in these areas, especially during periods of Santa Ana winds, are particularly catastrophic.

To prevent the spread of wildfires, the U.S. Forest Service, the California Department of Forestry, and private landowners have established numerous fuel and fire breaks, particularly where wildland areas adjoin communities and other developments. These fuel and fire breaks are wide swaths, sometimes several miles long, where vegetation is partially or completely removed. Other methods of fire prevention include the use of controlled or "prescribed" burns in the early spring or late fall. These carefully planned burns during wet months reduce the amount of flammable vegetation that would normally exist during peak fire hazard seasons.

Although arson accounts for the origin of many California wildfires, most fires on public lands are ignited by lightning or by accidental causes such as downed or shorted power lines, sparks from railroad trains, campfires, the use of machines or firearms, and discarded cigarettes and matches. During periods of high fire danger, some California park lands may be closed, or campfires prohibited. Because wildfires are easiest to extinguish while they are still small, any fires should be immediately reported to local fire prevention authorities.

Los Angeles County
MALIBU PIER-TOPANGA BEACH

NAME	LOCATION	Entrance/Parking Fee	Parking	Restrooms	Lifeguard	Campground	Showers	Firepits	Stairs to Beach	Path to Beach	Bike Path	Hiking Trail	Facilities for Disabled	Boating Facilities	Fishing	Equestrian Trail	Sandy Beach	Dunes	Rocky Shore	Upland from Beach	Stream Corridor	Bluff	Wetland
Surfrider Beach (Malibu Lagoon State Beach)	23200 block of Pacific Coast Hwy., Malibu	•	•	•	•										•		•				•		•
Malibu Pier	23000 block of Pacific Coast Hwy., Malibu	•	•											•	•								
Zonker Harris Accessway	22700 block of Pacific Coast Hwy., Malibu									•							•						
Walkway to the Beach	21200 block of Pacific Coast Hwy., Malibu									•							•						
Stairway to the Beach	20300 block of Pacific Coast Hwy., Malibu								•								•						
Stairway to the Beach	19900 block of Pacific Coast Hwy., Malibu								•								•						
Las Tunas State Beach	19400 block of Pacific Coast Hwy., Malibu		•	•											•		•		•			•	
Topanga State Beach	18500 block of Pacific Coast Hwy., Malibu	•	•	•	•										•		•		•			•	•

SURFRIDER BEACH (MALIBU LAGOON STATE BEACH): 35 acres with 2/3 mile of ocean frontage. Very popular surfing and swimming beach adjacent to Malibu Pier; diving area. Fee parking lot $3/car; some free roadside parking. Call: (213) 457-9891. Malibu Lagoon has recently been restored; facilities include picnic tables and interpretive trails for individuals and groups. Guided tours are available for groups; the new parking lot at the west end of the beach is for groups only. For information, call: (213) 706-1310.
Mass Transit: Rapid Transit District (RTD) Route 434.

MALIBU PIER: 700-foot pier built in 1903 and reconstructed in 1946; now owned by the state. The pier is open 6 AM-8 PM. Fishing licenses, bait and tackle are available at the Malibu Sport Fishing Landing, open 6 AM-5 PM, (213) 456-8030. Sport fishing boats, excursion boat, and restaurant also available at the pier. Fee parking lot; roadside parking.
Mass Transit: RTD Route 434.

ZONKER HARRIS ACCESSWAY: 10-foot wide cement walkway leads to the beach; private property on either side. Do not trespass.
Mass Transit: RTD Route 434.

WALKWAY TO THE BEACH: 10-foot wide cement walkway leads to the beach; private property on either side. Do not trespass.
Mass Transit: RTD Route 434.

STAIRWAYS TO THE BEACH: Public stairways lead to the beach; private property on either side. Do not trespass.
Mass Transit: RTD Route 434.

LAS TUNAS STATE BEACH: Narrow, sandy, two-acre beach, sometimes rocky, below the bluff; swimmers and divers should beware of the metal groins in the water which hold the sand. Unpaved parking area. For information, call: (213) 457-9891.
Mass Transit: RTD Route 434.

TOPANGA STATE BEACH: Narrow, sandy beach, sometimes rocky, below the bluff; 21.5 acres of beach with 1.1 acres of ocean frontage. Recently acquired by the state. Popular surfing area near Topanga Creek. $3 parking fee. Call: (213) 394-3266.
Mass Transit: RTD Route 434.

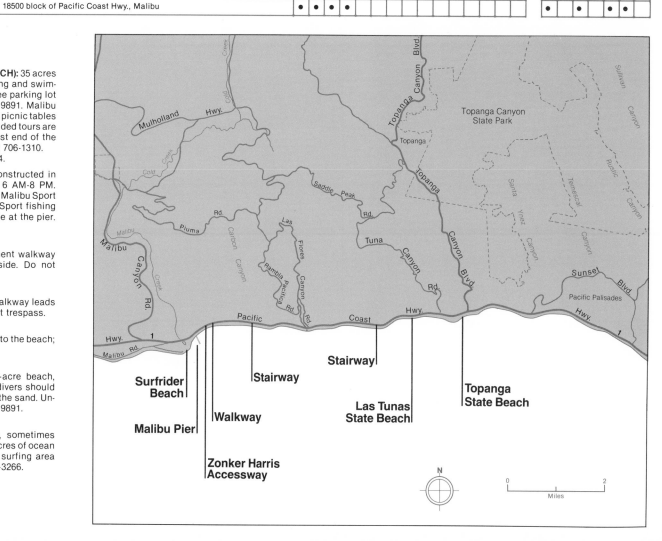

Santa Monica Mountains

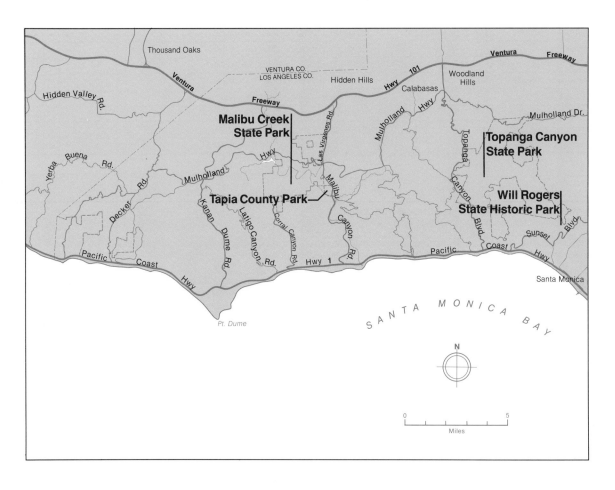

Los Angeles County
SANTA MONICA MOUNTAINS

NAME	LOCATION	Entrance/Parking Fee	Parking	Restrooms	Lifeguard	Campground	Showers	Firepits	Stairs to Beach	Path to Beach	Bike Path	Hiking Trail	Facilities for Disabled	Boating Facilities	Fishing	Equestrian Trail	Sandy Beach	Dunes	Rocky Shore	Upland from Beach	Stream Corridor	Bluff	Wetland
Malibu Creek State Park	28754 Mulholland Dr., Agoura	•	•	•								•			•	•				•	•		
Tapia County Park	Piuma Rd. and Malibu Canyon Rd., Malibu		•	•				•				•	•			•				•	•		
Topanga Canyon State Park	20825 Entrada Rd., Topanga	•	•	•								•				•				•	•		
Will Rogers State Historic Park	14235 Sunset Blvd., Pacific Palisades	•	•	•								•	•			•				•			

FACILITIES   **ENVIRONMENT**

The Santa Monica Mountains run east and west from the Los Angeles River to the Oxnard Plain. The dramatic contrast between the natural and scenic environment of the mountains, and the intensely developed urban areas of Los Angeles and the San Fernando Valley makes the Santa Monicas an extremely valuable resource, particularly as a recreational area.

The mountains offer panoramic views of the ocean from the summits, some of which are as high as 2,000 feet, and provide a large open space area; much of the Santa Monica Mountains is still wild and undeveloped. Mulholland Drive and Highway follow the crest of the mountains for nearly 50 miles, from Hollywood to the ocean at Leo Carrillo State Beach, providing a major scenic access route.

The Santa Monica Mountains National Recreation Area (SMMNRA), consisting of 150,000 acres within the mountains and along the coast, is an area of the National Park System established in November, 1978 to preserve the mountains' natural, cultural, and scenic resources and provide recreational and educational opportunities for the public. Several areas within the SMMNRA are currently open to the public for hiking and picnicking; there are also free ranger-led hikes in some of these areas. The National Park Service hopes to acquire more public land within the SMMNRA and develop additional recreational facilities. For information, write or call the SMMNRA at 22900 Ventura Blvd., Suite 140, Woodland Hills 91364, (213) 888-3440.

The mountains are covered by chaparral and other dense vegetation such as sage, scrub oak, and sumac, which become very dry in summer and create a major fire hazard. Brush fires which spread easily are frequent occurrences; visitors are urged to use extreme caution when making fires, and to use only designated firepit or grill areas.

The State Department of Parks and Recreation owns and operates several state parks in the mountains. Their Santa Monica Mountain Area Headquarters is at 2860A Camino Dos Rios, Newbury Park 91320. For information, call: (213) 706-1310 or (805) 499-2112.

MALIBU CREEK STATE PARK: 4,000 acres, 700' elevation; includes Malibu Creek, two-acre Century Lake, woodlands, canyons, volcanic rock, waterfall areas, and Kaslow, Udell, and Liberty Canyon Natural Preserves. Nearly 15 miles of hiking and equestrian trails; picnicking permitted. Formerly Twentieth Century Fox's movie set, called Century Ranch. Parking lot fee $2/car; no cars allowed in the park. For information, call: (213) 706-1310.

TAPIA COUNTY PARK: Adjacent to Malibu Creek; 94.5 acres of land. Facilities include picnic tables and grills, a sports field, and equestrian/hiking trails. One of the more developed parks in the Santa Monica Mountains.

TOPANGA CANYON STATE PARK: Take Topanga Canyon Rd. to Entrada Rd. to get to the park; watch carefully. 9,000 pristine acres with woodlands and meadows, 35 miles of trails and fire roads, picnic areas, and a small stream. Panoramic views of the San Fernando Valley and the ocean from Eagle Rock. Day use fee $2. (213) 706-1310.
Mass Transit: RTD Route 434.

WILL ROGERS STATE HISTORIC PARK: 187-acre park; former ranch of the late Will Rogers, famous cowboy humorist. Main house, open 10 AM-5 PM, displays possessions and momentos; Visitor Center shows a 12-minute film of his life. Saturday polo matches, free of charge, held in the summer on the polo field, weather permitting. Hiking and equestrian trails; no fires allowed. Restrooms are wheelchair accessible. Park open 8 AM-7 PM in the summer; 8 AM-5 PM in the winter. Parking fee $2/car. Call: (213) 454-8212 or 706-1310.
Mass Transit: RTD Routes 2, 176, and 601.

Santa Monica Mountains, Mouth of Malibu Creek

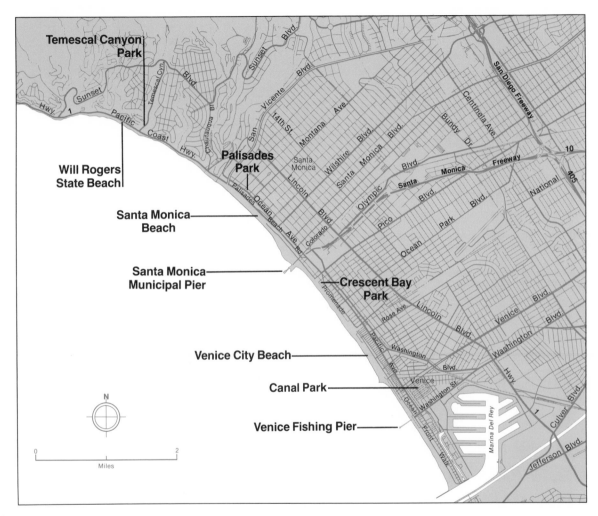

Temescal Canyon Park

Sunset Blvd.

Temescal Cyn. Blvd.

Hwy. 1

Sunset

Pacific Coast Hwy.

Chautauqua Bl.

San Vicente Blvd.

14th St.

Montana Ave.

Wilshire Blvd.

Santa Monica Blvd.

Santa Monica

Lincoln Blvd.

Will Rogers State Beach

Palisades Park

Palisades Ocean Beach Ave.

Olympic Blvd.

Santa Monica Blvd.

Colorado

Pico Blvd.

Santa Monica Beach

Ocean Park Blvd.

Santa Monica Municipal Pier

Crescent Bay Park

Promenade

Rose Ave.

Lincoln Blvd.

Venice Blvd.

Washington Blvd.

Venice City Beach

Pacific Ave.

Washington Blvd.

Canal Park

Venice

Washington St.

Venice Fishing Pier

Ocean Front Walk

Marina Del Rey

Centinela Ave.

Bundy Dr.

San Diego Freeway

10

Santa Monica Freeway

405

National

Hwy. 1

Culver Blvd.

Jefferson Blvd.

N

0   2
Miles

Los Angeles County
PACIFIC PALISADES/SANTA MONICA/VENICE

NAME	LOCATION	Entrance/Parking Fee	Parking	Restrooms	Lifeguard	Campground	Showers	Firepits	Stairs to Beach	Path to Beach	Bike Path	Hiking Trail	Facilities for Disabled	Boating Facilities	Fishing	Equestrian Trail	Sandy Beach	Dunes	Rocky Shore	Upland from Beach	Stream Corridor	Bluff	Wetland
Will Rogers State Beach	16000 block of Pacific Coast Hwy., Pacific Palisades	•	•	•	•										•		•						
Temescal Canyon Park	Temescal Canyon Rd. and Pacific Coast Hwy., Pacific Palisades		•	•																		•	
Palisades Park	Ocean Ave., from Colorado Ave. to Adelaide Dr., Santa Monica		•	•							•									•		•	
Santa Monica Beach	W. of Pacific Coast Hwy., Santa Monica	•	•	•					•		•						•					•	
Santa Monica Municipal Pier	Colorado and Ocean Aves., Santa Monica	•	•							•				•	•		•						
Crescent Bay Park	1800 Promenade, Santa Monica		•																			•	
Venice City Beach	1531 Ocean Front Walk, Venice	•	•	•	•						•		•		•		•						
Canal Park	Linnie Canal and Dell Ave., Venice																				•		
Venice Fishing Pier	Foot of Washington St., Venice	•	•							•					•								

WILL ROGERS STATE BEACH: Wide, sandy beach, several miles long, with volleyball courts and food facilities; diving and surfing. Named for the cowboy humorist Will Rogers. $3 parking fee. For information, call: (213) 394-3266.
Mass Transit: Rapid Transit District (RTD) Routes 2, 176, 434, and 601. Santa Monica Municipal Bus Lines (MBL) Route 9.

TEMESCAL CANYON PARK: In the bottom of Temescal Canyon, on both sides of Temescal Canyon Rd.; the park extends one mile up the canyon to Pacific Palisades High School. View of the ocean; picnicking. Free roadside parking.
Mass Transit: RTD Routes 2 and 434.

PALISADES PARK: On the bluff above the Pacific Coast Highway overlooking Santa Monica Beach. Facilities include benches, shuffleboard courts, a walkway, and a Senior Recreation Center which is open Mon.-Fri. 9 AM-4 PM and Sat. and Sun. 11 AM-4 PM. Camera Obscura near Arizona St. is open daily. Several bicycle/pedestrian overpasses lead from the park down to the beach.
Mass Transit: RTD Routes 4, 20, 22, 75, 308, 309, and 434. Santa Monica MBL Routes 1, 7, and 10.

SANTA MONICA BEACH: Extremely wide, sandy beach below the bluff, divided by the Santa Monica Pier into north and south beaches. Facilities include picnic tables, playground and gymnastic equipment, and volleyball courts; popular surfing area. $3 parking fee. Access to the beach is from the parking lots or via bicycle/pedestrian overpasses from Palisades Park. A promenade extends the length of the south beach and part of the north beach. For information, call: (213) 394-3266. The South Bay Bicycle Trail begins at California St., about a mile north of the pier, and runs south for 19 miles to Torrance Beach.
Mass Transit: RTD Routes 4, 20, 22, 75, 308, 309, and 434. Santa Monica MBL Routes 1, 7, and 10.

SANTA MONICA MUNICIPAL PIER: Entrance at Colorado and Ocean Avenues. Pier features amusement arcade, restaurants and food concessions, shops, and the famous carousel. Facilities include a boat hoist: cap. 3 tons to 30 feet, rowboat and motorboat rentals, charter fishing boats, fishing licenses, bait and tackle. Harbormaster: (213) 395-1425. Fee parking in the beach lots; limited parking also available on the adjacent Newcomb Pier. Two stairways, one on the north side and one on the south, lead from the pier to the beach.
Mass Transit: RTD Routes 4, 20, 22, 75, 308, 309, and 434. Santa Monica MBL Routes 1, 7, and 10.

CRESCENT BAY PARK: Small grassy park south of the pier; parking on the street or in the beach lot.
Mass Transit: RTD Route 75. Santa Monica MBL Routes 1, 7, and 10.

VENICE CITY BEACH: Wide, sandy, 238-acre beach with playground and picnic area; diving and grunion. $3 parking fee. Call: (213) 394-3266. Ocean Front Walk, the walkway adjacent to the beach, has shops, restaurants, and street merchants, and is popular with rollerskaters, bicyclists, skateboarders, etc. The Venice Pavilion at the foot of Windward Ave. has murals, picnic tables, an auditorium, and a rollerskating area, and is wheelchair accessible by ramp.
Mass Transit: RTD Routes 75, 313, 604, 605, and 828. Santa Monica MBL Routes 1 and 2. Culver City Municipal Bus Lines (MBL) Route 1.

CANAL PARK: Small, grassy mini-park along Linnie Canal; no facilities.
Mass Transit: RTD Routes 75, 313, 604, 605, and 828.

VENICE FISHING PIER: 1,100-foot municipal pier with food concession and fish cleaning facility, open 24 hours; parking fee.
Mass Transit: RTD Routes 604, 605, and 828. Culver City MBL Route 1.

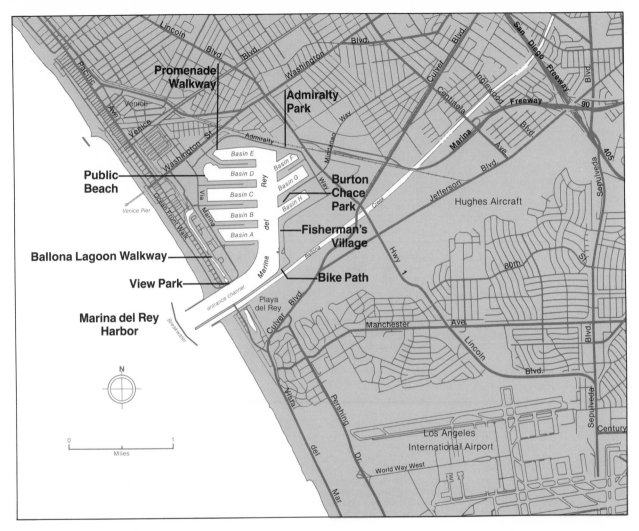

Promenade
Walkway

Admiralty
Park

Public
Beach

Burton
Chace
Park

Fisherman's
Village

Ballona Lagoon Walkway

View Park

Bike Path

Marina del Rey
Harbor

Basin E
Basin D
Basin C
Basin B
Basin A

Basin F
Basin G
Basin H

Lincoln
Blvd.

Washington
Blvd.

Culver
Blvd.

Inglewood

San Diego Freeway

Blvd.

Freeway

90

Washington
St.

Venice

Venice

Pacific
Ave.

Ocean Front Walk

Venice Pier

Admiralty

Via Marina

Marina del Rey

Mindanao
Way

Marina

Marina
Way

Creek

Jefferson

Blvd.

Hughes Aircraft

Sepulveda

405

Ballona

Hwy 1

80th

St.

entrance channel

Playa
del Rey

Culver
Blvd.

Manchester

Ave.

Lincoln

Blvd.

Blvd.

Sepulveda

Century

Breakwater

Vista

Pershing

Dr.

del

Mar

Los Angeles
International Airport

World Way West

N

0   1
Miles

Los Angeles County

MARINA DEL REY

NAME	LOCATION	Entrance/Parking Fee	Parking	Restrooms	Lifeguard	Campground	Showers	Firepits	Stairs to Beach	Path to Beach	Bike Path	Hiking Trail	Facilities for Disabled	Boating Facilities	Fishing	Equestrian Trail	Sandy Beach	Dunes	Rocky Shore	Upland from Beach	Stream Corridor	Bluff	Wetland
Ballona Lagoon Walkway	E. side of Ballona Lagoon																			•			•
Marina del Rey Harbor	South of Venice, Marina del Rey		•	•						•		•	•	•			•			•			•
Main Channel View Park	Along entrance channel, Marina del Rey														•				•	•			
Public Beach	End of Basin D, Panay Way, Marina del Rey	•	•	•	•						•		•				•						
Promenade Walkway	In front of Marina City Club, Marina del Rey																			•			
Admiralty Park	Admiralty Way, Marina del Rey	•	•								•									•			
Burton Chace Park	Basin H, W. end of Mindanao Way, Marina del Rey	•	•	•			•								•					•			
Fisherman's Village	Basin H, Fiji Way, Marina del Rey		•	•										•	•					•			
Marina del Rey Bike Path	Around perimeter of Harbor, Marina del Rey												•							•			

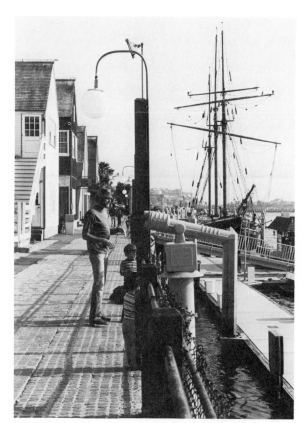

Fisherman's Village

BALLONA LAGOON WALKWAY: A public walkway on the east side of the lagoon.
Mass Transit: Rapid Transit District (RTD) Routes 605 and 828.

MARINA DEL REY HARBOR: Built in 1960; the largest artificial small-craft harbor in the world, with more than 6,000 private pleasure craft. Facilities include public boat slips (waiting list), marine supplies, hoists, fuel docks, and fishing charter boats. There are also shops, restaurants, hotels, and seven yacht clubs. A public boat launch ramp at Basin H, Fiji Way, is 10-lanes concrete with floating docks; open 24 hours. Fee for parking and use of ramp. Adjacent to the ramp is a public dry storage boating facility; fee. There are also private facilities for boat rentals and dry boat storage. Special events include the Christmas Boat Parade, the annual boat show at Burton Chace Park, and the California Cup Race.

Guest berths with water, electricity, restrooms, and showers are available at Basin H; transients report to the Harbormaster for berth assignment. Advance reservations recommended. The Harbormaster is on the east side of the bend in the main channel. Mailing address: Administration Bldg., Fiji Way, Marina del Rey 90291. Call: (213) 823-4571. The Marina Information Center is at Admiralty Way and Mindanao Way: 4701 Admiralty Way, Marina del Rey 90291, (213) 822-0119. The harbor is also the home of the Marina del Rey Chamber of Commerce: (213) 821-0555.
Mass Transit: RTD Routes 220, 605, 606, and 828. Santa Monica Municipal Bus Lines (MBL) Route 3.

There is public access along most of the bulkheads in the harbor. Other accessways are listed below.

MAIN CHANNEL VIEW PARK: Walkway with benches and view piers along the north side of the entrance channel of the harbor; jetties on either side. The park is used for fishing, biking, and walking.
Mass Transit: RTD Routes 605 and 828.

PUBLIC BEACH: Swimming beach and hand launching, open all year. Free for hand-launched, non-motorized boats weighing less than 200 lbs. A ramp for the disabled leads to the water; wheelchairs provided free of charge for use on the ramp.
Mass Transit: RTD Routes 605 and 828.

PROMENADE WALKWAY: Public accessway along the bulkhead in front of the Marina City Club. Walkway open 6 AM-9 PM; the Marina City Club is private.
Mass Transit: RTD Routes 605 and 828.

ADMIRALTY PARK: A linear, grassy park along Admiralty Way between Lincoln Blvd. and Washington St.; view of the marina. Parking fee. The Marina del Rey Bike Path runs along one edge.
Mass Transit: RTD Routes 605 and 828.

BURTON CHACE PARK: Eight-acre park with a panoramic view of the main channel. Transient boat docks, picnic shelter, watchtower, fishing dock, and fish cleaning facility. Annual in-the-water boat show. Parking at the park is free only on weekdays during the daytime.
Mass Transit: RTD Routes 220, 605, and 828. Santa Monica MBL Route 3.

FISHERMAN'S VILLAGE: Commercial area which offers shops, galleries, restaurants; sail, power, and sport fishing boat charters and rentals; fishing licenses, bait and tackle; and a view of the harbor. For information, call: (213) 823-5411. Parking fee. Harbor cruises on the Marina Belle, which leaves every hour between 10 AM and 6 PM from the Boat House in the southern part of Fisherman's Village, 13727 Fiji Way; (213) 822-1151.
Mass Transit: RTD Routes 220 and 606.

MARINA DEL REY BIKE PATH: Bike path along the perimeter of the harbor.

Bicycling

California's coast is one of the most scenic areas in the state for bicycling. Throughout the year, particularly in summer, bicyclists tour along the coast, or use bicycles simply to get to the beach.

California has extensive bikeway systems along the coast, ranging from the 1,000-mile long Pacific Coast Bicentennial Route to numerous bike paths (paved paths exclusively for the use of bicycles) and bike lanes (special lanes delineated by a painted line on the road) that provide access to and between local beaches and coastal parks. Bicycle racks are frequently provided at beaches and parks.

The Pacific Coast Bicentennial Route, designated in recognition of the nation's Bicentennial celebration in 1976, runs near the coast from the Oregon border to Mexico, offering spectacular vistas and veering inland only when there is no other suitable roadway. The route ranges from freeway shoulders to exclusive bike paths, while the topography varies from steep hills in the north to flat ocean terraces in the south.

The Bicentennial Route passes numerous historic sites, state parks and beaches, plus several national parks. Many of these parks provide special camping sites for bicyclists, charging an overnight fee of approximately 50¢. There are also low-cost accommodations and bicycle facilities at most of the coastal hostels.

For more detailed information and maps covering the entire route, request the *Pacific Coast Bicentennial Route Guide,* and send $2.12 to:

Caltrans Publication Unit
6002 Folsom Boulevard
Sacramento, CA 95819   (916) 445-3520

For maps and information on local and regional bikeways, contact the main Caltrans office:

Office of Bicycle Facilities
Division of Highways
P.O. Box 1499
Sacramento, CA 95807   (916) 322-4314

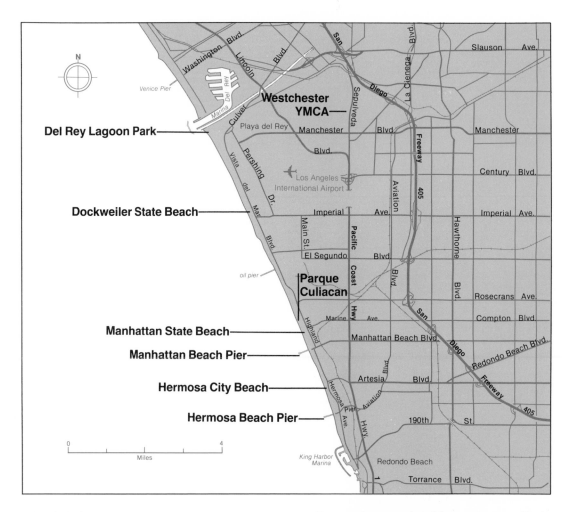

Bicycle Safety:

1. Ride defensively. Never assume motorists are aware of you; many drivers are so busy watching other cars that they don't notice bicycles.

2. Obey the same rules and regulations as motorists.

3. Stay as far to the right side of the road as safely possible, except to pass or on one-way streets.

4. Keep an eye out for parked cars with people inside; someone may open a door or the car may pull out into traffic suddenly.

5. Beware of cars turning right across your path; the driver may not know you're there.

6. Let other drivers know what you're doing: use hand signals, and always ride in a straight line.

7. Keep your bicycle in good condition; check tires (pressure and tread), brake shoes, chain, and all cables frequently.

For the complete set of laws pertaining to bicycle operation, refer to section 21200 of the California Vehicle Code.

Los Angeles County
PLAYA DEL REY
MANHATTAN BEACH/HERMOSA BEACH

NAME	LOCATION	Entrance/Parking Fee	Parking	Restrooms	Lifeguard	Campground	Showers	Firepits	Stairs to Beach	Path to Beach	Bike Path	Hiking Trail	Facilities for Disabled	Boating Facilities	Fishing	Equestrian Trail	Sandy Beach	Dunes	Rocky Shore	Upland from Beach	Stream Corridor	Bluff	Wetland
Westchester YMCA	8015 S. Sepulveda Blvd., Los Angeles	•	•	•		•														•			
Del Rey Lagoon Park	6660 Esplanade, Playa del Rey		•	•				•		•				•					•	•		•	
Dockweiler State Beach	Runs from Harbor Channel to Vista del Mar and Grand Ave.	•	•	•	•	•			•	•	•		•		•		•	•				•	
Parque Culiacan	26th St. and Manhattan Ave., Manhattan Beach		•																			•	
Manhattan State Beach	W. of the Strand, Manhattan Beach	•	•	•					•		•		•				•						
Manhattan Beach Municipal Pier	Foot of Manhattan Beach Blvd., Manhattan Beach	•	•												•								
Hermosa City Beach	W. of the Strand, Hermosa Beach	•	•	•							•		•				•						
Hermosa Beach Municipal Pier	Foot of Pier Ave., Hermosa Beach		•	•											•								

WESTCHESTER YMCA: Run as a hostel; approximately three miles northeast of Dockweiler State Beach. Sleeps 35; $5.25 for members, $6.25 for non-members. No kitchen. Must be over 18 years old. Advance booking required for groups; open mid-June through mid-September. (213) 776-0922.
Mass Transit: Rapid Transit District (RTD) Route 871 to Manchester and Sepulveda Blvd.; walk four blocks north on Sepulveda to 80th Street. Take RTD Route 88 from the L.A. International Airport; Route 88 offers Bike 'N' Ride Service – buses on this line are equipped with bicycle racks.

DEL REY LAGOON PARK: Approximately 13 acres; grassy area around the lagoon. Facilities include picnic tables, playground, baseball diamond, and basketball courts. Small boat launch on the lagoon; no swimming. Access to the beach along Ballona Creek.
Mass Transit: RTD Routes 220 and 606.

DOCKWEILER STATE BEACH: Extremely wide, sandy, 255-acre beach behind the airport. The beach runs south from Harbor Channel to the foot of Grand Ave. and also extends 1,500 feet north of Harbor Channel. To get to the main entrance, take the Imperial Highway west to the end. Facilities include a picnic area and volleyball courts; diving. $3 parking fee.

There are wheelchair ramps leading from the parking area to the Strand at 41st and 43rd Streets; there are also parking stalls for the disabled. The new R.V. campground, located at the south end of the beach, has 158 spaces, an on-site restroom, and a sewage disposal unit; no hookups. $8/vehicle; must check in by 10 PM. Call: (213) 322-5008 or 372-2166.
Mass Transit: RTD Routes 115, 116, 220, and 606.

PARQUE CULIACAN: Three-acre grassy park on the bluff; basketball court. Adjacent to the County Lifeguard Headquarters along the Strand.
Mass Transit: RTD Routes 606 and 871.

MANHATTAN STATE BEACH: 44-acre sandy beach with access ramps for the disabled, volleyball courts, and a playground; diving and surfing. Parking fee $3. For information, call: (213) 372-2166. The Strand, which is a cement pedestrian walkway, extends the length of the beach; the South Bay Bicycle Trail runs adjacent to the Strand.
Mass Transit: RTD Routes 125, 606, 861, and 871. The City of Manhattan Beach operates a dial-a-ride bus program for senior citizens and disabled persons, Mon.-Fri. 9 AM-12 PM and 1 PM-4PM; 25¢/trip (within city limits only). Call: (213) 545-3500.

MANHATTAN BEACH MUNICIPAL PIER: 900-foot pier, open 24 hours. Parking fee.
Mass Transit: RTD Routes 606, 861, and 871.

HERMOSA CITY BEACH: Wide, sandy, 110-acre beach with volleyball courts and swing sets; diving and surfing. (213) 372-2166. The Strand, a pedestrian walkway, and the adjacent South Bay Bicycle Trail run the length of the beach.
Mass Transit: RTD Routes 130, 606, and 871. The City of Hermosa Beach runs a free bus; Routes 1 and 2 both stop near the beach.

HERMOSA BEACH MUNICIPAL PIER: 1,320-foot pier with snack bar and bait and tackle shop. Bait shop open year-round; call Hermosa Sportfishing: (213) 372-2124. Pier open 24 hours.
Mass Transit: RTD Routes 130, 606, and 871. Hermosa Beach Bus Routes 1 and 2.

Hermosa City Beach

King Harbor

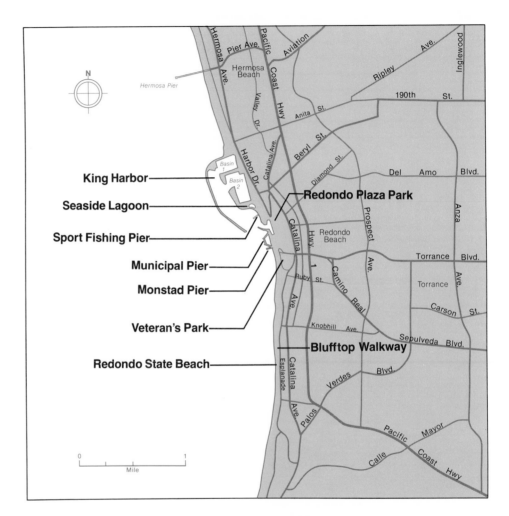

King Harbor

Seaside Lagoon

Sport Fishing Pier

Redondo Plaza Park

Municipal Pier

Monstad Pier

Veteran's Park

Blufftop Walkway

Redondo State Beach

NAME	LOCATION	Entrance/Parking Fee	Parking	Restrooms	Lifeguard	Campground	Showers	Firepits	Stairs to Beach	Path to Beach	Bike Path	Hiking Trail	Facilities for Disabled	Boating Facilities	Fishing	Equestrian Trail	Sandy Beach	Dunes	Rocky Shore	Upland from Beach	Stream Corridor	Bluff	Wetland
King Harbor	W. of Harbor Dr., Redondo Beach	•	•	•							•			•	•								
Seaside Lagoon	200 Portofino Way, Redondo Beach	•	•																				•
Redondo Sport Fishing Pier	W. of Harbor Dr., N. of Basin #3, Redondo Beach	•	•												•								
Redondo Plaza Park	Between Harbor Dr. and Catalina Ave., Redondo Beach												•							•		•	
Redondo Beach Municipal Pier	Foot of Torrance Blvd., Redondo Beach	•	•												•								
Monstad Pier	Foot of Torrance Blvd., Redondo Beach	•	•												•								
Veteran's Park	Foot of Torrance Blvd., Redondo Beach	•	•																	•			
Redondo State Beach	W. of Esplanade, Redondo Beach	•	•	•	•				•		•		•		•		•					•	
Blufftop Walkway	W. of Esplanade, Redondo Beach									•	•									•		•	

KING HARBOR: Municipal small-craft harbor with three basins, accommodating more than 1,400 boats. See Harbormaster for transient berthing; office at the entrance to Basin 2. Mailing address: Box 270, Redondo Beach 90277. Call: (213) 372-1175, ex. 239. Harbor facilities include slips, marinas, marine supplies, hoists, fuel docks, charter boat rentals, shops, and restaurants. Parking fee. Adjacent to the Seaside Lagoon is a small hand-carry boat launching ramp. Seasonal whale watching boat trips available.

Basin 3 includes a large commercial-recreational area associated with the Pier Complex, known as the International Boardwalk, which has an amusement arcade; the Pier Complex consists of the Pier approach, the Monstad Pier, the Municipal Pier, the International Boardwalk, and a parking structure. Public walkways extend around each basin and throughout the harbor and pier area. The South Bay Bicycle Trail is east of the harbor. **Mass Transit:** Rapid Transit District (RTD) Routes 130, 867, and 871. Torrance Transit System (TTS) Routes 1 and 3 to Coral Way.

SEASIDE LAGOON: Located between Harbor Basins 2 and 3; a 2½-acre sand-bottom, warm saltwater swimming lagoon. Parking fee. Open 10 AM-6 PM, May 29-September. (213) 376-9905. **Mass Transit:** RTD Routes 130, 867, and 871. TTS Routes 1 and 3 to Coral Way.

REDONDO SPORT FISHING PIER: 200-foot privately owned pier with bait and tackle shop, equipment sales and rentals, and snack bar. Parking fee. Pier open 24 hours. For information on whale watching cruises, call: (213) 372-3566. **Mass Transit:** RTD Routes 130, 867, and 871. TTS Routes 1 and 3 to Coral Way.

REDONDO PLAZA PARK: Small grassy park on a bluff east of Harbor Basin 3 with benches and a viewing area; provides access to King Harbor. An underground parking garage between the park and the harbor is under construction. **Mass Transit:** RTD Routes 130, 607, 814, 867, and 871. TTS Routes 1 and 3 to Coral Way.

REDONDO BEACH MUNICIPAL PIER: Also known as Horseshoe Pier; has commercial facilities such as restaurants and shops. Large parking structure located behind the pier; fee. **Mass Transit:** RTD Routes 130, 607, 814, 867, and 871. TTS Routes 1 and 3 to Coral Way.

MONSTAD PIER: 300-foot privately owned pier, open 24 hours, with bait and tackle shop and restaurant. Admission fee. **Mass Transit:** RTD Routes 130, 607, 814, 867, and 871. TTS Routes 1 and 3 to Coral Way.

VETERAN'S PARK: 6.3-acre public park; stairs lead from the park to Redondo Beach. **Mass Transit:** RTD Routes 130, 607, 814, 867, and 871. TTS Routes 1 and 3 to Coral Way.

REDONDO STATE BEACH: Extremely wide, sandy, 85-acre beach below the bluff with volleyball courts; a walkway and the South Bay Bicycle Trail run parallel the length of the beach. A number of stairways, walkways, and ramps lead down to the beach from Harbor Dr. and from Esplanade. Metered parking along Esplanade. (213) 372-2166. **Mass Transit:** RTD Routes 130, 607, 814, 867, and 871. TTS Routes 1 and 3 to Coral Way.

BLUFFTOP WALKWAY: Parallels Esplanade 50 feet above the shoreline and runs north from the Torrance City boundary to Knob Hill Ave., where a stairway leads down to another walkway which continues north to the Pier Complex. **Mass Transit:** RTD Routes 130, 607, 814, 867, and 871. TTS Routes 1 and 3 to Coral Way.

Redondo Beach Municipal Pier

Point Vicente Fishing Access

Point Vicente Lighthouse

Scenic Overlook, Palos Verdes Estates

Los Angeles County
TORRANCE/PALOS VERDES

NAME	LOCATION	Entrance/Parking Fee	Parking	Restrooms	Lifeguard	Campground	Showers	Firepits	Stairs to Beach	Path to Beach	Bike Path	Hiking Trail	Facilities for Disabled	Boating Facilities	Fishing	Equestrian Trail	Sandy Beach	Dunes	Rocky Shore	Upland from Beach	Stream Corridor	Bluff	Wetland
Torrance County Beach	Along Paseo de la Playa, Torrance	●	●	●	●				●	●					●		●					●	
Palos Verdes Estates Shoreline Preserve	Entire shoreline of Palos Verdes Estates		●							●					●		●		●	●		●	
Malaga Cove	Off Paseo del Mar, E. of Via Arroyo, Palos Verdes Estates		●							●					●		●					●	
Path to Beach	At Flat Rock Pt., 600 block of Paseo del Mar, Palos Verdes Estates		●							●					●							●	
Overlook at Bluff Cove	1300 block of Paseo del Mar, Palos Verdes Estates		●																●			●	
Point Vicente County Park	Palos Verdes Dr. West, S. of Hawthorne Blvd., Rancho Palos Verdes		●										●						●	●		●	
Point Vicente Fishing Access	E. of Point Vicente County Park, Rancho Palos Verdes		●	●						●	●				●				●			●	

TORRANCE COUNTY BEACH: The beach is accessible through the parking lot; at the north end from Redondo Beach; and at the south end via a pathway in Palos Verdes Estates, just south of the City of Torrance's southern border. $3 parking fee; diving and surfing. (213) 372-2166. The South Bay Bicycle Trail ends at Torrance Beach, having run south for 19 miles from California St. at Santa Monica Beach.
Mass Transit: Rapid Transit District (RTD) Routes 814 and 869. Torrance Transit Lines (TTS) Route 4 along Palos Verdes Blvd.; walk west to the beach; no Sunday bus service.

PALOS VERDES ESTATES SHORELINE PRESERVE: Established in 1969; includes 130 acres of city-owned blufftop parkland and submerged lands, running the full length of the city's 4-1/2 mile shoreline. The blufftop parklands are undeveloped and have no facilities; ample street parking exists. Many scenic overlooks and paths along the blufftop. Most of the shoreline is rocky and the footpaths down the cliff are usually very steep and hazardous. Tidepools; skin and scuba diving. Popular surfing spots at Malaga Cove, Bluff Cove, and Lunada Bay.
Mass Transit: RTD Routes 814 and 869.

MALAGA COVE: Take the beach access road off Paseo del Mar. Scenic viewpoint at the gazebo above the cove; a paved accessway leads down to the beach. Free parking. Malaga Cove has the only sandy beach on the Peninsula; swimming and surfing. The beach is also known as "RAT" Beach — Right After Torrance; access from Torrance County Beach by walking south.
Mass Transit: RTD Routes 814 and 869.

PATH TO BEACH: At Flat Rock Point a partially paved path leads down to Bluff Cove, which is a popular surfing and diving area.
Mass Transit: RTD Route 869.

OVERLOOK AT BLUFF COVE: Free parking lot on the blufftop; view of the shoreline.
Mass Transit: RTD Route 869.

POINT VICENTE COUNTY PARK: Currently an undeveloped area north of the Point Vicente Lighthouse; will become a regional park. The Lighthouse, which is at the Coast Guard Station, was built in 1926 and is now open to the public Tuesday and Thursday afternoons.
Mass Transit: RTD Routes 813 and 869.

POINT VICENTE FISHING ACCESS: A wide dirt path leads down to a rocky beach; popular area for fishing, and scuba and skin diving.
Mass Transit: RTD Routes 813 and 869.

Tidepools

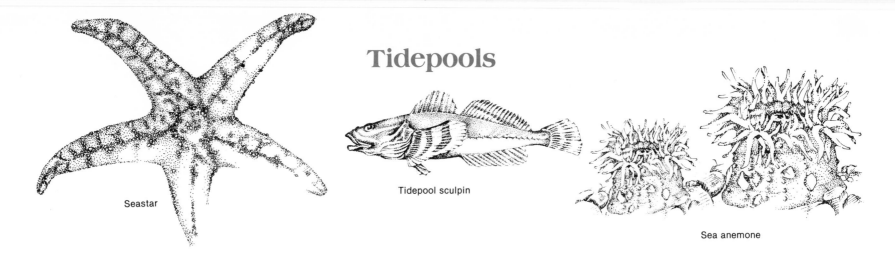

Seastar

Tidepool sculpin

Sea anemone

Tidepools are rocky pockets which retain water when the tide recedes; they are found on rocky shores in the intertidal zone, the area between high and low tides. Tidepools are habitat for a myriad of marine life forms which live in the crevices, ledges, and caves of the tidepool, such as barnacles, sea urchins, anemones, starfish, limpets, mussels, snails, clams, periwinkles, chitons, oysters, scallops, crabs, squid, abalone, shrimp, and other invertebrates, and fish such as gobies and sculpins.

The intertidal marine area is divided into four life zones according to the amount of exposure to air; the ability of each species to live in a particular zone depends upon their relative air tolerance. Other factors include the type of food source, predation by other species, and amounts of required sunlight.

The splash zone, the highest zone, gets the least amount of water and contains such biota as periwinkles and green algae; the upper intertidal zone, which is usually only under water during high tide, supports such organisms as acorn barnacles, limpets, and chitons; the middle intertidal zone, typically covered and uncovered twice a day, contains mussels, gooseneck barnacles, and rockweed; and the low intertidal zone, usually uncovered only by "minus" tides, supports the greatest diversity of life forms including abalone, starfish, sea urchins, and anemones.

There are four types of food gatherers in tidepools: predators, such as starfish, sea anemones, and barnacles; filter feeders, such as mussels and clams, which pump water through their filters and digest plankton and bits of plant; algae eaters, such as snails, limpets, and abalone, which feed on kelp and other algae; and scavengers such as crabs, which eat waste food.

Each species in the intertidal zone must be adapted to prevent dehydration and asphyxiation when exposed to air at low tide, and be able to protect itself from wave shock; these adaptations have evolved over millions of years. In the last 50 years people have caused a tremendous amount of change in the environment which these intertidal biota are unable to cope with. Thermal and chemical waste discharges from urban and industrial activities as well as oil spills have severely disrupted many of California's tidepool habitats.

However, the greatest damage to tidepools is probably from people who trample through them and overturn rocks, exposing the organisms to light, dessication, and predation. Marine life removed from its natural environment usually cannot survive.

As a result, the Department of Fish and Game has adopted regulations to protect tidal invertebrates and it is now a crime to remove living organisms from tidepools except those species designated in the regulations. A valid California Sport Fishing License is required to take the invertebrates listed, and there is a bag limit of 35 on all organisms for which the take is authorized and for which there is not a bag limit otherwise established.

Tidepool visitors should consult tide tables, which may be found on the weather page of many coastal newspapers, and should keep a close watch on the waves and the tide while observing tidepools; many rocky shore areas along the California coast are hazardous.

Los Angeles County
MARINELAND/POINT FERMIN

NAME	LOCATION	Entrance/Parking Fee	Parking	Restrooms	Lifeguard	Campground	Showers	Firepits	Stairs to Beach	Path to Beach	Bike Path	Hiking Trail	Facilities for Disabled	Boating Facilities	Fishing	Equestrian Trail	Sandy Beach	Dunes	Rocky Shore	Upland from Beach	Stream Corridor	Bluff	Wetland
Marineland	6600 Palos Verdes Dr. South, Rancho Palos Verdes	•	•	•													•	•		•			
Abalone Cove County Beach	Palos Verdes Dr. South, W. of Narcissa Dr., Rancho Palos Verdes		•	•	•					•					•		•		•			•	
Abalone Cove Ecological Reserve	Palos Verdes Dr. South, W. of Narcissa Dr., Rancho Palos Verdes		•	•						•									•			•	
Royal Palms State Beach	Western Ave. and Paseo del Mar, San Pedro	•	•	•	•					•			•				•		•			•	
Los Angeles International Hostel	1502 Palos Verdes Dr. North, Harbor City	•	•	•																•			
Wilder Annex (Point Fermin Park)	Paseo del Mar and Meyler St., San Pedro		•	•						•			•				•	•				•	
Point Fermin Park and Lighthouse	Paseo del Mar and Gaffey St., San Pedro		•	•				•	•								•	•				•	

MARINELAND: Large water zoo at the southwest tip of the Palos Verdes Peninsula, with aquariums, sea collections, shows, and exhibits including performing sea lions, dolphins, and killer whales. Sky Tower, a circular revolving elevator, rises 344 feet above sea level for a spectacular view of the coast; small fee. Food available. Free parking; admission charge. For information, call: (213) 541-5663.
Mass Transit: Rapid Transit District (RTD) Routes 813 and 869.

ABALONE COVE COUNTY BEACH: Unpaved parking lot; dirt path leads down to the beach and tidepools. The old paved road and parking lot have been closed due to earth movement. The beach is a popular surfing and diving spot; steep cliffs. Call: (213) 372-2166. Wayfarer's Chapel across Palos Verdes Dr. South is an unusual and beautiful chapel designed by Lloyd Wright (son of Frank Lloyd Wright) in 1946, made of redwood, stone, and glass with a 50-foot tower.
Mass Transit: RTD Route 869.

ABALONE COVE ECOLOGICAL RESERVE: A designated portion of Abalone Cove County Beach; take the same dirt road down to the water.
Mass Transit: RTD Route 869.

ROYAL PALMS STATE BEACH: The Royal Palms Hotel was situated here until it was washed out by a storm in the 1920's; majestic palms and garden terraces remain. Popular surfing spot; lifeguards summer only. Steep, rugged cliffs; tidepools. $3 parking fee. County-operated White's Point Beach is directly east. Call: (213) 372-2166.

LOS ANGELES INTERNATIONAL HOSTEL: Approximately five miles north of Royal Palms State Beach. 70 beds, fully equipped kitchen; $5.50/night for members, $7.50/night for non-members. Open all year. (213) 831-8109.
Mass Transit: RTD Routes 232 and 849.

WILDER ANNEX: The western portion of Point Fermin Park; blufftop park with a paved path to the beach. Street parking only.
Mass Transit: RTD Route 810.

POINT FERMIN PARK AND LIGHTHOUSE: 37 landscaped acres on a bluff overlooking the ocean and L.A. Harbor. Facilities include picnic tables, playground, benches, a small amphitheater, and the Point Fermin Cetacean and Community Building. Whale watch station open Sat. and Sun. 9 AM-4 PM; free 20-minute whale movie. Two improved trails, one accessible from Barbara or Leland Streets, the other accessible from Meyler or Roxbury Streets, lead down the bluff to the shoreline. Point Fermin Lighthouse, built in 1874, is not open to the public.
Mass Transit: RTD Route 810.

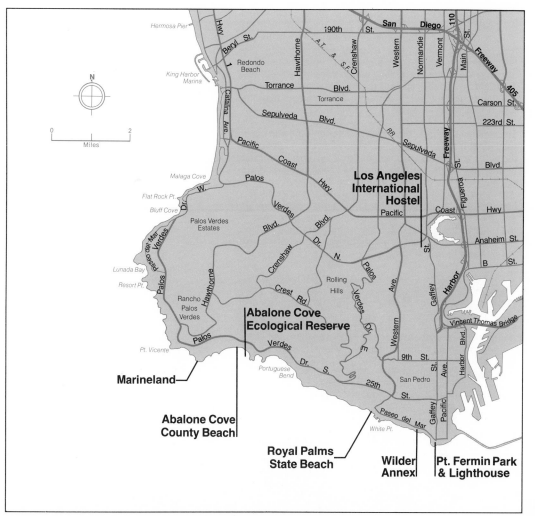

Grunion

O f all the thousands of fish who live in the sea, only the grunion lays its eggs on land. Grunion are small, silvery fish, related to topsmelt, who come ashore to spawn from March through August, just after highest high tide. California grunion are found generally between Morro Bay and Abreojos, Baja California; they live three to four years and reach a length of six inches or more. The periods when the grunion lay their eggs are called grunion runs, since the grunion come ashore in masses.

Spawning occurs on the second, third, and fourth nights following the peak tides of the 14-day lunar cycle, when the tides that follow will be lower than those of the night before. Females begin to spawn each night just after the tide turns, so the eggs will not be washed away. The female drills into the damp sand with her tail until she is buried up to the pectoral fins, which anchor her in place. Then she lays her eggs into the hole she has dug, while the male curls himself around her and releases his milt, which fertilizes the eggs.

The newly laid eggs, buried a few inches below the surface, are buried further beneath the sand by the action of the tides and waves. Grunion develop within a protective membrane which surrounds the fertilized eggs, and are ready to hatch in about nine days, but must wait until the tide is high enough to reach the eggs. 10-14 days after fertilization the next series of very high tides occurs and an enzyme activated by the agitation of the surf causes the eggs to hatch; the newborn grunion are then carried out to sea by the waves. In about a year the grunion are mature and ready to spawn.

Young females lay about 1,000 eggs at each spawning, while older females can lay up to 3,000 eggs; older females may spawn as many as eight times during the season, thus spawning as many as 24,000 eggs in one season. Spawning runs last about three hours. The name grunion probably comes from the Spanish word gruñón, meaning "one who grunts," since female grunion have been heard to make faint sounds like squeaks or grunts just after spawning.

Grunion may be collected by hand in March, June, July, and August by persons having a valid California fishing permit; no permit is required for those under 16. The Cabrillo Marine Museum sponsors a Grunion Run Program several nights a month during the spawning season, which includes a bonfire on the beach and discussion while waiting for the grunion run.

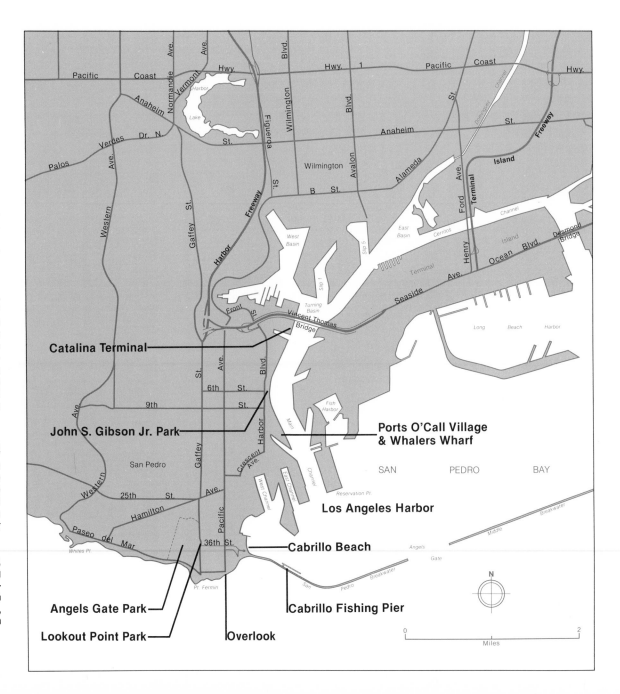

Los Angeles County
SAN PEDRO/LOS ANGELES HARBOR

NAME	LOCATION	Entrance/Parking Fee	Parking	Restrooms	Lifeguard	Campground	Showers	Firepits	Stairs to Beach	Path to Beach	Bike Path	Hiking Trail	Facilities for Disabled	Boating Facilities	Fishing	Equestrian Trail	Sandy Beach	Dunes	Rocky Shore	Upland from Beach	Stream Corridor	Bluff	Wetland
Angels Gate Park	930 Paseo del Mar, San Pedro		•	•															•			•	
Lookout Point Park	Gaffey St., 34th-36th Streets, San Pedro		•																•			•	
Overlook	Pacific Ave. and Sheppard St., San Pedro		•																•			•	
Cabrillo Beach	40th St. and Stephen M. White Dr., San Pedro	•	•	•	•		•						•	•			•		•				
Cabrillo Fishing Pier	1/4 mi. past beach, inside breakwater, San Pedro	•	•	•											•				•				
Ports O' Call Village and Whalers Wharf	Berth 77, L.A. Harbor, San Pedro		•												•					•			
John S. Gibson, Jr. Park	6th St. and Sampson Way, San Pedro		•																	•		•	
Los Angeles Harbor	W. end of San Pedro Bay	•	•											•	•					•			
Catalina Terminal	Berths 94-95, L.A. Harbor, San Pedro	•	•												•					•			

ANGELS GATE PARK: View of the ocean and of Pt. Fermin. The park has three parts: a play area with basketball and volleyball courts; a historic site with a pagoda housing the Friendship Bell given by the Republic of Korea in 1976 to commemorate the U.S. Bicentennial; and the old Fort McArthur site, used for recreational activities. (213) 548-7710. Gaffey Pool on 33rd and Gaffey St. is open to the public, summers only, for a small fee; (213) 833-9557.
Mass Transit: Rapid Transit District (RTD) Route 810.

LOOKOUT POINT PARK: Small overlook area with a view of San Pedro Bay; coin-operated telescopes.
Mass Transit: RTD Route 810.

CABRILLO BEACH: Stillwater beach inside the breakwater, and surf beach on the ocean; diving and surfing. Facilities include picnic tables, snack bar, and volleyball courts; on the harbor side is a public boat launching ramp, four-lanes concrete, open 24 hours. $3 parking fee. Call: (213) 372-2166.

The free Cabrillo Marine Museum, started in the 1920's by the lifeguards, has recently moved to a new, larger building across the parking lot from the old building. The museum has marine displays, ship models, navigation equipment, harbor and maritime lore, etc. New facilities include an auditorium, laboratories, classrooms, gift shop, and an exhibition hall with interpretive displays and 32 aquaria containing marine plants and animals. Open Tuesday-Sunday 10 AM-5 PM. Museum: 3720 Stephen M. White Dr., (213) 548-7562. The museum also sponsors guided tidepool tours at the Point Fermin Marine Life Refuge, whale watches on half-day boat trips, Cabrillo Day celebrations, Channel Island boat trips, and grunion run programs. For information on whale watching charter boats, call: (213) 832-4444.
Mass Transit: RTD Route 810.

CABRILLO FISHING PIER: 1,200-foot municipal fishing pier with bait shop; north of the Cabrillo Beach breakwater. Parking fee. Pier open daily. (213) 832-1179.
Mass Transit: RTD Route 810.

PORTS O'CALL VILLAGE AND WHALERS WHARF: Faces the main channel of the harbor. Ports O'Call Village is a facsimile of an old California seaport, with restaurants and shops; Village Boat House offers daily cruises of the harbor area. Open 11 AM-9 PM daily all year. Call: (213) 831-0287. For information on whale watching cruises, call: (213) 547-9916. Whalers Wharf simulates a 19th century New England seaport with shops, restaurants, and cobbled streets; helicopter rides and harbor and dinner cruises available. Open 11 AM-9 PM daily all year.
Mass Transit: Long Beach Transit (LBT) Route 14. RTD Route 872.

JOHN S. GIBSON, JR. PARK: Small grassy park overlooking L.A. Harbor; stairway access to the harbor down the cliff face. Los Angeles Maritime Museum, in the remodeled ferry building at the south end of the park (at Berth 84), contains a pictorial history of the Los Angeles Harbor area, marine artifacts, ship models, and a view of the harbor from the promenade deck. Museum open daily, Mon.-Fri. 9 AM-4 PM, weekends 12:30 PM-4 PM. Admission free; donations accepted. Museum: (213) 548-7618.
Mass Transit: LBT Route 14. RTD Routes 841 and 872.

LOS ANGELES HARBOR: One of the world's largest artificial harbors, with 7,000 acres of land and water, and 28 miles of waterfront. The harbor has three districts – San Pedro, Wilmington, and Terminal Island; the Vincent Thomas Bridge joins the San Pedro and Terminal Island districts. Nation's largest commercial fishing fleet and canning center, with cargo and passenger terminals, shipyards, marinas, and slips. Facilities include dry storage, hoists, cranes, fuel dock, fishing licenses, bait and tackle. Charter boats and marine supplies available.
Mass Transit: LBT Route 14. RTD Routes 841 and 872.

CATALINA TERMINAL: Take the Harbor Freeway south to the Catalina Island exit; the terminal is located under the west end of the Vincent Thomas Bridge. Parking fee. Catalina Cruises runs daily ferries to Avalon and Two Harbors June-September. Ferries take approximately two hours to get to Catalina. CC Berth 95-96, P.O. Box 1948, San Pedro 90733; (213) 514-3838. For information on whale watching cruises, call: (213) 775-6111.
Mass Transit: LBT Route 14.

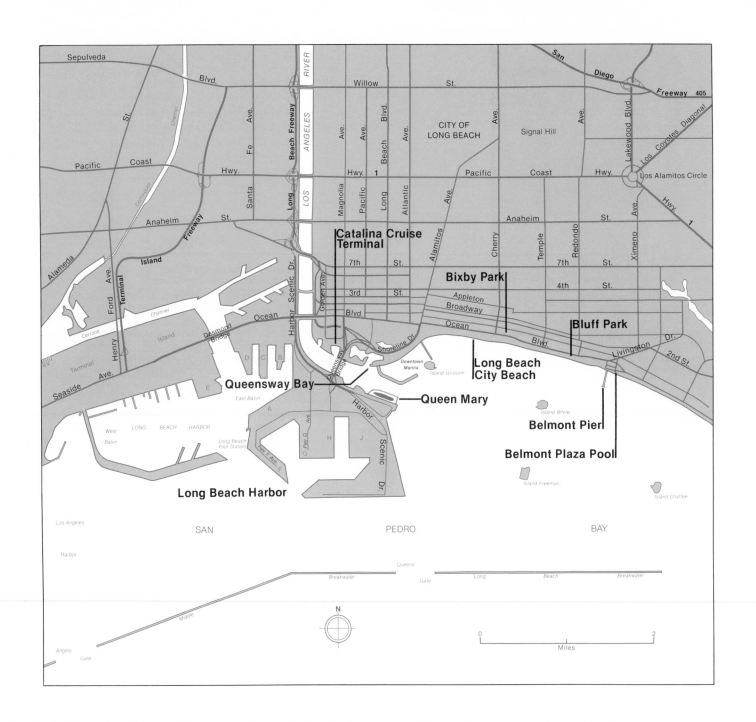

Los Angeles County

CITY OF LONG BEACH

NAME	LOCATION	Entrance/Parking Fee	Parking	Restrooms	Lifeguard	Campground	Showers	Firepits	Stairs to Beach	Path to Beach	Bike Path	Hiking Trail	Facilities for Disabled	Boating Facilities	Fishing	Equestrian Trail	Sandy Beach	Dunes	Rocky Shore	Upland from Beach	Stream Corridor	Bluff	Wetland
Long Beach Harbor	E. end of San Pedro Bay, Long Beach	•	•											•	•				•				
Queen Mary	Pier J, Long Beach Harbor	•	•	•																			
Queensway Bay	Mouth of Los Angeles River, Long Beach		•	•										•					•				
Terminal for Long Beach/Catalina Cruises	Queensway Landing, 330 Golden Shores Blvd., Long Beach	•	•											•									
Long Beach City Beach	Seaward of Ocean Blvd., Long Beach	•	•	•	•				•						•		•					•	
Bixby Park	Ocean Blvd. and Cherry Ave., Long Beach		•	•				•	•				•							•		•	
Bluff Park	Ocean Blvd. between 20th and Redondo, Long Beach		•						•		•				•					•		•	
Belmont Pier	Ocean Blvd. and 39th Place, Long Beach	•	•	•																			
Belmont Plaza Recreation Pool	E. of Belmont Pier, Long Beach	•	•	•			•																

LONG BEACH HARBOR: Artificial harbor in the eastern part of San Pedro Bay with extensive cargo-handling facilities, slips, supplies, and repair yards. Charterboats and boat cruises; fishing licenses, bait and tackle available. There are hotels and restaurants along Queensway Bay.
Mass Transit: Long Beach Transit (LBT) Routes 11, 12, and 14. Rapid Transit District (RTD) Route 456.

THE QUEEN MARY: One-time luxury liner; the largest passenger ship ever built, with a crew of 1,200 and weighing over 80,000 tons. The Queen Mary was launched in 1934 at Clydebank, Scotland and retired in 1964; now permanently berthed in Long Beach as a tourist attraction and a hotel. Hotel: (213) 435-3511. The ship has restaurants, shops, and the Cousteau "Living Sea" Museum, an undersea marine exhibition created by Jacques Cousteau. Fee for tour and museum: (213) 435-4747. The *Spruce Goose*, the largest airplane ever built, is located adjacent to the Queen Mary inside an aluminum dome about 13 stories high. The airplane, built by Howard Hughes, is made entirely of wood, and will be available for public viewing in May, 1983. Call: (213) 435-7766.
Mass Transit: LBT Route 12.

QUEENSWAY BAY: Boating and water-skiing. The Golden Avenue launching ramp, at the south end of Golden Ave. off Ocean Blvd., is 16-lanes concrete, open 24 hours all year; fee. The new small boat harbor, called the Shoreline Harbor Marina, has 131 slips, and is located east of the swimming lagoon. Scheduled for completion by summer 1983 are the larger Downtown Marina with approximately 1,694 slips, the Shoreline Aquatic Park, and associated commercial development. Facilities include restrooms, parking areas, bicycle and pedestrian paths, picnic areas, a children's play area, boat rentals at the lagoon, observation and fishing bridges onto Queensway Bay, and a fully-equipped 70-site R.V. campground at the western end of the park. Marina Headquarters is located at the end of the eastern jetty. Call: (213) 437-0377.
Mass Transit: LBT Routes 11, 12, and 14. RTD Route 456.

TERMINAL FOR LONG BEACH/CATALINA CRUISES: Take the Long Beach Freeway south almost to the end; take the first downtown exit, then the Golden Shore Exit. The Terminal is at Queensway Landing. Daily ferries to Avalon and Two Harbors September-June. (213) 775-6111.
Mass Transit: LBT Route 11. RTD Route 456.

LONG BEACH CITY BEACH: Wide, sandy beach seaward of Ocean Blvd., which runs for several miles from 1st Place to 72nd Place. The western end of the beach is below a bluff; stairways to the beach are at the ends of 2nd, 3rd, 5th, 8th, 9th, 10th, 12th, and 14th Places. Facilities include volleyball courts, concessions, and several pay parking lots. Very little surf, as the beach is inside the harbor breakwater.
Mass Transit: LBT Routes 2 and 12.

BIXBY PARK: 10 acres. Street parking alongside the park; pay parking lot below the bluffs. Facilities include picnic tables, benches, a playground, shuffleboard courts, and a bandshell with frequent concerts. Recreation Center heavily used by senior citizens for social events, dances, card-playing, etc. A tunnel leading to the beach goes underneath Ocean Blvd.
Mass Transit: LBT Routes 2, 11, and 12.

BLUFF PARK: Linear, grassy park above the beach, along the south side of Ocean Boulevard. Street parking. Long Beach Museum of Art is at 2300 E. Ocean Blvd. at the east end of Bluff Park; open Wednesday-Sunday 12 PM-5 PM; (213) 439-2119. Stairway to the beach at the end of 20th Place right near the museum.
Mass Transit: LBT Route 12.

BELMONT PIER: 1,300-foot municipal pier, open 5 AM-10 PM. Parking fee; benches, bait shop, and snack bar. Bait shop open 7 AM-8 PM; call: (213) 434-6781.
Mass Transit: LBT Route 12.

BELMONT PLAZA RECREATION POOL: Indoor pool designed for Olympic-class swimming and diving events; used in training U.S. athletes for international events; also used for locally-run recreational swimming and diving programs. Picnic tables and playground outside; volleyball courts on the beach. Parking fee.
Mass Transit: LBT Route 12.

Long Beach Harbor

Bayshore Walk

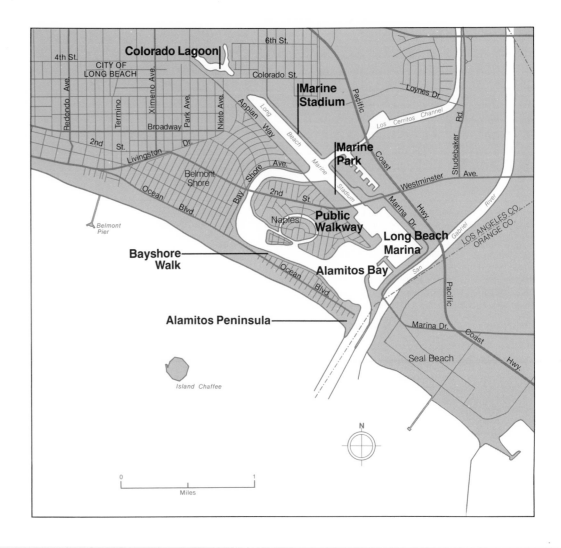

6th St.

4th St.

Colorado Lagoon

CITY OF
LONG BEACH

Colorado St.

Redondo Ave.

Termino

Ximeno Ave.

Park Ave.

Broadway

Nieto Ave.

Appian Way

Long Beach

**Marine
Stadium**

Pacific

Loynes Dr.

Los Cerritos Channel

Studebaker

Rd.

2nd St.

Livingston Dr.

**Marine
Park**

Marine Stadium

Coast

Westminster

Ave.

Ocean Blvd.

Belmont
Shore

Bay Shore Ave.

2nd St.

Marina Dr.

Hwy.

San Gabriel River

LOS ANGELES CO.
ORANGE CO.

Belmont
Pier

Naples

**Public
Walkway**

**Long Beach
Marina**

**Bayshore
Walk**

Alamitos Bay

San

Pacific

Alamitos Peninsula

Marina Dr.

Coast

Seal Beach

Hwy.

Island Chaffee

N

0   1
Miles

224

NAME	LOCATION	FACILITIES														ENVIRONMENT						
		Entrance/Parking Fee	Parking	Restrooms	Lifeguard	Campground	Showers	Firepits	Stairs to Beach	Path to Beach	Bike Path	Hiking Trail	Facilities for Disabled	Boating Facilities	Fishing	Equestrian Trail	Sandy Beach	Dunes	Rocky Shore	Upland from Beach	Stream Corridor	Bluff	Wetland
Bayshore Walk	From 55th-69th Place, Long Beach																•						
Alamitos Peninsula	Off Ocean Blvd., 54th Place to 72nd Place, Long Beach	•	•	•	•			•						•			•		•	•			
Alamitos Bay	W. of the San Gabriel River, Long Beach		•											•	•		•			•			
Long Beach Marina	N.E. end of Alamitos Bay, Long Beach	•	•	•										•									
Public Walkway	Around Naples, Long Beach																			•			
Marine Park	N. of Davies Bridge, Long Beach	•	•	•	•						•			•			•						
Marine Stadium	Appian Way and 2nd Street, Long Beach	•	•	•	•									•	•		•					•	
Colorado Lagoon	Appian Way and 4th Street, Long Beach	•	•	•	•		•			•							•						•

BAYSHORE WALK: Public walkway runs alongside Alamitos Bay from 55th-69th Place on the bay side of the Alamitos Peninsula. **Mass Transit:** Long Beach Transit (LBT) Route 8 (limited service).

ALAMITOS PENINSULA: Extends from 54th Place to the entrance channel of the bay. There is a sandy and rocky beach on the ocean side; fee parking lot at 72nd Place and Ocean Boulevard. Fishing from the jetty; surfing. Parking lot and small sailboat launching ramp at Claremont Ave. and Ocean Blvd. just west of the peninsula; fee. **Mass Transit:** LBT Route 8 (limited service) to 72nd Place and Ocean Blvd.

ALAMITOS BAY: Contains three marinas with berthing capacity for 2,000 boats; facilities include four hoists, a hand boat launch, restaurants, shops, yacht clubs, and a sailing center. Water-skiing permitted. Swimming at Alamitos Bay Beach, a narrow sandy beach south of 2nd St. on the bay side. Bayshore Playground at Ocean Blvd. and Peninsula Place has basketball and handball courts. The Marine Department office is on the east side of the entrance channel, 205 Marina Dr., Long Beach 90803, (213) 594-0951. **Mass Transit:** LBT Routes 5 and 12; limited service on Route 8. Rapid Transit District (RTD) Routes 266 and 755.

LONG BEACH MARINA: 158 acres. Public berths, supplies, and services; facilities include ramp-launching areas, hoists, and fuel dock. No slips available and there is a very long waiting list; temporary berthing for visitors on a first come, first served basis for up to 15 days in any month. Mooring controlled by the Marine Department, whose office is on the east side of the entrance channel, 205 Marina Dr., Long Beach 90803, (213) 594-0951.

Events include an annual Christmas parade of lighted boats and floats. Seaport Village, on the east side of the entrance channel, is a waterfront shopping and restaurant complex. **Mass Transit:** LBT Routes 5 and 12. RTD Routes 266 and 755.

PUBLIC WALKWAY: Naples is composed of three islands in Alamitos Bay separated by canals; the walkway extends around most of Naples, along the bay or canals, except along the southwest edges of the large island and Treasure Island (the smallest island). Overlook Park at Naples Plaza and Vista del Golfo has benches, a small grassy area, and a view of the bay. **Mass Transit:** LBT Routes 5 and 12. RTD Routes 266 and 755.

MARINE PARK: Located at the southeast end of Marine Stadium; narrow sandy beach and grassy area. Parking fee. **Mass Transit:** LBT Routes 5 and 12. RTD Routes 266 and 755.

MARINE STADIUM: Built in the 1920's and used for the 1932 Olympics. The Stadium is a long rectangular body of sea water, approximately 1 mile long and .1 mile wide, connected to Alamitos Bay; now used for commercial water sport events.

On the southwest side are beaches and facilities for small boat and water-ski launching, a parking lot, and grandstands; the public launching ramp is near the intersection of Appian Way and Nieto Ave., eight-lanes concrete, open all year 8 AM-sunset

(unless race events are scheduled). The northeast side has a parking lot, grandstands, rowing center, boathouse, and docks; the public launching ramp is parallel to the north approach to the Davies Bridge, 12-lanes concrete, open 24 hours year-round. Scheduled events include the International Sea Festival, Girl and Boy Scout mariners, university and other rowing races, etc.

A new park is currently under construction north of Marine Stadium and south of Colorado Lagoon, between Nieto and Havana Avenues. Planned facilities include two small parking lots, baseball and soccer fields, and a children's play area. **Mass Transit:** LBT Routes 5 and 12; limited service on Route 8. RTD Routes 266 and 755.

COLORADO LAGOON: 40 acres of water and land; the tidal lagoon receives sea water from Marine Stadium. Sandy beach, playgrounds, floating causeways; popular spot for clamming. Parking fee. Picnicking at Recreation Park just north of the Lagoon, which contains a large golf course. **Mass Transit:** LBT Routes 8 and 9. RTD Routes 149, 266, and 755.

Alamitos Bay

Santa Catalina Island

Santa Catalina Island, Avalon Bay

Catalina Island is 21 miles long, 8 miles wide at its widest point, and has a resident population of about 2,200. The island was discovered in 1542 by Cabrillo, and again in 1602 by Vizcaíno. It's now a popular tourist spot with mountains, canyons, and beaches; herds of buffalo, wild boar, and goats run free in the interior. Catalina is 22 miles off the coast of Los Angeles, and can be reached by air or sea.

To get around on the island, bicycles can be rented, and taxis and buses can be hired. Tours include cruises, bus tours, and inland motor tours, and visit such sites as the Casino in Avalon, the Undersea Gardens (in a glass bottom boat) just offshore from Avalon, and El Rancho Escondido in the interior, where purebred Arabian horses are raised and trained. For hotel reservations and more information about transportation and tours, contact the Avalon Chamber of Commerce on the Pleasure Pier, P.O. Box 217, Avalon 90704, (213) 510-1520; or the Visitor's Information & Services Center, P.O. Box 1159, Avalon 90704, (213) 510-2500.

The Santa Catalina Island Conservancy, a non-profit foundation, owns 86% of the Island's 76 square miles and manages it as a preserve. Permits are required for hiking and bicycling into the interior and are available free in Avalon at the Conservancy office, 206 Metropole Avenue, (213) 510-1421, and at the Information Center, 302 Crescent Avenue, (213) 510-2500; at the Cove and Camp Agency at Two Harbors, (213) 510-0303; and at the Airport in the Sky, (213) 510-0143.

Fresh water is available only at certain spots; hikers and backpackers are advised to carry water. Backpackers must camp in designated campgrounds; fees are charged and permits and reservations required. Campers under 18 must be accompanied by an adult. Pets are not allowed in any campground or in the interior. (See specific campground entries for more information on particular campgrounds). Skin and scuba diving is permitted; licenses, rentals, and air refills are available at Avalon and at Two Harbors. Private boats must pay mooring fees when landing ashore; transient mooring rentals are on a first come, first served basis.

Transportation to Catalina:

CATALINA CRUISES: Daily from Long Beach to Avalon and Two Harbors September-June, and from San Pedro June-September. Long Beach: (213) 775-6111; Catalina Landing, 330 Golden Shores Blvd., Long Beach 90802. San Pedro: (213) 514-3838; Catalina Terminal, Berth 95-96, P.O. Box 1948, San Pedro 90733.

CATALINA PASSENGER SERVICE: The 425-passenger *Catalina Holiday* runs daily April-October from the Balboa Pavilion in Newport Harbor to Avalon. Newport Harbor: (714) 673-5245. Avalon: (213) 510-0451.

CATALINA EXPRESS: Runs commuter boats year-round from San Pedro to Avalon and Two Harbors. San Pedro: (213) 519-1212. Avalon: 510-1212.

HELITRANS COMMUTER: Helicopters fly daily from the Catalina Terminal in San Pedro to Avalon. Call (213) 548-1314, or toll free (from southern California only): 1-800-262-1472.

PIPER AIR CENTER: Airplanes fly daily from the Long Beach Airport to Airport in the Sky. Long Beach: (213) 420-3500.

CAT ALL SEASONS AIR PACIFIC: Airplanes leave from the Long Beach Airport and fly to Airport in the Sky. Long Beach: (213) 420-1883. Avalon: (213) 510-1644.

EAGLE AIRLINES: Airplanes fly from Long Beach and Los Angeles International to Airport in the Sky. Long Beach: (213) 420-2655.

AIRPORT IN THE SKY, where both commercial and private planes land, is located 25 minutes from Avalon by bus service. Open daily. For information, call: (213) 510-0143.

FACILITIES **ENVIRONMENT**

NAME	LOCATION	Entrance/Parking Fee	Parking	Restrooms	Lifeguard	Campground	Showers	Firepits	Stairs to Beach	Path to Beach	Bike Path	Hiking Trail	Facilities for Disabled	Boating Facilities	Fishing	Equestrian Trail	Sandy Beach	Dunes	Rocky Shore	Upland from Beach	Stream Corridor	Bluff	Wetland
Avalon Bay	E. end of the Island, on the leeward side		•	•										•	•		•						
Descanso Beach	N. of Avalon Bay, Avalon	•		•									•				•						
Crescent Beach	Avalon Bay, Avalon		•	•													•						
Bird Park	Avalon Canyon Rd., Avalon	•		•		•	•	•					•		•					•			
Toyon Junction	On Old Stage Rd., 3.9 mi. from Avalon			•									•		•					•			
Black Jack Campground	9.4 mi. N.W. of Avalon	•		•		•		•					•		•					•			

AVALON BAY: Avalon Harbor is within the bay; no berths; moor to buoys. See the Harbormaster (on the Pleasure Pier) for temporary mooring assignments. Harbormaster: (213) 510-0303, 24 hours. Pleasure Pier in the south part of the bay has concessions, equipment rentals, and hoist. Diving supplies sold and rented on the pier. Fuel dock adjacent to the Casino, open daily: (213) 510-0046. Also available are marine supplies, fishing licenses, bait and tackle. Water-skiing and diving are permitted in the bay.

Nearby in Avalon are golf and tennis courts, stables, bike rentals, and a miniature golf course. The Casino, at the west end of the bay, is a popular tourist attraction and contains a ballroom, theater, and museum.

The Wrigley Memorial and Botanical Garden, at 1400 Avalon Canyon Rd., is 1.7 miles from downtown Avalon; walk or take a tram. 37.85 acres, open 8 AM-5 PM year-round. Small fee. The Memorial, completed in 1934, is an imposing structure of stone, marble, and tile; the Botanical Garden below features cactus, succulents, and other native Catalina plants. The Memorial and Garden commemorate William Wrigley Jr., founder of the Wrigley Chewing Gum Company, who purchased control of the Santa Catalina Island Company in 1919 and spent the rest of his life improving Catalina . **Mass Transit:** Ferry to Avalon.

DESCANSO BEACH: Private beach club; available to the public for daily fee or season membership. Cabanas, snack bar. (213) 510-0484 or 775-2589.
Mass Transit: Ferry to Avalon.

CRESCENT BEACH: Sandy, surf-free beach. Bath House at 228 Crescent provides showers, lockers, and a laundry.
Mass Transit: Ferry to Avalon.

BIRD PARK: Accommodates 75 campers. Fee is $4/person; reservations required. Call (213) 510-0688 or write L.A. County Department of Parks and Recreation, P.O. Box 1133, Avalon 90704.
Mass Transit: Ferry to Avalon.

TOYON JUNCTION: Picnic area; water available.
Mass Transit: Ferry to Avalon, hike 3.9 miles.

BLACK JACK CAMPGROUND: At 1500' elevation; water and picnic tables. Fee $4.00/adult, 40¢/child under 14; permit and reservations required. Group rates. Call (213) 510-0688 or write L.A. County Department of Parks and Recreation, P.O. Box 1133, Avalon 90704.
Mass Transit: Ferry to Avalon, hike 7.9 miles to Black Jack Junction, then 1.5 miles on the trail to the campground.

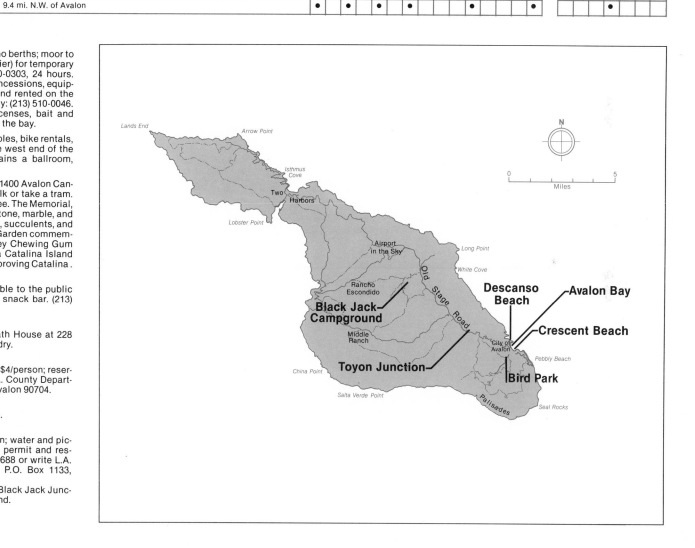

Santa Catalina Island, Little Fisherman's Cove

Little Fisherman's Cove

Little Fisherman's Cove Campground

Los Angeles County
SANTA CATALINA ISLAND WEST

NAME	LOCATION	Entrance/Parking Fee	Parking	Restrooms	Lifeguard	Campground	Showers	Firepits	Stairs to Beach	Path to Beach	Bike Path	Hiking Trail	Facilities for Disabled	Boating Facilities	Fishing	Equestrian Trail	Sandy Beach	Dunes	Rocky Shore	Upland from Beach	Stream Corridor	Bluff	Wetland
Little Fisherman's Cove Campground	Little Fisherman's Cove, Two Harbors	•	•	•		•						•		•	•		•						
Parson's Landing Campground	Parson's Landing, N.W. end of the Island	•	•	•								•		•	•		•						
Two Harbors (Isthmus)	N.W. part of the Island, on the leeward side			•	•	•						•		•	•	•	•						
Little Harbor Campground	Little Harbor, on the windward side of the Island	•	•	•	•	•	•					•		•	•		•						
Ben Weston Beach	W. end of Middle Canyon Trail, windward side of the Island														•		•						

FACILITIES **ENVIRONMENT**

Map

Parson's Landing Campground

Little Fisherman's Cove Campground

Two Harbors

Little Harbor Campground

Ben Weston Beach

Lands End · Arrow Point · Isthmus Cove · Two Harbors · Lobster Point · Airport in the Sky · Long Point · White Cove · Rancho Escondido · Old Stage Road · Middle Ranch · City of Avalon · Pebbly Beach · China Point · Salta Verde Point · Palisades · Seal Rocks

N

0 — 5
Miles

LITTLE FISHERMAN'S COVE CAMPGROUND: Campsites at the water's edge; facilities include tables, open cold showers, fresh water, and firewood for sale. Ranger on duty. Fee $4/person; permit and reservations required. Call Catalina Cove & Camp Agency: (213) 510-0303. Restaurant, bar, snack bar, and dive shop located nearby in Two Harbors.
Mass Transit: Ferry to Two Harbors.

PARSON'S LANDING CAMPGROUND: Facilities include picnic tables, cooking areas, limited fresh water, and charcoal for sale; the campground is near the beach. Ranger on duty. Fee $4/person; permit and reservations required. Call Cove & Camp Agency: (213) 510-0303. There are two moorings at Parson's Landing.
Mass Transit: Ferry to Two Harbors, hike seven miles to Parson's Landing.

TWO HARBORS (ISTHMUS): 12 miles by water from Avalon; mooring assignments are on a first come, first served basis. The Cove & Camp Agency, whose headquarters are at Two Harbors, lease moorings for the entire island (except Avalon). Landing cards are required in order to land ashore. Cove & Camp Agency: (213) 510-0303.

Facilities at Two Harbors include fuel dock and dinghy dock; restaurant, bar, snack bar, diveshop, and general store; boat and motor rentals, and shoreboat service. Fishing licenses, bait and tackle also available; water-skiing in Isthmus Cove.
Mass Transit: Ferry to Two Harbors.

LITTLE HARBOR CAMPGROUND: In a sheltered cove on the windward side of the Island; wide, sandy beach offers swimming and surfing. Fee $4/adult, 40¢/child under 14; permit and reservations required. Call (213) 510-0688 or write L.A. County Department of Parks and Recreation, P.O. Box 1133, Avalon 90704.
Mass Transit: Ferry to Two Harbors, hike 6.8 miles.

BEN WESTON BEACH: Beach and picnic area.
Mass Transit: Ferry to Two Harbors, hike 11.6 miles.

Laguna Beach

Orange County

Orange County is well known for its excellent surfing conditions at Huntington Beach, the yacht harbor at Newport Beach, and the artists' community at Laguna Beach. Since the first American settlement in the late 1800's, the Orange County coast has been a resort area for nearby residents due to its year-round warm weather, high cliffs, wide beaches, and sandy coves. This pleasant environment provides opportunities for swimming, sunbathing, boating, fishing, diving, and surfing.

From Seal Beach to Newport Beach, the broad sandy beaches are backed by low-lying plains and wetlands. Several of these wetlands have been established as nature preserves, such as Bolsa Chica Ecological Reserve and Upper Newport Bay Ecological Reserve.

In the late 1800's, a wharf was built at Newport, which transformed the quiet little village into a bustling community and initiated an era of shipping and trade. McFaddens Pier has since been rebuilt, but many of the original buildings still exist and are being renovated as part of Cannery Village, a cluster of shops.

At about the same time the first wharf was built, the first commercial grove of orange trees was planted. Most of the orange trees are now gone, due to the rapid growth of homes and businesses in the county. The harbors, however, are still flourishing. Huntington Harbor, Newport Harbor, and Dana Point Harbor are all popular destinations for private sailboats and yachts, and Newport and Dana Point Harbors also have commercial fishing boat rentals and whale watching trips.

Newport Harbor was one of the earliest summer resorts in southern California; the Balboa Pavilion, built in 1905 and designed to be a "magnificent pleasure pavilion," was the terminus of a streetcar line which originated in Los Angeles. The pavilion was used by fashionable guests as a boathouse, and later as a gambling casino and dancehall; today it remains as a prominent Victorian landmark, housing a restaurant, gift shop, and banquet room.

South of Newport Beach, uplifted marine terraces form cliffs at the water's edge, providing numerous coves for swimming and diving. Laguna Beach comprises a cluster of these coves, with the town centered near the longest beach, called Main Beach. In the early 1900's the rugged terrain and dramatic headlands drew painters to the area, who established Laguna Beach as a center for artists. The city now has shops, galleries, and an art festival each summer which lasts several weeks.

Located inland from San Clemente, San Juan Capistrano, established in 1776, was the first Spanish mission in Orange County. The Gabrieleño and Juaneño Indians were the original inhabitants of the Orange County coast, and while most of the Indians perished from exposure to European diseases, a band of Juaneño Indians still lives in the area. Archaeological remains of the Juaneño culture have been found in the new Crystal Cove State Park.

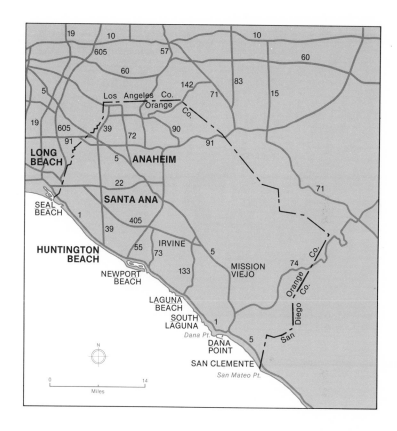

For more information on coastal towns in Orange County, write or call the appropriate Chamber of Commerce: Huntington Beach Chamber of Commerce, Seacliff Village, 2213 Main St. #32, Huntington Beach 92648, (714) 536-8888; Newport Beach Convention and Visitors Bureau, 1470 Jamboree Rd., Newport Beach 92660, (714) 644-8460; Laguna Beach Chamber of Commerce, P.O. Box 83, San Juan Capistrano 92693, (714) 494-1018; Dana Point Chamber of Commerce, 33621 Del Obispo, Dana Point 92629, (714) 496-1555; or San Clemente Chamber of Commerce, P.O. Box 338, 1100 N. El Camino Real, San Clemente 92672, (714) 492-1131.

For transit information call the Orange County Transit District: (714) 636-RIDE.

Seal Beach

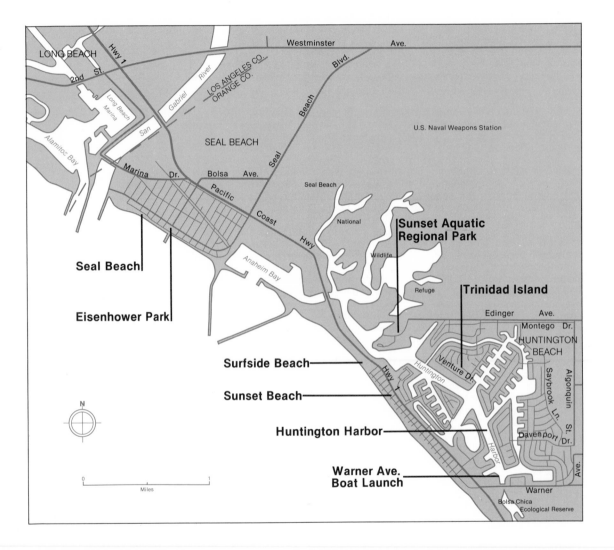

LONG BEACH

Westminster   Ave.

Hwy 1

2nd   St.

San Gabriel River

LOS ANGELES CO.
ORANGE CO.

Long Beach Marina

Alamitoc Bay

San

SEAL BEACH

Seal Beach Blvd.

U.S. Naval Weapons Station

Marina   Dr.

Bolsa   Ave.

Pacific

Seal Beach National

**Sunset Aquatic
Regional Park**

Coast

Anaheim Bay

Wildlife

Seal Beach

Hwy

Trinidad Island

Refuge

Eisenhower Park

Edinger   Ave.

Montego   Dr.

HUNTINGTON
BEACH

Surfside Beach

Venture Dr.

Huntington

Sunset Beach

Hwy 1

Saybrook Ln.

Algonquin   St.

Huntington Harbor

Davenport   Dr.

N

Harbor

Warner   Ave.

**Warner Ave.
Boat Launch**

Warner

Bolsa Chica
Ecological Reserve

0   1
Miles

Orange County
SEAL BEACH and HUNTINGTON HARBOR

FACILITIES **ENVIRONMENT**

NAME	LOCATION	Entrance/Parking Fee	Parking	Restrooms	Lifeguard	Campground	Showers	Firepits	Stairs to Beach	Path to Beach	Bike Path	Hiking Trail	Facilities for Disabled	Boating Facilities	Fishing	Equestrian Trail	Sandy Beach	Dunes	Rocky Shore	Upland from Beach	Stream Corridor	Bluff	Wetland
Seal Beach	S. of Ocean Ave., Seal Beach		•	•	•			•							•		•						
Eisenhower Park	Main St. and Ocean Ave., Seal Beach		•					•									•			•			
Surfside Beach	Anderson Ave. and Pacific Coast Hwy., Surfside																•						
Sunset Beach	W. of Pacific Ave., Huntington Beach		•	•	•			•			•				•		•						
Huntington Harbor	E. of Pacific Coast Hwy., Huntington Beach		•							•	•			•	•		•						
Warner Avenue Boat Launch	N. of Warner Ave., 1/8 mi. E. of Pacific Coast Hwy., Huntington Beach	•	•											•									
Trinidad Island	Trinidad Ave., Huntington Beach		•	•						•	•				•		•		•				
Sunset Aquatic Regional Park	2901 Edinger Ave., Huntington Beach		•	•										•	•								

SEAL BEACH: All street ends between 1st and Electric lead to the beach. Parking lot at 1st and Main Street. The pier which divides the beach in half is floodlit at night and is a focal point for fishermen and surfers. Pier information: (213) 431-1374. Lifeguard station: (213) 431-3567. **Mass Transit:** Orange County Transit District (OCTD) #1, #50, and #60. Long Beach Transit (LBT) Route 5. Southern California Rapid Transit District (RTD) Route 829.

EISENHOWER PARK: Grassy park at the foot of Main St. **Mass Transit:** OCTD #50 and #60. LBT Route 5.

SURFSIDE BEACH: Pedestrian and bicycle access only through the Anderson St. gate of the private Surfside community. No public parking. **Mass Transit:** OCTD #1 stops at Anderson St.

SUNSET BEACH: 27 street ends between Anderson and Warner Ave. lead to the beach. Grassy strip one block east, with a bike path, restrooms, and parking areas, runs the length of the beach. Beach area has volleyball nets. Surfing is allowed on part of the beach. **Mass Transit:** OCTD #1, #70, and #72.

HUNTINGTON HARBOR: A private harbor with docks adjacent to waterfront homes; entry is from Anaheim Bay. There are 263 commercial marina slips; other public commercial facilities include dry storage, boat hoist, launch ramps, repair and maintenance yard, fuel, marine supplies, and boat sales. Motels, grocery stores, and shops near the marina. Harbormaster: (213) 592-2869, (714) 846-2873, or (714) 843-3800. Small public beaches are at the east end of 11th Ave., at the intersection of Davenport and Edgewater Streets, and at Humboldt Dr. and Mandalay. **Mass Transit:** OCTD #1 and #70.

WARNER AVENUE BOAT LAUNCH: City-operated public boat ramp and metered parking area. **Mass Transit:** OCTD #1 and #70.

TRINIDAD ISLAND: Small residential island with a public fishing dock off Venture Dr. and a waterfront park at the corner of Trinidad Ave. and Typhoon Lane. A bike path and walkway parallels Venture Dr. and Typhoon Lane along the harbor, and meanders through the center of the island. Respect private property; do not trespass.

SUNSET AQUATIC REGIONAL PARK: A public small boat harbor at the end of Edinger Road. Ocean access is from Anaheim Bay. Grassy areas with pathways and picnic tables overlook the bay. There are 300 privately owned boat slips; guest slip rentals available. Concrete eight-lane boat ramp is open 24 hours with a fee for use. Dry storage, haul-out and repair facilities. (213) 592-2833. The park is adjacent to Seal Beach National Wildlife Refuge, 1,200 acres of salt marshes which belong to the U.S. Naval Weapons Station.

Seal Beach Pier

Huntington Beach

Edinger   Ave.
Heil   Ave.
Warner   Ave.
FOUNTAIN VALLEY

Bolsa Chica
Slater   Ave.

Ecological
Talbert   Ave.

Reserve
HUNTINGTON
BEACH   Ellis

Garfield   Blvd.

Huntington Sea Cliff Country Club

Yorktown

Bolsa Chica State Beach

Adams

Santa Ana River Trail

Bike Path/Walkway

Indianapolis   Ave.

COSTA MESA

Colonial Inn Hostel

Atlanta   Ave.

Wilson   St.

Huntington Pier

Hamilton   Ave.

Victoria   St.

Huntington City Beach

19th   St.

Huntington State Beach

N

0   2
Miles

NAME	LOCATION	Entrance/Parking Fee	Parking	Restrooms	Lifeguard	Campground	Showers	Firepits	Stairs to Beach	Path to Beach	Bike Path	Hiking Trail	Facilities for Disabled	Boating Facilities	Fishing	Equestrian Trail	Sandy Beach	Dunes	Rocky Shore	Upland from Beach	Stream Corridor	Bluff	Wetland
Bolsa Chica Ecological Reserve	E. of Pacific Coast Hwy., S. of Warner Ave., Huntington Beach		●																				●
Bolsa Chica State Beach	W. of Pacific Coast Hwy., between Warner Ave. and Huntington Pier, Huntington Beach	●	●	●	●	●	●		●	●		●		●		●		●				●	●
Bike Path/Walkway	W. of Pacific Coast Hwy., Huntington Beach										●												
Colonial Inn Hostel	421 8th St., Huntington Beach	●	●	●			●													●			
Huntington Pier	Main St. and Pacific Coast Hwy., Huntington Beach		●	●											●								
Huntington City Beach	W. of Pacific Coast Hwy., between Main St. and Beach Blvd., Huntington Beach	●	●	●	●		●						●		●		●						
Huntington State Beach	W. of Pacific Coast Hwy., Beach Blvd. to Santa Ana River, Huntington Beach	●	●	●	●		●			●	●		●		●		●						
Santa Ana River Trail	Along Santa Ana River, Huntington Beach										●					●					●	●	

BOLSA CHICA ECOLOGICAL RESERVE: 1,200-acre marsh area in which three endangered bird species can be seen: Savanna sparrow, clapper rail, and California least tern. Most of the marsh is private land. There are two parking lot viewing areas; one is at Pacific Coast Highway across from the main Bolsa Chica Beach entrance, and one is at Pacific Coast Highway and Warner Avenue. Loop trail with interpretive signs starts at the parking lot across from the beach entrance.
Mass Transit: Orange County Transit District (OCTD) #1.

BOLSA CHICA STATE BEACH: Six-mile long beach; only the northern three miles are developed with facilities. The northern end has fee parking lots, picnic areas, food concessions, cold showers, and a ramp for the disabled which runs across the sand. 50 en route camping spaces are available; $6 fee per vehicle. The southern end has steep cliffs between the road and beach; accessways are at Golden West St., 17th, 14th, 11th, and 9th Streets. A bike path/walkway extends the entire length of the beach. Clamming, diving, and fishing are popular here. Grunion runs occur between March and August. (714) 848-1566.
Mass Transit: OCTD #1.

BIKE PATH/WALKWAY: A long cement path extends the length of Bolsa Chica State Beach, through Huntington City and State Beaches, and connects to the Santa Ana River Trail. To get to the River Trail, cross Highway 1 at Brookhurst St., and follow the river channel.

COLONIAL INN HOSTEL: New 40 bed hostel four blocks from the beach. Overnight fee is $6.25 for members, $8.25 for non-members. Open all year; facilities include showers, fully equipped kitchen, and a storage shed for bicycles. Call ahead for availability. (714) 536-9184.
Mass Transit: OCTD #1 and #25.

HUNTINGTON PIER: The 1,800-foot pier, which was built in 1914, has three snack bars and a bait and tackle shop, and is floodlit at night for fishing and surfing.
Mass Transit: OCTD #1, #25, #29, #35, #37, and #76.

HUNTINGTON CITY BEACH: Site of international surfing competitions; concessions, wave-rider rentals, and volleyball courts are available. Surfing allowed in the morning or on uncrowded days only. Lifeguards on duty all year. Lifeguard station: (714) 536-5281. Between September 15 and May 31, R.V. camping is allowed for a fee. No hookups on site; sewage station. Entrance is off Pacific Coast Highway opposite Lake Avenue. Information and reservations: City of Huntington Beach–Sunset Vista, P.O. Box 190, Huntington Beach 92648, (714) 536-5281, –5280.
Mass Transit: OCTD #1, #25, #29, #37, and #76.

HUNTINGTON STATE BEACH: A three-mile long sandy beach. Facilities include picnic areas, volleyball nets, food concessions, outdoor cold showers, two ramps on the sand for the disabled, and a two-mile bike path/promenade. Fee parking lots at Beach Boulevard. En route camping; $6 fee per vehicle. Pedestrian access through gates at Newland, Magnolia, and Brookhurst Streets. Pismo clams are found here, and a five-acre least tern (an endangered bird species) preserve is nearby. Rangers and lifeguards are on duty all year. (714) 536-3053.
Mass Transit: OCTD #1 and #35.

SANTA ANA RIVER TRAIL: This bicycle and equestrian trail follows the west side of the Santa Ana River from the southern end to Adams St., then crosses over to the east side. The trail ultimately ends in Yorba Linda.

Huntington Beach Pier

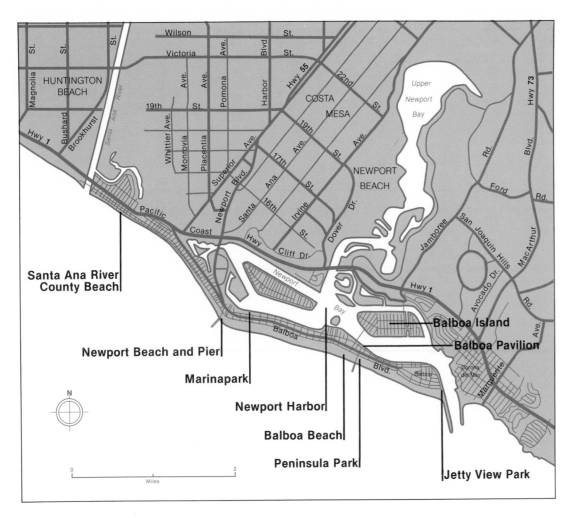

Santa Ana River
County Beach

Newport Beach and Pier

Marinapark

Newport Harbor

Balboa Beach

Peninsula Park

Balboa Island

Balboa Pavilion

Jetty View Park

NAME	LOCATION	Entrance/Parking Fee	Parking	Restrooms	Lifeguard	Campground	Showers	Firepits	Stairs to Beach	Path to Beach	Bike Path	Hiking Trail	Facilities for Disabled	Boating Facilities	Fishing	Equestrian Trail	Sandy Beach	Dunes	Rocky Shore	Upland from Beach	Stream Corridor	Bluff	Wetland
Santa Ana River County Beach	W. of Seashore Dr., Newport Beach		•		•					•							•						
Newport Beach and Pier	W. of Ocean Front, S. of McFadden Lane, Newport Beach	•	•	•	•		•			•					•		•						
Marinapark	Balboa Blvd. and 16th St., Newport Beach		•											•			•			•			
Newport Harbor	N.E. of Balboa Blvd., Newport Beach		•	•										•	•								
Balboa Beach	W. of Balboa Blvd., Balboa		•	•	•			•	•	•	•		•				•						
Peninsula Park	S. end of Main St., Balboa		•	•									•									•	
Jetty View Park	S. end of Channel Rd., Balboa		•										•				•		•				
Balboa Pavilion	N. end of Main St., Balboa			•										•	•								
Balboa Island	Marine Ave., Newport Beach		•	•						•				•	•		•			•			

SANTA ANA RIVER COUNTY BEACH: Street ends between Summit St. and 61st St. lead to the beach.
Mass Transit: Orange County Transit District (OCTD) #1.

NEWPORT BEACH: The 5-1/4 mile beach is narrow at the north end and wide at the southern end. Surfing allowed near 30th St. in the afternoon. Volleyball nets, outdoor showers, and an ocean front boardwalk are located near the pier. McFaddens Pier is the center for morning surfing and fishing activities; the Newport Dory Fishing Fleet returns around 9:30 AM on the north side of the pier to sell their catch on the beach. Tackle shops and the Cannery Village shopping area are nearby.

West Newport Park, one block inland from the beach at 58th and Seashore Dr., has grassy areas, playground, tennis and racquetball courts. Another playground directly on the beach is in front of Newport Harbor Elementary School between 13th and 14th Streets.
Mass Transit: OCTD #1, #43, #53, and #65.

MARINAPARK: Small boat launching area with picnic tables.
Mass Transit: OCTD #53 and #65.

NEWPORT HARBOR: Large yachting harbor with 1,160 residential piers, 2,220 commercial slips and side ties, and 1,050 bay moorings. Facilities include dry storage, gas docks and service stations, shipyards, engine and hull maintenance, marine supplies, and sewage pump-outs. Harbormaster: 1901 Bayside Dr., Corona Del Mar 92625. (714) 834-2654.

There are numerous small parks, vistas, and walkways around the harbor. Two of note in the Northern Harbor are Channel Park, at 44th and Balboa Ave., which has a grassy area and a playground adjacent to a small sandy beach, and Lido Park, at Lafayette and 31st St., which is a small harbor viewing area with benches and trees.
Mass Transit: OCTD #1, #53, and #65.

BALBOA BEACH: The ocean beach extends the length of the peninsula; most street ends lead to the beach. There is a bike path/walkway along the ocean. Concession and other facilities are at the Balboa Pier area.
Mass Transit: OCTD #53 and #65.

PENINSULA PARK: Adjacent to Balboa Pier and Beach. Grassy areas, gazebo, baseball diamonds, and picnic tables.
Mass Transit: OCTD #53 and #65.

JETTY VIEW PARK: Shaded park between the West Jetty and Balboa Beach.

BALBOA PAVILION: The large pavilion is the hub of Newport Harbor. A restaurant, gift shop, and banquet room operate in the building. It is also the terminal for Catalina Island tours, harbor cruises, whale watching trips, and charter boats. (714) 673-5245. Other facilities include boat and motor rentals, fishing licenses, and bait and tackle sales. A boardwalk runs from the pavilion to the Newport Harbor Yacht Club along the bay.
Mass Transit: OCTD #53 and #65.

BALBOA ISLAND: Small island in Newport Harbor. A bayfront boardwalk circles the island with periodic small beaches and boat slips. There is a bridge to the island on the north side; an auto ferry connects the island to Balboa Peninsula on the south side. Ferry information: (714) 673-1070.

Balboa Pavilion, Newport Bay

Little Corona Del Mar

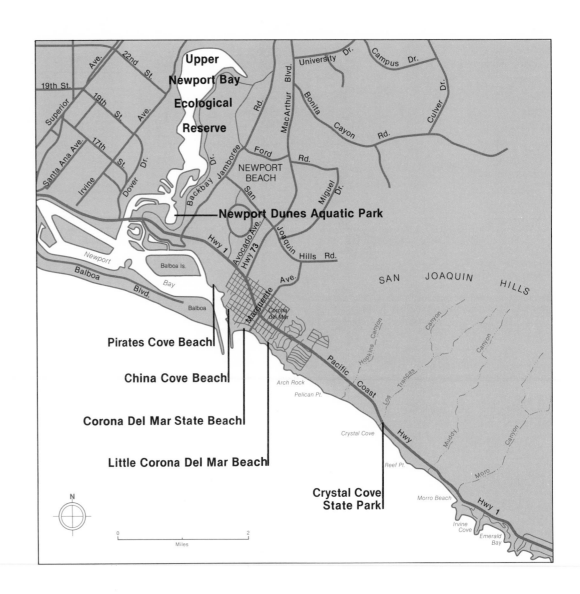

Orange County
UPPER NEWPORT/CORONA DEL MAR

NAME	LOCATION	Entrance/Parking Fee	Parking	Restrooms	Lifeguard	Campground	Showers	Firepits	Stairs to Beach	Path to Beach	Bike Path	Hiking Trail	Facilities for Disabled	Boating Facilities	Fishing	Equestrian Trail	Sandy Beach	Dunes	Rocky Shore	Upland from Beach	Stream Corridor	Bluff	Wetland
Newport Dunes Aquatic Park	Bayside Dr., Newport Beach	●	●	●	●	●		●						●	●		●			●			
Upper Newport Bay Ecological Reserve	West of Back Bay Dr., Newport Beach		●																				●
Pirates Cove Beach	Bayside Dr., Corona Del Mar																●						
China Cove Beach	Between Dahlia and Carnation Streets, Corona Del Mar				●				●	●							●						
Corona Del Mar State Beach	Ocean Blvd. and Iris Ave., Corona Del Mar	●	●	●	●			●					●				●	●					
Little Corona Del Mar Beach	Ocean Blvd. and Poppy Ave., Corona Del Mar			●	●								●				●		●			●	
Crystal Cove State Park	W. of Pacific Coast Hwy., between Arch Rock and Irvine Cove	●	●	●	●					●							●		●			●	

NEWPORT DUNES AQUATIC PARK: A 15-acre lagoon with swimming, boating, and camping facilities. Day use fee. Facilities include dressing rooms, picnic tables, playground, wading pool, outdoor showers, and fire rings; cabanas and other beach equipment can be rented. 14-lane boat ramp, fuel dock, slips, dry storage, and marine repairs are available as well as paddleboards, kayaks, sea cycles, and sailboat rentals.

Camping facilities include 64 R.V. spaces with full hookups and 80 R.V. spaces with water and electricity. Organized groups can tent camp on the beach. There is a fee for overnight camping. For information, call: (714) 644-0510.

UPPER NEWPORT BAY ECOLOGICAL RESERVE: Estuary and mudflat wildlife reserve. Backbay Dr. runs along the east side; a trail from the University of California at Irvine runs along the west side of the reserve to North Star Beach. Remain on established trails and roads. Friends of Upper Newport Bay offers interpretive bird tours Saturdays during the winter: P.O. Box 2001, Newport Beach 92663.

PIRATES COVE BEACH: Sandy beach adjacent to the Coast Guard Station, which is at 1911 Bayside Dr.
Mass Transit: Bank of Newport Shuttle Bus leaves from 2101 Pacific Coast Highway every half hour Sat. 1 PM-6 PM, Sundays and bank holidays 9 AM-6 PM. Parking is available at the bank. Shuttle bus goes to Pirates Cove Beach, China Cove Beach, Corona Del Mar Beach, and Little Corona Del Mar Beach.

CHINA COVE BEACH: Sandy cove along the harbor channel.
Mass Transit: Bank of Newport Shuttle Bus stops at the top of the bluff.

CORONA DEL MAR STATE BEACH: Popular large sandy beach just east of the east jetty at the entrance to Newport Harbor. Fee parking lot at the beach; metered parking on the bluff. A concrete path leads to the beach from the bluff at the foot of Orchid Avenue. Rock jetty area used by snorklers and surfers. Beach facilities include picnic tables, volleyball nets, outdoor showers, dressing rooms, food concessions, and rental store. (714) 237-7411.
Mass Transit: Orange County Transit District (OCTD) #1 and #57. Bank of Newport Shuttle Bus.

LITTLE CORONA DEL MAR BEACH: A walkway leads down to the beach from Poppy Avenue. Newport Marine Life Refuge is offshore; tours offered. Information: (714) 640-2156.
Mass Transit: Bank of Newport Shuttle Bus stops at the top of the walkway.

CRYSTAL COVE STATE PARK: A new state park with a 3-1/4 mile coastline, grassy terraces, and sandy beaches and coves. The Pelican Point area at the northern end of the park has a fee parking lot and three walkways to the beach. Access at Crystal Cove is through the small community of beach houses. There is a fee parking lot at Reef Point, and two paths to the beach; there is also access to the southern end of the park at Moro Beach. Trails are planned for Moro Canyon, inland of Moro Beach. The offshore area adjacent to the park has been designated an underwater park for divers. For information, call: (714) 237-7411.
Mass Transit: OCTD #1 and #57.

Crystal Cove State Park

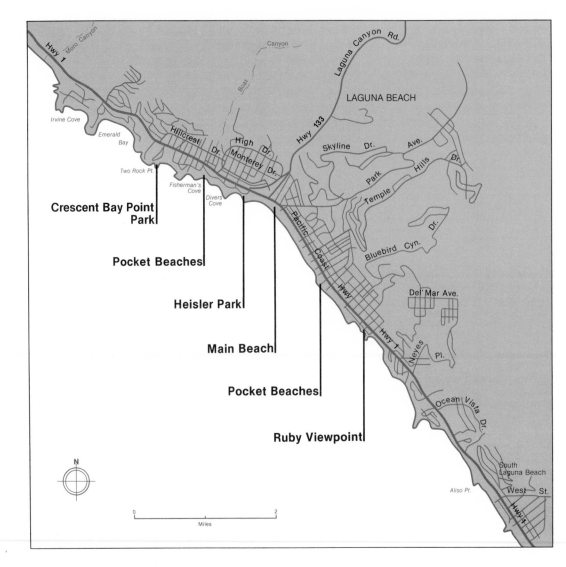

Crescent Bay Point Park

Pocket Beaches

Heisler Park

Main Beach

Pocket Beaches

Ruby Viewpoint

LAGUNA BEACH

Irvine Cove

Emerald Bay

Two Rock Pt.

Fisherman's Cove

Divers Cove

Hillcrest Dr.

High Dr.

Monterey Dr.

Moro Canyon

Hwy 1

Canyon

Boat

Laguna Canyon Rd.

Hwy 133

Skyline Dr.

Park

Temple

Hills

Ave.

Dr.

Pacific Coast Hwy

Bluebird Cyn.

Del Mar Ave.

Neves Pl.

Ocean Vista Dr.

Hwy 1

South Laguna Beach

Aliso Pt.

West St.

Hwy 1

N

0   2
Miles

NAME	LOCATION	Entrance/Parking Fee	Parking	Restrooms	Lifeguard	Campground	Showers	Firepits	Stairs to Beach	Path to Beach	Bike Path	Hiking Trail	Facilities for Disabled	Boating Facilities	Fishing	Equestrian Trail	Sandy Beach	Dunes	Rocky Shore	Upland from Beach	Stream Corridor	Bluff	Wetland
Crescent Bay Point Park	W. end of Crescent Bay Dr., Laguna Beach		•										•						•			•	
Pocket Beaches	W. of Cliff Dr., Laguna Beach	•	•	•	•				•	•							•						
Heisler Park	W. of Cliff Dr., 400 block, Laguna Beach	•	•	•				•	•	•							•		•			•	
Main Beach	W. end of Broadway, W. of Pacific Coast Hwy., Laguna Beach	•	•	•	•			•	•	•	•		•		•		•						
Pocket Beaches	Street ends W. of Pacific Coast Hwy., Laguna Beach			•					•	•			•				•	•				•	
Ruby Viewpoint	W. end of Ruby St., Laguna Beach																		•			•	

CRESCENT BAY POINT PARK: Accessible to disabled persons. View of Laguna Beach and Seal Rock.
Mass Transit: Orange County Transit District (OCTD) #1 and #57. Laguna Beach (LB) #581.

POCKET BEACHES: Several small coves can be reached by walkways off Cliff Dr.: Crescent Bay is accessible from a stairway off Circle Way, and a ramp off Barranco St.; Shaws Cove from the west end of Fairview Dr.; Fishermans Cove from a walkway in the 600 block; Divers Cove from a walkway in the 500 block; Picnic Beach from the west end of Myrtle St.; and Rock Pile Beach from the west end of Jasmine Street. Picnic Beach and Rock Pile Beach have restrooms. Glenn E. Vedder Ecological Reserve is offshore from Divers Cove.
Mass Transit: OCTD #1 and #57. LB #581.

HEISLER PARK: Grassy area on the bluff above Picnic Beach and Rock Pile Beach. Sandbox, picnic tables, shuffleboard, and lawn bowling available. Heisler Park Marine Life Refuge is offshore.
Mass Transit: OCTD #1 and #57. LB #581.

MAIN BEACH: Access from Cliff Dr., Broadway, Ocean, and Laguna Streets. Long beach and grassy area with a boardwalk, benches and tables, playground, basketball and volleyball courts. Laguna Beach Marine Life Refuge is offshore.
Mass Transit: OCTD #1 and #57. LB #581, #582, and #583.

POCKET BEACHES: The following street ends, from north to south starting just south of the main beach, have paths and/or stairs to small sandy beaches: Sleepy Hollow, Cleo St., St. Ann's St., Thalia St., Anita St., Oak St., Brooks St., Cress St., Mountain Rd., Bluebird Canyon Rd., Agate St., Pearl St., Diamond St., Moss St., Victoria Dr., and Dumond Drive. A wooden viewing platform at the end of Thalia St. includes tables and benches and is wheelchair accessible. There is a scenic overlook at the end of Oak Street. Respect private property; do not trespass.
Mass Transit: OCTD #1. LB #581.

RUBY VIEWPOINT: Overlooks the ocean. No beach access.
Mass Transit: OCTD #1. LB #581.

Main Beach, Laguna Beach

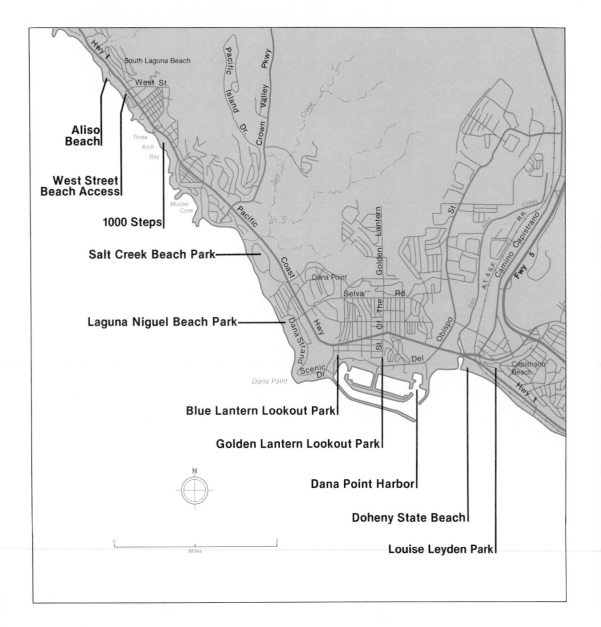

Aliso Beach

West Street Beach Access

1000 Steps

Salt Creek Beach Park

Laguna Niguel Beach Park

Blue Lantern Lookout Park

Golden Lantern Lookout Park

Dana Point Harbor

Doheny State Beach

Louise Leyden Park

South Laguna Beach

West St.

Hwy 1

Pacific Island Dr.

Crown Valley Pkwy

Creek

Three Arch Bay

Mussel Cove

Salt

Pacific

Coast

Dana Point

Golden Lantern

St.

B.R. Creek

Camino Capistrano

Fwy 5

A.T. & S.F.

Selva

Rd.

St. Of The

Obispo

San

Dana Strand Hwy

Scenic Dr.

Del

Dana Point

Capistrano Beach

Hwy 1

N

0 ————————— 2
Miles

Laguna Niguel Beach Park

Orange County
SOUTH LAGUNA/DANA POINT

NAME	LOCATION	Entrance/Parking Fee	Parking	Restrooms	Lifeguard	Campground	Showers	Firepits	Stairs to Beach	Path to Beach	Bike Path	Hiking Trail	Facilities for Disabled	Boating Facilities	Fishing	Equestrian Trail	Sandy Beach	Dunes	Rocky Shore	Upland from Beach	Stream Corridor	Bluff	Wetland
Aliso Beach County Park	31000 block of Pacific Coast Hwy., South Laguna	•	•	•	•		•		•		•		•		•		•						
West Street Beach Access	W. of Pacific Coast Hwy. and West St., South Laguna							•	•				•				•					•	
1000 Steps	Pacific Coast Hwy., opposite 9th Ave., South Laguna								•								•					•	
Salt Creek Beach Park	Pacific Coast Hwy. and Whitewater Dr., South Laguna	•	•	•					•	•			•				•			•			
Laguna Niguel Beach Park	Selva Rd., Laguna Niguel	•	•	•						•			•				•					•	
Blue Lantern Lookout Park	S. end of Blue Lantern St., Dana Point		•																•			•	
Golden Lantern Lookout Park	End of Street of the Golden Lantern, Dana Point		•										•						•			•	
Dana Point Harbor	Del Obispo and Island Way, Dana Point		•	•						•			•	•	•		•						
Doheny State Beach	Del Obispo and Pacific Coast Hwy., Dana Point	•	•	•	•	•	•	•			•				•	•	•				•		
Louise Leyden Park	End of Villa Verde, off Camino Capistrano, Capistrano Beach		•																•			•	

ALISO BEACH COUNTY PARK: Facilities include a picnic area, bike trail, cold showers, and concessions. Restrooms are wheelchair accessible. Parking fee. There is a 3/4-mile long fishing pier with a snack bar and tackle shop. Popular surfing area. There are also two walkways to a southern cove of the park from the 31300 block of Pacific Coast Hwy., and another from Camel Point Drive. Respect private property; do not trespass.
Mass Transit: Orange County Transit District (OCTD) #1. Laguna Beach (LB) #581.

WEST STREET BEACH ACCESS: A stairway at the end of West St. and another stairway at the Coast Royale condominium building 200 feet north of West St. lead to a sandy beach.
Mass Transit: OCTD #1. LB #581.

1000 STEPS: A long stairway leads down the bluff to the beach.
Mass Transit: OCTD #1. LB #581.

SALT CREEK BEACH PARK: Upland facilities include fee parking, concessions, and restrooms. Beach area has firepits, picnic area, and restrooms. A long road leads to the beach from the parking lot; vehicles are not allowed down to the beach. Popular surfing area.
Mass Transit: OCTD #1 and #85.

LAGUNA NIGUEL BEACH PARK: Southern entrance to Salt Creek Beach Park. The parking lot is closed during the winter, but the path to the beach is open all year.
Mass Transit: OCTD #1 and #85.

BLUE LANTERN LOOKOUT PARK: View of Dana Point Harbor; the park is dedicated to Ken Sampson.
Mass Transit: OCTD #1 and #85.

GOLDEN LANTERN LOOKOUT PARK: Landscaped blufftop park with benches overlooking Dana Point Harbor. A walkway accessible to the disabled leads from the blufftop down to Del Obispo Street and the Dana Point Harbor.
Mass Transit: OCTD #1 and #85.

DANA POINT HARBOR: Once a major port for square-rigged ships, the new artificial harbor named for author Richard Henry Dana has extensive boating and recreational facilities. At the northern end of the harbor one can walk to the jetty and the offshore Dana Point Marine Life Refuge. There are grassy areas with picnic tables along Dana Cove Rd. and Dana Dr., and a small stillwater swimming beach off Ensenada Place. Restaurants and small shops line a boardwalk along the marina.

Boating facilities include guest slips, 15-lane launch ramp, dry storage, hoist, engine and hull maintenance, fuel, marine supplies, boat charters, sport fishing and whale watching trips. Information: (714) 496-5794. Scuba diving and breakwater fishing; sailing lessons, bike rentals, and trailer space are available. Harbor Patrol: (714) 496-2242.
Mass Transit: OCTD #1 and #85 stop near the harbor.

DOHENY STATE BEACH: Campground and day use area; fee for use. Day use area has a five-acre lawn with picnic tables, group picnic areas, fire rings, changing rooms, food and supply concessions. Surfing is allowed at the north end of the beach. The offshore area has been designated an underwater park for divers. Campground area has 115 campsites with fire rings, tables and drinking water, and a trailer sanitation station. (714) 496-6171. Doheny State Marine Life Refuge is offshore. The San Juan Creek Bike Trail, which runs along the west side of the creek, and the equestrian trail along the east side begin just north of Doheny State Beach and continue north along the creek.
Mass Transit: OCTD #1 and #85.

LOUISE LEYDEN PARK: An overlook with a walkway and benches; grassy areas. View of Doheny State Beach and Dana Point Harbor.

Dana Point Harbor from Blue Lantern Lookout Park

San Clemente Municipal Pier

Leslie Park

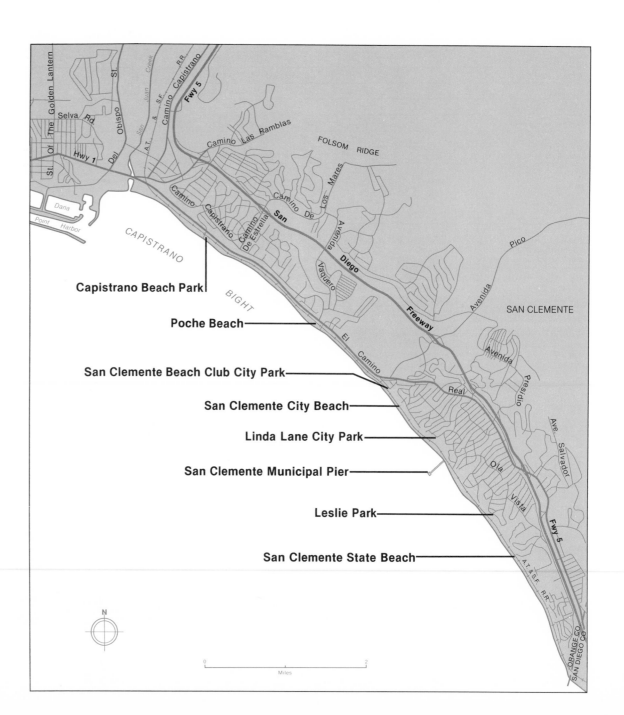

Capistrano Beach Park

Poche Beach

San Clemente Beach Club City Park

San Clemente City Beach

Linda Lane City Park

San Clemente Municipal Pier

Leslie Park

San Clemente State Beach

Miles

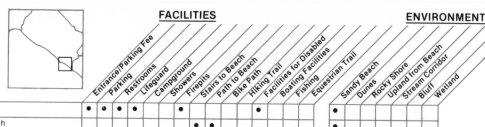

NAME	LOCATION	Entrance/Parking Fee	Parking	Restrooms	Lifeguard	Campground	Showers	Firepits	Stairs to Beach	Path to Beach	Bike Path	Hiking Trail	Facilities for Disabled	Boating Facilities	Fishing	Equestrian Trail	Sandy Beach	Dunes	Rocky Shore	Upland from Beach	Stream Corridor	Bluff	Wetland
Capistrano Beach Park	El Camino Real and Palisade Dr., Capistrano Beach	●	●	●	●		●						●				●						
Poche Beach	Camino Capistrano and Pacific Coast Highway, Capistrano Beach								●	●							●						
San Clemente Beach Club City Park	Avenida Estacion, San Clemente		●	●	●		●	●		●					●		●						
San Clemente City Beach	Beach area from Ave. Estacion to San Clemente State Beach, San Clemente		●	●			●	●		●							●						
Linda Lane City Park	Linda Lane, San Clemente		●	●	●					●							●			●			
San Clemente Municipal Pier	W. end of Avenida Del Mar, San Clemente	●	●	●	●			●							●		●						
Leslie Park	Calle Los Alamos and Calle Roca Vista, San Clemente		●																●			●	
San Clemente State Beach	Off Avenida Calafia, San Clemente	●	●		●	●	●	●		●							●					●	

CAPISTRANO BEACH PARK: Fee for parking. Restrooms are wheelchair accessible.
Mass Transit: Orange County Transit District (OCTD) #1, #85, and #91.

POCHE BEACH: A stairway at the end of Camino Capistrano on the inland side of Pacific Coast Highway leads to an underpass beneath the highway and the railroad tracks. Follow the path to a sandy beach.
Mass Transit: OCTD #1, #85, and #91.

SAN CLEMENTE BEACH CLUB CITY PARK: Facilities include picnic tables, snack bar, and playground; public pool with dressing room and showers. Beach Club hall rental: (714) 492-5101 x265.
Mass Transit: OCTD #91.

SAN CLEMENTE CITY BEACH: A city-maintained beach in San Clemente runs from the city boundary in the north to beyond the municipal pier in the south. The west ends of Dije Court, Buena Vista at W. El Portal, and W. Escalones at W. Mar each have ramps and/or stairs which lead to the beach north of the pier. The railroad tracks must be crossed at grade to reach the beach.

There are three more paths to the beach south of the pier. A pedestrian railroad overpass crosses to the beach at the foot of Esplanade; there are cold showers and picnic tables at the beach. An unmaintained dirt path down a steep slope from Calle Los Alamos near Calle Lasuen also leads to the beach; the entrance is hard to find and is between bushes and behind a telephone pole. Railroad tracks must be crossed to reach the beach.

A third access is a tunnel which crosses under railroad tracks and leads to the beach from the north end of Plaza a la Playa. In each case there is limited on-street parking.
Mass Transit: OCTD #91 stops several blocks away.

LINDA LANE CITY PARK: An upland park which slopes down to the beach; playground and picnic area. A storm drain tunnel under the train tracks provides access to the beach.

SAN CLEMENTE MUNICIPAL PIER: A popular fishing pier with food concessions and bait and tackle shops. The beach area has picnic facilities and volleyball nets. Lifeguard station: (714) 492-1011. There is one underpass to the beach; all other access is across railroad tracks.
Mass Transit: OCTD #91. AMTRAK trains stop right at the pier.

LESLIE PARK: A small park overlooking San Clemente Beaches; no beach access. Limited on-street parking.
Mass Transit: OCTD #91 stops several blocks away.

SAN CLEMENTE STATE BEACH: Day use area has a metered parking lot, picnic areas with grills and tables, and restrooms. Fire rings are on the beach, which is reached by steep paths down the bluffs. It is unsafe to stray from established trails. The ocean has rip currents; check conditions before swimming. Surfing is allowed at the north end of the beach. There is also access to the beach at the foot of Avenida Calafia, either by a tunnel or by crossing the railroad tracks at grade.

The general campsites have stoves, cupboards, tables, and water. Trailer campsites have water, electrical, and sewer hookups. Each campground has hot showers, restrooms, and laundry tubs. There is a group campground for up to 50 people. Camping fee. For information, call: (714) 492-3156.
Mass Transit: OCTD #91.

San Clemente City Beach

Coronado Shores Beach

San Diego County

In 1542, the European explorer Juan Rodríguez Cabrillo spent six days in San Diego Bay, landed on Point Loma, and named the area San Miguel. In 1602, Sebastián Vizcaíno, a merchant navigator who was charting the California coast for the Spanish government, visited the same spot and renamed it San Diego, giving the county in the southwest corner of the United States its present name. Today, thousands of people visit Point Loma to watch the migration of the California gray whale to its winter breeding grounds in the Gulf of California.

Maritime interests have since taken advantage of the shelter provided by the landlocked San Diego Bay. The bay has a long history as the home port for a large commercial fishing fleet. During World War I the U.S. Navy established headquarters for the 11th Naval District in the bay; today, the facilities in San Diego Bay constitute the largest naval base on the west coast. In addition to the commercial and military shipping activity, a number of sportfishing charters operate out of the bay, and numerous marinas and launching facilities provide berthing space and services for a large portion of southern California's boating population.

San Diego County's 76 miles of shoreline include virtually every kind of coastal landscape. The north county coast consists primarily of a series of long, sandy beaches backed by steep eroded bluffs ranging in elevation from a few feet to more than 100 feet above sea level. The La Jolla coastline south includes a number of rocky headlands, coves, and points whose beaches are transformed into tidepools during low tide periods. Some of the largest and best remaining examples of coastal wetlands in southern California are located in San Diego; examples include Los Penasquitos Marsh in the Torrey Pines State Reserve, and the Tia Juana River Estuary near the U.S. Mexico border.

Like all of southern California, the mild Mediterranean climate has had a major influence on the county's development. Many coastal communities were originally established as agricultural centers. Pacific Beach, a residential community located only eight miles north of downtown San Diego, was considered a farming district as recently as the late 1930's. Principal crops throughout the county include citrus fruits, avocados, flowers, and vegetables. Along the coast, major agricultural areas are located on the terraces and flood plains north of Del Mar; large farms also operate inland of San Diego Bay, near Chula Vista.

Summer air temperatures average in the mid 70s; water temperatures average in the mid 60s, with higher temperatures in sheltered coves and bays. These mild air and water temperatures, combined with a short rainy season and diverse coastal topography, make San Diego County's beaches popular for sun bathing, swimming, surfing, surf and rock fishing, diving, and tidepool exploring. The San Diego coast also supports a large recreational boating community. Marinas and launching facilities from Oceanside to Chula Vista provide opportunities for thousands of people to enjoy boating activities.

The variety of aquatic recreation activities available in San Diego County is demonstrated dramatically at Mission Bay. The bay, previously known as False Bay because ships would mistake its entrance for the entrance to San Diego Bay to the south, originally was a salt marsh and estuary system at the mouth of the San Diego River. In 1946, construction began to convert the wetland into a boating and water recreation complex. Today, Mission Bay contains dock facilities and slips for more than 1,900 boats, as well as sheltered swimming bays, water-skiing areas, picnic areas, campgrounds, playgrounds, and fishing spots.

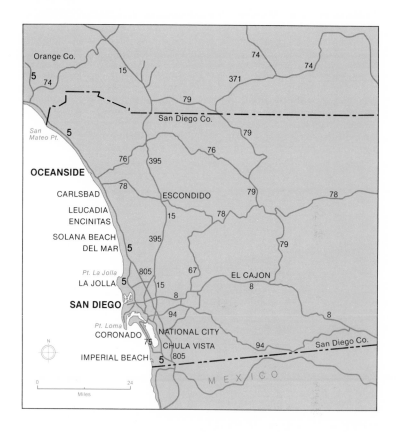

For more information on San Diego County, write or call the San Diego Convention and Visitors Bureau, 1200 3rd Avenue, Suite 824, San Diego 92101; (619) 232-3101 (offices) or (619) 239-9696 (recorded visitor information). More detailed information can also be obtained from the local Chamber of Commerce office in the area you plan to visit. For transit information from Oceanside to Del Mar, call the North County Transit District at (619) 484-2550 in Del Mar and Solana Beach, and (619) 438-2550 in Oceanside and Carlsbad. For transit information in areas south of Del Mar, call San Diego Transit at (619) 233-3004. For transit information in Coronado, call: (619) 232-8505.

The winter storms of 1982/83 were particularly severe in San Diego County, and many stairways and other coastal facilities were damaged. Repairs will be completed as soon as possible, depending on the availability of funds.

Coastal Industry

The various physical characteristics and resources of California's coastal environment provide an opportunity for the development of diverse industrial operations.

Geologic formations along portions of the coast and beneath the continental shelf offshore contain petroleum resources that have been extracted since the turn of the century; other coastal resources that have been extracted commercially include sand and kelp. As the use of coastal resources has increased and expanded, shoreside facilities have been developed to refine and process the raw materials into marketable products. For example, many petroleum refineries are located in the Los Angeles basin between El Segundo and Long Beach, and a number of kelp processing plants operate within the Port of San Diego.

Electric power plants and sewage treatment facilities have also been located along the coast in order to take advantage of the large volumes of water provided by the ocean. Power plants require copious amounts of water to cool circulating steam, while sewage treatment plants use the ocean as a location for the disposal of treated effluent.

Commercial shipping and the trades that support it constitute a major portion of California's coastal industry.

California's ports have served as the principal gateways for the import and export of raw materials and finished goods such as petroleum, ores, agricultural products, and automobiles. Support industries at many ports include tanker terminals, shipbuilding and repair facilities, truck and railroad terminals, and seafood processing plants and canneries.

Although the operations at various industrial facilities may differ significantly, many coastal dependent or coastal related facilities employ heavy equipment, high voltage power lines, or potentially hazardous substances in their operation. Consequently, many of these facilities are closed to the public. To promote public safety and prevent interference with the functions of coastal industries, please respect fences, warning signs, and other barriers installed by the operators of the facilities when using beaches near these facilities.

San Onofre Nuclear Generating Station

San Diego County
CAMP PENDLETON

NAME	LOCATION	Entrance/Parking Fee	Parking	Restrooms	Lifeguard	Campground	Showers	Firepits	Stairs to Beach	Path to Beach	Bike Path	Hiking Trail	Facilities for Disabled	Boating Facilities	Fishing	Equestrian Trail	Sandy Beach	Dunes	Rocky Shore	Upland from Beach	Stream Corridor	Bluff	Wetland
San Onofre State Beach (North)	S.W. of I-5 at Basilone Rd., San Onofre	●	●	●	●		●								●		●		●	●	●		
San Onofre State Beach (South)	S.W. of I-5, 2.5 mi. S. of Basilone Rd. off-ramp, San Onofre	●	●	●	●	●	●			●	●	●			●		●		●	●		●	
Bike Path	Along I-5 from San Clemente to S. entrance of Camp Pendleton										●									●			
Las Flores Viewpoint	W. of I-5, 5 mi. S. of San Onofre		●																	●			
Camp Pendleton Beach Access	W. of I-5 at Las Pulgas Rd., Camp Pendleton	●	●	●		●									●		●					●	
Aliso Creek Roadside Rest	W. of I-5, 6 mi. N. of Oceanside		●	●										●						●			

SAN ONOFRE STATE BEACH NORTH: Wide, sandy beach below steep bluffs; enter by turning off Basilone Rd. at the Nuclear Visitor Center. Open 6 AM-12 midnight (summer), 7 AM-10 PM (winter); $3 day use fee. Popular beach for surfing, clamming, and surf fishing. Riparian plant life and migratory birds can be observed at the mouth of San Mateo Creek, located at the north end of the beach. Trestles Beach, also at the north end, is a popular surfing spot. State Parks and Recreation plans to open a campground off Cristianitas Rd., northeast of San Onofre State Beach, by summer of 1984.

A public walkway, located along the seawall of the San Onofre Nuclear Generating Station, links San Onofre State Beach North and South. Use of this walkway is restricted to passage between the two state beaches; no loitering is permitted. The walkway is open only during daylight hours on weekends and major holidays from June through September. The walkway will be open daily following the completion of construction of the plant, sometime in 1984. There are no public access restrictions to the beach below the mean high tide line.

Access to the scenic, isolated arroyos fronting the ocean south of the generating station is permitted for viewing and hiking purposes only.

SAN ONOFRE STATE BEACH SOUTH: There is a campground along the abandoned highway on the bluffs above the beach, with 272 trailer spaces; facilities include restrooms, outside showers, supply store (open only in summer), and a trailer sanitary station (no individual hookups); $6 camping fee. 40 primitive tent spaces are available at the Echo Arch hike-in camp, located on a terrace between the blufftop and the beach; open April to November; $3 camping fee. En route campsites are also available; $6 fee. There are several hiking trails from the campgrounds to the beach, with panoramic views of the coast and whale watching spots. For information, call: (714) 492-4872 or 492-0802.

BIKE PATH: Runs adjacent to Interstate 5 and provides bicycle access to San Onofre State Beach.

LAS FLORES VIEWPOINT: Parking area with a view of the adjacent bluffs and the beach.

CAMP PENDLETON BEACH ACCESS: Restricted public access by lottery to Las Pulgas (Red) Beach for surf fishing and self-contained R.V. camping only; no swimming or surfing. To apply for a beach access permit, send two self-addressed, stamped postcards, listing your name and the names of your immediate family members, to: Director, Natural Resources Office, Marine Corps Base, Camp Pendleton 92055. Applications for permits are accepted only during the month of November, and drawings are held the first week in December. 1,000 applications are selected for the first period, from February 1 to July 31, and another 1,000 applications selected for the second period, from August 1 to January 31. There is a fee for permits. For more information, call: (619) 725-3360.

ALISO CREEK ROADSIDE REST: Landscaped area with picnic tables, a dog run, and a map display showing local points of interest.

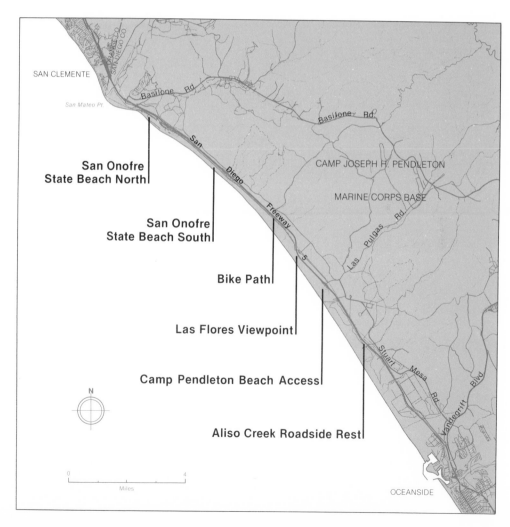

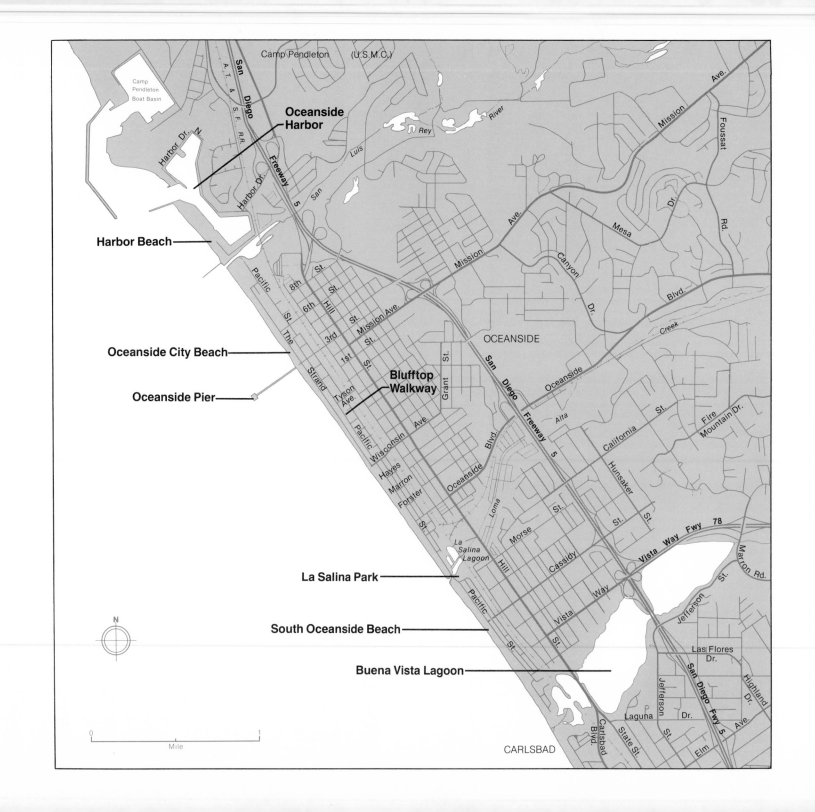

NAME	LOCATION	Entrance/Parking Fee	Parking	Restrooms	Lifeguard	Campground	Showers	Firepits	Stairs to Beach	Path to Beach	Bike Path	Hiking Trail	Facilities for Disabled	Boating Facilities	Fishing	Equestrian Trail	Sandy Beach	Dunes	Rocky Shore	Upland from Beach	Stream Corridor	Bluff	Wetland
Oceanside Harbor	Along Harbor Dr., Oceanside	•	•	•										•	•								
Harbor Beach	Corner of Harbor Dr. South and Pacific St., Oceanside	•	•		•										•		•						
Oceanside City Beach	Along The Strand, between San Luis Rey River and Witherby St., Oceanside	•	•	•	•		•		•	•					•		•		•			•	
Oceanside Pier	W. end of 3rd St., Oceanside		•	•			•						•		•		•					•	
Blufftop Walkway	Along Pacific St., between 2nd St. and Wisconsin Ave., Oceanside												•									•	
La Salina Park	N.E. corner of Pacific and Morse Streets, Oceanside		•	•																	•		•
South Oceanside Beach	W. of Pacific St., between Morse and Eaton Streets, Oceanside								•						•		•					•	
Buena Vista Lagoon	E. and W. of I-5, 2.5 mi. S. of downtown Oceanside		•												•						•		•

OCEANSIDE HARBOR: Small-craft harbor operated by Oceanside Harbor District, with berthing for about 800 vessels. Transients arrange berthing at the Harbormaster office on the east side of the harbor, opposite the channel entrance. Harbormaster: 1540 Harbor Dr. North, Oceanside 92054; (619) 722-1418. Harbor facilities and services include shops, restaurants, fuel dock, fishing pier, marine supplies, haul-out yard, charter sportfishing boats, fishing licenses, bait and tackle. Whale watching trips available from January 1-March 31; call (619) 722-2133. Boat launching ramp on the west side of the harbor, with five concrete lanes, open 24 hours all year; $2 fee for parking and launching.
Mass Transit: North County Transit District (NCTD) bus #303 and #312.

HARBOR BEACH: Wide, sandy beach; surf and rock fishing. Some free parking available. Lifeguards on duty only during the summer.
Mass Transit: NCTD bus #303 and #312.

OCEANSIDE CITY BEACH: Popular beach for swimming, surfing, and surf fishing; ramps or stairways located at some street ends between 9th and Witherby Streets provide access to the beach. There are public parking lots near the Oceanside Pier, at the end of 3rd St.; parking fee at some lots. Outdoor showers are also available at the end of 3rd Street. A private motor home campground (no trailers or tents) is located at 6th St. and The Strand; overnight fee.
Mass Transit: NCTD bus #312.

OCEANSIDE PIER: 1,900-foot long municipal pier, lighted at night, with fish cleaning facilities; no vehicles allowed on the pier.
Mass Transit: NCTD bus #312.

BLUFFTOP WALKWAY: Landscaped concrete walkway along the blufftop with benches and a view of the coast.
Mass Transit: NCTD bus #312.

LA SALINA PARK: Across Pacific St. from Buccaneer Beach, a unit of Oceanside City Beach. A concrete path along the bank of the wetland leads beneath the railroad trestle to Hill St.; a variety of bird species can be seen from the path. Playground equipment located south of the wetland.
Mass Transit: NCTD bus #312.

SOUTH OCEANSIDE BEACH: Swimming, surfing, and surf fishing. Access to the beach is via public stairs at the end of Cassidy St., and at the 1600 block of Pacific St.
Mass Transit: NCTD bus #312.

BUENA VISTA LAGOON: Natural reserve and bird sanctuary; fishing is permitted. Many points around the perimeter of the wetland from which to view plant and animal life. Parking is available along Jefferson St. between I-5 and Rte. 78.
Mass Transit: NCTD bus #302, #311, #312, #320, and #322.

Oceanside Pier

Oceanside City Beach, Along the Strand

Amtrak San Diegan

Several times a day, Amtrak's passenger train, the San Diegan, travels between Los Angeles and San Diego. For about one hour of this two hour and forty minute trip, the San Diegan travels along the Orange and San Diego County shorelines, providing unobstructed views of the coast between Dana Point in Orange County and the Del Mar area of San Diego County.

About 25 minutes out of the Santa Ana station going south (seven minutes out of San Clemente going north), the San Diegan meets the coast at Capistrano Beach, which is located just south of Dana Point. The Dana Point Harbor breakwater is visible from the San Diegan just before the train turns south to parallel the shoreline. Dana Point was named after the author Richard Henry Dana, who vividly described this area of the coast in his book *Two Years Before the Mast,* written in 1840.

The San Diegan arrives at San Clemente about five minutes after reaching the coast (15 minutes out of Oceanside going north). Four trains stop at San Clemente Beach and Municipal Pier every day; the 1,100-foot long pier is a popular fishing spot. Five minutes after leaving the San Clemente Pier (about 10 minutes out of Oceanside going north), the San Diegan passes the San Onofre Nuclear Generating Station. The power plant consists of three pressurized water reactor units. Unit 1 has been operating since 1968; the reactor is contained in a 140-foot high cylindrical structure located in the northern part of the facility. The nuclear reactors for Units 2 and 3, scheduled to be operating in 1982 and 1983 respectively, are contained in the 170-foot high dome-shaped structures situated south of Unit 1. When operating at full capacity, the power plant will provide electrical power for more than a million people, and more than two million gallons of ocean water will be used per minute to condense reactor-produced steam after the steam turns the generating turbines.

After passing San Onofre going south (just out of Oceanside going north), the San Diegan begins its run through the Camp Pendleton Marine Corps Base. The base extends along 17 miles of shoreline, and is a major center for amphibious landing operations and other advanced training programs; occasionally, train passengers may see military exercises taking place on either side of the train.

The San Diegan passes the Oceanside Harbor and arrives at the Oceanside station immediately after leaving Camp Pendleton (about 20 minutes out of Del Mar going north). The City of Oceanside was incorporated in 1888, during one of Southern California's railroad booms. By the 1920's, Oceanside was known as a beach resort and an agricultural produce distribution center.

Between Oceanside and Del Mar, the San Diegan travels along the mid-San Diego County coast and passes through the towns of Carlsbad, Encinitas, and Leucadia. This area has long been one of the country's major centers for the production of cut flowers, shrubs, bulbs, and other ornamental plants. The coastal landscape here is characterized by narrow beaches backed by high coastal bluffs, except where natural drainage areas meet the ocean. Some of the best examples of California's remaining coastal wetlands are found in these drainage basins; the San Diegan passes along or across a total of five coastal marshes and lagoons between Oceanside and Del Mar.

About 20 minutes out of Oceanside (30 minutes out of San Diego going north), the San Diegan passes the Del Mar Race Track and San Diego County Fairground complex, located on the north side of the San Dieguito River estuary; the race track and fairgrounds are visible from the inland side of the train. The San Diegan continues for a short distance to the Del Mar station; for the first 1-1/2 miles south of the Del Mar Station, the San Diegan travels immediately adjacent to the coast, less than 100 feet from the edges of the sea cliffs.

About three minutes out of Del Mar (27 minutes out of San Diego going north), the San Diegan travels inland along the Los Penasquitos Marsh Natural Preserve, a part of Torrey Pines State Park. The marsh contains valuable habitat for rare and endangered bird species such as the California least tern, and is also a nesting and feeding place for waterfowl and other migratory birds.

Between the coast at Los Penasquitos Marsh and the downtown San Diego station, the San Diegan follows an inland route. Minutes before reaching the station, the San Diegan passes inland of Mission Bay, the largest aquatic park on the West Coast. The downtown San Diego station is only four blocks from the bay edge, and is located near the Broadway Pier, the Maritime Museum, and other bayside points of interest.

For scheduling, fares, or other information on the San Diegan, look for the Amtrak listing in the white pages of your telephone directory.

Amtrak San Diegan

San Diego County
CARLSBAD

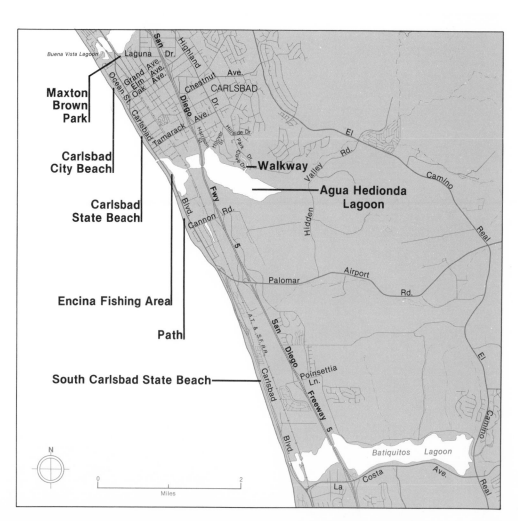

NAME	LOCATION	Entrance/Parking Fee	Parking	Restrooms	Lifeguard	Campground	Showers	Firepits	Stairs to Beach	Path to Beach	Bike Path	Hiking Trail	Facilities for Disabled	Boating Facilities	Fishing	Equestrian Trail	Sandy Beach	Dunes	Rocky Shore	Upland from Beach	Stream Corridor	Bluff	Wetland
Maxton Brown Park	500 Laguna Dr., Carlsbad		•																	•			•
Carlsbad City Beach	W. of Ocean St., between Cypress and Elm Avenues, Carlsbad		•	•					•						•		•		•				
Carlsbad State Beach	W. of Carlsbad Blvd. at Tamarack Ave., Carlsbad		•	•	•					•					•		•		•			•	
Agua Hedionda Lagoon	E. and W. of I-5, 1.4 mi. S. of Carlsbad Civic Center, Carlsbad	•	•											•	•								•
Walkway to Lagoon	S. end of Cove Dr., Carlsbad									•													•
Encina Fishing Area	E. side of Carlsbad Blvd., at the mouth of Agua Hedionda Lagoon, Carlsbad		•												•				•				•
Path to Beach	W. of Carlsbad Blvd., adjacent to the S.D.G.&E. Power Plant, Carlsbad		•							•							•						
South Carlsbad State Beach	W. of Carlsbad Blvd. at Ponto Dr., Carlsbad	•	•	•	•	•	•			•					•		•		•	•		•	

MAXTON BROWN PARK: Located on the shore of Buena Vista Lagoon; landscaped picnic area and panoramic views of the lagoon. On-street parking. For information, call: (619) 438-5571.
Mass Transit: North County Transit District (NCTD) bus #301 and #322.

CARLSBAD CITY BEACH: Access to the beach is provided by stairways located at the ends of Cedar, Grand, and Elm Avenues, and Ocean Street. Popular beach for swimming, surfing, and surf fishing; portions of the beach are rocky. Lifeguards during the summer only. On-street parking.
Mass Transit: NCTD bus #301 and #321.

CARLSBAD STATE BEACH: Sandy and rocky beach backed by bluffs. Free parking along the blufftop, at the end of Tamarack Avenue, and along Carlsbad Boulevard. Popular uses include swimming, surfing, diving, and rock and surf fishing; lifeguards during summer only. For information, call: (619) 729-8947.
Mass Transit: NCTD bus #301 and #321.

AGUA HEDIONDA LAGOON: Calm water within the lagoon makes it a popular swimming and fishing spot. Cove Dr. leads to a small sandy beach and a concrete public walkway above the lagoon, located adjacent to the western condominium development. Free parking and access near the dirt road at the end of Hoover Street. The Snug Harbor Marina is also located on the lagoon at 4215 Harrison St., Carlsbad 92008. Facilities include a three-lane concrete boat launching ramp and a fuel dock, a guest dock, boat and motor sales, snack bar, and a picnic area. The lagoon is used for water-skiing; skis can be rented at the marina. Entrance and parking fee for vehicular access into the marina.
Mass Transit: NCTD bus #301 and #321.

ENCINA FISHING AREA: This dirt parking area above a rocky seawall provides fishing access to Agua Hedionda Lagoon. Private property; permission to pass revocable by owner. No overnight parking.
Mass Transit: NCTD bus #301 and #321.

SOUTH CARLSBAD STATE BEACH: 226 campsites are located along the bluffs overlooking the beach and ocean. Campsites can accommodate trailers up to 28 feet long; each is equipped with a table, stove, and cupboard. Other facilities include fresh water, hot showers, restrooms, laundromat during the summer and most holidays, grocery and bait store, beach equipment rentals, and a trailer sanitation station (no individual hookups). Some campsites are wheelchair accessible. Access from the blufftop to the beach is provided by stairways; the beach is noted for swimming, surfing, surf fishing, and skin diving. Limited day use parking within the park; roadside parking is available along Carlsbad Blvd. at San Marcos Creek. $6 camping fee; $3 day use fee. Information: (619) 729-8947.
Mass Transit: NCTD bus #301.

Surfing

Surfing is the sport of riding a wave as it breaks along the shoreline. This sport has been practiced for hundreds of years; Captain James Cook observed natives surfing when he visited the Sandwich (Hawaiian) Islands in 1778. Surfing became known on the California coast during the early 1900's. However, the sport was seen as an activity for the truly hardy, and caught on slowly; a major reason for this was that early surfboards were 14- to 18-foot long redwood planks that weighed up to 150 lbs.

With the advent of lightweight balsa boards in the 1940's and polyurethane boards in the 1950's, the popularity of surfing increased significantly. A modern surfboard is five to nine feet long and may weigh as little as 12 pounds. Today, there are also a number of variations to the sport; kayaks, canoes, small sailboats, inflated rubber mats, and other floating objects are used to ride waves. However, using a surfboard and body surfing (riding waves without the aid of any floating object) are still the most popular forms of surfing.

Regardless of the particular type of surfing one does, the basic principles are the same. The surfer heads toward the shore just ahead of an incoming, unbroken wave. As the wave moves forward and catches up to the surfer, the surfboard (or body, boat, raft, etc.) starts to slide down the face of the wave. At this point the surfer has caught the wave and now must stay just ahead of the breaking portion of the wave to maintain the ride; this is done by shifting body weight to maneuver the board in the appropriate direction.

The most highly regarded surfing spots are usually locations where waves either approach the shore at an angle or are refracted around a point, jetty, or other protruding landform. In these locations incoming waves reach the breaking point in stages. The portion of the wave closest to the beach or in the shallowest water breaks first; the remaining portions of the wave break in succession as they move toward the shore.

Surfers nearest the breaking portion of a wave have the right-of-way; don't try to catch a wave in front of someone. In crowded surfing areas, watch out for unattended boards; try to hold on to your own board at all times to protect yourself and others from injury.

Most public beach areas where surfing is popular have designated surfing areas or times; look for signs that indicate where and when surfing is allowed, or ask a lifeguard. Body surfing is usually permitted in any swimming area. Rip currents are common in many surfing areas; if caught in a rip current, swim or paddle parallel to the shore to escape the current.

There are a number of popular surfing beaches in California. In San Diego County, San Onofre and Windansea Beaches are frequented by surfers. Other well-known southern California surfing areas include Newport and Huntington Beaches in Orange County, Malibu and Leo Carrillo Beaches in Los Angeles County, and the Rincon area in Ventura County. Excellent surfing conditions also exist farther north; Steamer Lane is a popular surfing spot in Santa Cruz County.

San Diego County

LEUCADIA/ENCINITAS

NAME	LOCATION	Entrance/Parking Fee	Parking	Restrooms	Lifeguard	Campground	Showers	Firepits	Stairs to Beach	Path to Beach	Bike Path	Hiking Trail	Facilities for Disabled	Boating Facilities	Fishing	Equestrian Trail	Sandy Beach	Dunes	Rocky Shore	Upland from Beach	Stream Corridor	Bluff	Wetland
Stairway to Beach	End of Grandview St., Leucadia		•	•					•								•	•				•	
Leucadia State Beach	W. of Neptune Ave., between Grandview St. and Leucadia Blvd., Leucadia		•	•			•	•	•				•				•	•				•	
Encinitas Beach County Park	Between Leucadia State Beach and Seaside Gardens County Park, Leucadia														•		•					•	
Seaside Gardens County Park	W. of Neptune Ave. at El Portal St., Leucadia		•		•				•								•					•	
Moonlight State Beach	4th St. at the W. end of B St., Leucadia		•	•	•				•				•				•					•	
Self-Realization Fellowship Hermitage Grounds	215 K St., Encinitas																			•		•	
Sea Cliff Roadside Park	W. of Old Hwy. 101 (1st St.), .9 mi. S. of Encinitas Blvd., Encinitas		•	•	•				•	•					•		•					•	

LEUCADIA STATE BEACH: Wide, sandy beach backed by bluffs; good surfing, swimming, surf fishing, and skin diving. Access to the north part of the beach is provided by a dirt trail at the end of Grandview St., where there is a parking lot. Parking is also available in a lot at the end of Leucadia Blvd.; the parking lot includes a viewing platform and a stairway and ramp leading to the beach. For information, call: (619) 729-8947.
Mass Transit: North County Transit District (NCTD) bus #301 and #361.

ENCINITAS BEACH COUNTY PARK: Sandy beach; popular for swimming and surf fishing. No access from the bluffs to the beach; to reach this area, walk south along the shore from Leucadia State Beach or north from Seaside Gardens County Park.
Mass Transit: NCTD bus #301 and #361.

SEASIDE GARDENS COUNTY PARK: A stairway provides access to this sandy beach, which is suitable for swimming, surfing, and surf fishing. On-street parking is available along Neptune Ave.
Mass Transit: NCTD bus #301 and #361.

MOONLIGHT STATE BEACH: Wide, sandy beach; popular for surfing, swimming, and surf fishing; lifeguard service year-round. Facilities include volleyball and tennis courts, equipment rentals, and a snack bar; parking lots are located at 4th and C Streets, and at the end of C Street. A blufftop viewing area with benches is at the end of D Street. For information, call: (619) 729-8947.
Mass Transit: NCTD bus #301, #309, and #361.

SELF-REALIZATION FELLOWSHIP HERMITAGE GROUNDS: Meditation area with panoramic views of the adjacent coastline. Open Tues.-Sat. 9 AM-5 PM; Sun. 11 AM-5 PM. Commercial photography and bathing attire are prohibited.
Mass Transit: NCTD bus #301 and #309.

SEA CLIFF ROADSIDE PARK: Small blufftop park with a grassy picnic area. Stairs lead to a narrow beach known as "Swami's," which is considered an excellent surfing spot; surf fishing, skin diving, and swimming are also popular. An outdoor shower is located near the base of the stairway.
Mass Transit: NCTD bus #301 and #309.

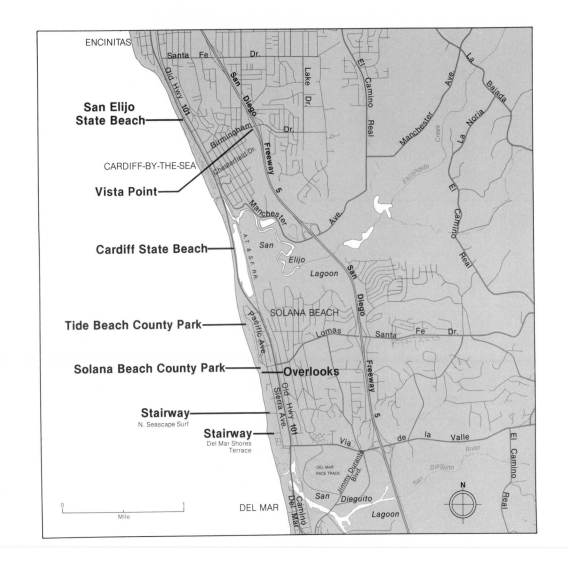

ENCINITAS

Santa Fe Dr.

San Elijo State Beach

CARDIFF-BY-THE-SEA

Vista Point

Cardiff State Beach

Tide Beach County Park

Solana Beach County Park **Overlooks**

Stairway
N. Seascape Surf

Stairway
Del Mar Shores Terrace

SOLANA BEACH

DEL MAR

0 Mile 1

N

Tide Beach County Park

Stairs at Del Mar Shores Terrace

San Diego County
CARDIFF/SOLANA BEACH

NAME	LOCATION	Entrance/Parking Fee	Parking	Restrooms	Lifeguard	Campground	Showers	Firepits	Stairs to Beach	Path to Beach	Bike Path	Hiking Trail	Facilities for Disabled	Boating Facilities	Fishing	Equestrian Trail	Sandy Beach	Dunes	Rocky Shore	Upland from Beach	Stream Corridor	Bluff	Wetland
San Elijo State Beach	Old Hwy. 101, N. of Chesterfield Dr., Cardiff-by-the-Sea	•	•	•	•	•	•	•	•						•		•		•			•	
Vista Point	San Diego Fwy. 5, S. of Birmingham Dr., Cardiff-by-the-Sea		•																			•	
Cardiff State Beach	Old Hwy. 101, directly W. of San Elijo Lagoon, Cardiff-by-the-Sea	•	•	•			•								•		•		•				•
Tide Beach County Park	Pacific Ave. at Solana Vista Dr., Solana Beach				•				•						•		•					•	
Solana Beach County Park	Sierra Ave. at Plaza St., Solana Beach		•	•	•					•					•		•					•	
Overlooks	S. of Solana Beach County Park parking lot, Solana Beach		•									•								•		•	
Stairway to Beach	Just S. of Dahlia St. on Sierra Ave., Solana Beach		•						•	•					•		•					•	
Stairway to Beach	N. end of Del Mar Shores Terrace, Solana Beach		•						•						•		•					•	

SAN ELIJO STATE BEACH: Features the southernmost developed campground in the State Beach Park System. The campground is located along the top of a bluff overlooking the beach; there are 171 campsites that can accommodate trailers up to 28 feet long. Each site includes a table, stove, and cupboard. Other facilities include restrooms, hot showers, grocery store, bait shop, and beach equipment rentals; laundry facilities are available during the summer and most holidays. Campground: (619) 753-5091. Stairways lead from the blufftop to the beach, which is popular for surf fishing, swimming, skin diving, and surfing. $6 camping fee. $3 fee for day use parking within the park; some parking is available along the highway. Information: (619) 729-8947.
Mass Transit: North County Transit District (NCTD) bus #301 and #309.

VISTA POINT: Accessible from the southbound lanes of San Diego Freeway 5. Overlooks the San Elijo Lagoon and Pacific Ocean.

CARDIFF STATE BEACH: Wide, sandy beach with tidepools at the south end. Popular beach for surfing, swimming, and surf fishing. Open 7 AM-5 PM. Lifeguard service only during the summer. For information, call: (619) 729-8947.
Mass Transit: NCTD bus #301, #308, and #309.

TIDE BEACH COUNTY PARK: A stairway down the bluff leads to a sandy beach; surfing, skin diving, swimming, and surf fishing. Lifeguards are on duty during the summer.
Mass Transit: NCTD bus #301 and #308.

SOLANA BEACH COUNTY PARK: A ramp provides access to a sandy beach; popular activities include catching grunion, skin diving, swimming, surfing, and surf fishing. Park facilities include basketball and shuffleboard courts. The Community Center Building (619-565-3600) and the lifeguard headquarters are located in the park; lifeguards are provided year-round.
Mass Transit: NCTD bus #301 and #308.

OVERLOOKS: A stairway at the south end of Solana Beach County Park leads up the bluff to the Las Brisas viewpoint; panoramic views of the ocean and the adjacent coastline from the trail. The Surfsong viewing access is located south of Las Brisas; benches and a landscaped garden make this a pleasant resting spot.

San Elijo State Beach

STAIRWAY TO BEACH: A 450-foot long paved sidewalk leads to a wooden stairway known as the North Seascape Surf Beach Access; the sandy beach below is popular for surfing, skin diving, surf fishing, swimming, and catching grunion.
Mass Transit: NCTD bus #301.

STAIRWAY TO BEACH: A stairway at the end of a 400-foot long paved walkway leads to a sandy beach; popular for surf fishing, catching grunion, swimming, and surfing. Parking lots are located along Sierra Ave. north and south of the accessway.
Mass Transit: NCTD bus #301.

Torrey Pines State Reserve

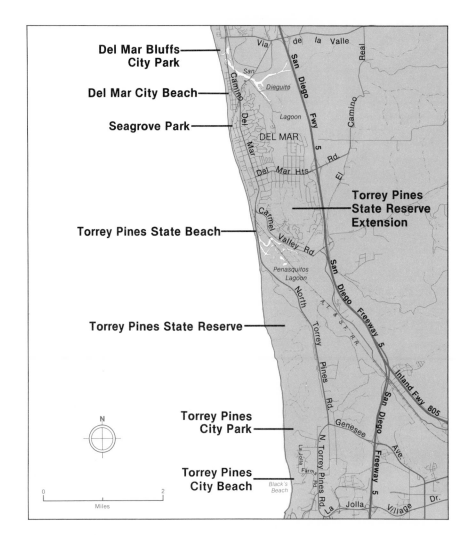

Del Mar Bluffs City Park

Del Mar City Beach

Seagrove Park

Torrey Pines State Reserve Extension

Torrey Pines State Beach

Torrey Pines State Reserve

Torrey Pines City Park

Torrey Pines City Beach

San Diego County

DEL MAR/TORREY PINES

NAME	LOCATION	Entrance/Parking Fee	Parking	Restrooms	Lifeguard	Campground	Showers	Firepits	Stairs to Beach	Path to Beach	Bike Path	Hiking Trail	Facilities for Disabled	Boating Facilities	Fishing	Equestrian Trail	Sandy Beach	Dunes	Rocky Shore	Upland from Beach	Stream Corridor	Bluff	Wetland
Del Mar Bluffs City Park	W. of Camino Del Mar, just N. of the San Dieguito River mouth, Del Mar		●												●		●					●	●
Del Mar City Beach	W. of Camino Del Mar, from 29th St. to Torrey Pines State Beach, Del Mar		●	●											●		●						
Seagrove Park	15th St. at Ocean Ave., Del Mar		●																			●	
Torrey Pines State Beach	McGonigle Rd., off Carmel Valley Rd., San Diego	●	●	●			●			●					●		●					●	●
Torrey Pines State Reserve Extension	W. of I-5, at the end of Del Mar Scenic Pkwy., San Diego		●									●	●							●			●
Torrey Pines State Reserve	W. of N. Torrey Pines Rd., 2 mi. N. of Genesee Ave., San Diego	●	●	●								●	●	●		●	●	●	●	●		●	●
Torrey Pines City Park	W. of N. Torrey Pines Rd., at the end of Torrey Pines Scenic Dr., San Diego		●												●					●		●	
Torrey Pines City Beach (Black's Beach)	La Jolla Farms Rd. at Blackgold Rd., San Diego		●							●					●		●					●	

DEL MAR BLUFFS CITY PARK: Sandy beach at the mouth of the San Dieguito River; noted for swimming and surf fishing. On-street parking only.
Mass Transit: North County Transit District (NCTD) bus #301.

DEL MAR CITY BEACH: Wide, sandy beach; good swimming and surfing; other activities include catching grunion and surf fishing. Beach access is at street ends from 29th St. to 18th Street. Off-street parking is located adjacent to the Amtrak station. Lifeguard service is provided year-round at 17th St., but only during the summer at 20th and 25th Streets.
Mass Transit: NCTD bus #301.

SEAGROVE PARK: Grassy area with benches on the bluffs overlooking the ocean.
Mass Transit: NCTD bus #301.

TORREY PINES STATE BEACH: Runs from 6th St. near Del Mar Heights Rd. south to Torrey Pines City Beach. Main parking area and beach access is at the North Beach area adjacent to the Los Penasquitos Lagoon. Popular activities at this wide, sandy beach include picnicking, swimming, surfing, surf fishing, clamming, and skin diving. A $3 parking fee is charged during the summer and on weekends. For information, call: (619) 729-8947.

TORREY PINES STATE RESERVE EXTENSION: Numerous trails through the Extension offer spectacular views of Los Penasquitos Lagoon and Salt Marsh, the main reserve, and the ocean. Rare plant and animal life, such as the white-tailed kite and the snowy plover, may also be observed along the trails. Parking is available at various street ends off of Del Mar Heights Road. At the end of Nogales Dr., the reserve extension and the Los Penasquitos Lagoon can be viewed from an undeveloped public overlook along the eastern edge of the bluff. Private property adjoins; do not trespass.

TORREY PINES STATE RESERVE: The reserve is situated on a series of steep bluffs interspersed with deep ravines; it is the only natural continental habitat for the world's rarest pine tree, the Torrey pine. The reserve contains two natural preserves: the Torrey Pines Natural Preserve has the finest stands of trees; the Los Penasquitos Marsh Natural Preserve, part of one of the few remaining salt marsh and lagoon areas in southern California, is the habitat of a number of rare and endangered bird species, such as the least tern and the light-footed clapper rail, and is an important feeding and nesting place for migratory waterfowl and shorebirds.

Torrey Pines State Reserve

Trails throughout the reserve provide opportunities for observing plant and animal life and viewing the adjacent coastline. Interpretive programs, trail maps, and plant and animal lists are available at the reserve office and museum; interpretive displays are located at various points within the reserve. The reserve accommodates a limited number of people in order to protect the natural resources; visitors may be asked to come back at a later time or date if the reserve is full; it is full most weekend afternoons. $3 day use fee. Information: (619) 755-2063.

TORREY PINES CITY PARK: The park is located on the bluffs overlooking the ocean; landslides have closed the extremely steep and hazardous paths at the north and south ends of the park which formerly led to Black's Beach. A radio-controlled model aircraft field and a glider port are located within the park; soaring is limited to licensed gliders. Hang gliding off the bluffs is also popular, and is limited to people rated by the American Hang Gliding Association.
Mass Transit: San Diego Transit Corporation (SDTC) bus #41.

TORREY PINES CITY BEACH (BLACK'S BEACH): The only safe access to this popular sandy beach backed by highly eroded bluffs is via a very steep road, for pedestrians only, which is located at the south end of Blackgold Road. The cliffs are very hazardous. The beach is noted for good swimming and surf fishing. Clothing optional. On-street parking only, limited to two hours.

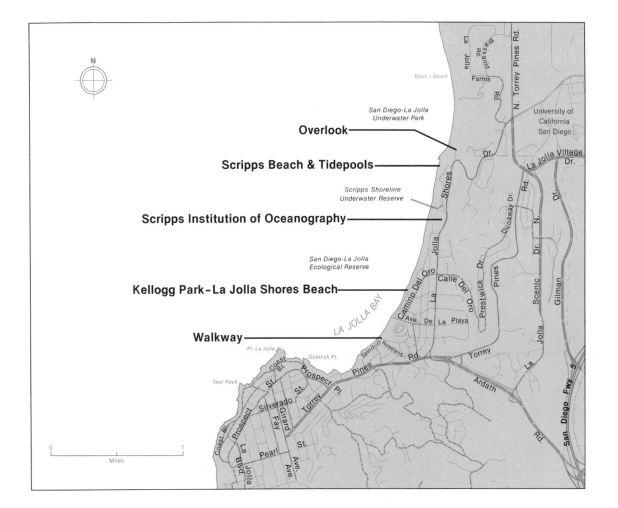

Overlook

Scripps Beach & Tidepools

Scripps Institution of Oceanography

Kellogg Park–La Jolla Shores Beach

Walkway

San Diego–La Jolla Underwater Park

Scripps Shoreline Underwater Reserve

San Diego–La Jolla Ecological Reserve

University of California San Diego

Black's Beach

La Jolla Farms

LA JOLLA BAY

Pt. La Jolla

Goldfish Pt.

Seal Rock

0   1
Miles

Scripps Pier

San Diego County
SCRIPPS/LA JOLLA

NAME	LOCATION	Entrance/Parking Fee	Parking	Restrooms	Lifeguard	Campground	Showers	Firepits	Stairs to Beach	Path to Beach	Bike Path	Hiking Trail	Facilities for Disabled	Boating Facilities	Fishing	Equestrian Trail	Sandy Beach	Dunes	Rocky Shore	Upland from Beach	Stream Corridor	Bluff	Wetland
Overlook	N. end of La Jolla Shores Lane, La Jolla	•																	•	•		•	
Scripps Beach and Tidepools	W. of La Jolla Shores Dr. at the Scripps Institution of Oceanography, La Jolla						•										•		•			•	
Scripps Institution of Oceanography	8602 La Jolla Shores Dr., La Jolla	•	•																•			•	
Underwater Reserves	From the S. end of the City of Del Mar to Goldfish Pt., La Jolla																		•				
Kellogg Park-La Jolla Shores Beach	Camino Del Oro at Calle Frescota, La Jolla	•	•	•									•	•			•						
Walkway to Beach	W. of Spindrift and Roseland Drives, La Jolla	•						•	•	•							•						

OVERLOOK: A short path leads to a blufftop overlook; views of the offshore marine reserves. On-street parking only. Private property adjoins; do not trespass.
Mass Transit: San Diego Transit Corporation (SDTC) bus #30.

SCRIPPS BEACH AND TIDEPOOLS: Sandy beach and tidepools popular for observing intertidal marine life; part of the Scripps Shoreline-Underwater Reserve, protected by the California Department of Fish and Game. Look, but do not touch the marine life.
Mass Transit: SDTC bus #30.

SCRIPPS INSTITUTION OF OCEANOGRAPHY: Facilities at the Institution include an aquarium and museum complex; open daily 9 AM-5 PM. An artificial tidepool, located near the entrance of the aquarium, contains marine flora and fauna representative of a naturally occurring tidepool ecosystem. In the aquarium, tanks containing examples of local, deep-sea, and tropical marine life are on display. Underwater video cameras provide views of activity in the nearby underwater marine reserves. The museum contains several models that demonstrate wave action and tide and current patterns. Tours and educational programs are available. No entrance fee, but donations are welcome. Information: (619) 452-4086.
Mass Transit: SDTC bus #30.

UNDERWATER RESERVES: The San Diego-La Jolla Underwater Park and Ecological Reserve, and the Scripps Shoreline-Underwater Reserve are located along the coast from the southern limits of the city of Del Mar south to Goldfish Point in La Jolla; these are protected marine life areas where a simple rule applies: look and enjoy, but do not touch or disturb the marine life present. At low tide much of the shoreline area is exposed, revealing numerous tidepools that support a diverse assemblage of marine plants and animals. Visitors to these areas are asked to respect the resources present and honor the applicable rules and regulations.

KELLOGG PARK-LA JOLLA SHORES BEACH: Wide, sandy beach with good swimming conditions; also noted for surfing, surf fishing, and skin diving. Native American artifacts have been recovered by divers near the north end of the beach. A boat launching area is located at the end of Avenida De La Playa, at the south end of the park.
Mass Transit: SDTC bus #30 and #34.

WALKWAY TO BEACH: A narrow concrete walkway and steps lead to a wide sandy beach at La Jolla Bay. Bathing and swimming only; no surfing allowed. On-street parking.
Mass Transit: SDTC bus #30 and #34.

Scripps Pier and Scripps Shoreline Reserve

Children's Pool Beach

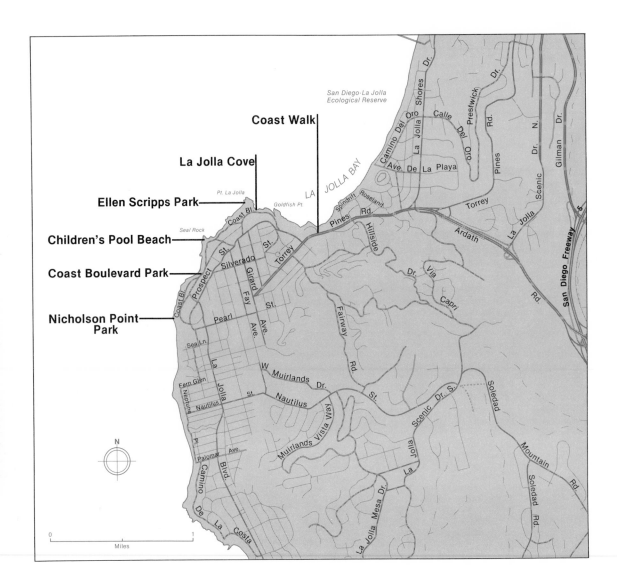

Coast Walk

La Jolla Cove

Ellen Scripps Park

Children's Pool Beach

Coast Boulevard Park

Nicholson Point
Park

San Diego-La Jolla
Ecological Reserve

LA JOLLA BAY

Pt. La Jolla

Goldfish Pt.

Seal Rock

N

0 _____ 1
Miles

NAME	LOCATION	Entrance/Parking Fee	Parking	Restrooms	Lifeguard	Campground	Showers	Firepits	Stairs to Beach	Path to Beach	Bike Path	Hiking Trail	Facilities for Disabled	Boating Facilities	Fishing	Equestrian Trail	Sandy Beach	Dunes	Rocky Shore	Upland from Beach	Stream Corridor	Bluff	Wetland
Coast Walk	Torrey Pines Rd. at Coast Walk and Coast Blvd., La Jolla		•						•	•		•							•			•	
La Jolla Cove	Coast Blvd., E. of Girard Ave., La Jolla		•	•	•		•								•		•					•	
Ellen Scripps Park	Coast Blvd. at Girard Ave., La Jolla		•	•					•	•									•			•	
Children's Pool Beach	Coast Blvd. at Jenner St., La Jolla		•	•	•										•		•					•	
Coast Boulevard Park	W. of Coast Blvd. at Cuvier St., La Jolla		•																•	•		•	
Nicholson Point Park	S. end of Coast Blvd., La Jolla		•						•	•					•		•		•			•	

COAST WALK: A dirt path along the La Jolla bluffs provides a panoramic view of the ocean, beach, and caves along the shoreline. The walk can be entered at Torrey Pines Rd., just east of the Prospect St. intersection, and at the Goldfish Point area, adjacent to 1325 Coast Boulevard. Stairs at Goldfish Point lead to tidepool areas. The shell shop at 1325 Coast Blvd. provides access via a human-made tunnel to one of the wave-created La Jolla caves; 75¢/adult, 50¢/child admission fee.

Free public parking is available during weekends and non-business hours at the Bank of America lot at Fay Ave. and Kline St., and serves coastal accessways from Coast Walk south to Nicholson Point Park.
Mass Transit: San Diego Transit Corporation (SDTC) bus #30 and #34.

LA JOLLA COVE: Small cove with a sandy beach; swimming, surf fishing, and skin diving. On-street parking.
Mass Transit: SDTC bus #34.

ELLEN SCRIPPS PARK: A grassy picnic area on the blufftop includes shuffleboard courts; a path and stairs down the bluff lead to a rocky beach.
Mass Transit: SDTC bus #34.

CHILDREN'S POOL BEACH: Strong rip currents often make this beach more hazardous than its name suggests; however, it is still a popular swimming and surf fishing spot. Lifeguards are on duty year-round. On-street parking.
Mass Transit: SDTC bus #30 and #34.

COAST BOULEVARD PARK: Improved shoreline park with picnic tables; a path down a low bluff leads to a rocky beach. Parking is available along nearby streets.
Mass Transit: SDTC bus #34.

NICHOLSON POINT PARK: A public path along the northwest side of a condominium complex at 100 Coast Blvd. provides the easiest access to this hard-to-reach beach; noted for skin diving, rock fishing, and surf fishing.
Mass Transit: SDTC bus #34.

La Jolla Caves, viewed from Coast Walk

263

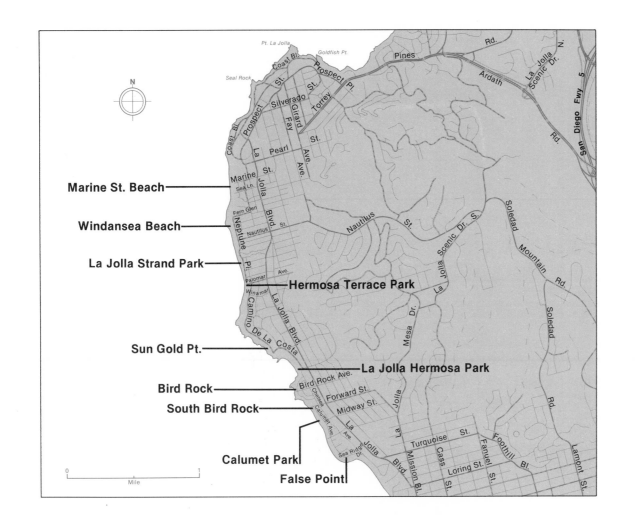

Marine St. Beach

Windansea Beach

La Jolla Strand Park

Hermosa Terrace Park

Sun Gold Pt.

La Jolla Hermosa Park

Bird Rock

South Bird Rock

Calumet Park

False Point

Windansea Beach

San Diego County
LA JOLLA

NAME	LOCATION	Entrance/Parking Fee	Parking	Restrooms	Lifeguard	Campground	Showers	Firepits	Stairs to Beach	Path to Beach	Bike Path	Hiking Trail	Facilities for Disabled	Boating Facilities	Fishing	Equestrian Trail	Sandy Beach	Dunes	Rocky Shore	Upland from Beach	Stream Corridor	Bluff	Wetland
Marine Street Beach	W. of La Jolla Blvd., at the end of Marine St., La Jolla		•						•	•					•		•		•				
Windansea Beach	W. of Neptune Pl., from Vista De La Playa to Bonair St., La Jolla		•						•	•							•		•				
La Jolla Strand Park	W. of Neptune Pl., from Playa Del Sur to Palomar Ave., La Jolla		•						•								•		•				
Hermosa Terrace Park	W. of Neptune Pl., at Palomar Ave., La Jolla		•							•							•		•				
Sun Gold Point	W. of Camino De La Costa, at Sun Gold Pt., La Jolla		•							•					•				•				
La Jolla Hermosa Park	Camino De La Costa at Chelsea Ave., La Jolla														•				•	•		•	
Bird Rock	W. of La Jolla Blvd., at the end of Bird Rock Ave., La Jolla		•							•					•				•			•	
South Bird Rock	W. of Calumet Ave., from Chelsea Pl. to Midway St., La Jolla		•							•					•				•				
Calumet Park	W. of Calumet Ave., between Midway St. and Colima Ct., La Jolla		•																	•		•	
False Point	Off Sea Ridge Dr. at the end of Linda Way, La Jolla		•							•					•				•				

MARINE STREET BEACH: Sandy beach popular for swimming, surfing, skin diving, and surf fishing. Stairways to the beach are located at the ends of Marine St. and Sea Lane; a paved walk at the end of Vista del Mar also leads to the beach. On-street parking only.
Mass Transit: San Diego Transit Corporation (SDTC) bus #30 and #34.

WINDANSEA BEACH: Also known as Neptune Park. This is one of the most popular surfing spots on the coast; swimming is also popular. At times, the waves are too large for inexperienced surfers and swimmers. A path at the end of Vista De La Playa leads to the beach; the beach is also accessible by stairways along Neptune Place south of Fern Glen. On-street parking only.
Mass Transit: SDTC bus #30 and #34.

LA JOLLA STRAND PARK: This seasonally sandy beach is noted for swimming and surfing. A stairway at the end of Playa Del Sur leads to the beach. Parking is available along nearby streets.
Mass Transit: SDTC bus #30 and #34.

HERMOSA TERRACE PARK: A paved path at the end of Winamar Ave. provides access to this swimming and surfing beach; the beach is rocky at times. On-street parking only.
Mass Transit: SDTC bus #30 and #34.

SUN GOLD POINT: Paths at the end of Sun Gold Point, Mira Monte Place, and Cortez Place lead to a rocky shoreline, which is a noted fishing spot. At low tide, a small cove just south of Sun Gold Point can be reached by walking along the shore. On-street parking only.
Mass Transit: SDTC bus #30 and #34.

LA JOLLA HERMOSA PARK: An unimproved park on the blufftop; the rocky beach below is reached by traversing a steep bluff face; rock fishing and skin diving.
Mass Transit: SDTC bus #30 and #34.

BIRD ROCK: This rocky point gets its name from the large guano-covered rock rising above the water just offshore. At low tide, exposed tidepools reveal interesting marine life. The area is also a popular fishing spot; surfing and skin diving here are recommended for experts only. Access is provided by a stairway at the end of Bird Rock Ave., and by steps cut into the bluff at the end of Moss Lane. Parking available along adjacent streets.
Mass Transit: SDTC bus #30 and #34.

SOUTH BIRD ROCK: Paths at the end of Chelsea Place, Midway St., and Forward St. lead to a rocky beach with tidepools; noted for fishing. On-street parking only.
Mass Transit: SDTC bus #30 and 34.

CALUMET PARK: A landscaped picnic area with benches situated on the bluffs above a cobblestone beach. No developed beach access. Parking available along Calumet Ave.
Mass Transit: SDTC bus #30 and 34.

FALSE POINT: Paths at the ends of Linda Way and Bandera St. provide access to a rocky shoreline, popular for fishing. On-street parking only.
Mass Transit: SDTC bus #30 and 34.

Sun Gold Point

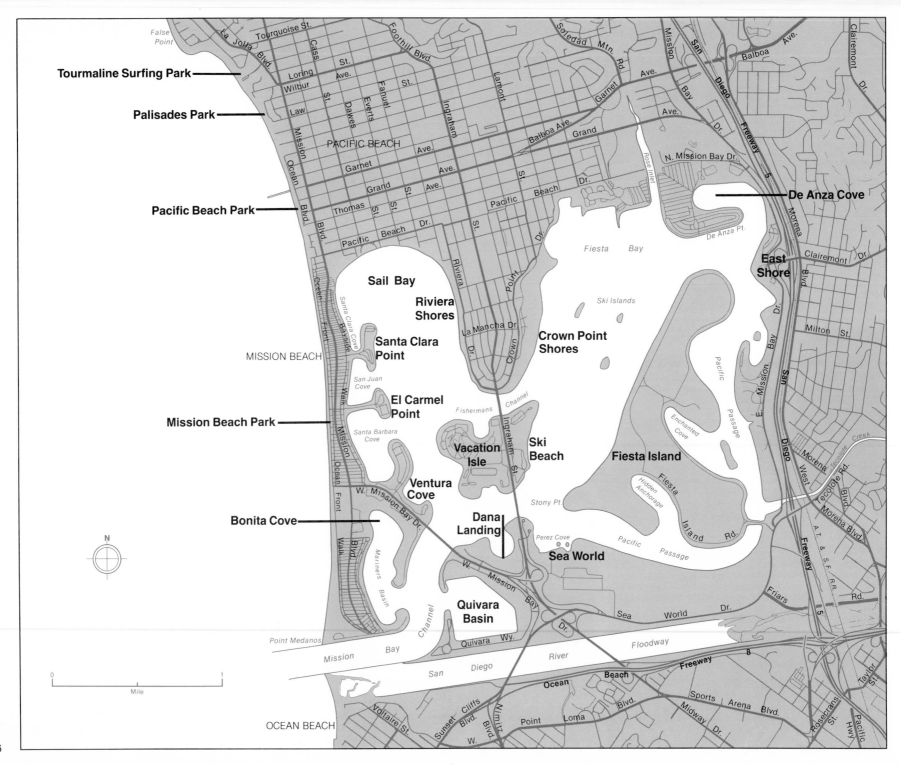

Tourmaline Surfing Park

Palisades Park

Pacific Beach Park

Mission Beach Park

Bonita Cove

PACIFIC BEACH

MISSION BEACH

OCEAN BEACH

De Anza Cove

East Shore

Sail Bay

Riviera Shores

Santa Clara Point

El Carmel Point

Vacation Isle

Ski Beach

Crown Point Shores

Fiesta Island

Ventura Cove

Dana Landing

Sea World

Quivara Basin

Fiesta Bay

Ski Islands

Pacific Passage

Enchanted Cove

Fiesta Island Rd.

Hidden Anchorage

Pacific Passage

Perez Cove

Stony Pt.

Fishermans Channel

San Juan Cove

Santa Barbara Cove

Santa Clara Cove

Mariner's Basin

Point Medanos

False Point

De Anza Pt.

Rose Inlet

N

0   1
           Mile

San Diego County
MISSION BAY

NAME	LOCATION	Entrance/Parking Fee	Parking	Restrooms	Lifeguard	Campground	Showers	Firepits	Stairs to Beach	Path to Beach	Bike Path	Hiking Trail	Facilities for Disabled	Boating Facilities	Fishing	Equestrian Trail	Sandy Beach	Dunes	Rocky Shore	Upland from Beach	Stream Corridor	Bluff	Wetland
Tourmaline Surfing Park	W. of La Jolla Blvd., at the end of Tourmaline St., La Jolla		•	•	•		•							•			•		•				
Palisades Park	W. of Mission Blvd., between Wilbur Ave. and Law St., Pacific Beach		•	•						•							•					•	
Pacific Beach Park	W. of Ocean Blvd., from Diamond St. to Thomas Ave., Pacific Beach		•	•	•					•					•		•						
Mission Beach Park	W. of Strand Way, from Santa Rita Pl. to the Mission Bay entrance channel, Mission Beach		•	•	•												•						
Sail Bay and Riviera Shores	S. of Pacific Beach Dr., between Mission Blvd. and Riviera Dr., Mission Bay		•						•	•				•			•						
Crown Point Shores	W. shore of Crown Pt. peninsula, Mission Bay		•	•				•						•			•						
De Anza Cove	N.E. corner of Mission Bay		•	•										•			•						
East Shore	Along E. Mission Bay Dr., from Clairemont Dr. to Fiesta Island Rd., Mission Bay		•	•										•	•		•						
Santa Clara Point and El Carmel Point	E. of Mission Blvd., at Santa Clara Pl. and El Carmel Pl., Mission Beach		•	•										•			•						
Vacation Isle and Ski Beach	Ingraham St. at Vacation Village Rd., Mission Bay		•	•			•							•	•		•						
Fiesta Island	Fiesta Island Rd. at E. Mission Bay Dr., Mission Bay		•					•				•		•			•						
Bonita Cove	W. Mission Bay Dr. at Mariners Way, Mission Bay		•	•													•						
Ventura Cove	W. Mission Bay Dr. at Gleason Rd., Mission Bay		•	•										•	•		•						
Dana Landing and Quivira Basin	Off W. Mission Bay Dr., at Dana Landing Rd. or Quivira Rd., Mission Bay		•	•										•	•						•		
Sea World	1720 S. Shores Rd., Mission Bay	•	•	•																			•

TOURMALINE SURFING PARK: Rocky beach, popular for surfing, fishing, and skin diving; swimming not permitted. Large waves break well off shore. Lifeguards summer only.
Mass Transit: San Diego Transit Corporation (SDTC) bus #30, #34, and #80.

PALISADES PARK: Paths lead from a grassy picnic area to a wide, sandy beach; no surfing from 11 AM-6 PM when swimmers are present. On-street parking.
Mass Transit: SDTC bus #9, #30, #34, and #80.

PACIFIC BEACH PARK: A landscaped picnic area overlooks the ocean; paths provide access to the sandy beach, which is used for surfing and swimming. Surfing is prohibited from 11 AM-6 PM when swimmers are present. Crystal Pier, located at the end of Garnet Ave., is open from 7 AM-5 PM for walking and fishing.
Mass Transit: SDTC bus #9, #27, #30, #34, and #80.

MISSION BEACH PARK: Sandy beach, with areas posted for surfing and body surfing. A paved boardwalk runs along the beach and is popular for walking, jogging, roller skating, and bicycling; skate and bike rentals are available along the boardwalk. Public parking areas are located at the old amusement park site, south of W. Mission Bay Dr. and Mission Blvd., and at the south end of Mission Boulevard. A number of shops and stores line the boardwalk south of W. Mission Bay Drive. Basketball courts and a play lawn are at the south end of the beach.
Mass Transit: SDTC bus #34 and #80.

Mission Bay City Park, the largest aquatic park on the west coast, encompasses the entire shoreline of Mission Bay; the following areas, except for Sea World, are all part of the park.

SAIL BAY AND RIVIERA SHORES: These areas make up the northwest portion of Mission Bay. The sandy beach areas, which are frequently submerged during high tide, are at the edge of a highly urbanized portion of Pacific Beach. The ends of Graham, Everts, Dawes, and E. and W. Briarfield Streets provide access to Sail Bay. Access to Riviera Shores is provided by stairs at the end of La Moncha Dr. and a path at 3862 Riviera Drive. Riviera Shores is a wide, sandy swimming beach with a water-ski take off and landing area. Only on-street parking is available.
Mass Transit: SDTC bus #9, #34, and #80.

CROWN POINT SHORES: Provides a sandy beach, picnic area, nature study area, physical fitness course, water-ski landing and take off areas, and a public loading dock. Special events include an annual sand castle building contest. Parking is available in three parking lots and along nearby streets.
Mass Transit: SDTC bus #9 to Ingraham St.

DE ANZA COVE: Includes a sandy beach and swimming area with lifeguard service, large grassy picnic areas, and a four-lane concrete boat ramp; the cove is used by swimmers and water-skiers. A trailer park is located at the west side of De Anza Point, and a private campground is near the cove at 2211 Pacific Beach Dr.

EAST SHORE: Facilities include the Visitor's Information Center, landscaped picnic areas, playgrounds, pathways, a physical fitness course, a snack bar, and a hotel; swimming and fishing at the sandy beach.

SANTA CLARA POINT AND EL CARMEL POINT: Santa Clara Point is in the western part of Mission Bay; facilities include the city's boat house, a concrete boat launch (one lane), boat slips, a recreation center, a baseball field, tennis courts, and multipurpose play courts. The Mission Bay Yacht Club, a parking area, and a sandy beach are located on El Carmel Point, about .4 mile south of Santa Clara Point. A public beach is located between the two points in San Juan Cove.
Mass Transit: SDTC bus #34 and #80.

VACATION ISLE AND SKI BEACH: Vacation Isle is bisected by Ingraham St.; the west side contains a hotel and golf course, public swimming area, boat rentals, youth camping area, and a model yacht basin. Ski Beach, located on the east side, is a noted water-skiing and boating spot, with a water-ski take off and landing area, a four-lane concrete boat launch, picnic areas, volleyball courts, a model airplane course, and a swimming beach.
Mass Transit: SDTC bus #9.

FIESTA ISLAND: The western and southern parts of this almost rural island are used for jet-skiing and fishing, and for viewing special aquatic events such as speedboat races. There are several swimming beaches around the island; a youth campground is located in the eastern portion of the island. An over-the-line softball tournament is held here annually.

BONITA COVE: Used for swimming, picnicking, over-the-line softball, and volleyball. Trails and a large playground are located along the cove; shops, restaurants, and recreation equipment rentals are within walking distance. The Bayside Walk begins south of Bonita Cove and continues north to Sail Bay.
Mass Transit: SDTC bus #34 and #80.

VENTURA COVE: Sandy beach and a grassy picnic area; the very calm waters make it a popular swimming spot for small children. Other facilities include a hotel-marina complex with bay excursion cruises; the hotel rents recreation equipment to its guests.
Mass Transit: SDTC bus #34 and #80.

DANA LANDING AND QUIVARA BASIN: The Dana Marina and the Dana Landing Public Ramp provide a 5-lane concrete boat ramp, open 24 hours, boat sales and service, fuel dock, and other marine services. For marina information, call (619) 222-6440. Sunset Point is a public park with picnic facilities, and is a popular fishing spot.

Quivara Basin includes a large grassy picnic area with excellent bay views, sportfishing and marina services, the Mission Bay Aquatic Center, and the port headquarters. The Mission Bay Marina, located in the basin, is open from 8 AM-5 PM, and includes a hoist with a 60-ton capacity; for marina information, call (619) 225-9627. A bike path runs from the basin east to Friars Rd., where it connects with another bike path that runs along E. Mission Bay Dr.
Mass Transit: SDTC bus #34 and #80.

SEA WORLD: A 75-acre aquarium and theme park located on the southern shore of Mission Bay. Attractions include marine life displays and shows, snack bars, and gift shops. (619) 224-3562.
Mass Transit: SDTC bus #9 and #80.

Diving

California's lengthy shoreline, generally favorable weather, and a diverse marine environment provide numerous opportunities for people to skin and scuba dive along the coast.

Skin diving is a relatively inexpensive way to view marine life and, where legal, to collect specimens. Typical skin diving equipment consists of swim fins, a mask, and a snorkel. A snorkel is a breathing tube that allows a person to swim at the water's surface and to look underwater without having to hold his or her breath. When diving below the range of the snorkel, however, one's breath must be held, and upon surfacing, the diver must first exhale to clear water out of the snorkel tube.

In some southern California locations the water is warm enough to dive without a wetsuit; however, for deeper dives, prolonged periods in the water, or dives in northern California, a wetsuit is a necessity. Any diver who becomes cold should get out of the water; diving while in poor physical condition can be dangerous.

The term "scuba" is an acronym for the words "self contained underwater breathing apparatus." Scuba gear was developed in the 1940's by Emil Gagnan and Jacques Cousteau. Basic scuba gear consists of a wetsuit, fins, an air tank that is strapped to a diver's back, and an air hose and regulator system that supplies and controls the flow of air to a diver's mouth. Scuba gear allows people to dive deeper and stay submerged for longer periods of time than is possible when skin diving.

Scuba diving involves certain potential hazards. For example, if a diver surfaces from a dive too quickly, air embolism (blockage of blood to the brain or heart by an air bubble) may occur, and the rapid change in water pressure may cause decompression sickness, commonly called "the bends." No one should scuba dive without first receiving expert instruction.

Diving is a safe, enjoyable experience for trained, qualified divers who abide by basic safety rules. Always dive with a companion, and be aware of your own physical limitations, as well as those of your companion. Use a diver's flag (a red flag with a white diagonal stripe) when diving is in progress; the flag notifies boaters that divers are in the water and to take heed. All divers should be familiar with decompression procedures, tables, and emergency action.

In a diving-related medical emergency, assistance by a physician trained in diving emergencies is absolutely necessary. Divers should be aware of the nearest medical facility equipped to handle such emergencies. The U.S. National Diving Accident Network (DAN), sponsored by Duke University in North Carolina, offers a 24-hour hotline service; the physicians on call will refer the caller to the nearest recompression chamber and trained staff. Phone: (919) 684-8111.

Divers should also be aware of fish and game laws pertaining to the area where they are diving. The California Department of Fish and Game publishes Ocean Fishing Maps that identify diving locations. In addition, many coastal communities contain dive shops that provide services, supplies, and information. Skin and scuba diving lessons are offered by private diving schools, at a number of colleges, and as special programs by many community recreation departments.

San Diego County

OCEAN BEACH

NAME	LOCATION	Entrance/Parking Fee	Parking	Restrooms	Lifeguard	Campground	Showers	Firepits	Stairs to Beach	Path to Beach	Bike Path	Hiking Trail	Facilities for Disabled	Boating Facilities	Fishing	Equestrian Trail	Sandy Beach	Dunes	Rocky Shore	Upland from Beach	Stream Corridor	Bluff	Wetland
Robb Field and Playground	W. of Sunset Cliffs Blvd., along W. Point Loma Blvd., Ocean Beach		•	•							•								•	•			
Ocean Beach Park	Between the ends of Niagara Ave. and Voltaire St., Ocean Beach		•	•	•		•							•			•		•				
Ocean Beach Fishing Pier	End of Niagara Ave., Ocean Beach		•	•						•					•		•						
Ocean Beach City Beach	Between Ocean Beach Pier and the end of Pescadero Ave., Ocean Beach									•							•				•		
Sunset Cliffs Park	Along Sunset Cliffs Blvd., from Pt. Loma Ave. to Ladera St., Ocean Beach		•						•	•		•			•		•		•	•		•	
Point Loma Hostel	3790 Udall St., Ocean Beach	•	•	•			•												•				

ROBB FIELD AND PLAYGROUND: A large athletic park at the mouth of the San Diego River; facilities for baseball, tennis, and basketball. Call for information and reservations: (619) 224-7581. A bike path runs along the river's south bank.
Mass Transit: San Diego Transit Corporation (SDTC) bus #35.

OCEAN BEACH PARK: Sandy beach with some tidepools, and a small grassy picnic area. The beach is noted for excellent surfing, but swimming and surf fishing are also popular. The north end of Ocean Beach Park is the only beach managed by the City of San Diego (other than the beaches at Fiesta Island) where dogs are allowed to be off their leashes during the day.
Mass Transit: SDTC bus #35.

OCEAN BEACH FISHING PIER: Long, T-shaped pier, located at the south end of Ocean Beach Park; facilities include bait and tackle shops and a fish cleaning area.
Mass Transit: SDTC bus #35.

OCEAN BEACH CITY BEACH: A series of small pocket beaches and tidepools along the coast from the Ocean Beach pier south to the end of Pescadero Ave.; sun bathing and surfing. Access is provided by stairs at the ends of Cable St. and Del Monte, Santa Cruz, Pescadero, and Bermuda Avenues.
Mass Transit: SDTC bus #35.

SUNSET CLIFFS PARK: A dirt path along the cliffs provides a spectacular view of the coastline. There are parking areas along Sunset Cliffs Blvd., and a parking lot is located at the end of Cornish Dr., at the south end of the park. Several steep trails lead from the parking lot down the cliff face to pocket beaches frequently used by experienced divers and surfers; these trails are highly eroded and can be dangerous. A stairway at the end of Ladera St. leads to a rocky beach. The park also contains some upland hiking trails among eucalyptus trees, which provide views of the beaches and tidepools below the cliffs.
Mass Transit: SDTC bus #35.

POINT LOMA HOSTEL: Centrally located between Mission Bay and San Diego Bay, about a mile east of Ocean Beach; accommodates 36 men and 24 women; guests are provided a room with bunk beds for 2 to 14 people. Fully equipped community kitchen; open at 4:30 PM, with an 11:00 PM curfew. Lodging is $6.50/night for hostel members, $8.50 for non-members. For reservations, send a deposit for the first night's lodging to: Reservation Desk, Point Loma Hostel, 3790 Udall St., San Diego 92107. Call: (619) 223-4778.
Mass Transit: SDTC bus #35.

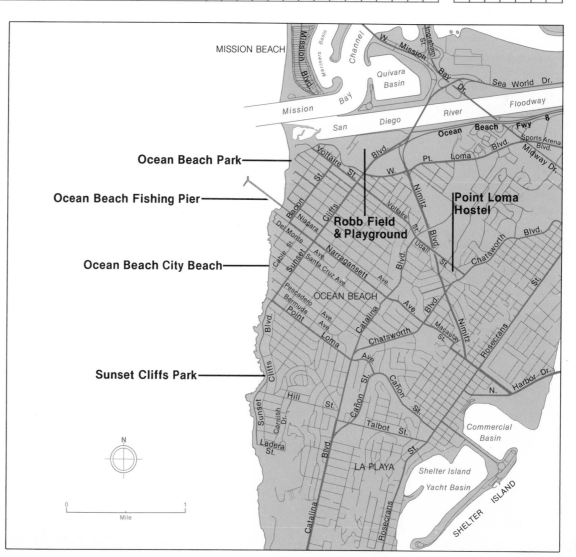

Kelp Harvesting

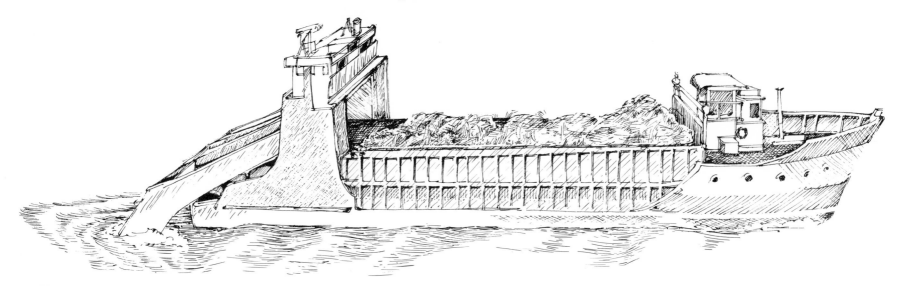

Kelp, a marine plant that provides food and habitat for diverse species of fish, marine invertebrates, and marine mammals, is also a valuable resource used in the manufacture of numerous everyday products.

Kelp is a type of alga. A number of species of kelp grow off the California coast, but giant kelp *(Macrocystis pyrifera)* is the most commercially important species. Giant kelp grows outside the surf zone to depths of 100 feet; the amount of sunlight that extends below 100 feet is not generally sufficient to sustain kelp growth. Giant kelp has no true roots, but uses root-like structures called holdfasts to anchor itself to hard rocky surfaces. Whereas terrestrial vegetation absorbs most of its nutrients through its root system, the entire kelp plant absorbs food; therefore, some of the largest and healthiest kelp beds grow in areas where strong ocean currents provide the kelp with a continuous supply of nutrients.

Giant kelp has an interesting reproductive cycle. Microscopic spores are released from the kelp beds, attach themselves to hard surfaces below the water surface, and germinate and grow into microscopic, filament-like male and female plants. Female eggs are fertilized by sperm released by the male plants; the fertilized egg then grows rapidly, and within a year develops into a plant recognizable as giant kelp. Young kelp plants double in size every three weeks. For a period of five to ten years a kelp plant continuously sends up new stalks, called stipes; giant kelp stipes live approximately six months and may grow as much as two feet in a day.

Giant kelp contains numerous useful elements and chemical compounds such as iodine, minerals, vitamins, and carbohydrates, making it a nutritious food supplement for humans and livestock. Kelp also contains very high concentrations of potassium, which is an important constituent in fertilizer and soaps.

Perhaps the most important substance found in kelp is a versatile compound called algin, which is used in countless manufacturing processes. Since algin absorbs large quantities of water relative to its volume, it is used in preparing commercial ice cream to prevent the formation of large ice crystals. Algin is able to suspend various compounds in solutions and, therefore, is useful in the manufacture of antibiotics, polishes, and paint products. Rubber companies use algin as a thickening and stabilizing agent in the manufacture of synthetic rubber products, such as latex. These are just a few examples of the more than one hundred food, industrial, and pharmaceutical products that contain algin.

In the United States the kelp harvesting industry is centered in southern California. The waters off the San Diego coast are an attractive harvesting location because expansive giant kelp beds and favorable weather conditions allow virtual year-round harvesting. Kelp harvesting is regulated by the California Department of Fish and Game; some kelp beds are leased by the State to individual companies through a competitive bidding process, while others are open to all harvesting companies. Harvesting companies pay the State a royalty based on the amount of kelp harvested.

Today kelp is harvested by specially designed barges which cut and collect as much as 300 tons of wet kelp in one outing. By law, kelp can be cut to a maximum depth of four feet below the water surface. Harvesting kelp in this manner promotes new kelp growth, because the removal of the top layer of kelp allows more sunlight to reach the rest of the plant. After the kelp is harvested, it is transported to onshore processing plants where it is converted into its various marketable forms.

San Diego County

POINT LOMA

NAME	LOCATION	Entrance/Parking Fee	Parking	Restrooms	Lifeguard	Campground	Showers	Firepits	Stairs to Beach	Path to Beach	Bike Path	Hiking Trail	Facilities for Disabled	Boating Facilities	Fishing	Equestrian Trail	Sandy Beach	Dunes	Rocky Shore	Upland from Beach	Stream Corridor	Bluff	Wetland
Commercial Basin	E. of Rosecrans St., N. of Shelter Island Dr., San Diego	•												•									
Shelter Island Yacht Basin	E. of Rosecrans St., S. of Shelter Island Dr., San Diego													•									
Shelter Island	Along Shelter Island Dr., San Diego	•	•											•	•	•	•						
La Playa	Along San Antonio Ave. and Pl., between Bessemer and Kellog Streets, San Diego																•						
Cabrillo National Monument	S. end of Cabrillo Memorial Dr., Point Loma	•	•						•			•	•		•				•	•		•	
Point Loma Ecological Reserve	Offshore W. side of Pt. Loma																						

COMMERCIAL BASIN: Home of a large fleet of commercial fishing vessels; can accommodate more than 800 small craft. Facilities include sportfishing services, a fueling dock, launching ramp, marine railway (800-ton capacity), marine supplies, and boat sales and service. The basin can be viewed from a public observation deck located on the west side of Shelter Island Dr., 400 feet north of the traffic circle. Information: (619) 291-3900.

Two docks are open to public use: the gangway and boat dock adjacent to 2515 Shelter Island Dr. may be used for viewing of the basin and moored boats; the wooden dock north of the intersection of Anchorage Lane and Shelter Island Dr., and adjacent to the Kettenburg Marine facilities, may be used for berthing of dinghies and viewing of the shipyards. Parking is available at Kettenburg Marine's peripheral parking areas after business hours and at the public parking lots on Shelter Island Dr.
Mass Transit: San Diego Transit Corporation (SDTC) bus #29.

SHELTER ISLAND YACHT BASIN: Contains a number of marinas and yacht clubs; can accommodate almost 2,000 small craft. Boating facilities include boat launches, a fuel dock, transient berthing and mooring areas, marine supplies, and boat sales and service. Information: (619) 291-3900.
Mass Transit: SDTC bus #29.

SHELTER ISLAND: The beach area of the island is popular for swimming, fishing, water-skiing, and picnicking. A landscaped walkway runs along the length of the island, just inland from a sandy beach; other features include a boat launch with ten concrete lanes and two hoists, a fishing pier, and picnic areas. A Coast Guard station is located at the south end of the island.
Mass Transit: SDTC bus #29.

LA PLAYA: Narrow, sandy beach located on the Point Loma peninsula just west of Shelter Island; excellent views of the bay and yacht basin. Access at the ends of Bessemer, Perry, Owens, McCall, Lawrence, and Kellog Streets. Swimming is prohibited within the marked yacht channel.
Mass Transit: SDTC bus #6 and #29.

CABRILLO NATIONAL MONUMENT: The monument commemorates Cabrillo's discovery of San Diego Bay. Major attractions include a visitor's center with exhibits, films, and a gift shop; the old Point Loma Lighthouse, built in 1854; and a telescope-equipped whale watching platform. Hiking trails overlooking the ocean and the bay lead to some of the finest tidepools in southern California. The monument is open daily from 9 AM-5:15 PM. Information: (619) 293-5450.
Mass Transit: SDTC bus #6.

POINT LOMA ECOLOGICAL RESERVE: Adjacent to Cabrillo National Monument. Only fin-fish can be taken in this underwater natural reserve.
Mass Transit: SDTC bus #6.

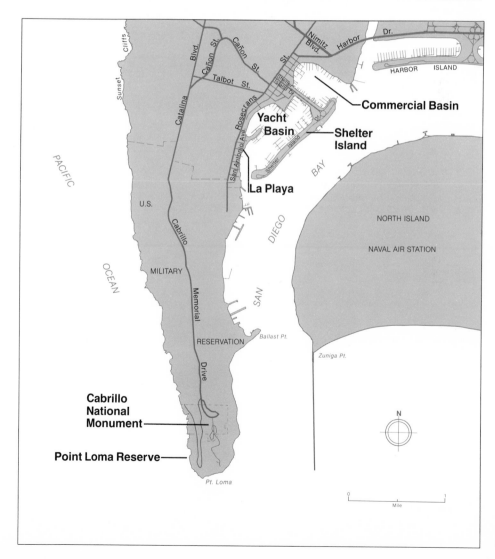

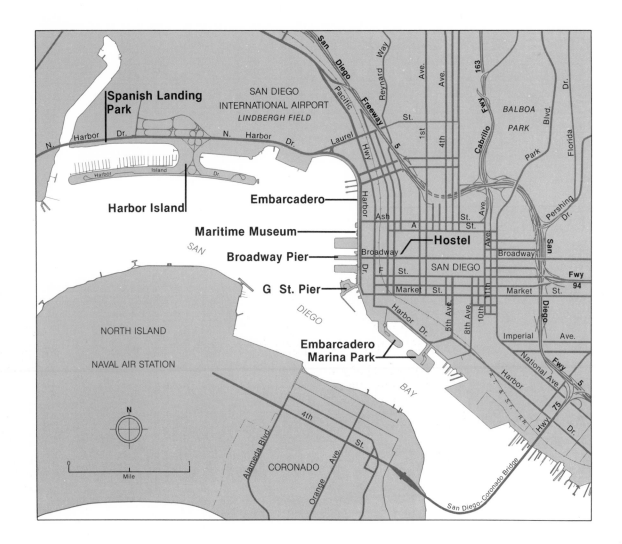

Spanish Landing Park

SAN DIEGO INTERNATIONAL AIRPORT
LINDBERGH FIELD

Harbor Island

Embarcadero

Maritime Museum

Broadway Pier

G St. Pier

Embarcadero Marina Park

Hostel

SAN DIEGO

BALBOA PARK

NORTH ISLAND

NAVAL AIR STATION

SAN DIEGO BAY

CORONADO

N

Mile

San Diego-Coronado Bridge

Embarcadero Marina Park

G Street Pier

San Diego County
CITY OF SAN DIEGO

NAME	LOCATION	Entrance/Parking Fee	Parking	Restrooms	Lifeguard	Campground	Showers	Firepits	Stairs to Beach	Path to Beach	Bike Path	Hiking Trail	Facilities for Disabled	Boating Facilities	Fishing	Equestrian Trail	Sandy Beach	Dunes	Rocky Shore	Upland from Beach	Stream Corridor	Bluff	Wetland
Spanish Landing Park	W. of Lindbergh Field, on N. Harbor Dr., San Diego		•	•											•		•						
Harbor Island	S. of Lindbergh Field, on Harbor Island Dr., San Diego		•	•										•	•								
Embarcadero	Along Harbor Dr., at the end of Hawthorne St., San Diego														•								
Maritime Museum	W. of Harbor Dr., at the end of Ash St., San Diego	•	•	•																			
Broadway Pier	W. end of Broadway, San Diego		•	•																			
G Street Pier	W. of N. Harbor Dr., at the end of G St., San Diego	•	•												•								
Embarcadero Marina Park	Harbor Dr. at the end of Kettner Blvd., San Diego		•	•										•	•							•	
Armed Services YMCA Hostel	500 W. Broadway, San Diego	•		•			•															•	

SPANISH LANDING PARK: The sandy beach located just south of the San Diego International Airport is a popular swimming spot; there is also a grassy picnic area near the shore. A concrete walkway along a seawall provides an opportunity for fishing, strolling, and enjoying views of the bay.

HARBOR ISLAND: Like Shelter Island, its neighbor to the southwest, Harbor Island functions primarily as a boating center; the various marinas can accommodate a total of about 1,000 vessels, and some marinas have guest berths or moorings. Other facilities include hotels, restaurants, shops, and boating sales and service businesses. A walkway extends along the entire length of the island, bordered by lawns with benches; noted for fine views of the bay and for rock fishing.
Mass Transit: SDTC bus #10.

EMBARCADERO: A walkway with benches along the east side of the bay provides views of the bay and Coronado. Commercial fishing boats unload here; other attractions include restaurants, fish markets, and shops. Harbor excursion boats also depart from the area.
Mass Transit: SDTC bus #2, #4, #7, #9, #20, #20A, #29, #34, #35, #90, and #110.

MARITIME MUSEUM: Consists of a display of three historical ships, the most famous of which is the 100-year old three masted bark named the Star of India. Admission fee: $3/adult, 50¢/child. Information: (619) 234-9153.
Mass Transit: Same as for the Embarcadero, plus San Diego Trolley.

BROADWAY PIER: The walkway along the pier offers fine views of activity on the bay. The U.S. Customs office is located at the end of the pier. One or more U.S. Navy ships are available for public tours on most weekends from 1 PM-4 PM; for information, call: (619) 235-3534.
Mass Transit: Same as for the Embarcadero, plus San Diego Trolley.

G STREET PIER: Fishing pier; the walkway is also used for strolling and viewing. Fee for parking.
Mass Transit: SDTC bus #2 and #7.

EMBARCADERO MARINA PARK: The park is divided into two sections, but is connected by a walkway along a seawall on the bay. The northern section has a lawn, picnic tables, path, and drinking fountains; popular activities include fishing and viewing. Enter from the Seaport Village Shopping Center on Harbor Drive. The entrance to the southern section is at the intersection of Harbor Dr. and Harbor St.; facilities include a grassy picnic area, paths, a fishing pier, basketball courts, and an athletic course.
Mass Transit: SDTC bus #7.

ARMED SERVICES YMCA HOSTEL: 100 private rooms and a dormitory; complete toilet, bath, and clothes washing facilities. Private rooms cost $15.78 or more/night ($13.66 for military); dorm lodging is $4.76/night for members, $6.76 for nonmembers ($4.50 for military), but you must bring your own linen. Storage of backpacks or other items costs 50¢/day. Open year-round. For further information, call: (619) 232-1133.
Mass Transit: Same as for the Embarcadero, plus San Diego Trolley.

Harbor Island

Shellfish

Shellfish comprise a significant and highly desirable resource off the California coast. Included in this category are crustaceans such as shrimp, prawns, crabs, and lobsters; and mollusks such as clams, oysters, abalone, mussels, and squid.

One of the most popular shellfish is abalone, many species of which are found along the state's entire coast. Adult abalone feed on algae such as kelp, and usually remain on a single rock for the duration of their lives. The shells are noted for their beauty and brilliance; archaeological evidence indicates that Native Americans used them for barter. Today, commercial abalone fishing is one of the largest shellfish industries in southern California; in northern California abalone are taken in large numbers by sports divers.

Typical predators of abalone, other than people and sea otters, are rock crabs who frequently pick the thick shells apart to get at the meat inside. Inhabitants of inshore rocky areas, rock crabs are common catches of pier and shore net fishermen. The larger and more commercially popular crab sold in restaurants and stores is the Dungeness crab, found within the state primarily in the San Francisco and Humboldt Bay areas.

California spiny lobster populations are located off the San Diego and southern California coasts, providing an important commercial shellfish. Spiny lobsters, in large groups of up to several hundred, typically inhabit rocky crevices and dens during the daytime; at night they forage singly, usually feeding on other crustaceans and mollusks.

The most commonly found mollusk in rocky areas is the mussel, often used for bait by fishermen, but also popular for eating. Mussels are filter feeders, and subsist on phytoplankton. During summer months, mussels and other bivalves may ingest and accumulate large amounts of certain toxic plankton, causing them to become poisonous to humans. Shellfish poisoning is not limited to mussels; sand crabs and razor, Washington, and gaper clams may also accumulate toxic plankton if they are in or near the ocean. Shellfish taken in inland bays are generally safe. However, always check with the environmental health sections of local or state health services agencies concerning quarantines before removing any of these shellfish. Mussels are usually quarantined between May 1 and October 31.

Although only one oyster species is native to California, several introduced species are grown in California using mariculture techniques. Natural reproduction of these non-native oysters is inhibited in California because of low water temperatures, requiring commercial oyster farms to artificially plant juvenile oysters. The Pacific oyster is the most successful in California, introduced originally from Japan; commercial Pacific oyster beds are grown in Encina Lagoon, Drakes Estero, and Humboldt, Tomales, and Morro Bays.

Squid, considered a shellfish because of its small internal shell, is one of the most important commercial catches off the Monterey coast. Schools of squid are typically caught at night, using floodlights or torches held above the water to attract them into submerged nets. California squid grow to as much as 12 inches in length, and feed on small fishes, shrimp, and other squid.

Bag limits, equipment, and fishing seasons for shellfish are regulated by the State Department of Fish and Game. For information, see the annual California Sport Fishing Regulations available from the Department of Fish and Game or at sporting goods stores.

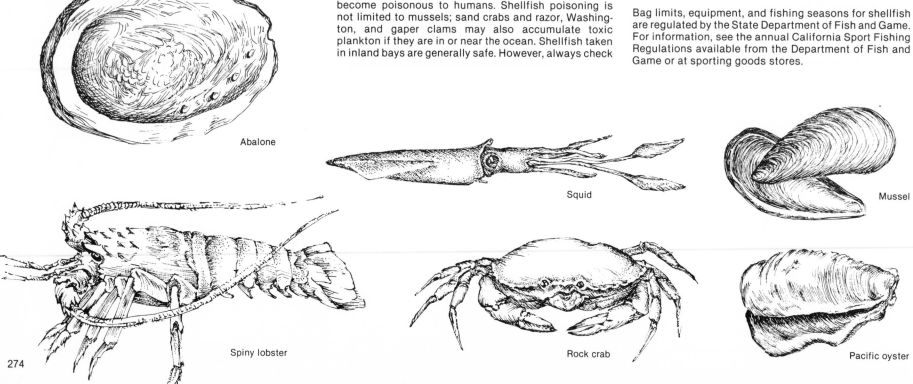

Abalone

Squid

Mussel

Spiny lobster

Rock crab

Pacific oyster

NAME	LOCATION	Entrance/Parking Fee	Parking	Restrooms	Lifeguard	Campground	Showers	Firepits	Stairs to Beach	Path to Beach	Bike Path	Hiking Trail	Facilities for Disabled	Boating Facilities	Fishing	Equestrian Trail	Sandy Beach	Dunes	Rocky Shore	Upland from Beach	Stream Corridor	Bluff	Wetland
"I" Park	"I" St. and 1st St., Coronado		•															•					
Path to Bay	On 1st St., between E and F Streets, Coronado		•						•	•							•						
Harbor View Park	1st and E Streets, Coronado		•															•	•				
Coronado Municipal Golf Course	Visalia Row and Glorietta Blvd., Coronado	•	•	•				•									•		•				
Glorietta Bay Marina	1715 Strand Way, Coronado	•	•	•										•	•								
Glorietta Bay Park	E. of Hwy. 75, at the S. end of Strand Way, Coronado	•	•	•				•						•	•								
Coronado City Beach	W. of Ocean Blvd., Coronado		•	•	•			•	•	•					•		•						
Coronado Shores Beach	Seaward of Coronado Shores Condominiums on Hwy. 75, Coronado		•							•			•		•		•						

"I" PARK: Small, beautifully landscaped park; provides a good view of the bay and the San Diego skyline. On-street parking only.
Mass Transit: San Diego Transit Corporation (SDTC) bus #9. Strand bus #901.

PATH TO BAY: A narrow pathway with stairs leads to the bay on the east side of Coronado; provides views of downtown San Diego. Private property adjoins the path; do not trespass. On-street parking only.
Mass Transit: Strand bus #901.

HARBOR VIEW PARK: Small, grassy park with benches; view of the downtown waterfront.
Mass Transit: Strand bus #901.

CORONADO MUNICIPAL GOLF COURSE: Situated along the shores of San Diego Bay; open year-round at 6:30 AM on weekends and 7 AM on weekdays. Golf course fee is $6.50. A dirt road adjacent to the golf course office provides pedestrian access to the narrow sandy beach along the bay. Do not trespass on the golf course lawn areas. (619) 435-3121.
Mass Transit: Strand bus #901.

GLORIETTA BAY MARINA: Glorietta Bay is the home of the Coronado Yacht Club. The Bay Marina is a full service facility with moorings and slips, a concrete boat launch ramp, power and sailboat rentals, a dry dock (five-ton capacity), and charter fishing boats. For information, call (619) 435-5203.
Mass Transit: Strand bus #901.

GLORIETTA BAY PARK: Park facilities include a playground, grassy picnic area, and concrete boat launch; the boat launch has three lanes and loading docks, and is open 24 hours a day year-round. The Coronado Municipal Swimming Pool is located next to the park; open M-F from 10 AM-1 PM and 6 PM-7 PM (winter) and 10 AM-4 PM daily, 6 PM-7 PM M-F (summer) for a fee of 75¢ (or $10.00 per month). Swimming pool: (619) 435-1397.
Mass Transit: Strand bus #901.

CORONADO CITY BEACH: Wide, sandy beach used for swimming, surfing, and surf fishing. A large grassy picnic area is located at Sunset Park, at the north end of Ocean Boulevard. On-street parking only.
Mass Transit: Strand bus #901.

CORONADO SHORES BEACH: The entrance and a public parking area are located at the Coronado Shores condominium development. Wide, sandy beach; heavily used for surfing, swimming, and surf fishing. A concrete promenade runs along the top of a seawall adjacent to the shore; excellent views. The promenade is accessible from Avenida del Sol, Avenida de las Arenas, and Avenida Lunar; a parking lot and wheelchair ramp is at the end of Avenida de las Arenas.
Mass Transit: Strand bus #901.

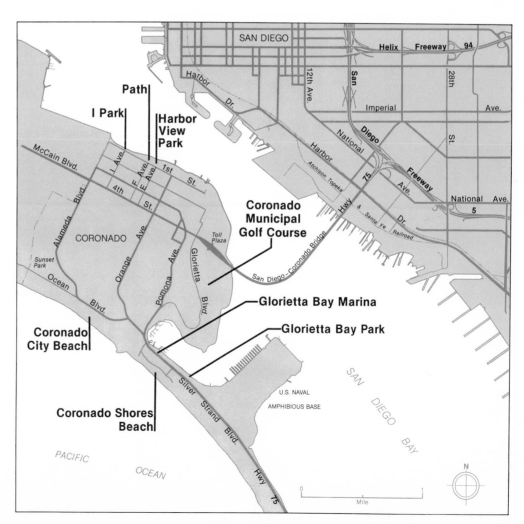

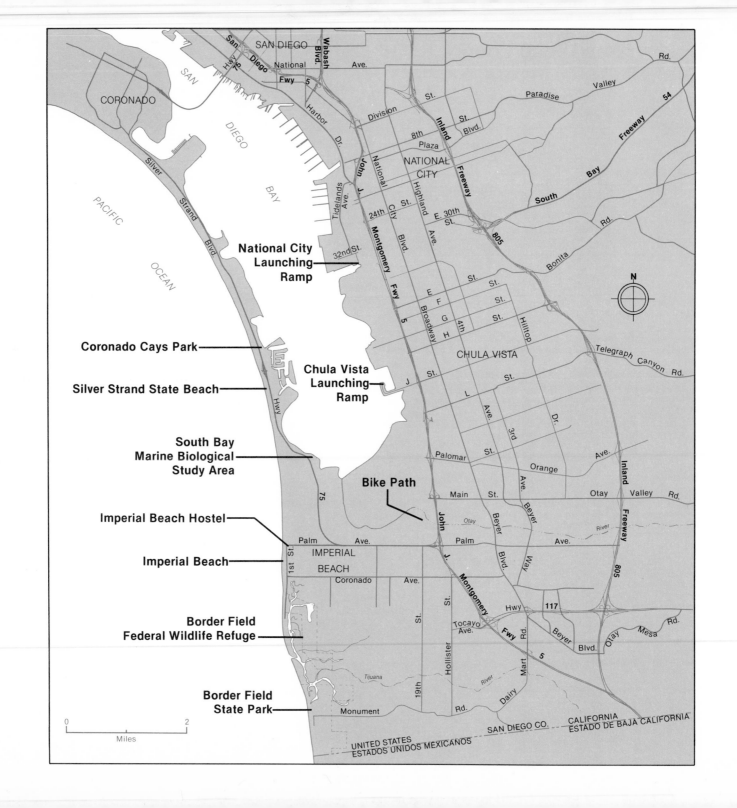

CORONADO

SAN

DIEGO

BAY

PACIFIC

OCEAN

Silver Strand Blvd.

SAN DIEGO

San Diego Fwy

Wabash Blvd.

National

San Diego Fwy 5

Harbor Dr.

John J.

Division

8th

Plaza

NATIONAL CITY

Inland Freeway

St.

Blvd.

National City Blvd.

Highland Ave.

24th St.

E. 30th St.

Tidelands Ave.

Montgomery Fwy

5

32nd St.

E St.

F St.

Broadway

G St.

H St.

4th St.

J St.

L Ave.

3rd St.

Palomar St.

Main St.

CHULA VISTA

Hilltop Dr.

Orange Ave.

Beyer Ave.

Otay

John

Palm

Beyer Blvd.

Palm Ave.

IMPERIAL BEACH

Coronado Ave.

J St.

Montgomery Fwy

Hollister St.

Tocayo Ave.

19th Rd.

Tijuana

River

Dairy Mart Rd.

Monument

Hwy 75

Hwy

1st St.

Palm Ave.

Otay River

Valley Rd.

Inland Freeway

805

805

117

Beyer Blvd.

Otay

Mesa Rd.

5

South Bay

Paradise Valley

Rd.

54

Bonita Rd.

Telegraph Canyon Rd.

CALIFORNIA
ESTADO DE BAJA CALIFORNIA

SAN DIEGO CO.

UNITED STATES
ESTADOS UNIDOS MEXICANOS

National City Launching Ramp

Coronado Cays Park

Silver Strand State Beach

Chula Vista Launching Ramp

South Bay Marine Biological Study Area

Bike Path

Imperial Beach Hostel

Imperial Beach

Border Field Federal Wildlife Refuge

Border Field State Park

N

0   2
Miles

NAME	LOCATION	Entrance/Parking Fee	Parking	Restrooms	Lifeguard	Campground	Showers	Firepits	Stairs to Beach	Path to Beach	Bike Path	Hiking Trail	Facilities for Disabled	Boating Facilities	Fishing	Equestrian Trail	Sandy Beach	Dunes	Rocky Shore	Upland from Beach	Stream Corridor	Bluff	Wetland
National City Launching Ramp	S. end of Goesno Pl., National City		•	•			•							•	•								
Chula Vista Launching Ramp	W. end of J St., Chula Vista		•	•			•				•			•	•								
Coronado Cays Park	Coronado Cays Blvd. at Halfpenny Lane, Coronado		•																	•			
Silver Strand State Beach	3500 Hwy. 75, Coronado	•	•	•	•	•	•	•	•				•		•		•	•					
South Bay Marine Biological Study Area	E. of Hwy. 75, .9 mi. N. of Imperial Beach City limits, Coronado		•																			•	•
Bike Path	E. of Imperial Beach, from the W. end of Main St. to the N. end of 19th St., San Diego										•												•
Imperial Beach Hostel	170 Palm Ave., Imperial Beach	•	•	•																•			
Imperial Beach	W. of Ocean Lane, from Carnation to Encanto Avenues, Imperial Beach		•	•	•							•		•			•						
Border Field Federal Wildlife Refuge	S. end of 1st St., Imperial Beach						•		•								•	•		•			•
Border Field State Park	W. end of Monument Rd., Imperial Beach		•	•	•			•		•		•			•	•	•	•		•	•		•

NATIONAL CITY LAUNCHING RAMP: Public ramp operated by the Port of San Diego. Facilities include a ten-lane concrete boat ramp, docks, trailer space, a landscaped picnic area, and a fishing platform. Open 24 hours. From I-5 take the 24th St. off-ramp west to Tidelands Ave., south on Tidelands to 32nd St., then east to Goesno Place. Information: (619) 291-3900.
Mass Transit: San Diego Transit Corporation (SDTC) bus #32.

CHULA VISTA LAUNCHING RAMP: Concrete boat launch with ten lanes; open 24 hours year-round. Facilities include docks, picnic areas, a playground, and a jogging and bicycle path. Noted for swimming, fishing, and water-skiing; however, swimming and skiing are prohibited within the launch basin. The old Chula Vista launching ramp (now closed) at the end of G St., and the end of F St., both provide pedestrian access to the South Bay tidal areas. Information: Port of San Diego, (619) 291-3900.

CORONADO CAYS PARK: Small park with playground, lawn, and benches. On-street parking only.
Mass Transit: Strand bus #901.

SILVER STRAND STATE BEACH: Sandy beach noted for swimming, surfing, clamming, surf fishing, and catching grunion; beachcombing is also popular due to the large quantity of shells found on the beach. Pedestrian tunnels connect the ocean beach with the bay shore, where the water is calmer and warmer. The ranger station contains exhibits of the area's plant and animal life. Other facilities include first-aid stations, and picnic areas with cabanas and tables; restrooms are wheelchair accessible. $3 day use fee; $6 fee for en route campsites. Information: (619) 435-5184.
Mass Transit: Strand bus #901.

SOUTH BAY MARINE BIOLOGICAL STUDY AREA: This nature refuge provides an opportunity to observe the plant and animal life of a wetland environment; many shorebirds and migratory waterfowl can be seen. Panoramic views of the southern San Diego Bay. Unpaved parking area.
Mass Transit: Strand bus #901.

BIKE PATH: Separated lanes accommodate two-way traffic. The path runs through the salt flats along the edge of the bay.

IMPERIAL BEACH HOSTEL: Located in a former firehouse one block from the ocean. The hostel accommodates up to 18 men and 12 women. Facilities include bunk beds, community kitchen, and a common room. Opens daily at 4:30 PM, curfew at 11:00 PM.

$6.00/night for members, $8.00 for non-members; $1 fee for blankets and sheets. Information and reservations: 170 Palm Ave., Imperial Beach 92032, (619) 423-8039.
Mass Transit: SDTC bus #33 and 33A. Strand bus #901.

IMPERIAL BEACH: Wide, sandy beach; popular for swimming and surf fishing. The waves here can be dangerously large; the renovated fishing pier at the end of Palm Ave. was previously destroyed by storms. There is a metered parking lot and wheelchair access at the intersection of Evergreen and 1st Streets. Street ends from Palm Ave. to Encanto Ave. also provide access and some on-street parking.
Mass Transit: SDTC bus #33 and #33A.

BORDER FIELD FEDERAL WILDLIFE REFUGE: Located at the mouth of the Tia Juana River; this area has been proposed as an estuarine sanctuary. Features include a large sandy beach, sand dunes, and a marsh area. Wetland wildlife can be observed here.
Mass Transit: SDTC bus #33 and #33A.

BORDER FIELD STATE PARK: Located at the southwest corner of the United States, bordering on Mexico and the Pacific Ocean. Equestrian/hiking trails lead to a two-mile long stretch of sandy beach; good swimming, clamming, and surf fishing. For information, call: (619) 428-3034. The Tia Juana River Estuary is located within the park, and is an important habitat for rare species of plants and animals.

Imperial Beach Pier

Afterword

This revised, expanded Guide is current as of Spring 1983, and is accurate to the best of our knowledge. All accessways were visited, and all information was verified using sources such as Local Coastal Programs, which were prepared by local governments in compliance with the Coastal Act of 1976. We also incorporated into this updated edition the comments and corrections supplied by various agencies and members of the public who wrote to us regarding the information in the first edition. Nevertheless, we are aware that conditions on the coast are constantly changing and that inaccuracies may still exist in the text.

If you think something is incorrect or has been omitted, please let us know. The Commission intends to continue publishing revised and expanded guides in the future, and would therefore appreciate any additional information you can provide. Please remember, however, that the Guide includes *only* those beaches which are managed for public use.

Address all comments to:

California Coastal Commission
631 Howard Street
San Francisco, CA 94105

Acknowledgements

CONTRIBUTORS

Louise McCorkle Adams	Tom Jackson	Carol Opotow
Rich Allen	Anna Kondolf	Wendy J. Phillippay
Deborah S. Benrubi	Evelyn Lee	Rick Rayburn
Gina M. Bentzley	Jack I. Liebster	Paul Thayer
William G. Broad	Cynthia K. Long	Martha K. Weiss
Michael Buck	Carl Martin	Jon Van Coops
Stewart M. Crone	Daniel S. Miller	Cy Yee
Mary Hudson	Gianmaria Mussio	John Zentner

Special thanks to the compositor of the *California Coastal Access Guide*, Marie L. Zimmermann of A-Offset Composition Service, San Francisco.

The editors wish to thank the staff of the University of California Press for assistance in preparation and revision of the guide.

Printed by the University of California Printing Department, Berkeley.

With grateful acknowledgement to Ansel Adams for the cover photograph.

Selected References

Allen, Richard K., *Common Intertidal Invertebrates of Southern California,* Peek Publications, Palo Alto, Ca., 1969.

American Youth Hostels Handbook 1983, American Youth Hostels, Inc., Washington, DC., 1983.

Anthrop, Donald F., *Redwood National and State Parks,* Naturegraph, Happy Camp, Ca., 1977.

Ashley, Frank and Mary Ashley, "Exploring Coronado — San Diego's 'Isolated' Peninsula," *California Traveler,* July 1982.

Bakker, Elna, *An Island Called California,* University of California Press, Berkeley, 1971.

Bancroft, Hubert Howe, *The History of California,* 7 Vol., Bancroft Press, San Rafael, Ca., 1888.

Bascom, Willard, *Waves and Beaches: The Dynamics of the Ocean Surface,* Anchor Books, Anchor Press/Doubleday, Garden City, N.Y., 1980.

Beachcombers Guide to the Pacific Coast, Sunset Books, Lane Publishing Co., Menlo Park, Ca., 1966.

Benet, James, *A Guide to San Francisco and the Bay Region,* Random House, New York, 1963.

Berssen, William, ed., *Pacific Boating Almanac,* Western Marine Enterprises, Inc., Ventura, Ca., 1981.

Bies Frank, "Surf Wars," *New West,* May 1981.

Brusca, Gary J. and Richard C. Brusca, *A Naturalist's Seashore Guide: Common Marine Life of the Northern California Coast and Adjacent Shores,* Mad River Press, Eureka, Ca., 1978.

California, A Guide to the Golden State, Federal Writers Project, State of California, American Guide Series, Hastings House, N.Y., 1939.

California Sport Fishing Regulations 1983, California Department of Fish and Game, Sacramento, 1983.

California State Parks, Sunset Books, Lane Publishing Co., Menlo Park, Ca., 1972.

California's Living Marine Resources and Their Utilization, California Department of Fish and Game, Sacramento, 1971.

Campground and Trailer Park Guide to the United States, Canada, and Mexico, Rand McNally, Skokie, Ill., 1980.

Catalog of California Seabird Colonies, U.S. Department of the Interior, Fish and Wildlife Service, Washington, D.C., 1980.

Clark, Eugenie, "Sharks: Magnificent and Misunderstood," *National Geographic,* Vol. 100, No. 2, August 1981.

Clausen, Lucy W., *Insect Fact and Folklore,* Collier Books, New York, 1954.

Cogswell, Howard L., *Water Birds of California,* University of California Press, Berkeley, 1977.

Concept Plan for Waterfowl Wintering Habitat Preservation: California Coast, U.S. Department of the Interior, Fish and Wildlife Service, Portland, Or., 1979.

Cuanang, Abe, "Shark! Big Game in the Bay," *Western Saltwater Fisherman,* December 1981.

Culliney, John L. and Edward S. Crockett, *Exploring Underwater, The Sierra Club Guide to Scuba and Snorkeling,* Sierra Club Books, San Francisco, 1980.

Dawson, E. Yale, *Seashore Plants of Northern California,* University of California Press, Berkeley, 1979.

Dawson, E. Yale, *Seashore Plants of Southern California,* University of California Press, Berkeley, 1962.

Dixon, Sarah and Peter Dixon, *West Coast Beaches: A Complete Guide,* E. P. Dutton, New York, 1979.

Doss, Margot Patterson, *San Francisco At Your Feet,* Grove Press, New York, 1964.

Doss, Margot Patterson, *The Bay Area At Your Feet,* Presidio Press, San Rafael, Ca., 1981.

Dougherty, Anita E., *Marine Mammals of California,* California Department of Fish and Game, Sacramento, 1972.

Durrenberger, Robert W. and Robert B. Johnson, *California: Patterns on the Land,* 5th ed., Mayfield Publishing Co., Palo Alto, Ca., 1976.

Easterbrook, Don J., *Principles of Geomorphology,* McGraw-Hill, New York, 1969.

Explore, a series of pamphlets for the Year of the Coast, U.S. Army Corps of Engineers, San Francisco, 1980.

Fagan, Brian M. and Graham Pomeroy, *Cruising Guide to the Channel Islands,* Capra Press and Western Marine Enterprises, Santa Barbara and Van Nuys, Ca., 1980.

Fire Weather, U.S. Department of Agriculture, Forest Service, Washington, D.C., 1970.

Fitch, John E., *Common Marine Bivalves of California,* Fish Bulletin 90, California Department of Fish and Game, 1953.

Fitch, John E. and R. Lavenberg, *Tidepool and Nearshore Fishes of California,* University of California Press, Berkeley, 1975.

Gordon, Burton L., *Monterey Bay Area: Natural History and Cultural Imprints,* Boxwood Press, Pacific Grove, Ca., 1974.

Griggs, Gary B. and John A. Gilchrist, *The Earth and Land Use Planning,* Duxbury Press, Belmont, Ca., 1977.

Gudde, Erwin G., *California Place Names,* University of California Press, Berkeley, 1974.

Guide to California Boating Facilities, California Department of Boating and Waterways, Sacramento, 1976.

Harrison, Richard J. and Judith E. King, *Marine Mammals,* Hutchinson and Co., London, 1965.

Hayden, Mike, *Exploring the North Coast from the Golden Gate to the Oregon Border,* Chronicle Books, San Francisco, 1976, 1982.

Hayden, Mike, *Guidebook to the Northern California Coast,* Ward Ritchie Press, Los Angeles, 1970.

Hedgpeth, Joel W. and Sam Hinton, *Common Seashore Life of Southern California,* Naturegraph Publishers, Inc., Happy Camp, Ca., 1961.

Hedgpeth, Joel W., *Introduction to Seashore Life of the San Francisco Bay Region and the Coast of Northern California,* University of California Press, Berkeley, 1962.

Hinton, Sam D., *Seashore Life of Southern California,* University of California Press, Berkeley, 1969.

Hittell, Theodore H., *History of California,* 4 Vol., N.J. Stone & Company, San Francisco, 1897.

Hoover, Mildred Brooke, Hero Eugene Rensch, and Ethel Grace Rensch, *Historic Spots in California,* 3rd ed., revised by William N. Abeloe, Stanford University Press, Stanford, Ca., 1966.

Hutchinson, W.H., *California: The Golden Shore by the Sundown Sea,* Star Publishing Company, Palo Alto, Ca., 1980.

Iacopi, Robert, ed., *Redwood Country and the Big Trees of the Sierra,* Sunset Books, Lane Publishing Co., Menlo Park, Ca., 1969.

Inventory of California Boating Facilities, Management Consulting Corporation for California Department of Navigation and Ocean Development, Sacramento, 1977.

Jackson, Ruth A., *Combing the Coast: San Francisco through Big Sur,* Chronicle Books, San Francisco, 1977.

Knox, Maxine and Mary Rodriguez, *Making the Most of the Monterey Peninsula and Big Sur,* Presidio Press, San Rafael, Ca., 1978.

Le Boeuf, Burney J. and Stephanie Kaza, eds., *The Natural History of Año Nuevo,* Boxwood Press, Pacific Grove, Ca., 1981.

Lee, Georgia et al., *An Uncommon Guide to San Luis Obispo County, California,* Padre Publications, San Luis Obispo, Ca., 1977.

Los Angeles: A Guide to the City and its Environment, Federal Writers Project, State of California, Hastings House, New York, 1951.

Los Angeles & Orange County Guide, Rand McNally & Company, 1980.

Lussier, Tomi Kay, *Big Sur: A Complete History and Guide,* Big Sur Publications, Monterey, Ca., 1979.

Magary, Alan and Kerstin Fraser Magary, *Across the Golden Gate,* Harper and Row, New York, 1980.

Marine Mammal and Seabird Survey of the Southern California Bight, University of California at Santa Cruz for U.S. Department of the Interior, Bureau of Land Management, Washington, D.C., 1978.

Mason, Jack, *Point Reyes, the Solemn Land,* North Shore Books, Inverness, Ca., 1970.

McWilliams, Carey, *Southern California: An Island on the Land,* Peregrine Smith, Inc., Santa Barbara, Ca. and Salt Lake City, 1973.

Miller, Daniel and Robert N. Lea, *A Guide to the Coastal Marine Fishes of California,* Fish Bulletin 157, California Department of Fish and Game, 1972.

Miller, Daniel J., "Shark Attacks," *Outdoor California,* November-December 1981.

Muller, Barbara D., *The Mendocino Coast,* Mendocino Community Land Trust, Inc., Mendocino, Ca., 1981.

Munz, Phillip A., *Shore Wildflowers of California, Oregon, and Washington,* University of California Press, Berkeley, 1973.

Nathenson, Si, "Sharks as Food," *Outdoor California,* November-December 1981.

Norris, Robert and Robert Webb, *Geology of California,* John Wiley & Sons, Inc., New York, 1976.

North, Wheeler J., *Underwater California,* University of California Press, Berkeley, 1976.

Oakeshott, Gordon, *California's Changing Landscapes: A Guide to the Geology of the State,* McGraw-Hill Book Co., New York, 1971.

Orr, Robert T., *Marine Mammals of California,* University of California Press, Berkeley, 1976.

Pacific Coast Bicentennial Bike Route Guide, California Department of Transportation, Sacramento, 1976.

Power, Dennis, ed., *The California Islands: Proceedings of a Multidisciplinary Symposium,* Santa Barbara Museum of Natural History, Santa Barbara, Ca., 1980.

A Primer of Offshore Operations, Petroleum Extension Service, University of Texas at Austin, 1976.

Redwood Empire Visitor's Guide, Redwood Empire Association, San Francisco, 1980, 1981.

Ricciuti, Edward R., *Dancers on the Beach, The Story of the Grunion,* Thomas Y. Crowell Co., New York, 1973.

Ricketts, Edward F., Jack Calvin, and Joel W. Hedgpeth, *Between Pacific Tides,* 4th ed., Stanford University Press, Stanford, Ca., 1968.

Salitore, Edward, ed., *California Information Almanac: Past, Present, Future,* California Almanac Company, Lakewood, Ca., 1973.

Smith, Clifton F., *A Flora of the Santa Barbara Region, California,* Santa Barbara Museum of Natural History, Santa Barbara, Ca., 1976.

Smith, Emil J. Jr. et al., *The Marine Life Refuges and Reserves of California,* Marine Resources Information Bulletin No. 1, California Department of Fish and Game, Sacramento, 1979.

Smith, Ralph I. and James T. Carlton, eds., *Light's Manual: Intertidal Invertebrates of the Central California Coast,* University of California Press, Berkeley, 1975.

Sowls, Arthur L. et al., *Catalog of California Seabird Colonies,* U. S. Fish and Wildlife Service, Office of Biological Services, Coastal Ecosystems Project (FWS/OBS-80/37), 1980.

A Summary of Knowledge of the Central and Northern California Coastal Zone and Offshore Areas, Winzler and Kelly for U.S. Department of the Interior, Bureau of Land Management, Washington, D.C., 1977.

A Summary of Knowledge of the Southern California Coastal Zone and Offshore Areas Vol. 1, Southern California Ocean Studies Consortium of the California State University and Colleges for U.S. Department of the Interior, Bureau of Land Management, Washington, D.C., 1974.

Sunset Travel Guide to Northern California, Sunset Books, Lane Publishing Co., Menlo Park, Ca., 1975.

Sunset Travel Guide to Southern California, Sunset Books, Lane Publishing Co., Menlo Park, Ca., 1979.

A Survey of the Marine Environment from Fort Ross, Sonoma County, to Point Lobos, Monterey County, California Department of Fish and Game, Sacramento, 1968.

Tasto, Robert N., *Marine Bivalves of the California Coast,* Marine Resources Leaflet No. 6, California Department of Fish and Game, Sacramento, 1974.

"Vanishing Giants: a Biography [of the California Gray Whale]," *Audubon,* January 1975.

Welles, Annette, *The Los Angeles Guide Book,* Sherbourne Press, Los Angeles, 1972.

Whitaker, Thomas W., ed., *Torrey Pines State Reserve,* The Torrey Pines Association, La Jolla, Ca., 1964.

The Why and How of Undersea Drilling, American Petroleum Institute, pamphlet, Washington, D.C., 1973.

Wieman, Harold, *Nature Walks on the San Luis Coast,* Padre Publications, San Luis Obispo, Ca., 1980.

Winlund, Edmond, *ChartGuide for Southern California,* ChartGuide, Anaheim, Ca., 1978.

Wood, Basil C., *The What, When and Where Guide to Southern California,* rev. ed., Doubleday, Garden City, N.Y., 1979.

Wurman, Richard Saul, *LA/Access,* Official Publication of the Los Angeles 200 Committee, Access Press, Inc., Los Angeles, 1981.

Index